A Pneumatology of Race in the Gospel of John

A Pneumatology of Race in the Gospel of John

An Ethnocritical Study

RODOLFO GALVAN ESTRADA III

☙PICKWICK *Publications* • Eugene, Oregon

A PNEUMATOLOGY OF RACE IN THE GOSPEL OF JOHN
An Ethnocritical Study

Copyright © 2019 Rodolfo Galvan Estrada III. All rights reserved. Except for brief quotations in critical publications or reviews, no part of this book may be reproduced in any manner without prior written permission from the publisher. Write: Permissions, Wipf and Stock Publishers, 199 W. 8th Ave., Suite 3, Eugene, OR 97401.

Pickwick Publications
An Imprint of Wipf and Stock Publishers
199 W. 8th Ave., Suite 3
Eugene, OR 97401

www.wipfandstock.com

PAPERBACK ISBN: 978-1-5326-7086-2
HARDCOVER ISBN: 978-1-5326-7087-9
EBOOK ISBN: 978-1-5326-7088-6

Cataloguing-in-Publication data:

Names: Estrada, Rodolfo Galvan, III.

Title: A pneumatology of race in the Gospel of John : an ethnocritical study. / Rodolfo Galvan Estrada III.

Description: Eugene, OR: Pickwick Publications, 2019 | Includes bibliographical references and index.

Identifiers: ISBN 978-1-5326-7086-2 (paperback) | ISBN 978-1-5326-7087-9 (hardcover) | ISBN 978-1-5326-7088-6 (ebook)

Subjects: LCSH: Bible. John—Criticism, interpretation, etc. | Ethnicity in the Bible. | Race—Religious aspects—Christianity. | Holy Spirit—Biblical teaching.

Classification: BS2615.6.E815 E78 2019 (print) | BS2615.6.E815 (ebook)

Manufactured in the U.S.A.   MARCH 5, 2021

This book would not be possible without the love of my life—Jessica Estrada. Thank you, my love, for always believing in me. You have been with me since I was an undergraduate student and journeyed with me throughout my entire academic life, always hearing my ideas and thoughts about this book. I appreciate you so much. Love you to the moon and beyond the mountains.

Contents

Acknowledgments | ix

Part I Ethnicity and the Spirit in Johannine Christianity | 1

    1 Journey Through the Issues of Johannine Pneumatology | 3

    2 Examining the Ethnic Background of the Fourth Gospel | 25

    3 Study of the Greco-Roman Ethnic Ideologies | 53

Part II Ethnicity and the Spirit in Jesus' Public Ministry | 95

    4 Study of the Spirit in Context | 97

    5 Interpreting the Anointing of the Spirit: John 1:32-33 | 107

    6 Creating and Subverting Genealogical Relations: John 3:1-10 | 130

    7 Advocating for a Pneumatic Non-Violent and Non-Segregation Worship: John 4:23-24 | 152

    8 Arguing Against Ethnic Kinship: John 6:62-63 | 169

    9 Native Resistance to the Greeks?: John 7:37-39 | 191

Part III Ethnicity and the Spirit—Παράκλητος in the Farewell Discourse and Conclusion of the Gospel | 211

    10 Discussion on Παράκλητος and Πνεῦμα τῆς Ἀληθείας in the Farewell Discourse | 213

    11 Responding to the Orphaned: John 14:16-17, 26 | 222

    12 Understanding the Paraclete in an Ethnically Hostile World: John 15:26-27; 16:7-15 | 245

    13 Delivering the Community from the Fear of the Other: John 20:19-23 | 270

    14 Yielding to the Holy Spirit | 288

Bibliography | 301

Index of Ancient Documents | 317

Acknowledgments

THE IDEA OF THIS BOOK FIRST STARTED IN 2008 WHEN I WAS a graduate student at Duke Divinity in Durham, North Carolina. I was from southern California and new to the history and realities of racism in the South. It was during these formative experiences in North Carolina, the same time that Barack Obama was being elected as President, that I realized that America still had a race problem. I also learned while in North Carolina that I was indeed a "Mexican" with an accent (or at least a non-southern accent). This was a difficult experience for my wife as well, who is a second-generation Latina. She came with me to North Carolina and supported me throughout my graduate education. I am forever indebted to her for enduring all the racial animosity and microaggressions that tainted our experience of the South. We indeed felt "ethnic" given that there were hardly any Latinx people in the city and university. I rarely met other Latinx students at Duke University and many at my wife's job had never met an educated Latina with a bachelor's degree. It was a difficult experience for us, but also one that opened our eyes to the ideas of race and ethnicity that were influencing and impacting Christian theology.

Years later, the issues of race and racism started to publicly emerge on a national scale with the Presidential election between Trump and Clinton in 2016. I started to write the first chapters of this book and investigate the role of race in the ancient world during this time. So, in a sense, this book emerges from the context of rising xenophobia, racial rhetoric against immigrants, and the theological justification for this hate by right-wing Christians. While I do not explore or intend to provide a summative answer to the problem of race for the church today, this study does look at how the early Christians would have answered this question. That is, what does the

Spirit have to do with race? How does the Spirit address the challenges of xenophobia and dehumanization of the ancient world? I believe the pneumatology of the gospel gives us this answer.

Even though this study was birthed in the pain of racism and hate against Mexicans, I also want to give special thanks to the Latinx students of LABI College in La Puente, California. I am very thankful for the opportunity to write and teach sections of these chapters throughout my teaching and deanship tenure at LABI College from 2010–2018. All the students at LABI College inspired me to write this book. In many ways, they helped me recognize that the ethnic context of the interpreter matters. LABI students give me hope that the future of the church is indeed Latinx. I also want to thank Mary Biroscak who poured through the drafts of these chapters. Her editing skills and attention to detail was so excellent. Thanks also to Rosemarie Guzman who helped me edit and finalize the final chapters.

R. G. ESTRADA III

Fontana, CA
February 1, 2021

PART I

Ethnicity and the Spirit in Johannine Christianity

1

Journey Through the Issues of Johannine Pneumatology

WAS THE PNEUMATOLOGY OF THE FOURTH GOSPEL SHAPED BY the racial ideologies and challenges of the Johannine community? This is a question that is not often asked when thinking about the influences and motivation for the Spirit references in the gospel. One would presume that ethnic ideologies and stereotypes only emerged after the colonialization of the Americas or when scientists of the eighteenth and nineteenth century began to classify people into different racial groups. Even more, some may contend that the problem of race and ethnicity is solely a problem limited to our context alone in the United States. Indeed, far right-wing nationalistic views have globally reemerged and racist rhetoric from political leaders such as Donald Trump have made the ever-present reality of racism a concern for Christians in our contemporary era. Cornel West notes that demagogues like Trump are "neither alien nor extraneous to American culture and history" but as "American as apple pie."[1] But this racial challenge and bigotry is not new. We must remember that racism goes further back than our American context. Ethnic ideologies, prejudices, and stereotypes have been around for a long time. It was the ancient Greeks who judged ethnic groups based upon the location of their birth and purity of their lineage. It is thus not difficult to imagine converts from various ethnic backgrounds, daring to join the Johannine community in the late first century, also dealing with these various views, fears, or suspicions toward one another. Yes, this is an imaginative exercise, like all reconstructive history.[2] Prevailing ideologies of

---

1. West, *Race Matters*, xviii.
2. Collingwood states, "The history of past thought, and therefore all history, is the

difference, not just theological disagreements, but specific racial views that separate and distinguish Jews, Samaritans, and Greeks from one another would have been a problem for emerging Christianity. This truly would be an ethnic challenge, especially since Christians dared to form a new community composed of members from different ethnic backgrounds, a community which we today call a "church."

So what shall we say about this Johannine "church," or what scholars also call the "Johannine community?" Did they have an ethnic problem? And since the Spirit is involved in the conversion of each believer through the maternal birthing activity of all members into this church (John 3:3–8), is the Spirit at all concerned with ethnic issues, community inclusion, and the formation or subversion of their ethnic identities? Or when we think about the challenges today, does the Spirit care about how we view one another and the ethnic ideologies that we hold? This last question I must admit is a topic for another book. But when we explore the portrait of the Spirit in the gospel and what scholars say, we are hard-pressed to find anyone thinking or talking about the ethnic challenges of the nascent Johannine community. Yet we find many clues in how the Johannine community would have been challenged to think about the ethnic issues of the Greco-Roman world, if only we look. These concerns of mine may seem anachronistic. I admit, this entire project is really birthed not only from an ardent desire to know what scripture says about ethnic relations, but also how the early Christians would have dealt with the ethnic challenges of their time and how their theology of the Spirit emerges and develops in response. One must seriously consider if the Johannine Spirit has anything to say about ethnic relations and ethnic ideologies that would have been a part of the social worldview of the first century. But first, who or what is the "Spirit" in the Fourth Gospel?

We must note that what clearly separates Johannine pneumatology from the Synoptic tradition is the rare use of the word παράκλητος and the phrase πνεῦμα τῆς ἀληθείας. The gospel furnishes us with a portrait of the Spirit that is distinguishable but not too far detached from the perspectives found in the Synoptic Gospels. The term παράκλητος is found on four occasions within the gospel (14:16, 26; 15:26; 16:7) and once in the letter (1 John 2:1). The phrase πνεῦμα τῆς ἀληθείας is noted to be with the disciples (14:17; 15:26; 16:13) and compared to the "spirit of error" in the Johannine letter (1 John 4:6). These two expressions are totally foreign to the Synoptic tradition, including the Old Testament. Yet they both hold a prominent role within the Farewell Discourse and are major aspects of

---

re-enactment of past thought in the historian's own mind" (Collingwood, *Idea of History*, 215).

Johannine pneumatology. When we compare the Spirit in the Johannine public ministry of Jesus to the Synoptic tradition, further differences become apparent. The Fourth Gospel does not draw attention to the Spirit's involvement in Jesus' entrance to the world as we find in the Synoptics (Matt 1:18–20; Luke 1:35). The prologue is absent of any pneumatic involvement, despite the strong allusion to Genesis 1:1–2. The Spirit is also not involved in filling or leading Jesus' ministry, nor emerging among people.[3] Neither is the Spirit involved in the expulsion of spirits in exorcisms and healings,[4] nor discussed in terms of blaspheming the Spirit.[5] Although this does not suggest that the traditions are radically divergent, they do reveal that the Fourth Gospel has a different understanding of the Spirit, despite the resemblances with the gospels. But why such a different articulation, emphasis, and theme?

John Christopher Thomas notices that the narrative development of the Spirit in the Fourth Gospel often receives little attention.[6] In many ways, it is overshadowed by the Paraclete sayings in the Farewell Discourse. The Spirit in the Johannine public ministry however concerns itself with topics on new birth, temple worship, a rejection of the flesh, and cross-cultural suspicion. The Paraclete is discussed in the context of the impending death of Jesus and the fear that Jesus would leave his disciples orphaned. Why does the Fourth Gospel depart from the Synoptic tradition and paint a new portrait of the Spirit in different contexts, including new descriptions of the Spirit as the Paraclete (παράκλητος) and Spirit of Truth (πνεῦμα τῆς ἀληθείας)? Or more specifically, what were the situations, social circumstances, or controversies that could have motivated such a new perspective for the Spirit? These questions have challenged scholars throughout the years and are the focus of our study. For there is something significant about the way in which the Spirit is described within the Fourth Gospel that reveals to us an underlying problem, one which this study argues includes an ethnic one. It is no trivial matter that the relationship between the Spirit and ethnicity is intimated throughout the public ministry of Jesus and continues into the Paraclete sayings and Johannine Pentecost. And as we will find within this study, this also provides a new opportunity for reimagining the Spirit's identity and activity in this emerging Christian community and context. Truly, at the end of this project we will come to realize that the theology of the Spirit in the

---

3. Matt 4:1; Mark 1:12; Luke 1:17, 41, 67; 4:1, 14.

4. Matt 12:28, 43; Mark 1:23–26; 5:2, 8; 7:25; 9:17–25; Luke 4:33; 8:29; 9:39–42; 13:11.

5. Matt 12:31–32; Mark 3:29; Luke 12:10.

6. Thomas, *Spirit of the New Testament*, 158.

gospel emerges in response to the racial views of the ancient world that were indeed a hostile part of their society.

Views of the Spirit in the Fourth Gospel

But does the Johannine portrait of the Spirit really have anything to say about ethnicity? If we solely focus upon the views of American scholars rarely is there anything mentioned, which is ironic given their history of colonization. Nevertheless, attempting to understand why the writer of the gospel would utilize different foci to describe the Spirit has compelled many scholars to examine the possible origins, circumstances, and situations that motivated a distinct pneumatology. Scholars have also recognized that this quest cannot be done in isolation from the context in which the gospel was written. Thus, when C. K. Barrett examines the Spirit, he does so in relation to Johannine Christology, the primitive Christian community, and eschatology.[7] He notices that at the end of the first century the earliest task of the Christian apologist was to explain why Jesus had not appeared in power and glory. Barrett believes that the explanation given was in terms of the Holy Spirit. That is, the eschatological problem and the profound religious experience led to the formulation of a theology on the Holy Spirit.[8] Barrett also finds that there was something about the Spirit in the ministry of Jesus that was distinct from the experience of the Johannine readers. He argues that to understand the pneumatology of the gospel, we must do so with the assumption that all statements on the Spirit are a reflective post-resurrection perspective.[9] According to Barrett, the Spirit is the eschatological continuum in which the work of Christ is carried out and the church is the proper sphere of the Spirit's activity.[10] Barrett's analysis provides us with early insights into deciphering the pneumatic language in the gospel. He also recognizes that even though some may claim that the Paraclete statements are insertions and foreign to the ideas of the writer, they are to be regarded as genuine. He suggests that the Paraclete activity is understood eschatologically and is made present through the activity of the church.[11] This not only helps ground our analysis in the church's context and reminds us that there was something different with the experience of the Spirit after the resurrection, it lays out some preliminary steps that help us imagine

7. Barrett, *St. John*, 74.
8. Barrett, "Holy Spirit," 1.
9. Barrett, "Holy Spirit," 5.
10. Barrett, *St. John*, 76–77.
11. Barrett, *St. John*, 76–78.

the context and circumstances that could have motivated such pneumatic expressions. However, Barrett's views on the Spirit are primarily understood through the prism of Johannine theological concerns.

Raymond Brown claims that the Johannine writer viewed the Spirit in a highly distinctive manner that necessitated a specific title. As such, he primarily focuses on the distinguishing role and portrayal of the Paraclete within the farewell discourse. Brown prefers to understand the Paraclete as a distinct element within Christian pneumatology.[12] The movement and ministry of the Paraclete, as Brown argues, shapes the overall pneumatology of the gospel. He examines the experiences of the Johannine community in order to discern the emergence of Johannine pneumatology. As he claims, this view of the Spirit was needed for a community that was dealing with the deaths of the apostolic eyewitnesses and the delay of the Parousia that caused a loss of faith. He even adds that the evangelist may have used the concept of the Paraclete to justify the Johannine proclamation.[13] Brown perceives that the context of the Johannine community gave a fuller understanding of the role and function of the Spirit. Similar to Barrett's analysis, he affirms that the Spirit provided believers with the presence of Jesus which enabled them to enjoy the eschatological benefits.[14]

Brown was not the only one who started to point out the need for constructing a pneumatology of the gospel in light of the experiences of the community. George Johnston believes that the description of the Spirit has roots in a polemical context. He agrees that the Hebrew scripture should be the primary background of our understanding of the Spirit.[15] His view, however, interprets the Spirit-Paraclete as a divine power or active agent of divine work.[16] He even adds that when God gives the "spirit of truth," this refers to nothing more than a "true spirit" or a power that God issues. The Spirit, in Johnston's view, is not the third person of the Trinity but the "power and influence" that proceeds from God in a "creative and redemptive mission."[17] Johnston understands the Paraclete as a Christ-like power under God's control.[18] He also states that "the spirit of truth, as Paraclete, acts on behalf of Christ and for the advantage of the disciples, and thus the most useful word

---

12. Brown, "Paraclete in the Fourth Gospel," 113.
13. Brown, *Community*, 28.
14. Brown, *John*, 2:1143.
15. Johnston, *Spirit-Paraclete*, 4.
16. Johnston, *Spirit-Paraclete*, 15.
17. Johnston, *Spirit-Paraclete*, 122.
18. Johnston, *Spirit-Paraclete*, 32.

for παράκλητος is representative."[19] This understanding of the Spirit leads Johnston to also find a hostile tone in the gospel's pneumatology. This tone, as he believes, was reflective of the Johannine community's dealing with those who elevated John the Baptist, experienced synagogue excommunication, venerated Moses, or held Docetic views.[20] What are the implications of this pneumatology? Johnston claims that the Johannine Spirit was thus articulated in order to stand in opposition to anyone who sought to displace the central role of Jesus with another spirit or intercessor such as an angel.[21] Confrontation and hostile theological views are the underlying influence of Johannine pneumatology according to Johnston.

Johnston is right to observe a polemical context within the gospel's pneumatic language. And as we notice with Brown and Barrett, this understanding of Johannine pneumatology was beginning to hint at the need for greater understanding of the gospel's primary context. We thus find Gary Burge's approach highlighting a context that emphasizes the importance of the Spirit-anointing of each member.[22] Burge agrees that the roles and activities of the Paraclete should lead us to preserve the uniqueness of the term.[23] He claims that the evangelist reconstructed a traditional Jewish image within the gospel for his own context, elevating the forensic metaphor and including the role of revelation.[24] Burge's pneumatology explores the Spirit in relation to other themes such as Christology, eschatology, sacramentalism, and witness. Like Barrett and Brown, Burge also argues that the Johannine community had a pneumatology that was entirely Christocentric. Since Jesus was a Spirit-anointed man, he must be emulated by the community that follows him.[25] The Spirit takes a prominent role in revealing, anointing, and empowering Jesus as the Messiah.[26] And since the Spirit was the seal that identifies Jesus as the Messiah, this also meant that the Johannine Christians bore the mark of the Spirit which affirms their identity and authority in Christ.[27]

In exploring the relationship between the Spirit and eschatology, Burge argues that what is being discussed is the life of the community with

19. Johnston, *Spirit-Paraclete*, 87.
20. Johnston, *Spirit-Paraclete*, 121.
21. Johnston, *Spirit-Paraclete*, 126.
22. Burge, *Anointed Community*, xvi.
23. Burge, *Anointed Community*, 9–10.
24. Burge, *Anointed Community*, 31.
25. Burge, *Anointed Community*, 41–45.
26. Burge, *Anointed Community*, 56.
27. Burge, *Anointed Community*, 85.

the presence of the Paraclete.²⁸ He believes that John is reinterpreting the church age as the eschatological age of the personalized Paraclete. Yet the Spirit-Paraclete is not an impersonal force as Johnston claims. It is the presence of Jesus while he is away. The gospel thus stresses a realized eschatology that holds to a future hope of Jesus' return.²⁹ In addition, Burge finds that this may reflect the gospel's correction of sacramental literalism or the institutionalization of the church that does not recognize the presence and power of the Spirit.³⁰ John's interest was therefore attempting to articulate a response to these issues and challenges through a pneumatic perspective. And finally, Burge concludes by pointing out that the mission of Christ will be carried out by the Spirit-led witness of the church.³¹ Mission is strictly Christocentric. As such, the witnessing and revealing activity of the Paraclete and the disciples are akin to the activity of Jesus and the Father. The Johannine community therefore carries on its mission in concert with the Spirit and confronts the hostile world through the power of the Spirit.³²

Burge offers a new interpretation of the Spirit considering the Johannine community's identity as the anointed community. He observes that the most important feature is the community's complete reshaping of the Spirit's image to early Christian pneumatic experiences.³³ As an anointed community, they too could recognize that Jesus' experience with the Spirit and encounter with the world was paradigmatic for their experiences. This was necessary given that the community was experiencing a delay of the Parousia and encountering liturgical challenges within the life of the church.

But were these experiences of the community solely related to the charismatic or theological challenges? Although the context of the community is explored in these various examined views, left unexamined is the concrete racial identity of this community. We can readily notice that there is a striking interpretation of the Spirit that reflects, shapes, or is influenced by how one views the Johannine context. Other recent scholars such as Craig Keener offers a refined approach to the study of the Spirit by detailing how it developed from Jewish pneumatology.³⁴ Keener observes that this pneumatological background gives one an understanding of the context and conflict within the Johannine community. He suggests that historically, the

---

28. Burge, *Anointed Community*, 114.
29. Burge, *Anointed Community*, 146.
30. Burge, *Anointed Community*, 169.
31. Burge, *Anointed Community*, 202.
32. Burge, *Anointed Community*, 206.
33. Burge, *Anointed Community*, 223.
34. Keener, *Spirit in the Gospels*, 1–26.

gospel is addressing a Jewish-Christian community that is both excluded from their local synagogue and facing pressure from Roman authorities to participate in the civic cult.[35] Similar to Johnston's views, Keener asserts that the gospel's pneumatology functions as a major component of John's polemic against a synagogue leadership and a cessationist stream within Judaism.[36] He also observes that the gospel's pneumatic language challenges Jewish purity rituals, proposes a spiritual proselyte baptism, and a new location for worship that transcends boundaries.[37] The gospel's pneumatology according to Keener developed as a polemic against Jewish liturgy and possible ecclesial sacramentalism, an observation that Johnston and Burge also make. Keener identifies the Spirit with the Jewish Spirit of purification and prophecy, a Spirit that was available to those who received the Spirit from Jesus.[38]

Other recent social-scientific interpreters of the Spirit in the gospel include Tricia Gates Brown. She insists that in order to grasp what Spirit means within the gospel we must enhance our knowledge of the socio-cultural context, which includes the experiences of the author and community.[39] Brown believes that the model of patron-client relations are a useful analysis for Johannine pneumatology, given that it illuminates the relationship between God, Jesus, the Spirit-Paraclete, and the Johannine community. Her analysis thus contends that Jesus provides the "spirit" in order to open up access to God. The Paraclete also provides access to Jesus and this all serves as a legitimate function for the author. The author and community can claim to know God because they have access to God's patronage through Jesus and the Spirit-Paraclete. In sum, Jesus and the Paraclete are brokers or mediators for the Johannine community and readers.[40]

Brown does not define the term "spirit" but simply remarks that it is abstract language.[41] She notes that the "spirit" is that which is in the realm of God, legitimates certain people by associating them with the God-realm, a benefit that Jesus confers, and received by those who are born anew as God's

---

35. Keener, *Spirit in the Gospels*, 135. See also Keener, "Function of Johannine Pneumatology," 1–57.

36. Keener, *Spirit in the Gospels*, 26.

37. Keener, *Spirit in the Gospels*, 137–39, 151–60.

38. Keener, *Spirit in the Gospels*, 162.

39. Brown, *Spirit in the Writings of John*, 1.

40. Brown, *Spirit in the Writings of John*, 55.

41. Brown, *Spirit in the Writings of John*, 5.

children.⁴² In other cases, the "spirit" is merely a brokered benefit,⁴³ something possessed, legitimizes the disciples as subordinate brokers,⁴⁴ denotes a spiritual realm,⁴⁵ or allows access to the kingdom of God.⁴⁶ Nonetheless, she insists that the "spirit" designates that which is the realm of God. Similar to this interpretation, the "Paraclete" also is impersonal and viewed as an abstract broker or mediator.⁴⁷ She does not think that the Paraclete language suggests personality but interprets the Paraclete as a representative who opposes the world's spirit-representatives.⁴⁸

Does Our Study of the Spirit Imply a Particular Context?

Now that we have explored some views of the Spirit in the gospel, common themes and interpretations emerge. C. K. Barrett identifies the importance of eschatology and its impact upon the Johannine community's understanding of the Spirit in their post-resurrection context. Raymond Brown observes that the Paraclete's presence replaces the presence of Christ and helps a community that was struggling with the delay of the Parousia and death of the apostles. George Johnston emphasizes the visibility of the Spirit as a power in the experience of preaching, prophesying, and teaching of the leaders. Gary Burge highlights the Christocentric emphasis of the Spirit and how each member of the Johannine community was marked by the Spirit and lived according to the pattern of the anointed Christ. Craig Keener reveals the Judaic background of the Spirit and how the Spirit was understood in relation to prophesy and purity. And finally, Trica Brown pulls us toward an early Roman social context that views the Spirit through the prism of patron-client relations. Other explorations of the Spirit not reviewed include

---

42. Brown, *Spirit in the Writings of John*, 168–69.
43. Brown, *Spirit in the Writings of John*, 108, 129, 163.
44. Brown, *Spirit in the Writings of John*, 113.
45. Brown, *Spirit in the Writings of John*, 122–25, 137, 151–52, 164.
46. Brown, *Spirit in the Writings of John*, 135.
47. Brown, *Spirit in the Writings of John*, 180, 201.
48. Brown, *Spirit in the Writings of John*, 199–200.

Otto Betz,[49] Felix Porsch,[50] Stephen Smalley,[51] Marianne Meye Thompson,[52] Andreas Köstenberger and Scott Swain,[53] Craig Koester,[54] Max Turner,[55] all who have a theological articulation of the Spirit with references to the circumstances and context of the community.

The literature rightly notices that the pneumatology of the gospel intersects with many motifs that are historical, social, and theological. It affirms that the activity of the Spirit includes revealing, teaching, convicting, reminding, and life-giving activities, all which indicate a community that was discerning the truth of the gospel for their context. Others notice the Johannine community continuing the mission of Jesus through empowerment of the Spirit. And some views highlight the theological significance of the Spirit for a community that was dealing with the death of its founder and the delay of the Parousia. These theological motifs associated with the Spirit are vital to our understanding of Johannine pneumatology. But they

---

49. Betz draws from Qumran literature to suggests that the Spirit is to be understood as an advocate in the legal sense. However, as he points out, the Paraclete does not function as an intercessor but is a prophetic teacher who continues Jesus' revelation. See Betz, *Der Paraklet*, 113–14, 117–214.

50. Porsch contends that the Paraclete sayings emerge from the conflict experiences of the church. Yet he finds that the Spirit realizes Jesus' revelation and stands in place of Jesus. See Porsch, *Pneuma und Wort*, 322–24.

51. Smalley suggests that some who came from a Hellenistic environment may have become uncomfortable with the claim that Jesus was fully human as well as uniquely related to God. As such, a unique pneumatology was needed given that Jesus' identity was becoming an ever-growing threat to the community. See Smalley, "Paraclete," 89–92.

52. Thompson challenges the assumption that the Spirit should be understood solely from a Christological perspective. She points out that the Spirit is a distinct way of envisioning God's activity and presence in the world which should lead us to understand the identity and character of God. Thompson contends that the essential role of the Spirit is to be a life-giver and bring the presence of the Father and Son to a community in need of assurance. See Thompson, *God of the Gospel of John*, 145–83; *John*, 318–22.

53. Köstenberger and Swain recognize that within Jesus' public ministry the Spirit largely resembles the Spirit's activity in the Synoptics. They argue that the fullest characterization of the Spirit is in the Farewell Discourse which centers upon a missional understanding. See Köstenberger and Swain, *Father, Son, and Spirit*, 90–136; Köstenberger, *Theology of John's Gospel*, 393–400.

54. Koester observes that the Spirit relates to several fundamental issues such as evoking faith, disclosing the presence of the risen Christ and Father in the community, empowering the community to discern Jesus' identity, and bearing witness. See Koester, *Word of Life*, 134–60.

55. Turner interprets the Spirit in the public ministry of Jesus as a Spirit of prophecy which includes revelation, wisdom, and teaching. Ironically, when discussing the revelatory activity of the Paraclete in 16:13, he undercuts his claim by saying that revelation concerning future events does not apply. See Turner, *Holy Spirit*, 57–88.

cannot be isolated from the social-cultural context of the gospel as Tricia Brown rightfully notes.

Those who have incorporated the gospel's context in their articulation of the Spirit have gravitated upon specific circumstances, whether the community was dealing with liturgical issues, a polemical context, the death of the founding leaders, or strife with the Jewish synagogue. The reviewed literature also explores the historical reality of the community, although some do so more vaguely than others, nonetheless agreeing that the significance of the Spirit cannot be understood apart from an understanding of a Johannine context. One cannot escape noticing that a robust pneumatological articulation is difficult without some interaction with, or preliminary understanding of the context in which the gospel was written. Wayne Meeks notices this issue when he states that the gospel is "unthinkable apart from a particular kind of religious community."[56] We thus should not be hesitant to presume that the gospel's pneumatology can lead us to a richer picture of the community. And likewise, a richer understanding of the gospel's background will inevitably inform our articulation and understanding of the Spirit. As Meeks remarks, the structural characteristics of the literature permit certain deductions about the community even though we have no independent information about the organization of the Johannine group.[57]

The Problem of an Appropriate Hermeneutical Context

Any development of Johannine pneumatology is influenced by or influences how we perceive the context of the Johannine readers. We cannot deny that the gospel implies a certain understanding of the Johannine community, a context that needs exploration in order to have a robust understanding of the Spirit. These dynamics go together. Johannine scholars have rightly noted that the Spirit emerges in a polemical context or in response to the community's experience with the Jewish synagogue.[58] But are there other potential ethnic realities that are not just theological? And can we be a bit more specific on the identity of this community or church that is presumed to be the readers of the gospel?[59] One reality that has yet to be explored includes the ethnic dynamics of the Greco-Roman world. That is, how ethnic

56. Meeks, "Man from Heaven," 76.

57. Meeks, "Man from Heaven," 76.

58. Smalley, "Paraclete" 289. See also Martyn, *History and Theology*, 46; Brown, *Community*, 41.

59. Kim, "Paraclete," 255–70, esp. 269.

and racial issues and perspectives could yield new insights or illuminate the need for a fresh articulation of the Spirit. Why a concern for an ethnic context? As previously mentioned, the notion of an ethnic identity and the hostile race relations are not something limited to our contemporary era—it was present within the context of emerging Christianity.[60]

This study will thus examine how the Fourth Gospel's articulation of the Spirit can be read in light of the ethnic challenges, prejudices, views, and stereotypes that were part of the social world of the Roman Empire. This does not assume that theological or synagogue tensions were irrelevant. It adopts the thesis that the theology of the Spirit was a contextual portrait for a community that was undergoing ethnic challenges. I am even tempted to press the focus even further and propose the following: The racism of the Greco-Roman world that crept into the community compelled the writer of the gospel to articulate a new understanding of the Spirit that would embrace and develop the community's ethnic understanding of itself and each other. But before one may wonder if this approach is misguided, or even if there is truly another need for an exploration of the Spirit within the gospel, I will first define what I mean by "ethnicity" and "race" while presenting the case that justifies this study. I also recognize that exploring the Spirit in the gospel is often challenging, given the inferences one makes about the social realities of the Johannine community. Yet I believe that this also provides a fresh opportunity for new intersections, synthesis, and convergence with Greco-Roman material. Within the plethora of Johannine research, common themes and patterns on the study of the Spirit are often repeated. However, we are also at a point were interdisciplinary questions and research on ethnicity are proposing new understandings of early Christianity. The notion of an ethnic or racial identity was not recently invented. It not only has implications for our study of the gospel but also New Testament literature.

Ethnicity and Race

The ancients knew of ethnic differences and used the term ἔθνος to describe themselves, distinguish people groups, descendants, or humanity in general.[61] In fact, the term "ethnicity" which we commonly use today originates from the Greek word ἔθνος. Jonathan Hall notices that although the

60. Sherwin-White, *Racial Prejudice in Imperial Rome*; Isaac, *Invention of Racism*; Buell, *Why This New Race*; "Challenges and Strategies," 33–51; Horrell, "Race, Nation, People," 123–43; McCoskey, *Race Antiquity and Its Legacy*; Kennedy, *Race and Ethnicity in the Classical World*; Schäfer, *Judeophobia*.

61. Bertram, "ἔθνος, ἐθνικός," *TDNT* 2:367.

term could be used to describe population groups, it also embraces a wider meaning that includes groups of young men, birds, and flies.[62] Throughout biblical literature, the term commonly refers to people groups, nations, or foreigners.[63] Karl Schmidt remarks that ἔθνος is a common word which probably comes from ἔθος which means "mass," "host," or "multitude." When applied to humanity, he suggests that it has an ethnographical sense and denotes the natural cohesion of a people group in general.[64] Schmidt also finds that there are about 60 times in the New Testament when the term generally refers to people. As such, he proposes that ἔθνος and λαός could be used interchangeably.[65]

Although we find the term within the New Testament used in reference to Gentiles, especially in the Pauline letters[66] and Revelation,[67] it is also applicable to the Jews. We cannot assume that the term is exclusively reserved to describe non-Jewish groups. Within the Fourth Gospel the ἔθνος refers to Jews.[68] Within Acts there is a diverse application of the term, although the majority of occurrences refer to non-Jewish people including Samaritans.[69] Though ἔθνος in biblical literature is commonly translated as "Gentiles," caution must precede our analysis because in some occasions, as we find in the Fourth Gospel, ἔθνος refers to the Jewish people. These uses nonetheless demonstrate that the notion of "ethnicity" was something observable and applied to distinct groups of people. It reflects an acknowledgment of group difference. In fact, John Balsdon finds that the Jews divided humanity into Jews and Gentiles (ἔθνος) just like the Greeks divided humanity

---

62. Hall, *Ethnic Identity*, 34–35. In Homer's *Iliad* the term is applied to young men (2.91; 3.32; 7.115; 11.724), birds (2.459), and flies (2.87, 469).

63. Bertram, "ἔθνος, ἐθνικός," *TDNT* 2:364–69.

64. Schmidt, "ἔθνος, ἐθνικός," *TDNT* 2:369.

65. Schmidt, "ἔθνος, ἐθνικός," *TDNT* 2:369.

66. Matt 4:15; 6:32; 10:5, 18; 12:18, 21; 20:19, 25; Mark 10:33, 42; Luke 2:32; 18:32; 22:25; Rom 1:5, 13; 2:14, 24; 3:29; 9:24, 30; 11:11–13, 25; 15:9–12, 16, 18, 27; 16:4; 1 Cor 1:23; 5:1; 10:20; 12:2; 2 Cor 11:26; Gal 1:16; 2:2, 8–9, 12, 14–15; 3:14; Eph 2:11; 3:1, 6, 8; 4:17; Col 1:27; 1 Thess 2:16; 4:5; 1 Tim 2:7; 3:16; 2 Tim 4:17; 1 Pet 2:12; 4:3.

67. Matt 24:7, 9; 14; 25:32; 28:19; Mark 11:17; 13:8, 10; Luke 7:5; 12:30; 21:10, 24–25; 23:2; 24:7; Rom 4:17–18; 10:19; 16:26; Gal 3:8; 1 Pet 2:9; Rev 2:26; 5:9; 7:9; 10:11; 11:2, 9, 18; 12:5; 13:7; 14:6, 8; 15:4; 16:19; 17:15; 18:3, 23; 19:15; 20:3, 8; 21:24, 26; 22:2.

68. John 11:48, 50–52; 18:35. Bertram suggests within the Fourth Gospel the Jews are equated with the world in "ἔθνος, ἐθνικός," *TDNT* 2:369–71.

69. Acts 2:5; 4:25, 27; 7:7, 45; 9:15; 10:35, 45; 11:1, 18; 13:19, 46–48; 14:2, 5, 16, 27; 15:3, 7, 12, 14, 17, 19, 23; 17:26; 18:6; 21:11, 19, 21, 25; 22:21; 26:17, 20, 23; 28:28. The few occasions for Jewish people include Acts 10:22; 24:2, 10, 17; 26:4; 28:19. The use for Samaritans is found in Acts 8:9.

into Greeks and barbarians.[70] Our understanding of the term is still limited. What defines the boundaries and identity of the ethnic groups? Is an "ethnic" simply someone who is different from one's own homogenous group?

Fredrik Barth believes that the term "ethnicity" refers to a group of people who are biologically self-perpetuating, share basic cultural values, have a bounded social field of communication and interaction, and have members who identify and are identified as belonging to that ethnic group.[71] Barth highlights the significance of the term in relation to these boundaries of common identification. Benjamin Isaac defines "ethnic group" as a people who share a long history, beliefs, traditions, distinguishable characteristics, and a cultural tradition of its own, including family, social customs, and manners.[72] Hall argues that an ethnic identity is socially constructed and subjectively perceived.[73] He notices that within ancient Greece, ethnicity was not solely a biological phenomenon. Similar to how we observe in biblical literature, Hall also finds that ethnicity was developed in opposition to other ethnic groups.[74] He proposes that the war with the Persians in 480–479 BCE was the leading cause that compelled the Greeks to define themselves as an ethnic group. Throughout the process of ethnic identification and definition, they constructed "ethnicity" in contrast to the stereotypes and "generalized image of the exotic, slavish, and unintelligible barbarian."[75]

Hall insists that while genetic traits, language, religion, or common cultural forms are important symbols of ethnic identity, they are not the defining criteria. They are merely reflective of established boundaries maintained throughout time.[76] What distinguishes ethnic groups from a social group, as Hall argues, is that ethnic groups subscribe to a myth of shared descent and association to a particular territory. Hall believes that this is why there is an emphasis on birth, not to determine one's ethnic identity, but in order to justify it by anchoring birth to a common descent.[77] Hall

---

70. Balsdon, *Romans and Aliens*, 234.

71. Barth, *Ethnic Groups and Boundaries*, 10–11. Wimmer defines "ethnicity" as a subjectivity felt belonging to a group that is distinguished by a shared culture and common ancestry (Wimmer, *Ethnic Boundary Making*, 7).

72. Isaac, *Invention of Racism*, 35.

73. Hall, *Ethnic Identity*, 19.

74. Hall, *Ethnic Identity*, 33.

75. Hall, *Ethnic Identity*, 45–47.

76. Hall, *Ethnic Identity*, 2, 25.

77. Hall, *Ethnic Identity*, 28.

believes that these two aspects, land and descent, are the most distinguishing characteristics of ethnic groups.[78]

As a result, to be an "ethnic" within the ancient world suggests that one was a member of a people group that distinguished itself from another's shared ancestry and territory. The person within an ethnic group defines their identity either in contrast or with an acknowledgment of difference to another ethnic group. Therefore, our use of the term within this study must be disabused from the notion that ethnicity relates to biological genetics or skin color. The ancients did not view ethnicity in this manner. Although they identified differences—whether cultural, religious, territorial, or myths of descent—they were not impenetrable boundaries. Ethnicity was used to define oneself in contrast to others. These boundaries were dynamic and fluid, socially constructed, and maintained through the observation, separation, or criticism of the other.

If ethnic groups are socially constructed and determined in contrast to other people groups, does this also apply to the concept of race? Ivan Hannaford notes that the word "race" is a recent invention that entered the Spanish, Italian, French, English and Scottish language during the period of 1200–1500 CE. He notes that it was after the French and American Revolution that the idea of race was fully conceptualized and became deeply embedded in our understandings and explanations of the world.[79] Critical race theorists have also led us to recognize that the notion of "race" does not exist. Richard Delgado and Jean Stefancic insist that it is not objective, inherent, or fixed, but the product of social thought and relation. That is, race is a category that society invents in order to distinguish and define groups of people from one another based on cultural, physical, and linguistic differences.[80] Denise McCoskey also adds that at its most basic, race is an ideological structure that organizes and classifies perceived human variations. She insists that the term refers to a division of people into broad categories that are demarcated according to differences such as skin color.[81]

Given the contemporary use of the term "race," its history, potential for misunderstanding, and similar definition with ethnicity, should we reject "race" language altogether? Denise Buell argues that although "race" and "ethnicity" are modern categories, we cannot assume that they were irrelevant to early Christians. She believes that we can explore early Christian strategies of self-definition that resonate with both ancient interpretations of

---

78. Hall, *Ethnic Identity*, 25.
79. Hannaford, *Race*, 6.
80. Delgado and Stefancic, *Critical Race Theory*, 8.
81. McCoskey, *Race Antiquity and Its Legacy*, 2.

cultural difference and modern ones.[82] In biblical literature the term "race" is a translation of the Greek word γένος. The term refers to posterity, family, people, kind, or species.[83] Γένος appears more frequently to describe people groups or humanity.[84] It is most commonly used in reference to the people of Israel[85] and on a few occasions for other groups.[86] Nonetheless, within the Septuagint it also refers to distinct vegetation,[87] creatures,[88] and to describe different kinds of music.[89] The term does not always suggest a particular people group but becomes a general word for a "kind of being" or "entity."

Γένος appears only 20 times in the New Testament with most occurrences found in Acts. The term highlights distinct people groups such as the Syrophoenician woman, Gentiles, Jewish people, and Christians.[90] It is also used in reference to fish, demons, and types of languages or tongues.[91] In most occasions, γένος is used in a general sense for descendants or offspring.[92] This enables us to recognize that γένος denotes a kind of heritage or birth identification to a species, family, or people group. Buell aptly suggests that the common use of the term would have signaled a group classification.[93] She insists that it demarcates a group whose membership would share certain characteristics such as ancestors, rights of inheritance, knowledge, ritual practice, and ways of life.[94] This broad application should lead us to recognize that γένος is primary classification language, as Buell insists. We notice that when applied to people, it suggests a "common birth," "heritage," or "ancestry." When applied to inanimate objects, it refers to a "type" or "kind."

Although race and ethnicity are difficult to precisely define and used synonymously throughout the contemporary era, I will also use them interchangeably. I recognize that ethnicity and race are subjective and objective

82. Buell, *Why This New Race*, xiii.
83. Büchsel, "γένος" *TDNT* 1:684–85.
84. Gen 17:14; 19:38; 25:17; 34:16; 35:29; Lev 20:17–18; 21:13–14, 17.
85. Exod 1:9; 5:14; Josh 4:14; 11:21; Job 8:8; Ps 7:8; 17:7; Esth 2:10; 3:13; 6:13; Isa 22:4; 42:6; 49:6; Dan 1:3, 6; Jdt 5:10; 6:2, 5, 19; 8:20, 32; 9:14; 11:10; 12:3; 13:20; 15:9; 16:17, 24.
86. Gen 11:6; 26:10; Job 40:30.
87. Gen 40:17; 2 Chr 16:14.
88. Gen 1:11–12, 21, 24–25; 6:20; 7:14; 8:19.
89. Jer 48:1; Dan 3:5.
90. Mark 7:26; 2 Cor 11:26; Gal 1:14; Phil 3:5;1 Pet 2:9.
91. Matt 13:47; Mark 9:29; 1 Cor 12:10, 28; 14:10.
92. Acts 4:36; 7:13, 19; 13:26; 17:28, 29; 18:2, 24; Rev 22:16.
93. Buell, *Why This New Race*, 1.
94. Buell, *Why This New Race*, 2.

terms. They are subjective because the boundaries of people groups are always shifting and determined by both insiders and outsiders. People groups share distinct identity markers such as culture, ancestry, religion, territory, and myths of descent. The boundaries are also fluid in that one can abandon or join another ethnic/racial group. Yet ethnicity and race are also objective in that there is a common heritage and ancestry related through birth and genealogy. These boundaries are fixed in the sense that there will be insiders who determine and demarcate who could be properly considered a member. That is, regardless of how one may perceive oneself, one could be categorized and placed among other ethnic and racial members. Since this study utilizes both terms, we must recognize their fluid but stable meanings.[95] This is important for our study because various ethnic groups appear in the gospel. And since this was an acknowledged reality in the ancient world, we must be cognizant of how ethnic groups and boundaries were perceived, observed, and maintained. Even more, we must also be aware how ethnic and racial views were challenged, criticized, and even subverted.

The Approach in this Study: Ethnocritical Method

In order to uncover these ethnic dynamics within the text I also want to explain how I arrive at my observations. I admit that the use of the historical-critical method has enabled interpreters to uncover information for our analysis and understanding of the text while also compelling us to read the literature within its primary setting.[96] This approach has fostered various proposals and concise investigations, especially in determining the circumstances and surrounding context of scripture. It has grounded theological research by anchoring texts in a historical framework that enables us to faithfully interpret biblical literature. However, as we begin our analysis of the Spirit and the ethnic realities of the ancient world, this approach is limited in finding the answers to our questions.

What other approach can we use then in interpreting the ethnic dynamics of the gospel? John Elliott notes that social-scientific criticism is that phase within the exegetical task that analyzes the social, cultural, and environmental context through the utilization of perspectives, theories, models, and research of the social sciences.[97] He reminds us that a text is a product of its social context. It encodes and communicates information

---

95. See Oware and James, "Ethnicity and Race," 99–102.
96. Krentz, *Historical-Critical Method*, 35–41; Miller, "Reading the Bible Historically," 17–32.
97. Elliott, *What Is Social-Scientific Criticism?*, 7.

about the system in which it was created and to which it responds.[98] Bruce Malina also agrees that meaning comes from the social system and is controlled by the context in which it was produced.[99] He remarks that language transmits a hidden load of shared assumptions, a collective and shared set of interpretations of reality that make up the culture of a particular group.[100] Wayne Meeks calls this approach a "hermeneutic of social embodiment." He insists that this hermeneutic entails a social strategy because texts function intelligibly within specific cultures. Meeks notes that if we do not have the adequate social context, the communication of the text is frustrated or distorted.[101] In other words, these social-scientific critics argue that to understand the text, we must understand the social dimensions of the text. There is no way to escape this fact because all texts are social exchanges and correctly interpreting them will be shaped by our grasp of the environment in which they were produced.

What is the social system that we must uncover in order to understand the text? Malina recognizes that it includes culture, social structures, and an accepted individual self-understanding, all which are the general ways a society provides a socially meaningful way of living.[102] A social-scientific approach compels us to recognize that any understanding of the Spirit will depend upon the socially conditioned environment of the Johannine community. But I also believe that our attempt to understand the Spirit must include an analysis of the ethnic scripts, views, ethos, and knowledge of the racial context within the Greco-Roman world. These concerns are crucial in helping us reimagine and reconstruct the situation of the texts we interpret.[103] Yet this approach is also similar to what literary critics describe as "ethnocritical" given the emphasis centers upon the intersection of ethnic attitudes, perspectives, prejudices, stereotypes, and groups within the social-cultural context of a text.[104] I utilize this ethnocritical approach,

---

98. Elliott, *What Is Social-Scientific Criticism?*, 9.

99. Malina, *Christian Origins and Cultural Anthropology*, 1–9; *Social World of Jesus*, 7.

100. Malina, *Christian Origins and Cultural Anthropology*, 2.

101. Meeks, "Hermeneutic of Social Embodiment," 192.

102. Malina, *Social World of Jesus*, 6; Elliott, "Social-Scientific Criticism of the New Testament," 5; Malina, "Normative Dissonance," 35–55.

103. Elliott, *What Is Social-Scientific Criticism?*, 15; Barton, "Historical Criticism and Social Scientific Perspective," 69–74.

104. The term utilized within this exegetical analysis is borrowed from Krupat's ethno-critical approach to Native American literature. His approach reads ethnic encounters within texts in such a way that it provokes an interrogation of and challenge to what we take as familiar and our own. See Krupat, *Ethnocriticism*, 3–5, 37. Critics have rightly noticed the difficulties in distinguishing between cultural readings and

not as an independent method, but in relation to other operations of the exegetical enterprise which includes insights from historical and narrative perspectives on the gospel.[105]

When we examine the Greco-Roman context of the gospel in the following chapter I argue that the Johannine community was composed of diverse ethnic members. They would have recognized ethnic differences and how different groups viewed and described one another, including the various ethnic characters within the gospel. We thus need to take ethnic questions into consideration if we want to have a richer access to the possible interpretation and understanding of the Spirit in the gospel. As such, questions about the ethnic identity of the writer, audience, and texts would include:[106]

1. What is the ethnic composition of the readers?
2. What can be inferred from the author's and readers' ethnic identity?
3. What are the ethnic scripts, traditions, and beliefs that readers are presumed to share with the author?
4. What ethnic perspectives does the text affirm, encourage, promote, exhort, or declare?

Questions that incorporate ethnic identity in relation to texts on the Spirit within the Fourth Gospel would also include:

5. How does the Spirit challenge, affirm, or reject the ethnic views—prejudicial or stereotypical—of the readers and characters within the text?
6. What ethnic codes, behavior patterns, or values are necessary to incorporate in our understanding of the Spirit?
7. What is the writer's strategy in articulating the Spirit for a context that held ethnic views and perspectives?

This is what I would consider as ethnocriticism. That is, an aim to understand text in light of the ethnic and racial challenges, negotiations, relationships, context, and ideologies. Fundamental to all these questions is the desire to understand the Spirit in light of an ethnic context of the Greco-Roman age. We seek to uncover how ethnic and racial views may have impacted the development, portrayal, articulation, and understanding of the Spirit in the gospel. Even more, we seek to find how the articulation of

---

ethnocriticism. See Wong, "In Search of a Dialogic Criticism," 159–64.

105. Powell, *What Is Narrative Criticism?*; Stibbe, *John as Storyteller*; O'Day, *Revelation*.

106. Questions adapted from Elliott, *What Is Social-Scientific Criticism?*, 70–73.

the Spirit addresses the possible challenges of ethnic and racial prejudices, views, and stereotypes that were a part of the social life and context of Johannine Christianity.

We cannot assume that ethnic relations, including the perceptions and prejudices from the modern world, were similar to those of ancient communities. At the same time, we must also reject the claim that there is no consistency or continuity in human behavior. Instead, we affirm that, as in all historical reconstruction, some generalities between the present and past have remained.[107] The aim of this analysis explores the ethnic scenarios we are to imagine in reading the biblical text, which is also the goal of social-scientific criticism.[108] By reading the text with these questions in mind, I believe that we will arrive at a more vibrant understanding of the context that will not only explain the episodes within Jesus' ministry, but the theological motifs of the Spirit and its distinguishing foci that is not just Christological but ethnocritical. In other words, it is not just about the Spirit's relationship with Jesus—although important—it is also the Spirit's relationship with ethnic humanity that must be explored.

The Spirit and the Ethnic Context

In the following chapters I will demonstrate how the ethnic perspectives of the Greco-Roman world benefit our analysis of the Spirit. In particular, the underlying thesis throughout this monograph proposes that ethnic hostilities were a significant concern for the community which prompted a new development and understanding of the Spirit. In addition, this thesis also presumes that the Johannine community was ethnically diverse and lived in a contentious world filled with prejudices and phobias. Therefore, the Johannine writer articulated a pneumatology in response to ethnic conflicts and prejudicial views that were experienced and perpetuated by the members of the community. Many of these members still held onto ethnic hostilities toward their Jewish brethren. Others experienced the prejudice and phobias from them. The writer clearly finds racial tension to be problematic for the formation of the Johannine community that had a wider ethnic mission. At the minimum, these members would include Jews, Samaritans, and Greeks. These members would have caught the ethnic implications of the gospel's pneumatology for their current climate.

The Spirit thus challenges them to reimagine their diverse ethnic identities and relationships with one another. But most importantly, the

---

107. Harvey, *Historian and the Believer*, 68–99.
108. Elliott, *What Is Social-Scientific Criticism?*, 5.

Spirit is involved in the rejection of ethnic superiority and ethnocentric views that these Johannine members experienced, harbored, and perhaps championed. We will notice therefore that the Spirit commissions Jesus for the redemption of all ethnic groups. The Spirit grounds all ethnic identity in the common maternal birthing experiences of believers and rejects all genealogical privileges or prestige. In a sense, the Spirit "ethnicizes" humanity into a new creation. The Spirit seeks to dwell with all people, despite the perceived ethnic lineage, intra-ethnic conflict, and perceptions of inferiority and questionable heritage. We will also explore how an ethnic inclusive invitation to partake of the Spirit-Paraclete is proclaimed despite intra-ethnic abandonment, rejection, and hostility with the world. This also means that to be "breathed upon" by the Spirit means that one is commissioned to go into the racialized world of people from diverse ethnic backgrounds. Self-segregation or rejection of the other is not a mark of the Spirit. And since the Spirit is actively involved in the life of a diverse ethnic Johannine community, their commission also means that they must reject violence, oppression, ethnocentric hostilities, prejudices, and stereotypical views common to the Greco-Roman world. And in many ways, this also means that racism and ethnocentric views and practices are activities that are anti-pneumatic.

What we find is that the Johannine articulation of the Spirit was written in such a way that it aimed to provide the common space that would unite, affirm, and challenge the various ethnic members' views of others within and outside the community. Fundamental to this exploration is the belief that understanding the ethnic ideologies of the Greco-Roman world will not only inform how we reconstruct the context of the gospel, but also help us understand the ethnic context in which this pneumatology emerged. Without such background, our analysis of the Spirit will fail to touch the real-life issues surrounding the world of emerging Johannine Christianity. In a sense, I am also proposing that we not only become focused upon a Spirit-Christology but also recognize that the gospel is articulating a racial-pneumatology. Said differently, the gospel provides the grounds for thinking and exploring the significance of a racialized pneumatology that interacts and concerns itself with the living experiences of ethnic people.

Journey Ahead

My thesis proposes an alternative way of understanding the Spirit. I raise the possibility that the ethnic ideologies of the Greco-Roman world must influence how we understand the pneumatic discourses. One could argue that this understanding of the Greco-Roman world does not demand that we reread the Spirit discourses. In addition, one may also recognize that this incorporation of ethnicity also assumes key aspects of the context and community of the gospel that need to be clearly argued. As a result, in chapter two we will examine the implied ethnic author, readers, provenance, and date of the gospel. This will present us with the needed background to expand our imagination of the gospel's ethnic context. This will also prepare us for chapter three, where we will explore more critically the ethnic ideologies of the ancient world. This includes examining Greco-Roman theories of ethnicity and how the Romans, Greeks, and Jews viewed one another. In part two, we will incorporate our findings into an exegetical analysis of the Spirit within the public ministry of Jesus. This includes the bestowal of the Spirit in John 1, Jesus' dialogue with Nicodemus in John 3, Jesus' encounter with the Samaritan woman in John 4, the bread of life discourse in John 6, and the invitation to partake of the Spirit in John 7. In part three, we will explore the Paraclete sayings with an attention to how the ethnic themes of kinship, orphans, and construction of the other as "world." This will also include an analysis of the Johannine Pentecost in John 20 and the significance of Jesus' commission. And finally, I finish by summarizing the findings of our research and propose a more robust understanding of the Spirit from the gospel. These concluding remarks aim to challenge us to rethink the pneumatology of the gospel for a diverse ethnic context today. This research hopes to continue the dialogue of ethnicity in scripture with an attention to the reality of race in the ancient world.

2

Examining the Ethnic Background of the Fourth Gospel

CHARLES DODD ASSERTS THAT EXEGESIS WILL ALWAYS DEMAND a basic assumption regarding the general aim and background of the book.[1] It has been customary for biblical scholars to use literary and historical methodologies to identify the author, readers, provenance, and date. The narrative critic Mark Stibbe agrees that there is always a need to have a historical dimension in reading scripture.[2] Others such as John Elliot insist that social-scientific analysis is always a component of the historical-critical method.[3] I however do not want to lose sight of another aspect, the notion that the Fourth Gospel was also read, communicated, and shaped by those who were not from a homogenous ethnic identity and context in Judea. This study seeks to press beyond historical background questions, although it includes it. Our goal is to locate the gospel within its proper historical milieu and detect the implied ethnic dynamics that may give us a fuller understanding of the gospel's context. This exploration will include the traditional historical approach but with a focus upon the following three questions:

1. What is the implied ethnic identity of the author?

2. What is the implied ethnic identity of the reader(s)?

3. How do the location and date shape our understanding of the ethnic context?

1. Dodd, *Interpretation*, 3.

2. Stibbe, *John as Storyteller*, 12; Powell, *What Is Narrative Criticism?*, 95–98.

3. Elliot, *What Is Social-Scientific Criticism?*, 11; Malina, *New Testament World*, 1–2; *Christian Origins and Cultural Anthropology*, 9.

In this chapter, we will focus on the various arguments for the author, readers, and context of the gospel. As we observe in the first question, we are not only seeking to discern the identity of the author. We want to explore clues that may uncover the author's ethnic identity. In the second question, we do not solely want to find out the intended audience but also unearth any implied ethnic readers. Third, we do not only want to locate the context of the gospel. We seek to discern the social and racial realities of this period. Investigating the historical background of the gospel in this manner will better suite our interpretation of the text from an ethnocritical perspective. It will help us to have a more coherent picture of the possible ethnic challenges, context, and concerns that may have shaped the Spirit language in the gospel.

The Ethnic Identity of the Author

The patristic tradition overwhelmingly affirms that the author of the Fourth Gospel is John the apostle. The earliest text attributing the gospel to the apostle is P66, which is dated around 200 CE by textual scholars.[4] At the end of the second century, Irenaeus confirms that John the apostle provided the gospel while in Ephesus.[5] He states, "John, the disciple of the Lord, who also had leaned upon His breast, did himself publish a gospel during his residence at Ephesus in Asia" (*Haer.* 3.1.1). The significance of Irenaeus's testimony is vital. According to Eusebius of Caesarea, Irenaeus also traces his knowledge of the gospel's author through the witness of Polycarp who was John's disciple. According to Eusebius, Irenaeus also states,

> I remember how he spoke of his intercourse with John and with others who had seen the Lord. How he repeated their words from memory, and how the things that he had heard them say about the Lord, his miracles and his teaching, things that he had heard direct from the eyewitness of the word of life, were proclaimed by Polycarp in complete harmony with scripture. (Eusebius, *Hist. eccl.* 5.20)

Eusebius and Irenaeus certainly believe that John the apostle was the author. Eusebius also adds that the apostle wrote the gospel because all previous gospels omitted the deeds that Jesus did at the beginning of his ministry.[6]

---

4. Aland and Aland, *Text of the New Testament* 87; Metzger, *Texts of the New Testament*, 39–40.

5. Irenaeus, *Haer.* 2.22.5; 3.1.1; 3.16.5; 3.22.2; 5.1.8.2.

6. Eusebius, *Hist. eccl.* 3.24.

Eusebius further cites others who affirm John's authorship. This includes Clement of Alexandria,[7] Dionysius of Alexandria,[8] and a letter that Polycrates sent to Bishop Victor in Rome.[9] It is also important to point out that Eusebius does suggests that there were two people with the name of John in Ephesus.[10] But J. Ramsey Michaels argues that Eusebius has an alternative motivation for mentioning these two people with similar names in Ephesus.[11] Other textual evidence that proposes John the apostle as the author is the Muratorian Fragment, which includes a communal participation in the remembrance of Jesus' life.[12] John the apostle is described as being exhorted by his disciples to write his account of the gospel. He states, "Fast with me for three days from today and then let us relate to each other whatever may be revealed to each of us."[13]

The early church fathers present strong evidence for John's authorship. Scholars recognize the strength that this external evidence puts forth even though they raise caution on its reliability.[14] When we explore the text of the gospel, internal clues point to an eyewitness dependence. The gospel claims to be dependent upon "one whom Jesus loved," also known as the Beloved Disciple. The Beloved Disciple is a mysterious character within the gospel. He is identified in 13:23 when Jesus was foretelling his betrayal, standing at the foot of the cross in 19:26, with Peter at the tomb in 20:2–10, fishing with Peter in 21:7, and walking with Peter and Jesus along the sea in 21:20–25. Raymond Brown initially observes that the best explanation for the identity of this figure is John the son of Zebedee.[15] But the appearance of this unknown figure throughout the narrative is puzzling. This is possibly the same unnamed disciple in 1:37–42 and the same person who was with Peter in the courtyard of the high priest after Jesus was arrested in 18:15–16. Brown first believed that this person was John the apostle given the close association with Peter, his presence with Jesus at the Last Supper, and was known to be one of the three disciples constantly with Jesus.[16] Although

---

7. Eusebius, *Hist. eccl.* 6.14.
8. Eusebius, *Hist. eccl.* 7.25.
9. Eusebius, *Hist. eccl.* 5.24.
10. Eusebius, *Hist. eccl.* 5.24
11. Michaels, *John*, 10–12.
12. Robbins, "Muratorian Fragment," *ABD* 4:928–29.
13. Bettenson and Maunder, *Documents of the Christian Church*, 31.
14. Brown, *John*, 1:xcii; Michaels, *John*, 6–12, 24; Barrett, *St. John*, 105–6; Beasley-Murray, *John*, lxvii–lxviii.
15. Brown, *John*, 1:xcvi.
16. Brown, *John*, 1:xcvi.

Brown later changes his view on the identity of the beloved disciple,[17] no other person from the twelve apostles matches this description like John.

This anonymous person, however, is described not only as someone whom Jesus loved, but also one who was close to Jesus (13:23) which reflects the similar language that describes the closeness Jesus has with the Father (1:18).[18] Does this suggest that the testimony of the Beloved is akin to the reliable revelation of the Father that Jesus provides? Michaels does not think so. He suggests that this closeness would have been something that all the disciples would have enjoyed.[19] Samuel Pérez Millos finds this expression as a figure of speech which would signify the Beloved's position of honor.[20] Leon Morris suggests that this description only implies that Jesus had a tender regard for this disciple.[21] And we find Rudolf Bultmann arguing that in this passage the Beloved is presented as an ideal figure who symbolically represents a Gentile Christianity that achieved its own true self-understanding. Since the Beloved is close to Jesus, as Bultmann argues, this also means that he can mediate Jesus' thought and thus demonstrate a superior understanding of Christianity over and against Peter who represents Jewish Christianity.[22] Bultmann indeed interjects a racial component in understanding and identifying the author. But must this be so?

Does the nearness of the Beloved to Jesus in 13:23 suggest that the Beloved should be held in high regard? One cannot avoid the comparison being made between the Beloved's closeness to Jesus and Jesus' closeness with the Father, given that they are both described with similar language in 1:18 and 13:23 (κόλπος). Pressing the similar descriptions too far would lead one to suppose that the Beloved had a superior revelation of Jesus' identity. This thus places the Beloved in tension and opposition not only with Peter, but with all the disciples, as we notice in Bultmann's view which positions Jews and Gentiles against each other. Certainly, the relationship between the Beloved and Peter is not hostile throughout the gospel. In fact, Barnabas Lindars suggests that the description of the Beloved's intimate access to Jesus is intended to compare the Beloved Disciple with Judas.[23] Both Judas

---

17. Brown, *Introduction*, 191; *Community*, 34.

18. In 13:23 and 1:18 the term κόλπος is utilized to describe the closeness that Jesus has with the father and the beloved disciple's closeness with Jesus.

19. Michaels, *John*, 749.

20. Millos, *Juan*, 1290.

21. Morris, *John*, 555n53.

22. Bultmann, *John*, 484–85.

23. Lindars, *John*, 458.

and the Beloved were close enough to Jesus which suggests that they were at his right and left side.

But for the sake of argument, if the Beloved Disciple is John the apostle, does this necessarily mean that he is the author of the gospel? R. Alan Culpepper does not believe so.[24] Culpepper notes that passages such as 19:25–27, 35 and 21:20–25 point to the text's dependence upon the Beloved Disciple.[25] In 19:25–27, 35 the Beloved Disciple is described as both a reliable witness and witness of the events. The gospel states,

> When Jesus saw his mother, and the disciple whom he loved standing near, he said to his mother, 'Woman, behold, your son!' Then he said to the disciple, 'Behold, your mother!' And from that hour the disciple took her to his own home. (19:25–27)
>
> He who saw it has borne witness—his testimony is true, and he knows that he tells the truth—that you also may believe. (19:35)

The third person pronoun "he" in v. 35 gives us and the readers the assurance that what is written in the gospel is dependent upon an eyewitness. In other words, the writer describes a situation that the Beloved Disciple experienced. This is not something that the author personally observed.

Contrary to Culpepper's claim, Keener argues that the Beloved Disciple and the third person narration are being combined within this verse. He claims that this should lead us to reject a posthumous editor.[26] That is, the Beloved Disciple was writing these truths and referencing himself in the third person. In fact, Keener argues that third-person authorial claims frequently appear in antiquity alongside first person ones. He points to the case of Thucydides and Polybius who use the first person pronoun "I" or "we" when they are observers and the third person pronoun when they are active participants in the narrative.[27] According to Keener, 19:35 confirms that the author is John the apostle who was also known as the Beloved Disciple.

However, can we ascertain that the author is speaking about himself within these verses as Keener asserts? Or is it possible, as Culpepper claims, that the text is describing another witness who was the source of the gospel? We find further clues that identify the identity of the Beloved Disciple in 21:20–24. The text reads,

> Peter turned and saw following them the disciple whom Jesus loved, who had lain close to his breast at the supper and had

24. Culpepper, *Anatomy*, 44; Also Brown, *Introduction*, 190–96.
25. Culpepper, *Anatomy*, 44–48.
26. Keener, *John*, 112; Morris, *John*, 726.
27. Keener, *John*, 105.

said, 'Lord, who is it that is going to betray you?' When Peter saw him, he said to Jesus, 'Lord, what about this man?' Jesus said to him, 'If it is my will that he remains until I come, what is that to you? Follow me!' The saying spread abroad among the brethren that this disciple was not to die. Yet Jesus did not say to him that he was not to die, but, 'If it is my will that he remains until I come, what is that to you?' This is the disciple who is bearing witness to these things, and who has written these things (ὁ γράψας ταῦτα), and we know that his testimony is true.

The scene describes Peter questioning Jesus about the Beloved Disciple's fate. Some scholars note that v. 23 appears to clarify the belief that the Beloved Disciple was dead.[28] Others claim that this text challenges the rumor that Jesus' return would occur before his death.[29] It is difficult to determine which is the likely option from this text alone. We find further information in v. 24 which describes the Beloved Disciples as the one "who is bearing witness to these things and who has written these things." The verse points to the Beloved Disciple as both the source and author of the text. Is this evidence of the Beloved disciple's view of himself? It may appear so, but we find some challenges. The term "γράψας" does not necessarily mean that the Beloved Disciple penned the gospel but can also suggests that he authorized or caused its writing.[30] That is, the Beloved Disciple previously "authorized these things" which are now being edited and revised into the final version of the gospel.

The literary evidence should lead us to believe that an editor was giving credit to the Beloved Disciple as the primary witness and source of the gospel. If we include the external tradition, we notice that the solution is not easily untangled, and we have yet to discuss the possibility of other figures.[31] Scholars such as Keener and Morris affirm that John the apostle was the author. Others such as R. Alan Culpepper, George Beasley-Murray, and Raymond Brown believe in the involvement of another author or authors. However, we must recognize that it is difficult to ignore the rationale for the third person pronouns when it would have made sense to use first person. In fact, Bultmann also points out that 21:24 is a part of the postscript of a redactor.[32] He observes that 21:24 reflects the notion that the Beloved Disciple

---

28. Brown, *John*, 1:xciv; Barrett, *St. John*, 488; Smith, *John*, 398; Culpepper, *Anatomy*, 45–47.

29. Keener, *John*, 1240; Morris, *John*, 775.

30. Barrett, *St. John*, 100–101; Brown, *John*, 1:cii.

31. Stibbe contends that the Beloved Disciple is Lazarus. See Stibbe, *John as Storyteller*, 77–82.

32. Bultmann, *John*, 700.

is clearly the authority behind the gospel.[33] The writer holds the Beloved Disciple as the primary source and the key eyewitness to the gospel.[34] Bultmann does not believe that he is in any position to say anything about the identity of the Beloved Disciple or writer. He simply asserts that the author is not John the apostle.

John the apostle was certainly not the author. But this does not explain why patristic evidence clearly points to the apostle. There is also another way of thinking about this puzzle—that the gospel itself was developed from an earlier version by John the apostle, who was also known as the Beloved, but completed in its final form at some period after his death.[35] Holding to a theory of an early draft is debatable[36] but this view helps us understand the references to a Beloved Disciple. Brown reminds us that we must distinguish between the author whose ideas the book expresses and the writer who composed the final work. That is, if a particular author was surrounded by a group of disciples who carried on his thought even after his death, their works could be attributed to him as the author.[37] This does not mean, as Robert Fortna also points out, that the editors rewrote the gospel to the point that it became beyond recognition.[38] Indeed, if the final editor of the gospel did not agree with the content of the original source there would have been no need to incorporate it into the final version.[39] This is why we can affirm that the Beloved Disciple is the authority behind the gospel but not the final editor.[40] And this also explains why patristic testimony viewed John the apostle as the author.

---

33. Bultmann, *John*, 717.

34. Bultmann, *John*, 483. Paul Anderson makes a similar point. See Anderson, *Riddles of the Fourth Gospel*, 48–49, 155.

35. The sign-source theory championed by Bultmann claims that the evangelist drew from a source that contained a collection of miracle stories (Bultmann, *John*, 113). Fortna attempts to reconstruct the sign source used by the evangelist (Fortna, *Gospel of Signs*, 99–100; "Source and Redaction," 152). See Faure, *Die alttestamentlichen Zitate*, 99–121; Temple, "Two Signs in the Fourth Gospel," 169–74. Ashton upholds a sign-source tradition but also suggests that a principle preacher was the one responsible for the main body of the gospel material. See Ashton, *Understanding*, 102–7; *Gospel of John and Christian Origins*, 3.

36. Smith, "Sources of the Gospel of John," 345; "Setting and Shape," 236; Lindars, *Behind the Fourth Gospel*, 43; Van Belle, *Signs Source in the Fourth Gospel*, 372–77; Brown, *John*, 1:xxxi–xxxii; Thompson, "Signs and Faith in the Fourth Gospel," 89–108.

37. Brown, *Introduction*, 190.

38. Fortna, *Gospel of Signs*, 14.

39. Van Belle, *Signs Source in the Fourth Gospel*, 372–77; Smith, "Sources of the Gospel of John," 346; Lindars, *Behind the Fourth Gospel*, 37.

40. Brown, *Introduction*, 192; Lindars, *Behind the Fourth Gospel*, 12.

This synthesis of the internal and external evidence provides a major significance to our understanding of the ethnic identity of the author. Claiming that John the apostle and his community of disciples were the sources and redactors of the gospel principally suggests that the memory of the Jesus tradition originated with Jewish Christians. In fact, Brown remarks that the knowledge of Jewish customs and historical insights within the gospel enables us to affirm that the gospel is rooted in a primitive historic memory of Jesus' mission.[41] The apostle was not an unnamed person void of ethnic perspectives, cultural views, or prejudices. Identifying a Jewish apostle as the primary source of the gospel urges us to remember that he was a real person who was situated with an ethnic identity. However, the identity of the primary author does not necessarily mean that his redactors and later editors carried his Jewish perspectives and barred outside factors, views, and perspectives that may run contrary. Nonetheless, this is why it would benefit our exegetical analysis of the gospel to consider how the Jewish racial perspectives permeate the thoughts, ideas, and points of view within the text. Although we are now more conscious of these realities in our reading of the gospel, there are still further questions to explore.

The Implied Ethnic Readers

Who were the readers of the Fourth Gospel? Or more specifically, what can we infer from the text about their racial identity? We are indebted to monumental work of scholars who have compelled us to think about a "Johannine community" that preserved the memory of the Jesus tradition. However, in examining the identity of this community, their circumstances, and possible situation that led to the emergence of the gospel, we find diverse views on the identity of these members. Views range from an excommunicated Jewish community, a Hellenistic audience, possible Samaritan members, or multiple audiences that change depending upon the period in which the gospel was composed. In this section, I will demonstrate how the evidence compels us to think about a diverse ethnic Johannine community as the primary readers.

We will first start with the insights of Dodd who asserts that the gospel appeals to a non-Christian public. He believes that a reader with no knowledge of Christianity beyond the minimum would understand the gospel intelligently.[42] That is, the implied readers were not necessarily Jewish-Christian believers, but those who were ready to convert if the gospel was

41. Brown, *Introduction*, 110.
42. Dodd, *Interpretation*, 6.

presented to them in terms that drew on their previous religious worldview.[43] He bases this claim by comparing the language of the gospel to the Hermetic literature that fused Platonic and Stoic thought into Greek-Egyptian wisdom literature.[44] Dodd also points out that the Hermetics would have understood the gospel's cosmological dualism, emphasis upon knowledge, the importance of a mediator, and ideas of rebirth.[45] This leads him to conclude that there were common backgrounds and religious thoughts with the readers.[46] Does this mean that the readers were non-Jewish? Not necessarily.

Although Dodd makes a strong case for a non-Christian reader, he also finds remarkable parallels between the gospel and Philo. Both Philo and the gospel describe God with language of light,[47] fountain of life,[48] and shepherd.[49] Dodd insists that Philo's treatment of the Logos is strikingly different from the gospel's view of Jesus as the incarnate Logos. As he rightfully points out, Philo does not consider the Logos as a personal guide, companion, personal object of faith, and love.[50] According to Philo, the Logos is only the thought of God, image of God, and agent in the creation of and ministry to the world.[51] This affinity with Hellenistic literature is not the only possible background that the gospel reveals. Dodd also notes that the author has familiarity with details of rabbinic exposition, conceptions of the Torah, a Jewish understanding of the Logos, Messiah, and Jewish practices which can illuminate our understanding of the gospel.[52] Although he admits these examples are speculative, they demonstrate how the gospel was acquainted with emerging rabbinic Judaism. But Dodd also argues that since the Gnostic readers in the second century were profoundly interested in the gospel, the readers may have belonged to the same religious climate.[53] They have a similar metaphysical dualism, need for a mediator, and ideas of redemption

---

43. Dodd, *Interpretation*, 9.

44. Dodd, *Interpretation*, 12–18. See also Barrett, *St. John*, 28–42; Smith, *Theology of the Gospel*, 12.

45. Dodd, *Interpretation*, 49.

46. Dodd, *Interpretation*, 53.

47. Philo, *Somn.* 1.75; John 1:9.

48. Philo, *Fug.* 198; *Spec. Leg.* 1.303; John 4:10, 14.

49. Philo, *Agr.* 1:50–53; John 10.

50. Dodd, *Interpretation*, 69, 73.

51. Philo, *Opif.* 1:20, 25; *Conf.* 1:97; *Deus.* 1:57.

52. Dodd, *Interpretation*, 78–96; Barrett, *St. John*, 27.

53. Dodd, *Interpretation*, 102–3.

through knowledge.[54] Dodd insists that the ideas of a Logos, light and darkness, redemption, and mediator between God and the world, is as much Gnostic as it is Johannine.[55] Yet in spite of a common background, Dodd concludes that what makes Johannine Christianity different is the divergent interpretation and understanding of this language.

In sum, Dodd recognizes that the background of the gospel shows affinities with certain tendencies in non-Christian thought. He claims that the author of the gospel sympathetically echoes a Hellenistic Judaism that is reflective of Philo. He believes that Gnosticism has the same roots of Johannine Christianity but asserts that the ideas stand in contrast to the gospel. And finally, Dodd agrees that the evangelist is aware of and partly sympathetic to the teachings of Rabbinic Judaism.[56] Dodd's understanding of the readers therefore leads us to envision a non-Jewish and non-Christian audience residing in a Hellenistic city such as Ephesus.[57] Or simply put, ethnic people who held Hellenistic religious ideas with a minimal understanding of Christianity. The primary readers were neither Jewish nor Jewish Christians.

How then should we assess Dodd's claim? Barnabas Lindars notes that the gospel's thought does not operate in a Greek philosophical mold but from a Jewish and Christian background. He concedes that it is probably written for Greeks, given that the author takes their way of thinking into account and uses expressions that appeal to Hellenistic seekers.[58] Oscar Cullmann however contends that the question for the environment of the gospel has been put in the form of an alternative, either Hellenism or Judaism. He proposes that the alternative of Palestinian Judaism or the Hellenistic Judaism of the diaspora is a false one. Cullmann insists that the region was much less homogeneous and faithfulness to the traditions of Judaism did not exclude the openness to non-Jewish influences.[59] The gospel shows itself to be very familiar with the topography of Jerusalem, Jewish worship, and customs. It also includes numerous references to Old Testament themes.[60] Could this evidence suggest that the readers were probably Jewish in origin? Cullmann provides a strong challenge to the claim that the readers were solely non-Jewish and non-Christian as Dodd proposes.

54. Dodd, *Interpretation*, 109.
55. Dodd, *Interpretation*, 112.
56. Dodd, *Interpretation*, 133.
57. Dodd, *Interpretation*, 9.
58. Lindars, *John*, 35–42.
59. Cullmann, *Johannine Circle*, 30–31.
60. Cullmann, *Johannine Circle*, 32.

In fact, J. Louis Martyn claims that readers include Jewish Christians who had a hostile relation with the synagogue.[61] He argues that the readers are a community who hear the Christian tradition in a manner that is shaped by the circumstances and experiences of synagogue excommunication. Martyn believes that the gospel is a new and unique interpretation that blends the historical circumstances of the community with the events that occurred during Jesus' life.[62] Martyn calls this blending a "two-level drama."[63] He believes that the gospel records the experiences of the church engaged in a traumatic interaction with the synagogue that resulted from their messianic confession of Jesus.[64] Who then were these expelled synagogue members? Martyn detects a gradual identification, separation, and eventual expulsion that took place at some point prior to the gospel. They include Jewish members who were within the synagogue but had no knowledge of the Gentile mission, and felt little alienation or social dislocation from Judaism.[65] In the early period of this community they were a Torah-observant Jewish community. They resided in the synagogue and hoped for a messianic prophet like Moses.[66] Martyn believes that some Jewish Christians came to the synagogue and began to preach that Jesus was this prophet. They possibly penned down the collection of Jesus' signs in order to aid their successful evangelistic effort. Martyn believes that the evangelistic success prompted the authorities to become suspicious of the Jewish Christians' faith.[67] As a result, these secret believers assumed that the only way to respond to the growing suspicion was to either hide their faith or become excommunicated from the synagogue.[68]

Martyn believes that it was during this time that an authoritative Jewish body in Jamnia reached a formal decision to outlaw public expressions of messianic faith in Jesus.[69] These authorities viewed the messianic believers within the synagogue as apostates who needed to be stopped. Therefore, they developed the *Benediction Against Heretics* around 85 CE in order to

---

61. Martyn, *History and Theology*, 66.
62. Martyn, *History and Theology*, 30.
63. Martyn, *History and Theology*, 40.
64. Martyn, *History and Theology*, 48–49.
65. Martyn, *History and Theology*, 153.
66. Martyn, *History and Theology*, 114.
67. Martyn, *History and Theology*, 150–54.
68. Martyn, *History and Theology*, 114.
69. Martyn, *History and Theology*, 49.

weld Judaism into a monolithic structure.[70] Martyn argues that in order to expose Jewish Christians within the synagogue they had to recite the prayer:

> For the apostates let there be no hope. And let the arrogant government be speedily uprooted in our days. Let the naẓerim and the heretics be destroyed in a moment. And let them be blotted out of the Book of Life and not be inscribed together with the righteous. Blessed art thou, O Lord, who humblest the arrogant. (*b. Ber.* 28b)[71]

Martyn asserts that this formal prayer detected those who wanted to hold a dual allegiance to Moses and Jesus while attempting to remain socially connected to the synagogue.[72] He presumes that the faithful believers in Jesus would not recite this prayer. As a result, they were eventually expelled from the synagogue.[73] Martyn thus finds that some members of the Johannine community experienced hostile persecution and death. The tyranny of the synagogue deepened their fear, distrust, and led to social dislocation and alienation. But these experiences also created a need for the penning of the gospel. It compelled them to search for a more mature understanding of Jesus' life as they forged a new identity as Jews who were now Christians.[74] The gospel is thus developed from previous editions following the post-expulsion period of the community.[75] In this sense, the readers of the gospel not only include synagogue excommunicates, but many Jewish Christians who exist in the synagogue's shadow. Who are the implied readers of the gospel? The ethnic implications of Martyn's analysis leads us to primarily affirm a Jewish audience that considers itself "Christian." This community was primarily Jewish and emerged from the synagogue by force. They also recognized that some of their members remained within the synagogue as secret believers.

The influence of Martyn's reconstruction of the Johannine community is noticeable in Raymond Brown's analysis who also agrees that the gospel could be read on several levels which reflects the story of both the Johannine community and Jesus.[76] Although Brown explores the history of the community beyond the gospel, we will only focus on the first two stages relevant to our study. Brown believes that in the first stage, during the

---

70. Martyn, *History and Theology*, 63.
71. Martyn, *History and Theology*, 62–63.
72. Martyn, *History and Theology*, 69–70.
73. Martyn, *History and Theology*, 152.
74. Martyn, *History and Theology*, 156–57.
75. Martyn, *History and Theology*, 157.
76. Brown, *Community*, 17.

mid-fifties and before the gospel was written, a community existed that was very diverse but consisted mainly of Jewish Christians.[77] The original members had a relative low Christology that later blossomed into a high Christology which led to inevitable conflict with synagogue leaders who regarded their views as blasphemy.[78] The original members of the community were Jews.[79] But other members joined, including anti-temple Jews and Samaritan converts.[80] Brown asserts that this newly formed community eventually became suspect to the Jewish synagogue authorities and was eventually expelled. Because of this expulsion, Brown detects that they could no longer worship with other Jews nor consider themselves Jews, even though they were Jews by ancestry. Brown believes that this experience explains why there is anti-Jewish language within the gospel. In other words, there is a blurring between the hostile experience of Jesus with the Jewish authorities and the hostile experiences of the Johannine Christians with the synagogue authorities (9:22; 16:2).[81] The Johannine Christians of Jewish descent no longer considered themselves to be Jews and eventually received a number of Gentiles into the community which led to its gradual diversification.[82]

The second stage of the Johannine community's history according to Brown takes place during the nineties, along with the composition of the gospel. Brown believes that the entrance of Gentiles into the Johannine community led to some adaptations of Johannine thought so that the gospel might be more intelligible and appealing.[83] Brown also infers from the translation of words such as "Messiah" and "Rabbi" that there were non-Jews within the Johannine community.[84] But he also insists that since the opposition to the Jews dominates chapters 5–12 and the opposition to the world dominates chapters 14–17, this could possibly reflect a chronology in the experience of the Johannine community. That is, they now encounter Gentile disbelief after the definitive break with the Jews.[85] Brown also finds various members that could be inferred from the gospel which includes crypto-Christians (9:22–23, 33–38; 12:42–43), disciples of John

77. Brown, *Community*, 40.
78. Brown, *Community*, 25.
79. Brown, *Community*, 27.
80. Brown, *Community*, 37–40. See also Bowman, *Samaritan Problem*, 57–89; Freed, "Did John Write his Gospel," 241–56; Purvis, "Fourth Gospel and the Samaritans," 161–98; Cullmann, *Johannine Circle*, 51.
81. Brown, *Community*, 41.
82. Brown, *Community*, 55.
83. Brown, *Community*, 59.
84. Brown, *Community*, 55.
85. Brown, *Community*, 63.

the Baptist (3:22–26),[86] and other Jewish Christians (6:60–66; 7:3–5; 8:31; 44–45; 10:12). He finds the possibility that there were Jewish Christians who also left the synagogue but did not join the Johannine community. These Jewish Christians had a low Christology, rejected the Johannine view of the Eucharist, and insisted on the importance of physical Jewish descent.[87] Although Brown outlines various ethnic groups in the Johannine community, he insists that the community was not sectarian. Instead, they insisted that entry into the kingdom was not based upon human lineage and thus welcomed all, including Samaritan converts. Yet the ethnic and theological tensions eventually led to a hostile relationship with the synagogue and final expulsion.[88] Brown therefore argues that when the gospel was written the Jewish persecution and issues with the synagogue had left deep scars within the Johannine psyche.

We thus notice from Brown's analysis that ethnic hostility resides in the gospel's negative reference about the Jews. We also observe that the community was a diverse ethnic group that at least included Jews, Greeks, and Samaritans. Brown paints a vivid picture of a diverse ethnic readership but does not spell out the implications this has for our understanding of the Johannine context.

Other solutions to the background of the gospel focus upon the issues within the text but without the full-blown historical reconstruction of the Johannine community as we find in Brown and Martyn. For example, Keener believes that the audience was primarily Jewish and was grappling with its alienation and conflict with respected Jewish leaders within the late first century of the Mediterranean world.[89] He affirms that the Johannine community consisted of Gentiles, but contrary to Dodd, believes they were not the primary audience. Instead, he posits the possibility that the Johannine community included members who would view themselves as God-fearing adherents of an ethnically Jewish religion.[90] But similar to Dodd's view, Culpepper argues that the audience is primarily a Gentile community. He arrives at this conclusion from a literary analysis of the text. He argues that the readers were not aware of the geography,[91] only competent in the Greek language given that Hebrew terms are translated (1:38, 41, 42; 5:2;

---

86. Brown, *Community*, 68–69.
87. Brown, *Community*, 78.
88. Brown, *Introduction*, 168.
89. Keener, *John*, 153.
90. Keener, *John*, 158–59.
91. Culpepper, *Anatomy*, 218.

9:7; 19:13, 17; 20:16),[92] and had an extensive knowledge of the Old Testament scripture, festivals, Jewish groups, and beliefs.[93] This suggests to Culpepper that the readers were not Jewish but Gentile Christians who knew little about Judaism.[94] This claim also resembles David Lamb's analysis. He approaches the gospel from a sociolinguistic perspective and posits that the tenor of the narrative implies an interpersonal relationship between the author and readers. The relationship between them is formal, which is contrary to the assumption that the gospel envisions a close-knit community.[95] In other words, he proposes that the audience came from various backgrounds and approached the text from different points of view.[96]

What if there is no implied community at all and the diverse implied readers suggest that the gospel was written for all people? Richard Bauckham most recently advocates this view. He challenges the current consensus which assumes that each gospel was written for a specific church or group of churches.[97] He believes that the assumption that the evangelists wrote their gospels for their church with a particular situation, character, and need, is too local and particularized.[98] He proposes another possibility, that the gospels were written for all Christians, not specific churches, and with the intention that the gospels should be circulated around all.[99] Bauckham makes a persuasive case in considering the wider and general audience of Christian believers as recipients of the gospel. He notes that the early Christian movement was not composed of isolated communities with little or no communication. The evangelist, or all writers of the gospels, would have written their gospel in light of known issues shared by several churches.[100] I agree with Bauckham's claim that the evangelists were addressing features of the Christian life and social circumstances that were fairly widespread during that time.[101] But his response to the idiosyncrasies in the gospel narrative merits some caution.

We must recall that the gospel makes synagogue excommunication claims that were not reflective of Jesus' own lifetime but contemporary

---

92. Culpepper, *Anatomy*, 219.
93. Culpepper, *Anatomy*, 222.
94. Culpepper, *Anatomy*, 224–27.
95. Lamb, *Text, Context, and the Johannine Community*, 173.
96. Lamb, *Text, Context, and the Johannine Community*, 203–4.
97. Bauckham, *Gospel*, 1.
98. Bauckham, *Gospel*, 11.
99. Bauckham, *Gospel*, 2.
100. Bauckham, *Gospel*, 37–38.
101. Bauckham, *Gospel*, 24.

issues of the writers. How then should we read the claim that the "Jews had already agreed" to excommunicate believers? This certainly was not true of every Christian community throughout the empire and is too widespread throughout the gospel to assume that it was only a minor point (9:22; 12:42; 16:2). Even more, the hostile encounter with the "Jews" throughout the narrative is not a ubiquitous experience of all Christians. Why would the writer of the gospel strike up this animosity, or at least cause the potentiality for a negative view toward the Jews, their own kinsmen, or neighbors? We cannot overlook the early patristic evidence that points to the local communities and regions as the source of the gospels. Early patristic testimony challenges Bauckham's claim that the gospels were written for all Christians. A cursory review of Eusebius's testimony provides substantial evidence that links the gospels to a particular audience.[102] Regardless of the historical accuracy of Eusebius's claim, or authenticity of the tradition, the simple fact that each gospel was addressed to different audiences in different regions should disabuse us from assuming that particular audiences are irrelevant and have no hermeneutical value. In fact, Margaret Mitchell argues that patristic literature appears to complicate, if not contradict Bauckham's blanket assertions.[103] She insists that it was not modern redaction critics who first introduced the idea of "gospel communities" but patristic interpreters. She demonstrates that the early church fathers were occupied in asking questions about where, when, and to whom each of the four gospels was originally written.[104] As such, solely because we cannot demonstrate with certainty that a particular community was in mind does not suggest that we adhere to a general or indefinite audience. The gospel provides clues and invites us to imagine the possible audience, its struggles, conflicts, and concerns. And as we have examined those who embark upon a pneumatology of the gospel, how we imagine the gospel also influences and impacts how we interpret the role of the Spirit. The hermeneutical relevance cannot be denied.

Who then are the implied readers of the gospel and what can we discern about their ethnic identity? Bauckham provides the option for a diverse readership but does not localize or concede the possibility that the gospel was written for a particular community. According to Dodd and Culpepper, the ethnic readers are primarily Gentiles who are deeply aware of Hellenistic religious ideas and thoughts with minimal understanding of Judaism.

---

102. Eusebius, *Hist. eccl.* 2.15.1–2; 2.16; 3.24.7; 3.39.16; 4.14; 6.14.5–7; 6.25.3–6; Origen, *Fr. Matt.* 1.8; Irenaeus, *Haer.* 3.1.1; 3.5.1; 3.11.1; Luke 1:3; Acts 1:1.

103. Mitchell, "Patristic Counter-Evidence," 46.

104. Mitchell, "Patristic Counter-Evidence," 77.

Neither Dodd, Culpepper, nor Lamb envision a Jew or Jewish-Christian as the primary reader. However, from the analysis of Martyn, Brown, and Keener, we can find evidence of conflict between Jewish Christians and the synagogue Judaism. How then should we assess these diverse views? Perhaps, as John Ashton points out, the best approach is to recognize the most natural inference: the writer is thinking about the people he knows best and among whom he lives.[105] And as Martyn argues with his analysis, we too cannot neglect the possibility that the community's concerns may have bled into the development, emphasis, and idiosyncrasies of the gospel.

When we explore the gospel itself, we cannot deny that it is laced with meetings between Jesus and people from diverse ethnic backgrounds. There are various characters who are described by their ethnic identity. During Jesus' journey to Jerusalem he meets a Samaritan woman and spends many days with the people of Samaria (4:2–42). The readers are made aware of the ethnic segregation between Jews and Samaritans (4:9). Jesus is also accused of leaving to the Greeks (7:35), and there is a rare visit of Greeks who come to the Jewish festival and desire to see Jesus (12:20–26). Still, Samaritans and Greeks are not the only racially referenced characters in the gospel. When the Pharisees discuss Jesus' miraculous activity, they mention the possibility that Jesus' miracles would lead the Romans to take away their place and nation (11:48).[106] We do not find such specific fear of possible violence or uprooting of the Jewish leadership in the Synoptic Gospels (Matt 24:15–16; Mark 13:14–15; Luke 21:24). Even Luke, who makes a vague reference to "Gentiles," does not pin the threat specifically on the Romans. In addition, we also find a remarkable dialogue filled with ethnic overtones of difference when Jesus was before Pilate. In fact, it is Pilate that puts the reality of ethnic identity and difference to the forefront of the conversation. Pilate asks, "am I not a Jew?" (John 18:35). In the Synoptics, we find no discussion or mention of ethnic difference. But in the Fourth Gospel, ethnic identity and difference take a pivotal role. It aims to confront Jesus with the reality that he was handed over by his own people (18:35–36).

Why does the gospel concern itself not only with these ethnic characters but also ethnic difference? Since Martyn suggests the possibility that the gospel blends the historical circumstances of the community with the events that occurred during Jesus' life, why can we not suppose that the ethnic identity of the Johannine community would also be represented by the ethnic members who encountered Jesus during his ministry? I believe

105. Ashton, *Gospel of John and Christian Origins*, 81.
106. However, τόπος, which is translated as "place," could be another way of discussing the place of the temple as noted in Acts 6:13; 7:7; 2 Macc 3:12, 18, 30; 3 Macc 1:9; 2:14.

just that. The gospel is written in such a way that the ethnic identity and concerns of the readers could be found in the narrative story of Jesus. The gospel implies a diverse ethnic audience and therefore makes sure that Jesus addresses ethnic issues and encounters people who are different.

The Fourth Gospel, however, is not unique in depicting encounters with other ethnic members. Jesus' encounter and ministry with non-Jews is attested in the Synoptics. But James Dunn remarks that the picture which emerges in the Synoptics is that of a Jesus who did not envisage a mission to the Gentiles but took for granted the likelihood that they would be included in the Kingdom of God.[107] E. P. Sanders also cautions us in assuming that Jesus was open to the Gentiles. He suspects that the tradition about Jesus had to be stretched in order to have him come into contact with them.[108] Sanders explains that although Jesus started a movement which came to see the Gentile mission as a logical extension of itself, Jesus himself had no explicit view, which is why there was much debate in early Christianity on this topic.[109] In comparison, the Fourth Gospel appears to have a racial conscience by including several distinguishing encounters and remarks not found in the Synoptics. First, the gospel makes various references to the "Jews" throughout the narrative as if they were a distinct racial group. This includes the scandalous assertion that the devil is their father (8:44) and continual warning from Jesus of synagogue excommunication (9:22; 12:42; 16:2). This harsh language about the Jews and frequent warning of synagogue persecution is not found in the Synoptics. The Synoptics do mention synagogue tensions (Matt 23:34; Mark 13:9; Luke 21:12), but they are not regularly repeated as in the Fourth Gospel. Even more, the Fourth Gospel uses the term ἔθνος for the Jewish people (11:48, 50–52; 18:35). This differs from the way in which the Jews are presented in the Synoptics. Only twice are the Jews referred to as ἔθνος in Luke's gospel (7:5; 23:2). The Johannine community knew of ethnic differences and ethnic group membership, even distinguishing themselves from other Jews.

Additionally, in the Fourth Gospel there is no anti-Gentile or anti-Samaritan rhetoric as we find in Matthew. Although the Synoptics include a post-resurrection commissioning scene to "all the nations" (Matt 28:19; Mark 16:15; Luke 24:47), nowhere does Jesus prohibit his disciples from avoiding Gentile or Samaritan regions during his ministry in the Fourth Gospel. Instead, Jesus fellowships with Samaritans, informs the disciples that they would reap a harvest amongst them (4:35–38), and does not

---

107. Dunn, *Jesus Remembered*, 539.
108. Sanders, *Jesus and Judaism*, 219.
109. Sanders, *Jesus and Judaism*, 220–21.

respond to the charge of being called a "Samaritan" (8:48). Although Luke portrays Samaritans in a positive light, the Fourth Gospel describes Jesus having concrete interactions and success in their region.

The Fourth Gospel raises the possibility that Jesus had "other sheep" who were not Jews but possibly Samaritans or Gentiles (10:16). The gospel also recounts a rare episode in which Greeks come to worship at the Jewish feast and desire to meet with Jesus (12:20–26). This is in contrast with the Synoptic tradition which notes that Jesus was expelled from the region of the Decapolis. Why would the Fourth Gospel omit this trip to the Decapolis if this could have resonated with some readers who may have been Greek? Perhaps the gospel did not want to give the impression that the Greeks rejected Jesus during his ministry, especially since some within the Johannine community had converted to become members of the Johannine community. Although they are left wondering if the Greeks eventually meet with Jesus, they already know that he was previously accused of leaving the Jews and going to the Greeks (7:35). Mark and Luke recount that people from the coastal region of Tyre and Sidon came to Jesus. It is however unclear if the visitors were Jews who lived in the region or simply Gentiles.

The Fourth Gospel is concerned with Jesus encountering people who are ethnically different. This differs from the attention and description of ethnic encounters we find in the Synoptics. But why is this gospel concerned about events in which Jesus is encountering, being pursued, or is made aware of distinct ethnic differences? How do we account for such an awareness of diverse ethnic identities, views, and openness to communicate to a broader audience in the ministry of Jesus within the gospel? Is this evidence that the Johannine community was composed of members who were from distinct ethnic backgrounds? Again, I answer in the affirmative. Most admit that the gospel was written with these readers in mind, whether Jews, Greeks, or Samaritans.[110] But I argue that these subtle comments, which may seem trivial, reveal an ethnic focus that reflects the diverse readership of the Fourth Gospel. This is not just about writing to a group of excommunicated Jews from the synagogue or Hellenized Jews. And in contrast to the Synoptic tradition, the Fourth Gospel has a concern for these ethnic groups within Jesus' ministry because this reflects the diverse ethnic identity of the

110. Those who posit a diverse readership would include Brown, *Community*, 37–40, 55; Bowman, *Samaritan Problem*, 57–89; Freed, "Did John Write his Gospel," 241–56; Purvis, "Fourth Gospel and the Samaritans," 161–98; Cullmann, *Johannine Circle*, 51; Keener, *John*, 158–59. Those who have solely a Gentile audience in mind include Dodd, *Interpretation*, 9; Culpepper, *Anatomy*, 224–27; Lamb, *Text, Context, and the Johannine Community*, 203–4. Those who argue for a Jewish readership include Martyn, *History and Theology*, 66; Ashton, *Understanding*, 100–133; Lindars, *Behind the Fourth Gospel*, 76–79.

readers. This reading agrees with Bauckham's proposal that the gospel was written for a broad audience but with a caveat. I believe that the presumed broad audience does not necessarily imply that a specific context, location, or original community was not in mind. Instead, the broad audience should lead us to envision a different way of reading the text from a multiethnic perspective.[111] The multiethnic identity of the Johannine community is the gospel's implied audience. The gospel is remembered, rewritten, and presented with diverse ethnic readers in mind.

Location and Date of the Gospel

The patristic testimony affirms that Ephesus is the primary location of the Fourth Gospel.[112] Although patristic evidence alone is insufficient to make a compelling case, there is internal evidence that gives the strong possibility that Ephesus or Asia Minor more broadly is the provenance of the gospel. First, the gospel has a particular polemic against John the Baptist, a tone that is not reflected in the Synoptics.[113] This may reflect an Ephesian community's awareness of John the Baptist's disciples as noted in Acts 19:1–7. Or as Joel Marcus and Raymond Brown argue, the gospel was written for followers of the Baptist who regarded the Baptist on the same level of Jesus.[114] Second, the gospel also reflects an incipient anti-docetic and anti-gnostic polemic that was associated with Ephesus.[115] This fits with Irenaeus's claim that the gospel was written in Ephesus to refute the teachings of Cerinthus who was a follower of Nicolaitan.[116] Third, the gospel's anti-synagogue motif in John (9:22; 12:42; 16:2) also fits with the issues that Apollo and Paul had in the synagogue as noted in Acts (18:24–28; 19:8–10). However, Keener believes that the bitter conflict in the synagogue between Jews and Jewish Christians was reflective of the whole Asian region.[117] This is an apt point that cannot be denied. In fact, even if we do hold that Ephesus was the primary location, we may not be sure what community and to whom in Ephesus the gospel

---

111. Motyer's intriguing essay suggest that we focus upon receiver concerns and the gospel's rhetorical impact. This, as he argues, would allow the text to point to possible external events and enable us to understand the text in its possible home environment. See Motyer, "Fourth Gospel and the Salvation of Israel," 84–87.

112. Eusebius, *Hist. eccl.* 3.18.1; 3.20.11; 3.23.4–19; 3.39; 5.24.

113. John 1:8, 24; 3:30.

114. Marcus, "Johannine Christians," 155–63; Brown, *Introduction*, 156.

115. Brown, *Introduction*, 124, 205.

116. Irenaeus, *Haer.* 3.11.1.

117. Keener, *John*, 148.

was being written, especially since the city had a historic association with Apollo, Paul, and Timothy.[118] Certainly, Jörg Frey suggests that by the end of the first century there were a variety of Christian communities within the Ephesian metropolis that had various theological profiles and identities.[119] But we also do notice that the gospel has a particular interest to Samaritans and possibly knew of their conversion. According to Robert Anderson and Terry Giles, Samaritans traveled beyond their region and were located even in the Greek island of Delos, 150 miles from Ephesus.[120] It is possible that Ephesus would have been an attractive location for Samaritans, especially since there was already a strong presence of Jewish Christians in the region. And although I agree with the traditional view that this gospel was written for a community in Ephesus, we still must ask, does this make a difference in our understanding of the gospel's context?

This is a difficult question to answer given that many of the circumstances could reflect a broader Asian context as Keener points out. Sjef Van Tilborg, however, argues that if we anchor the gospel in an Ephesian social-cultural context it brings new meanings and understanding to the gospel.[121] For example, Tilborg observes that the way people perceive Jesus is akin to how the Ephesians dealt with their political, religious, and philosophical figures.[122] In Ephesus there are "savior" inscriptions that honor Zeus and Roman commanders, and Artemis has various titles such as "God," and "lord." As Tilborg discovers, the language has semantic parallel to the titles used for Jesus, especially Thomas's confession of Jesus as "Lord and God."[123] In addition, Tilborg notices that the gospel is embedded in a city life similar to the city of Ephesus.[124] He recognizes that Jerusalem and Ephesus were known as temple cities, described with similar language (ἱερόν ναός), include various sacrificial activities, and maintain distinct monetary practices.[125] This urban description would have largely resonated with an Ephesian reader.

How then do we assess this proposal? Although the ancient patristic witnesses and the internal clues that Tilborg proposes give the probability

118. Acts 18:19-21, 24-28; 19:1-20; Eph 1:1; 1 Tim 1:3; Rev 2:1-7.

119. Frey, "Toward Reconfiguring Our Views," 223.

120. Anderson and Giles, *Keepers*, 29-30; Kraabel, "New Evidence of a Samaritan Diaspora," 44-46. Trümper recognizes the difficulties in proving that the synagogue was for Jews or Samaritans but asserts that both groups were present. See Trümper, "Oldest Original Synagogue," 513-98.

121. Tilborg, *Reading John in Ephesus*, 3.

122. Tilborg, *Reading John in Ephesus*, 33.

123. Tilborg, *Reading John in Ephesus*, 47-51, 56.

124. Tilborg, *Reading John in Ephesus*, 63.

125. Tilborg, *Reading John in Ephesus*, 69-74.

of an Ephesian context, one is still compelled to ask if the location really makes a difference. Leon Morris does not think so.[126] Keener joins him by arguing that the final location of the gospel's composition is not necessary for interpreting the gospel, given that it was also representative of other Greco-Roman cities in the eastern Mediterranean.[127] It is true that we cannot be certain of the gospel's precise location. It is also correct that Ephesus reflects various aspects that are ubiquitous to many Hellenistic cities, something that Tilborg acknowledges as well. Although we cannot be certain, the external evidence from church fathers and internal clues point to the probability that Ephesus was the primary location. This does not mean that other cities such as Alexandria or Syria are not possible locations. But it is difficult to explain away the early testimonial and correlation that the gospel has with Ephesus.

Assuming with a certain level of confidence that Ephesus was the primary location, what time period within the first century could also help us understand the Johannine community's context? Was this gospel written during an early period akin to the Pauline mission or a later period after the publication of the Synoptics? We have already proposed that the gospel originates with John the apostle. But there is also something important in our discussion on the gospel's date. To put it simply, the date of the gospel will help us determine if the author and readers of the gospel were dealing with issues within emerging Christianity that were akin to the early Pauline mission or a period in which Christianity was developing its own identity apart from normative Judaism in the late first century.

Even though many scholars claim that the implied circumstances of the gospel and theology support a late date, we find Morris sharply disagreeing. He argues that the theology of the gospel is just as developed as the theology of Paul's epistle to the Romans. Second, he disagrees with the claim that the language of synagogue excommunication is a sign of a later date given that this practice had been occurring since Ezra 10:8.[128] Third, he notices that if the gospel was written last then it is difficult to account for the failure to intertextually refer to the Synoptics.[129] Lastly, he also observes that there are expressions within the gospel that reflect an early date. For example, in John 5:2 we read that "there is" and not "there was" a pool called Bethesda. He believes that the present tense of the verb suggests that the pool was in existence during the writing of the gospel, thus proving that Jerusalem had

---

126. Morris, *John*, 55.
127. Keener, *John*, 146.
128. Morris, *John*, 434–35.
129. Morris, *John*, 27.

not been destroyed.¹³⁰ These factors indicate to Morris that the gospel was written before the disastrous event of the Jerusalem temple.¹³¹

How then are we to assess Morris's rebuttal of the claim that the gospel was composed in the late first century? Believing that the theology of the gospel provides evidence for a later or early date is rightly debatable. In addition, the internal evidence of synagogue excommunication is also difficult to determine, as Jonathan Bernier and James Dunn also notice.¹³² Thus the first two issues that Morris raises are certainly valid arguments that can lead us to favor an early date. However, there are other factors that need to be taken into account before we concur with Morris's assessment.

First, favoring a later date reflects external evidence such as Eusebius's account that John the apostle had knowledge of the Synoptics.¹³³ D. Moody Smith points out that this patristic tradition seems to defend the gospel's relation to the Synoptics which was a problem that the early church attempted to resolve.¹³⁴ This not only explains why the gospel was written last and differs from the Synoptics. It proposes a distinct tradition emerging from the apostle John. What can explain this external support that favors both a later date and separate tradition from the Synoptics? Morris does not adequately address this issue nor the reason why such patristic tradition would exist.

Second, Morris's claim that the Fourth Gospel does not refer to the Synoptic Gospels and fails to reflect its tradition is misrepresented. Johannine scholars recognize that there are several editions of the Fourth Gospel, which are also described as the σημεῖα-source.¹³⁵ Bultmann believes that it was not only the foundational narrative account that led to the eventual emergence of the gospel. It has a style that is distinguishable from the language of the evangelist and main discourse.¹³⁶ Brown posits a theory on the composition of the gospel which includes three distinct historical stages of the gospel's development, including the raw material of Jesus' activity, a later perceptive faith enlightened by the resurrection, and the redactor's rearrangement of the Beloved Disciple's material.¹³⁷ Morris's charges that there are expressions in the gospel that denote an early date may instead reflect

130. Morris, *John*, 28.
131. Morris, *John*, 26.
132. Bernier, "Jesus, Ἀποσυνάγωγος, and Modes of Religiosity," 127–33; Dunn, *Neither Jew nor Greek*, 78.
133. Eusebius, *Hist. eccl.* 3.24.
134. Smith, *John Among the Gospels*, 6–8.
135. Fortna, *Gospel of Signs*, 99–100.
136. Bultmann, *John*, 113.
137. Brown, *John*, 1:xliv–xlvii. A similar argument is made in Anderson, *Riddles of the Fourth Gospel*, 125–55.

the writer's preservation of early material or as Tilborg's analysis suggests, a way of writing for Ephesian readers.[138] In other words, the final form we now have is the polished work of the editor. The work of the editor is evident in the awkwardness of intrusive passages, aporias, and inconsistencies.[139] These are not signs of an early date, but evidence of a distinct tradition, multiple revisions, and theological emphasis that suited the needs of a different community.

Morris's claim that if the gospel was written last it should have some dependence on the Synoptics can thus be explained another way. There is no reason to suppose that only one Jesus tradition existed. Instead, the composition of the gospel gives credence that there were various Jesus traditions, some of which were just as primitive as others. In other words, just because the gospel does not utilize the Synoptics does not mean that the writer was unaware of the tradition. Despite this response to Morris's claims, identifying a precise date is difficult. Yet, it is more reasonable to propose a later date for the gospel's composition after exploring the patristic testimony and internal evidence. Textually, we also know that the gospel could not have been written later than the second century. John Rylands Manuscript P52, which includes John 18:31–33, 37–38, is the oldest copy of any portion of the New Testament. This manuscript is dated between 100–150 CE.[140] Its existence in such an early period within the second century demonstrates that the gospel was in wide circulation in Egypt.[141] What we can affirm is that the gospel was known within one generation of the apostles and preserved by a community that relied upon the witness of John the Beloved Disciple. As such, the best historical judgment leads us to conclude that the gospel was written between 70–100 CE. This position takes into account the patristic evidence of the gospel, the internal clues that point to a period after the destruction of the Jerusalem temple, and the manuscript evidence within the textual tradition.

---

138. Tilborg, *Reading John in Ephesus*, 3, 67–74.

139. For example, language of the personified "word," "grace," and "fullness" in the prologue is not found anywhere else in the gospel (1:1–18); the two endings of the gospel (20:30–31; 21:25); Jesus concludes his remarks and gives orders to depart which does not occur until three chapters later (14:31; 18:1); John the Baptist's followers were present to hear Jesus' mission but fail to know anything later in the narrative (1:29–34; 3:26–30); only two signs are recorded, although Jesus performs many of them (2:11; 4:54); Jesus is in Jerusalem at the beginning of chapter 3 but then departs to Judea (3:22); and Jesus is described as going into hiding but then is speaking in public (12:36; 12:44–50).

140. Metzger, *Texts of the New Testament*, 38–39.

141. Metzger, *Texts of the New Testament*, 39.

Putting forth a late date for the gospel compels us to think about the circumstances and issues of emerging Christianity in a milieu post-70 CE, a period described as the "parting of the ways." Although the "parting of the ways" is a scholarly term, Shaye Cohen reminds us that the separation between Judaism and Christianity is about people, societies and institutions, not truth claims or abstractions.[142] In this gradual separation, Cohen asserts that as the communities became more and more Gentile and hostile toward Jews, it was their ethnically Jewish Christian members who had to decide if they were prepared to remain or maintain their position within the Jewish community.[143] We must keep in mind that this was not a casual decision to make nor was the rupture and separation similar in each region or community. The gradual separation between Judaism and Christianity in the late first century underwent many local circumstances that would have been felt differently by various communities. Strikingly, this tension is also evident in the gospel with its description of synagogue excommunication and Jesus' experiences of continual hostility with Jews that develops throughout the narrative.

In addition, Dunn also reminds us that Christianity as a distinctive entity was not named until the second decade of the second century.[144] He proposes that we should neither think of Judaism and Christianity in the first two centuries as defined entities nor assume that they were uniform movements.[145] Although Christianity in its beginning was Jewish, Dunn remarks that the period between the Jewish revolts (70–135 CE) and beyond was critical for the redefinition of Judaism and Christianity. He finds Christianity emerging from a competing struggle to define itself over and against its Jewish heritage, ideas, and faith.[146] Dunn points out that in the late first century there are many indications of strains and stresses between the Jewish believers in Jesus and the Jewish survivors of the first Jewish revolt. He believes that the local historical context of John 9:22 and Rev. 2:9; 3:9 is evidence of a serious rupture between the churches and synagogues during this period.[147]

The concern of Christianity to emerge independently and construct an identity in contrast to Judaism is a frequent theme noted by scholars. Daniel Boyarin also finds this concern developed in light of the need to define

---

142. Cohen, *From the Maccabees to the Mishnah*, 231.
143. Cohen, *From the Maccabees to the Mishnah*, 233.
144. Dunn, *Neither Jew Nor Greek*, 600.
145. Dunn, *Neither Jew Nor Greek*, 598–99.
146. Dunn, *Neither Jew Nor Greek*, 40.
147. Dunn, *Neither Jew Nor Greek*, 649.

orthodoxy. It was heresiology, as Boyarin suggests, which contributed to the self-definition of Christians over and against Judaism.[148] He proposes that Christianity during this period began to see itself as a community defined by adherence to a certain canon of doctrine and practice.[149] Even more, Boyarin admits that it was the threat of Gentile Christianity in Asia Minor that may have given rise to popular curses on Gentile Christians and to the reviling of Christ in the synagogues.[150] As Boyarin finds, this pressure from Gentile Christianity in Asia Minor stimulated Jewish hostilities and forced Gentile Christians to produce the need for clearer articulations of separation from Judaism.[151] These tensions that Boyarin describes remarkably resembles the synagogue language of the gospel, a point that Martyn and Brown also propose.

Why this brief review of the "parting of the ways" during the late first century? I believe that it is during this period that the gospel emerges as an important gospel for a multiethnic community that was experiencing the pressure to ethnically separate, understand its ethnic relation with Jews, and define itself apart from Judaism and the Jewish synagogue.[152] And as we have reviewed from scholars such as Dunn, Cohen, and Boyarin, the context of the gospel was during the history of emerging Christianity when unity with Judaism was starting to tear. Truly, the gospel appears to reflect the beginning stages of synagogue tension, persecution, and need to define Jesus' identity and relationship with Judaism. What then are the ethnic implications of this context for our understanding of the Johannine Spirit? Perhaps the ethnic motifs serve to force the Johannine community to separate from their Jewish kin and friends?[153] But before we continue to fully answer this question, let us review our findings.

The Ethnic Context of the Fourth Gospel

This analysis of the gospel's background enables us to envision a community and context that was rooted in an ethnic environment. The gospel stems from the memory of John, a Jewish apostle who was also known as the Beloved Disciple. This is not solely based on internal evidence alone but includes patristic witnesses such as Irenaeus, Clement of Alexandria, and

---

148. Boyarin, *Border Lines*, 7–14.
149. Boyarin, *Border Lines*, 17.
150. Boyarin, *Border Lines*, 71.
151. Boyarin, *Border Lines*, 73.
152. Smith, *Theology of the Gospel*, 55–56.
153. Reinhartz, "Story and History," 125–26.

Eusebius. However, John the Beloved Disciple is not the final writer of the gospel. Although he is the reliable source of the gospel, the final version of the gospel was possibly compiled by those who recognized him as a worthy witness. This also means that the gospel was composed within one generation of the Beloved Disciple's death but no later than this.

What about the readers? The translation of Jewish terms and references to Jewish practices and customs reveals that the readers would have been minimally acquainted with Judaism. But the gospel also demonstrates some affinities with non-Christian thought, given that the text reflects an ability to communicate to both Jewish and non-Jewish readers. In our analysis of the Johannine community there are clues that affirm the ethnic diversity of the community. This membership included at least Jews, Samaritans, and Greeks. Still, this should not lead us to assume that this community was void of ethnic tensions. The themes, hostility with the Jewish religious leadership, and anachronistic references to synagogue expulsion compels us to recognize that this community had recently undergone a traumatic expulsion from the Jewish community. This expulsion still lingered in the memory of the community and the gospel reflects a unique interpretation that blends this circumstance with the memory of Jesus' life and ministry.

Locating the precise destination of the gospel is difficult. The patristic witnesses nonetheless point us to Ephesus as the primary location. This enables us to imagine a context that was urban, diverse, and Hellenistic. The readers' environment would have been familiar with Jewish thought but also suitable to make connections between Jesus' teachings to the Hellenistic, imperial, and religious landscape of the Greco-Roman world. Ephesus provides a contextual setting for imagining the significance of Jesus as an itinerant teacher who encountered people from diverse ethnic backgrounds. The external and internal evidence also leads us to conclude that the gospel was written in the late first century when there was a quest for self-definition, a realization of immediate ethnic diversity because of evangelization, and continual tension with the synagogue. Many Jewish Christians still regarded themselves a part of a Jesus movement. But it was also during this time that these Jews and other ethnic members would have encountered challenges and tensions with the Jewish synagogue community.

This background on the gospel challenges us to think about the writer, readers, location, and period in which the gospel was written with ethnic people in mind. Examining these ethnic dynamics, such as how groups viewed and related to one another, provides a concrete reference point in our interpretation of the Spirit in gospel. This concern for an ethnic context does not derive solely from a desire to read scripture anew. Nor does it stem from my own self-conscience identity and understanding of myself as a Latino scholar in a predominantly White field, although I cannot deny that some aspects of my writing attempts to de-center Whiteness.[154] But most importantly, ethnicity matters because the primary readers had an ethnic identity. The gospel provides evidence of a Johannine community that includes members from diverse ethnic backgrounds and context. These ethnic readers are the ones who read and hear the pneumatic language from within their particularized setting and experiences as members of both the Johannine community and Greco-Roman world. And it is this ethnic environment and setting that we will now turn.

---

154. For further discussion on this topic related to theological education and hermeneutics, see Estrada, "Contextualized Hermeneutic," 341–55; "Renewing Theological Education," 134–57. See also Patrick Reyes, who also outlines the challenges in participating in the academy as scholars of color in Reyes, "Religious Education, Race, Dreams, and the Guild," 1–10.

3

Study of the Greco-Roman Ethnic Ideologies

IN THE PREVIOUS CHAPTER I ARGUE THAT THE BACKGROUND of the Fourth Gospel enables us to envision a multiethnic Johannine community that lived during the end of the first century in the Roman Empire. Scholars have rightly pointed out that the Johannine community was a diverse community that included at least Jews, Samaritans, and Greeks. I seek to explore the implications of this claim. That is, to suppose the background of the gospel includes an ethnically diverse community, we must examine how the ancients perceive and construct the ethnic other. As Denise Buell remarks, to speak of ethnicity we are also striving to understand interactions that have real, material, and embodied forms.[1] We thus seek to explore how a multiethnic Johannine community would have ethnically viewed one another and how these elements shape our reading of the pneumatic texts of the gospel. But first, what was the status of ethnic relations in the ancient world? And most importantly, what are the ethnic scripts we need to know in order to interpret the Johannine narrative, especially as it applies to the Spirit? These are the fundamental questions that this chapter seeks to examine.

The Greco-Roman World of Ethnic Difference

Understanding ethnic language and relations in the ancient Greco-Roman world does not come without its difficulties.[2] Our experiences of ethnic

1. Buell, "Challenges and Strategies," 35.
2. See Boatwright, *Peoples of the Roman World*, 14–15; Cosgrove, "Did Paul Value

relations may cloud our analysis of the relations in the ancient world, both in assuming that they did not matter or in assuming that they mattered at every place and situation. But despite this possible limitation, we will find that ethnic issues of identity and relations were a concern for the ancients. We cannot afford to assume that early Christianity sought to transcend and thus eradicate these differences.[3] Three main topics related to the ethnic context of the ancient world will thus be our focus. First, I will argue that it is false to assume that the Greco-Roman world knew nothing of ethnic identity, difference, or prejudice. The second part of this chapter will examine two dominant views that shape how the ancients viewed the other: environment and lineage. Third, since Christianity emerged from a Jewish context and community, I will also explore Roman and Greek views of the Jews. My aim is not to explore the essence of ethnic identity in the ancient world but to understand how the ancients perceived, rationalized, and viewed ethnic groups, especially when it illuminates our understanding of the Johannine narrative.

It must be noted that since this study will explore a range of Greco-Roman writers, this means that we will encounter some who express extreme hostility toward foreigners. I do not assume that all people in the ancient world upheld negative views. Some writers made positive comments about various ethnic groups. Admiration did exist. However, race relations are not a zero-sum game. Admiration of a group does not negate the influence and words of critics. If positive statements were made this does not mean we can erase, excuse, or regard vitriolic comments as forms of exaggerations or totally inconsequential.[4] Instead, they provide evidence that not all were suspicious or had a hatred of ethnic people. But together, both the negative and positive views in literature reveal interpretive possibilities for our understanding of both the ethnic context of the Johannine community and how the Spirit was heard by these Johannine members. We thus must ask, did those within the ancient world describe, relate, or hold contempt for one another based upon perceived ethnic differences? Or asked differently,

---

Ethnicity?," 268–70.

3. Harnack believes that Paul's mission is to move Christianity from an ethnocentric religion to a universal one. See Harnack, *What Is Christianity*, 176–82. See also Buell, *Why This New Race*, 151–52; "Rethinking the Relevance of Race," 453; "Early Christian Universalism" 121–28.

4. Snowden does not find "race" in the ancient world having any consequence in judging a person's worth (Snowden, *Blacks in Antiquity*, 216–18). Gruen admits that there were periodic expressions of superiority, control, and occasional removal of Jews, but contends that these were exceptional circumstances rather the norm (Gruen, *Diaspora*, 19; *Rethinking the Other*). Cohen recognizes anti-Jewish sentiment but does not find it as having a major significance (Cohen, *Beginning of Jewishness*, 54).

how did the ancients view, value, and rationalize their perspectives of the ethnically other?

Adrian Sherwin-White remarks that it is commonplace to assert that the ancients knew nothing of color and racial prejudice by pointing to the assimilation of foreigners into the Greco-Roman culture.[5] That is, since the Romans readily extended citizenship and absorbed various ethnic groups, we may be inclined to presume that hostilities and fears toward foreigners did not exist. This is what Ivan Hannaford claims when he states that our framework of race and ethnicity have led us to inappropriately assume that the idea was present in ancient Greek and Roman era.[6] His claim is however not reflective of the evidence. Denise McCoskey in fact asserts that although the ancients did not utilize skin color to justify ethnic suppression or oppression, this does not mean that the ancients did not think racially nor have a brand of racial ideology.[7] We find many Greek and Roman writers recognizing and describing ethnic groups.[8] Classicists trace the history of perceived racial differences to the Greek civilization.[9] Indeed, the Greeks made logical arguments of their own sense of superiority against those whom they deemed inferior. They notice that these prejudicial attitudes were systematically analyzed, given a firm basis for them in nature, and justified on a rational level.[10]

---

5. Sherwin-White, *Racial Prejudice in Imperial Rome*, 1. See Pliny, *Nat.* 3.39.

6. Hannaford, *Race*, 4–8.

7. McCoskey, *Race Antiquity and Its Legacy*, 9. This claim is contrary to Snowden, who believes that the absence of color prejudice means the absence of racial antipathy or prejudice. See Snowden, *Blacks in Antiquity*, 2; *Before Color Prejudice*, 63. Hannaford also believes that Greek color theories may have led to an absence of color prejudice. That is, difference in color depended upon sight and different degrees of moisture within the subject. See Hannaford, *Race*, 39–47.

Aristotle states, "Hair, plumage, skin of horses, cattle, sheep, men, and all other living creatures are white and grey and red and black for the same reason; white when the moisture which possesses its own natural color dries up, and black on the other hand when the moisture about the skin at birth, as happens in all other cases, grows black when it grows old and has lasted a long time because of its quantity. For the complexion and the skin of all such is black. Those are grey, red, yellow, and other colors, which dry before the moisture in them changes completely to black. Those in whom this change takes place unevenly have all kinds of variegated colors" (Aristotle, *De col.* 6.1).

8. Rebecca Kennedy notes that the terms *genos, ethnos, ethne,* and *phule* were all variously used to denote race, an ethnic group, or a political or some other social or cultural unit. See Kennedy, *Race and Ethnicity in the Classical World*, xiv.

9. Radin, *Jews Among*, 49; Sherwin-White, *Racial Prejudice in Imperial Rome*, 1–12; Balsdon, *Romans and Aliens*, 30; Isaac, *Invention of Racism*, 1; Eliav-Feldon et al., *Origins of Racism*, 9; McCoskey, *Race Antiquity and Its Legacy*, 1; Kennedy, *Race and Ethnicity in the Classical World*, xiii–xv.

10. Eliav-Feldon et al., *Origins of Racism*, 9. This is contrary to Hannaford, who

One of the earliest scholars on the study of Jewish ethnic relations in antiquity is Max Radin. He agrees with current theorists that we should reject the modern understanding of race based on biological theories.[11] Radin notices that ethnic views of superiority or inferiority in the ancient world, including racial prejudices, pride of blood, and contempt for slave nations was present and found voice in the ancient literature.[12] In fact, Greek identity emerged in distinction from the barbarian. The barbarian identity was defined in relation to the baseline of the Greek identity, which was assumed to be civilized and intelligible.[13] It was Homer who first described foreigners as barbarians (βαρβαρόφωνος) because of their speech.[14] Herodotus later outlines the Greek identity to include a common descent, language, religious observance, and way of life.[15] Those who did not have any of these distinguishing Greek identity markers, as Robert Browning asserts, were thus considered barbarians.[16] Although Isocrates later suggests that to be called a Greek meant that one was sharing in the Greek culture and not only birth,[17] this did not prevent the Greeks from distinguishing themselves from other ethnic groups. Even when the Romans were in contact with the Greeks, the Greeks still considered the Romans as barbarians.[18] It is claimed that Socrates attributed to fate three things concerning his identity. He said, "that I was born a human being and not one of the brutes. Next, that I was born a man and not a woman. Third, a Greek and not a barbarian."[19] Although Socrates did not write any documents, he made an impact upon his followers who preserved his philosophical

---

finds the Greek writers more concerned about constructing ideas of the person's role within the political life of the city. Hannaford does admit that many writers since the sixteenth century utilized Greek thought to construct racial ideologies. See Hannaford, *Race*, 17–60.

11. Radin, *Jews Among*, 48.

12. Radin, *Jews Among*, 49.

13. Radin, *Jews Among*, 49–51.

14. Homer, *Il.* 2.867. Jonathan Hall notices that it has yet to be demonstrated that there was an awareness of a common Hellenic language and heritage throughout the Mediterranean (Hall, *Hellenicity*, 113–15). Nippel also notes that originally the concept of the barbarian was not necessarily connected with a sense of superiority (Nippel, "Construction of the Other," 281).

15. Herodotus, 8.144.2.

16. Browning, "Greeks and Others," 259.

17. Isocrates, *Paneg.* 50.

18. Pliny, *Nat.* 29.7.15; Livy, 31.29.15.

19. Diogenes Laertius was a biographer of ancient Greek philosophers. Although we cannot take his statements as definitive, he alleges that Socrates asserted this belief (1.33).

views.[20] Whether or not they adequately reflect the original thought of the historical Socrates is debatable. Nonetheless, we do find this Greek view of foreigners, racial hierarchy, and superiority, which is relevant to our study. In this passage preserved by Diogenes Laertius, Socrates admits that there are ethnic benefits that are contingent upon a Greek identity, ones that are not gained by skill, character, or intellect, but merely by chance.

Regarding the Romans, Radin notes that their attitude toward other nations was based on the grounds of arrogance. He insists that they did not tend to encourage genealogical purity given that many had no quarrel with anyone who desired to be Roman.[21] However, solely because some desired to be Roman does not suggest that condescending attitudes toward ethnic groups were absent. Mary Boatwright notices that while the Greeks defined barbarianism in terms of language, the Romans defined it in terms of customs and behavior, not race.[22] She also points out that while there was a tendency to assimilate, there was also a persistent effort to retain non-Roman names, languages, customs, and religion which reveals that many retained their distinct identity despite incorporation into Rome.[23]

Sherwin-White points to Strabo, a Greek geographer and historian, who makes striking comments about various people who lived within the Roman Empire. Specifically, Strabo expresses cultural prejudice against the Iberians and Keltiberians. He states, "they do not lead a civilized life, but pass their days in poverty, only acting on the animal impulse, and living most corruptly."[24] Strabo also finds the Gauls having a "barbarous and absurd custom, common however with many nations of the north."[25] This condescending attitude and stereotypical description of these ethnic groups are specifically aimed toward those who did not reflect Roman life and practice. Sherwin-White also finds similar remarks in Julius Ceasar's *Gallic Wars* which describes the Gauls as "savage people and of great bravery."[26] There

---

20. Socrates as a figure in Greek history primarily comes from the writings of Aristophanes, Plato, and Xenophon. These writers do indeed present different portraits of Socrates. For example, Socrates's courtroom defense is recounted by both Plato and Xenophon, who present different views. Plato attempts to explain Socrates's apparent courtroom failure whereas Xenophon admits that Socrates was indeed arrogant. See Danzig, "Apologizing for Socrates," 281–321; Morrison, "Socrates," 101–118.

21. Radin, *Jews Among*, 53.

22. Boatwright, *Peoples of the Roman World*, 18. See Cicero, *Resp.* 1.58.

23. Boatwright, *Peoples of the Roman World*, 27.

24. Strabo, *Geogr.* 3.4.16.

25. Strabo, *Geogr.* 4.4.3–5.

26. Sherwin-White, *Racial Prejudice in Imperial Rome*, 33; Julius Caesar, *Gallic War*, 2.15.

is both a negative and positive portrayal of the Gauls in this statement. Yet Sherwin-White observes that Tacitus has a change in attitude toward foreigners, which is not a commendation for virtues, but due to the fact that Tacitus praises qualities that are essentially Roman.[27] While describing the German's military capability, Tacitus remarks, "They have plenty of judgment and acumen, as measured by the German standard. . . . They can also rise to an unusual achievement, usually reserved for Roman discipline."[28] Sherwin-White also notices that those nearest to Rome receive the most acclamation while those who are remote are described with condescending remarks.[29] This is evident in Tacitus's description of the Harri people who are regarded as savages who are strange to look at,[30] the Fenni people who are described as absolute beasts, wild, and poor, and in the descriptive remarks of the Germans who are mentioned as lazy barbarians, failing to question the reason why amber glass is collected from the beach.[31] Tacitus's comments convince Sherwin-White that racial prejudice against the northern people existed in the Greco-Roman world. He senses that this repulsion only dissipates when the ethnic groups develop Roman customs.[32] In other words, as long as the Gauls, Germans, and other remote ethnic groups assimilated to the Roman way of life then prejudice would abate. Foreign elements not reflective of the Roman way of life were thus considered barbarous.

John Balsdon focuses on how the Romans regarded, communicated, and viewed ethnic groups. He suggests that the Romans had a form of arrogance which he describes as a "cultural and moral snobbery."[33] Balsdon finds the Romans describing themselves as the home of empire and glory, the light of the world, the citadel of humanity, and claiming to be God's own people.[34] Their beliefs about themselves also included the assumption that their conquest of foreigners was a just act done for their own good.[35] Similar to Sherwin-White's analysis, Balsdon asserts that since the Romans held a lofty view of themselves, they tended to classify ethnic people on

---

27. Sherwin-White, *Racial Prejudice in Imperial Rome*, 36.
28. Tacitus, *Germ.* 30.2.
29. Sherwin-White, *Racial Prejudice in Imperial Rome*, 38.
30. Tacitus, *Germ.* 43.6.
31. Tacitus, *Germ.* 46.
32. Sherwin-White, *Racial Prejudice in Imperial Rome*, 60.
33. Balsdon, *Romans and Aliens*, 27.
34. Balsdon, *Romans and Aliens*, 2–10.
35. Balsdon, *Romans and Aliens*, 4.

a social scale based upon the distance they lived from Rome.[36] There was a geographical bias that shaped their perceptions of others. The Romans viewed themselves as the social center of the universe with the senatorial society treating anyone born outside the city as dirt.[37] Since there was no rival to Rome, this pride gave them a sense of superiority over the conquered, including the Greeks.

The Romans and Greeks had a love-hate relationship. Balsdon notes that since the Greeks divided humanity between themselves and barbarians, this meant that the Romans were on the wrong side of this division.[38] The Romans perceived the Greeks as unreliable, irresponsible, crooks, deceptive, self-indulgent, loquacious, and intellectually and culturally conceited. The Romans also used the phrase "to play the Greek" to describe their sexual lifestyle.[39] This contrasted with the Roman identity which viewed itself with a sense of gravitas.[40] This negative perception of the Greeks does not presume that positive acclamations failed to exist. The Greeks had a positive impact upon the Romans in the areas of grammar, rhetoric, philosophy, and medicine.[41] But Balsdon also notices that the Romans had an inferiority complex.[42] Greek contributions to scholarship, language, and culture were appreciated but not something that the Romans would boast about.[43]

One can thus notice in Balsdon's analysis that Roman prejudicial attitude was not limited solely to foreigners in the remote regions of the empire. It was also directed to the Greeks. Is this attitude, perception, and sense of cultural and racial superiority akin to what we commonly refer to as racism today? Recent scholars such as Benjamin Isaac agree but use the phrase "proto-racism." Isaac argues that this early form of racism was very common in the Greco-Roman world. He believes that these racial views became the prototype for modern racism which developed in the eighteenth and nineteenth century.[44] But he suggests that Greek and Roman antiquity did not know the sort of racism familiar to the modern world. Like Sherwin-White and Balsdon previously mention, Isaac also finds a range of

---

36. Balsdon, *Romans and Aliens*, 24–25.
37. Balsdon, *Romans and Aliens*, 29.
38. Balsdon, *Romans and Aliens*, 30.
39. Balsdon, *Romans and Aliens*, 33–43.
40. Balsdon, *Romans and Aliens*, 31.
41. Balsdon, *Romans and Aliens*, 36–38.
42. Balsdon, *Romans and Aliens*, 43.
43. Balsdon, *Romans and Aliens*, 44.
44. Isaac, *Invention of Racism*, 1.

prejudices, phobias, and hostilities towards foreigners.[45] The Romans and the Greeks had negative views of foreigners and each other. Isaac points to Pliny's remark, "through conquering we have been conquered"[46] as proof on how the Romans perceived foreign immigrants in Italy.[47] Isaac also cites Cato who espouses various negative views about the Greeks. Cato claims that the Greeks are a corrupting influence upon Romans, "worthless and foolish," and have given the Romans literature that is "perverse." In addition, Cato states that the Greeks conspire with medicine to murder Romans, whom they call "barbarians."[48] Isaac agrees with Baldson that there was a Roman contempt of Greeks.[49] Foreigners were not the only people of scorn. The Romans disliked the Greeks, even though they were culturally indebted to them.

But Isaac also regards this Roman sentiment toward ethnic groups as a reflection of those who held that Rome was losing its prestige. Or said another way, there was a sense that foreigners were making Rome lose its greatness. And thus to make Rome great again, they needed to divert their xenophobic attacks on foreigners. Certainly, Isaac points out that the Romans regularly expelled foreigners when they were considered undesirable or did not adapt to the Roman way of life.[50] Livy remarks,

> How often, in the times of our fathers and our grandfathers, has the task been assigned to the magistrates of forbidding the introduction of foreign cults, of excluding dabblers in sacrifices and fortune tellers from the forum, the circus, and the city, of searching out and burning books of prophecies, and of annulling every system of sacrifice except that performed in the Roman way. For men wisest in all divine and human law used to judge that nothing was so potent in destroying religion as where sacrifices were performed, not by native, but by foreign ritual. I have thought that this warning should be given you, that no religious fear may disturb your minds when you see us suppressing the Bacchanalia and breaking up these nightly meetings. (39.16.8–10)

Livy's comments not only include a rejection of non-Roman cults, but a rejection of foreigners themselves. The Romans believed they were justified in

---

45. Isaac, *Invention of Racism*, 37.
46. Pliny *Nat.* 24.1.
47. Isaac, *Invention of Racism*, 226.
48. Pliny, *Nat.* 29.8–14.
49. Isaac, *Invention of Racism*, 227–29.
50. Isaac, *Invention of Racism*, 235.

suppressing and expelling practitioners on the belief that foreign elements were a grave threat. Livy admits that expulsion, persecution of foreign ritual, and burning of sacred literature is warranted simply because it is "not performed in the Roman way." But it was not solely foreigners' sacred literature and people who were oppressed and rejected from the forum, circus, or city. Isaac also reveals that Greeks, Macedonians, Egyptians, Jews, and astrologers underwent similar experiences.[51]

Denise McCoskey explores ethnic representation and formation in the ancient world. She insists that the Greeks and the Romans were neither color blind nor promoted any fundamental racial opposition between "white" or "black."[52] They regularly employed a framework that organized and classified human diversity.[53] Similar to Radin's and Balsdon's observations, she notes that the term "barbarian," which was first used to label non-Greek speakers, eventually collapsed all human variation into a single racial opposition.[54] This includes the assumption that barbarians are subservient, prone to live under tyrannical governments, and characterized by excess, passion, emotions, and cowardice. This is in contrast to the Greeks who claimed to live by democratic principles and champion values such as self-control, reason, and bravery. Although this Greek-barbarian dichotomy was common in ancient Greek literature, McCoskey asserts that it did not wane under Roman rule but continued to structure ideas of racial difference for centuries to come.[55]

Similar to Boatwright and Sherwin-White's claim, McCoskey also recognizes that solely because the Romans assimilated various ethnic groups does not mean that they were void of differences and notions of superiority. She agrees that the Romans did create new modes of differentiation that was based upon a citizenship not linked to ethnic identity.[56] McCoskey cautions however that this should not indicate a lack of distinction between ethnic groups. Citizenship did not dissolve ethnic prejudices. She points to Cicero's comments on universal commonality and difference as proof that ethnic identity and citizenship concerns continued to hold meaning alongside one another.[57] Cicero states,

---

51. Isaac, *Invention of Racism*, 238; Pliny, *Nat.* 7.30; Polybius, *Hist.* 27.6; Livy, 42.48; Suetonius, *Claud.* 25.4; *Tib.* 36; Tacitus, *Ann.* 2.85.
52. McCoskey, *Race Antiquity and Its Legacy*, 24.
53. McCoskey, *Race Antiquity and Its Legacy*, 24.
54. McCoskey, *Race Antiquity and Its Legacy*, 54.
55. McCoskey, *Race Antiquity and Its Legacy*, 55–56.
56. McCoskey, *Race Antiquity and Its Legacy*, 68.
57. McCoskey, *Race Antiquity and Its Legacy*, 70.

> There are a great many degrees of closeness or remoteness in human society. To proceed beyond the universal bond of our common humanity, there is the closer one of belonging to the same people, tribe, and tongue, by which men are very closely bound together, it is a still closer relation to be citizens of the same city-state, for fellow-citizens have much in common—forum, temples, colonnades, streets, statutes laws, courts, rights of suffrage, to say nothing of social and friendly circles and diverse business relations with many. But a still closer social union exists between kindred.[58]

Cicero affirms that there are levels of relation more esteemed than others. He divided the world into three human categories: Greeks, Italians, and barbarians, with the barbarian as one who had an inferior condition rather than an inferior nature.[59]

McCoskey's analysis also includes how ethnics are represented in common vessels, arches, and colonnades. She notices that in the fifth century, Athenian artists depicted the legendary wars with the Amazons with eastern stereotypes which include flamboyant pantsuits in frenetic patterns.[60] Other graphic depictions include the "Eurymedon Vase," an Attic vase that displays the Greek defeat of the Persians. The vessel commemorates the defeat of the Persians with an image of a Greek hunter chasing a Persian man in order to sexually assault him. Amy Smith adds that the vase reminds the viewer of the submissive position of the Persians, the immediate outcome of the battle, and the political consequences of Athenian power over barbarians on the eastern reaches of the Greek world.[61] Later Persian descriptions, as McCoskey notes, also continued to reflect the conventions established by Athenian art and ideology.[62] Persians were portrayed as hierarchical,

---

58. Cicero, *Off.* 1.53. He also later comments, "For it means much to share in common the same family traditions, the same forms of domestic worship, and the same ancestral tombs" (*Off.* 1.55). See also Quintilian, who preferred speaking in a manner that reflected a genuine Roman accent. He states, "Our voice and all our words should be such as to reveal the native of this city, so that our speech may seem to be of genuine Roman origin, and not merely to have been presented with Roman citizenship" (*Inst.* 8.1.3).

59. McCoskey, *Race Antiquity and Its Legacy*, 7; Cicero, *Fin.* 2.49.

60. McCoskey, *Race Antiquity and Its Legacy*, 143.

61. Smith, "Eurymedon," 139. See also Shapiro, "Invention of Persian," 66–71; Lissarrague, "Athenian Image of the Foreigner," 118–19.

62. McCoskey, *Race Antiquity and Its Legacy*, 144.

luxurious, and emotional.⁶³ These images ranged from attitudes of extreme ambivalence, condescension, admiration, attraction, and repulsion.⁶⁴

Despite the historic tension between the Greeks and Persians, ethnic representations were not limited to them alone. Romans displayed the defeated ethnic groups in triumphs and columns. These were civil ceremonies and public processions that celebrated the achievements of a Roman leader who had successfully completed a war.⁶⁵ McCoskey claims that central to this triumph includes the flaunting of wealth, degradation of human captives, and the demonstration of Roman reach in various territories.⁶⁶ Triumphal arches and columns not only memorialized victorious events, they memorialized the foreign people who were conquered. We thus find the Arch of Titus commemorating the defeat of the Jews, Trajan's Column which highlights the Dacian wars, and the Column of Marcus Aurelius which shows victory over the Danubian tribes. How these Roman war memorials were interpreted is difficult to determine given that they evoke a plurality of meanings.⁶⁷ Nonetheless, McCoskey's insights help us recognize the various depiction of ethnic groups that were preserved in material culture.

When we turn to Roman literature, we find various ethnic remarks about the Egyptians within Juvenal's writings. Juvenal notices that the Egyptians worship various animals which include the crocodile, cats, fish, and dogs. As he lists these various animals, they are all contrasted with the worship of the Roman god Diana.⁶⁸ This comparison creates an impression that the Egyptians follow irreverent worship practices. Juvenal eventually describes the Egyptians as crazy (*demens*), cruel (*saevior*), and barbarous (*barbara*).⁶⁹

In order to demonstrate differences between the Egyptians and Romans, Juvenal details an incident that occurred between the people of Omboi and Tentrya. He states that these people loath one another and believe that only they worship the true gods. On one occasion, a riot broke out between them and a person who was captured by a mob was cut up into many pieces and eaten. Juvenal asserts that in this cannibalistic act the people did not boil or roast the captured individual, perhaps it was too

---

63. McCoskey, *Race Antiquity and Its Legacy*, 145.
64. Shapiro, "Invention of Persian," 58.
65. See Hope, "Trophies and Tombstones," 79–97; Brandfon, "Arch of Titus," 6–27.
66. McCoskey, *Race Antiquity and Its Legacy*, 156–57.
67. Hope, "Trophies and Tombstones," 94.
68. Juvenal, *Sat.* 15.1.
69. Juvenal, *Sat.* 15.1, 45, 110.

"tedious to wait for a fire."[70] Although the account is horrific, Juvenal states in a sarcastic tone that "at least the fire was not defiled."[71] In reflection of this incident Juvenal asks,

> What calamity drove these Egyptians to the deed? What extremity of hunger, what beleaguering army, compelled them to so monstrous and infamous a crime? Was the land of Memphis to run dry, could they do anything else than this to shame the Nile for being slow to rise? No dread Cimbrians or Britons, no savage Scythians or monstrous Agathyrsians, ever raged so furiously as this unwarlike and worthless rabble that hoists tiny sails on crockery ships, and plies puny oars on boats of painted earthenware. (15.120–30)

One can thus notice in Juvenal's description that he finds the Egyptians as people who perform the most savage acts in comparison to other known barbarians. He claims that no crime can be devised for this cannibalistic people, whose "anger and hunger are one and the same."[72]

How then do we explain Juvenal's perception of the Egyptians? McCoskey suggests that Juvenal commonly portrays the Egyptians with stock stereotypes of eastern people, including striking prejudicial comments about Egyptian religious practices.[73] She asserts that Juvenal's account of the Egyptians is designed to provoke Roman disgust by mocking their practices and expressing a hierarchy of racial difference between northern and southern people.[74] Edward Courtney also comments that Juvenal's descriptions are noted to portray the Egyptians with a low value of life and respect to worthless things.[75] Courtney even observes that one of Juvenal's theme is to show from Egyptian practices that human history is regressive, not progressive.[76] Juvenal's descriptions of Egyptians clearly reflect a satirical disdain of foreigners from a Roman perspective. While his comments are satirical in nature, this does not absolve Juvenal from his ethnically offensive comments.

Although McCoskey reviews various ethnic representations and perceptions, she also reminds us that not all discussion should lead to racism or ethnic prejudice in the ancient world. Frank Snowden also notices that

70. Juvenal, *Sat.* 15.80.
71. Juvenal, *Sat.* 15.80–90.
72. Juvenal, *Sat.* 15.130.
73. McCoskey, *Race Antiquity and Its Legacy*, 154.
74. McCoskey, *Race Antiquity and Its Legacy*, 155–56.
75. Courtney, *Commentary on the Satires of Juvenal*, 522.
76. Courtney, *Commentary on the Satires of Juvenal*, 522.

although the Greeks and Romans discussed, artistically designed, and described the bodily characteristics of the Ethiopians, they did not attach a special stigma to color nor develop a special racial theory about the inferiority of darker people.[77] He finds the mention of the Ethiopians having dark skin color and certain physical features explained in terms of their environment and relation to the sun.[78] As such, Snowden remarks that "blackness" and "Ethiopian" were synonymous in the ancient world.[79]

Snowden does admit that the history of Greco-Roman image of other people reveals instances of conflicting attitudes, even within the same author.[80] He remarks that it was Diodorus of Sicily who made the distinction between the savage Ethiopians and the civilized ones.[81] Diodorus affirms the widespread reputation of the Ethiopians for their worship, early knowledge of worship, and reception of divine favor.[82] Snowden also argues that to regard the classical reference to Ethiopians in Egypt as valueless or believe that the Greco-Roman image of the Ethiopians was a glorification of a distant, unknown, or mysterious people is to miss the mark.[83] He points to Homer as the earliest Greek writer who praised the Ethiopians for their piety and being beloved by the gods. This provides proof for Snowden that the ancient Greeks and Romans did not establish color as an obstacle to integration in society.[84]

McCoskey however insists that we do find the desire to designate groups as racially other alongside the desire to dominate in the ancient world.[85] Isaac also informs us that what makes racism different from ethnic or religious prejudice is in the nature of its ideological framework.[86] He notes that racism assumes the existence of physical and mental qualities that are hereditary and not subject to change. Ethnic or religious prejudice involves perceptions toward groups who have common mind sets and patterns of behavior that can change.[87] Simply put, he views racism to include

77. Snowden, *Blacks in Antiquity*, 176.
78. Snowden, *Blacks in Antiquity*, 2–6.
79. Snowden, *Blacks in Antiquity*, 5.
80. Snowden, *Blacks in Antiquity*, 169. Thompson makes a similar point in Thompson, "Roman Perception of Blacks," 26–27.
81. Snowden, *Blacks in Antiquity*, 109; Diodorus, 3.2.4–3.1.
82. Snowden, *Blacks in Antiquity*, 145–149; Diodorus, 3.2.2–3.3.1; Lucian, *Jupp trag.* 37; *Prom.* 17.
83. Snowden, *Blacks in Antiquity*, 119.
84. Snowden, *Blacks in Antiquity*, 216–18.
85. McCoskey, *Race Antiquity and Its Legacy*, 31–32.
86. Isaac, "Racism," 34.
87. Isaac, "Racism," 34.

key assumptions about human nature or physical characteristics while ethnic prejudice deals with criticism of culture or customs. But Isaac contends that the similarities between racial, ethnic prejudice, and xenophobia include the fact that they are forms of hostility toward foreigners. He asserts that this usually includes aggression or fear and is the result of the human tendency to generalize and simplify ethnic groups as a single individual and personality.[88] Were these issues prominent in the Greco-Roman world? As the literary excerpts and scholars reviewed thus far suggests—absolutely.

How must we interpret these various perceptions, critical attitudes, acts of expulsion, and condescending views of foreigners, including the Roman views of Greeks? The ancient writers and scholars surveyed provide firm evidence that ethnic hostilities and prejudice existed in the ancient Greco-Roman world. Ethnic description of one particular individual were applied to all people of that group. The characterization was stereotypically casted upon each ethnic member. In the ancient world individuals were known according to the collective personality. Bruce Malina explains that the ancients refer to and view themselves in terms of specific group or category qualities. There was a tendency to presume that the person's character as specified in unique and distinct groups was fixed and unchanging.[89] This not only created the potential for positive stereotypes of ethnic groups, but negative ones as well. Malina insists that this was possible because every individual was embedded within a group and shared the same qualities of the family, tribe, village, or ethnic group. As a result of viewing and characterizing collective groups, Malina finds that to know one group member is to know the whole group, because the individual was symptomatic and representative of the larger group that he or she was embedded.[90] This manner of viewing the relationship between the individual and the corporate group shapes our understanding of ethnic prejudice, race relations, and ethnic stereotypes in the ancient world. This corporate understanding of the people groups certainly fosters an environment for racial categorization and assumptions. These are realities that we cannot deny nor presume were absent in the Greco-Roman world.

We find various ancient Greek and Roman writers not only identifying diverse ethnic people but expressing critical and prejudicial views toward them. Racial ideologies are found as early in Greek contact with the Persians. Barbarians were portrayed as being antithetical to the baseline of a Greek

---

88. Isaac, *Invention of Racism*, 3.

89. Malina, *New Testament World*, 64; Titus 1:12; Matt 11:21–24; 23:37; Luke 10:13–15; 13:34; Mark 6:3; 14:70; John 1:46; Rom 3:2–29; 9:24; 11:14; 1 Cor 1:22–24; 9:20; 10:32; Gal 2:13–15; Philo, *Flacc.* 29; Josephus, *Life*, 352; *Ag. Ap.* 2.69.

90. Malina, *New Testament World*, 65.

identity. And even though racial identity in the ancient world was fluid, it was often defined in relation to the other. The dominate ethnic group described other ethnic people as barbarians, savages, animals, fools, and displayed public monuments to celebrate their humiliation. These claims not only resonated with existing stereotypes and perceptions, they reveal the racial views held by the dominant ethnic groups within Greco-Roman society. We notice that Juvenal depicts the Egyptians with horrors. Livy boldly justifies the expulsion of foreigners who did not adopt the Roman customs. Cato makes anti-Greek remarks. Pliny recognizes that through the conquering of the known world the Romans have been conquered by foreigners. Tacitus harbors ethnic prejudice toward groups that do not practice the Roman way of life. And we find Strabo having a strong repugnance for elements which he deems to be savagery. These perspectives should disabuse us from the notion that ethnic hostilities, phobias, and prejudices did not exist within the Greco-Roman world. They in fact reflect the way in which the ancients characterized people according to ethnic stereotypes.

Environmental Views on Ethnicity

Since racial perceptions in the ancient world existed and included various prejudices and tensions with foreigners, what was the underlying rationale for these views? What reasons were used to justify their attitudes, behaviors, and violence toward ethnic groups? What were the specific criteria that enabled them to make judgments of inferiority? One of the most common factors used to justify ethnic views was based on an ancient environmental theory.

As mentioned earlier, Balsdon notes that the Romans attributed the differences amongst people as deriving from proximity to the sun or remoteness from it. As such, the southern people such as the Ethiopians, Numidian, and Mauritanians were considered small and suffering from blood deficiencies which made them bad fighters.[91] Northerners, on the other hand, were tall, deep-voiced, pale-faced, and full-blooded fighters who were courageous but foolish in battle. Simply put, Balsdon surmises that the Romans were superior to the northerners in terms of intelligence and superior to the southerners in terms of physical strength.[92] Contrary to Snowden, David Goldenberg insists that environmental theories led to anti-black sentiment in the ancient world. He observes that the Greek and Roman environmental theories implicitly held an ethnocentric character,

91. Balsdon, *Romans and Aliens*, 59.
92. Balsdon, *Romans and Aliens*, 60.

which viewed skin color as an aberrant result of extreme environmental conditions.[93] This enabled Greeks and Romans to view both dark skin and light skin as aesthetically unpleasing.[94] But Goldenberg insists that the hostility exhibited toward Blacks in the ancient world was not limited to them alone. Another group that was singled out for their skin color included the Scythians who resided in the extreme north and were known for having light skin color and large bodies.[95] Environmental theories were thus a major factor in justifying superiority over ethnic groups in various regions and locations. This not only helped explain the reason for ethnic difference. It justified their superiority over people which included the use of military ventures and conquer of foreigners.[96]

The ancients firmly believed that one's environment, which includes climate and terrain, impacted and correlated to the character and physical appearance of various ethnic groups. The origins of environmental determinism can be traced to Hippocrates's *Airs Waters Places*. The writing is addressed to physicians who desire to successfully practice medicine in various regions. Hippocrates begins the writing by informing the readers that each region has its own weather with distinct soil and inhabitants.[97] He explains that those in cities who are exposed to hot winds have a flabby physique, are poor eaters and drinkers, have moist heads full of phlegm, and include unhealthy women.[98] On the other hand, those who reside in the north and experience cold winds are more liable to internal lacerations, have hard digestive organs, and eat much but drink little.[99] In comparison to both these extremes, those that live in moderate temperatures are considered healthier. He claims,

> Those that lie toward the risings of the sun are likely to be healthier than those facing the north and those exposed to the hot winds. . . . In the first place, the heat and the cold are more

---

93. Goldenberg, "Racism, Color Symbolism, and Color Prejudice," 90. Haley also argues that it is too simplistic to assume the Romans had no skin color prejudice. She proposes that the Romans were aware of skin color difference and that it was one factor out of many in the social construction of difference. See Haley, "Be Not Afraid of the Dark," 27–49.

94. Goldenberg, "Racism, Color Symbolism, and Color Prejudice," 91; Balsdon, *Romans and Aliens*, 215.

95. Goldenberg, "Racism, Color Symbolism, and Color Prejudice," 92; Balsdon, *Romans and Aliens*, 215–19; Sherwin-White, *Racial Prejudice in Imperial Rome*, 57–58.

96. McCoskey, *Race Antiquity and Its Legacy*, 45–48; Isaac, "Racism," 38–41.

97. Hippocrates, *Aer.* 1.10.

98. Hippocrates, *Aer.* 3.1–40.

99. Hippocrates, *Aer.* 4.1–48.

> moderate. Then the waters that face the risings of the sun must be clear, sweet-smelling, soft and delightful, in such a city. For the sun, shining down upon them when it rises, purifies them. The persons of the inhabitants are of better complexion and more blooming than elsewhere, unless some disease prevents this. They are clear-voiced, and with better temper and intelligence than those who are exposed to the north, just as all things growing there are better.... The women there very readily conceive and have easy deliveries. (5.10–28)

One thus notices that a moderate climate produces healthier, beautiful, and more intelligent people. In addition, the women in a moderate climate are not described as having any difficulties giving birth. Even if people who reside in a moderate climate get sick, Hippocrates explains that the diseases are fewer and less severe. These environmental differences reveal that the climates in the north and south directly impact the intelligence, health, and complexion of ethnic groups. One cannot avoid being sicker and aesthetically unpleasing if one resides in either a northern or southern area.

After describing the water and changes in season, Hippocrates compares the people of Asia and Europe in order to demonstrate how climate affects character and appearance. He claims that although the geography of Asia is not uniform, the milder and gentler people who are well nourished and of finer physique reside in the regions that are less wild.[100] He suggests,

> Where the seasons experience the most violent and the most frequent changes, the land too is very wild and very uneven ... but where the seasons do not alter much the land is very even. So it is too with the inhabitants if you will examine the matter. (13.10–20)

Hippocrates recognizes that living in a harsh climate will impact the character of people who reside in the region. This explains why the Asiatics are less warlike and gentle in comparison to the Europeans who are considered to have fierce passion.[101] Yet those who reside in Asia, whether Greek or non-Greek, are considered independent and warlike. To account for why this happens in Asia, he again explains that it is contingent upon the environment. He notices that one "will find that Asiatics also differ from one another, some being superior, others inferior. The reason for this, as I have said above, is the changes of the seasons" (16.40–43). Thus, inferiority and superiority, including the inclination of being ruled by a despot, can be

---

100. Hippocrates, *Aer.* 12.10–20.
101. Hippocrates, *Aer.* 16.1–10.

explained in terms of the environment's impact upon various ethnic groups. This is applicable not only to those who reside in Asia but also to the Egyptians, Libyans, and Scythians.[102]

Hippocrates insists that neither bodily nor mental endurance is possible where the changes in season are not violent.[103] This is also why some people are more prone to cowardliness and laziness. He claims,

> The same thing applies to character. In such a climate arise wildness, unsociability and spirit. For the frequent shocks to the mind impart wildness, destroying tameness and gentleness. For this reason, I think that the Europeans are also more courageous than the Asiatics. (23.20–30)

Hippocrates finds a strong correlation between one's environment and character, which also includes the reason why Europeans are not ruled by kings but have a rugged individualistic, intelligent, brave, and warlike temperament.[104] The terrain of the region, whether it is mountainous, barren, or watery, has an immediate impact upon the character of the ethnic groups that reside in the region. This also includes the impact of violent weather, which in Hippocrates's view has a formational influence upon the development of courage and endurance.

We also notice that Hippocrates assumes that soft terrain would produce weak people.[105] A soft terrain leads to the development of people who are fleshy, inarticulate, lazy, cowardly, and thick-witted regarding the arts. This is in contrast to those who reside in areas that are bare, waterless, rough, and experience violent winter storms and hot summers. Those people who live in harsh conditions are considered lean, articulate, energetic, vigilant, courageous, intelligent, and independent in character and temper.[106] Why such a view that land has a direct impact upon the people who dwell upon it? Hippocrates argues that "the things also that grow in the earth all assimilate themselves to the earth."[107]

Hippocrates's writing is therefore not only an ethnographic survey of various inhabitants and the geographical region in which they reside, but judgments about the character, intelligence, and bodies of various ethnic groups. Environmental determinism is assumed throughout Hippocrates's

---

102. Hippocrates, *Aer.* 13.1; 17.1; 18.1.
103. Hippocrates, *Aer.* 19.30.
104. Hippocrates, *Aer.* 24.1–67.
105. Hippocrates, *Aer.* 24.40–50.
106. Hippocrates, *Aer.* 24.50–59.
107. Hippocrates, *Aer.* 24.60.

writing. Different ethnic groups are thus categorized and ranked according to the conditions in which they live. There are vast stereotypes placed upon all the various groups he describes. And without traveling to the distant locations, the readers of *Airs Waters Places* are given a manual that guides how they should perceive, and perhaps discriminate, the various people they encounter.

Hippocrates's environmental determinism had a major influence on the following ancient writers. Plato held the belief that Athens was divinely situated in a region with a moderate climate that would produce wise people.[108] He observes that some regions "are naturally superior to others for the breeding of men of a good or bad type." Other areas are more suitable for living because the wind, sun, water, and soil not only affect the body but are "equally able to effect similar results in their souls as well."[109] We also find Aristotle reflecting similar views when he discusses the character of various people in comparison to the Greeks. He indicates that those living in cold climates and in Europe are full of courage but lack intelligence, skill, political organization, and ability to rule over others. Those in Asia are intelligent but cowardly, always in a perpetual state of subjection and enslavement. However, the Greeks who reside between Asia and Europe are geographically positioned in the best location. As a result, this environment has benefited them with a superiority over their neighbors. Aristotle states,

> The Greek race participates in both characters, just as it occupies the middle position geographically, for it is both spirited and intelligent; hence it continues to be free and to have very good political institutions, and to be capable of ruling all mankind if it attains constitutional unity. (*Pol.* 7.1327b)

Aristotle does not only turn to environmental factors to justify the superiority of the Greeks. He makes a close connection between the character of people and their region. He bluntly asserts that "those men who dwell in the north have stiff hair and are courageous while those who dwell further south are cowardly and have soft hair."[110] His assumption of Greek superiority is noticeable in his discriminatory remarks on those who live in the north and south. From a Greek perspective, one is either courageous and ignorant or cowardly and intelligent. As a foreigner, one could not be courageous and intelligent. This combination simply was not possible due to environmental reasons. In other words, no matter how much one attempted

---

108. Plato, *Tim.* 24c.
109. Plato, *Leg.* 747d–e.
110. Aristotle, *Physiogn.* 806b15.

to gain knowledge or military skill, one will always be inferior to the Greeks simply for not being born in Greece.

The Greek historian Polybius also reflects this environmental view of foreigners. To explains the reason why the Arcadians are austere, he points to their cold and gloomy climate. He assumes that,

> We mortals have an irresistible tendency to yield to climatic influences. And to this cause, and *no other*, may be traced the great distinctions which prevail amongst us in character, physical formation, and complexion, as well as in most of our habits, varying with nationality or wide local separation. (*Hist.* 4.21)

We can notice how for Polybius the environment and "no other" is the root cause of difference in terms of physical appearance and character. Other writers in the first century make similar observations. Vitruvius remarks that those who dwell near the southern axis are supplied with a limited amount of blood because of their closeness to the sun. This closeness thus explains why they are cowards in battle, short, dark, have curly hair, and have black eyes.[111] The climate also has positive effects on others such as making their minds sharp, clever in making plans, and astute because of the air they breathe.[112] On the other hand, those in the north do not experience the sun's heat, thus removing moisture from their bodies. They have a lot of blood supply which makes them brave and have tall, larger bodies, straight red hair, and blue eyes.[113] He also comments that they are mentally sluggish given that they experience a cold climate.[114]

Vitruvius's view of ethnic groups stems from an assumed correlation between the environment and character of people residing in the southern or northern region. Foreigners are either cowards or mentally deficient. His views aim to explain why the Romans are the most superior people suited to rule the known world. He justifies this belief on the assumption that the Romans are geographically positioned directly in the center of the world.[115] He states,

> The races of Italy are the most perfectly constituted in both respects—in bodily form and in mental activity to correspond to their valor. Exactly as the planet Jupiter is itself temperate, its course lying midway between Mars, which is very hot, and

111. Vitruvius, *On Architecture*, 6.1.3–4.
112. Vitruvius, *On Architecture*, 6.1.9–10.
113. Vitruvius, *On Architecture*, 6.1.3–5.
114. Vitruvius, *On Architecture*, 6.1.9.
115. Vitruvius, *On Architecture*, 6.1.10.

Saturn, which is very cold, so Italy, lying between the north and the south, is a combination of what is found on each side, and her preeminence is well regulated and indisputable. And so by her wisdom she breaks the courageous onsets of the barbarians, and by her strength of hand thwarts the devices of the southerners. Hence, it was the divine intelligence that set the city of the Roman people in a peerless and temperate country, in order that it might acquire the right to command the whole world. (6.1.11)

The same argument Aristotle uses to explain why the Greeks are capable to rule the entire world, Vitruvius utilizes to argue why the Romans have acquired the right to rule the world. This right, in Vitruvius's view, is based upon their superior environmental location that is between the extreme locations of the north and south. This view is also echoed by Pliny who, when describing those within the middle of the empire, points out that a healthy mix of warm and cold climate creates people who are moderate in size and color. This environment explains the differences of the people in the north and south whom he describes as wild or lackluster. The empires that arise from the middle of the world, as Pliny argues, include people who have gentle customs, clear thought, and temperaments capable of understanding all of nature. In effect, the empires in the middle of the world govern the rest of the world because their environment is unlike northern or southern regions which produce people with savage natures.[116]

The belief of racial superiority in the ancient Greco-Roman world was based on environmental factors. These were factors that were beyond the control of the individual or ethnic group. Not all agreed with this conviction. In the second century, we find Apuleius protesting these environmental theories because he believed that they were irrational.[117] Environmental determinism, however, continued to be a belief about people who resided in the distant geographical locations. In fact, Publius Flavius Vegetius insists that Roman military recruits should be chosen from more temperate climates because those recruits would possess greater bravery and intelligence in comparison to recruits from the north or south.[118] In a sense, it is possible that both the Greeks and Romans conquered the Mediterranean world on the assumption that the extreme environments could not produce people who were capable of overcoming their military strength and intellectual superiority. This environmental view leads to the supposition that conquered ethnic groups were either too weak to successfully revolt, or too ignorant to

116. Pliny, *Nat.* 2.80; Also Cicero, *Div.* 2.97; Ptolemy, *Tetra.* 2.2.
117. Apuleius, *Apol.* 24.
118. Vegetius, *De Re Militari*, 1.2.

devise a way to rebel. Therefore, all non-Roman or non-Greeks were always in a perpetual state of inferiority due to the environmental conditions of their homeland. Ethnic groups were impaired due to the environmental effect upon their bodies and mental disposition.

Genealogical Views of Ethnicity

Environmental determinism was not the only view that promoted the belief that certain people were either inferior or superior. We also find a prevailing assumption about genealogical purity and its significance for ethnic identity. Although what distinguished ethnic groups from one another included the collective name, culture, or history, these were not the most important features. Jonathan Hall argues that a shared memory of a specific land and the common myth of descent were the distinctive characteristics of ethnic groups.[119] This, as Hall believes, led to a concern to trace one's birth through genealogical relations. This activity was not done solely to determine one's ethnic identity, but in order to anchor one's individual standing to a common descent of a particular ethnic group.[120] This also means that the maintenance of boundaries between ethnic groups revolved around genealogical maintenance. For the Greeks, Hall believes that these myths were genealogical instruments by which ethnic groups could situate themselves in space and time, and reaffirm their identity by appeals to eponymous ancestors.[121] Genealogical accuracy, however, was irrelevant. What really mattered, as Hall argues, was that the claim for shared descent was consensually agreed.[122] Hall thus finds that these myths were fluid and fluctuated when deemed convenient.[123]

Why such a concern for tracing one's ancestral origins? Genealogical myths were vital ethnic instruments for the construction and maintenance of group identity. They defined, proclaimed, and regulated how ethnic groups perceived themselves and their relations to others. We find Thucydides utilizing Homer's writings in tracing Greek origins to Hellen and his children who unified all the Greek cities. Prior to this period, the Greeks were not yet brought under a single name.[124] Thucydides also describes the origin of the Roman people and how they came from various Greek tribes, Trojans who

119. Hall, *Ethnic Identity*, 25.
120. Hall, *Ethnic Identity*, 28.
121. Hall, *Ethnic Identity*, 41.
122. Hall, *Ethnic Identity*, 25.
123. Hall, *Ethnic Identity*, 41.
124. Thucydides, 1.3.

fled the war, and barbarians who arrived in Sicily.[125] But this perspective on Roman origins was not well received. We thus find Dionysius of Halicarnassus arguing that the Roman ancestors were no barbarians, refugees, or immigrants. The Romans were descendants of the ancient Greek people.[126] The belief that the Romans descended from the Trojans is also affirmed by Vergil.[127] In addition, Livy retells the story of Trojans who arrived in Sicily after the war. He asserts that the Trojans, led by Aeneas, founded a city and renamed themselves as Latins.[128] Livy notes that after several generations, two twin boys were born and abandoned. They were sent adrift into a flowing river but by fate, were rescued and nursed by a wolf.[129] One of the boys named Romulus eventually emerged as a leader and united the people through the giving of laws.[130] Although the certitude of these myths is difficult to prove, the retelling and defense of one's ancestral origins not only provides the ability to define oneself in relation to others, but is also reinvented to reflect a more prestigious origin.

This concern for anchoring one's identity in a prestigious genealogical lineage was not limited to Greek and Romans. Josephus also records a letter that was sent from the King Areus of Sparta to Onias the Jewish high priest. The king claims that the Judeans and the Lacedaemonians are of the same race through the ancestry of Abraham. As a result of shared genealogy, the Spartans would support and consider any Jewish affairs equal to their own.[131] The actual genealogical link between Sparta with the Jews is questionable. Indeed, Jan Bremmer asserts that although real diplomatic contacts never took place, the correspondence reveals a Jewish desire to prove the importance of the Jews within the world at large.[132] In a sense, this Jewish genealogical myth attempts to give the Jews a larger significance by aligning their origins with the Spartans. This attempt to dignify one's genealogical lineage is also manifested in Herod's genealogy. Although Herod was considered by some a Jew,[133] it was also known that he did not truly descend from a Jewish family.[134] In fact, Josephus remarks that Nicholas of

---

125. Thucydides, 6.2–6.
126. Dionysius of Halicarnassus, *Ant. rom.* 1.89.
127. Vergil, *Aen.* 3.161–71.
128. Livy, *From the Founding of the City*, 1.1–2.
129. Livy, *From the Founding of the City*, 1.4.
130. Livy, *From the Founding of the City*, 1.8.
131. Josephus, *Ant.* 12.225–27.
132. Bremmer, "Spartans and Jews," 56.
133. Plutarch, *Alex.* 61.3; Josephus, *Ant.* 15.311, 382, 385; *J.W.* 2.226.
134. Josephus, *J.W.* 1.123; 3.636–38; *Ant.* 13.257–58; 14.403.

Damascus reinvented Herod's genealogy in order to link his identity to a Jewish family who came from Babylon.[135]

Hall also finds that genealogical myths, which included invoking claims to territory and ancestral rights, also played some part in access and exclusion to citizen status.[136] In Euripides's *Ion*, a Greek tragedy about an orphan named Ion, we find startling revelations on what it means to be a foreigner and have a mixed ethnic identity in Athens. Ion remarks,

> It is said that the famous Athenians are natives of the land, not a foreign race, so that I shall burst in on them with two ailments, my father a foreigner, and myself of bastard birth. And with this reproach, if I am insignificant, I shall be called no one and nothing, if I rush into the highest rank of the city, and seek to be someone, I will be hated by the powerless. . . . To them I will seem laughable and foolish if I am not at rest in a city full of fear. If I attain the reputation of those who are . . . and useful in the city, the more I will be guarded against, in the votes. It is likely to be this way, father, those who hold cities and high rank are most hostile to their rivals. (585–605)

Ion recognizes that he is not a pure Athenian but of mixed ancestry. This self-awareness leaves him with a major social disadvantage. Regardless of his rise to influence and reputation, he would still be despised, laughed, and considered foolish. Ion continues,

> But one part of my fortune is lacking, if I do not find my mother, my life will not be endurable, father. If it is right to pray for it, my mother would be an Athenian, so that from her I might have freedom to speak my mind. For one who bursts as a stranger into a city unmixed in race, even if he is called a citizen, must keep a slavish mouth closed, and does not feel free to speak. (670–75)

Ion's remarks include the struggle of an orphan who desires to be of pure Athenian ancestry. He finds that his life is difficult without some clarity on his ancestral origins. But although Ion's true identity is later revealed, his life reveals the reality of Athenian oppression toward those who had questionable ancestral backgrounds. Ion thus reflects the experience of many who were considered inferior due to their mixed lineage and questionable relation to Greek heritage.

---

135. Josephus, *Ant.* 14.9.
136. Hall, *Ethnic Identity*, 65.

This concern for a pure genealogical lineage is also echoed in what Theseus, the king of Athens, said to the king of Argos for allowing his daughter to marry a foreign man. Theseus states, "doing so, you have mingled your clear line with a muddy one and sorely wounded your house."[137] Since the Athenian people were of pure ancestry, they had disdain toward those who had a foreign ethnic identity. This Greek preference for a pure lineage is also exemplified in Plato's recommendations for human reproduction. In Plato's Timaeus, it was believed that for humanity to reach its full potential, inferior people and noble people could not intermingle and produce offspring. Even more, the offspring of inferior people were to be secretly assigned to another city and parentally abandoned.[138] In the Republic, Plato advocates for a monitored and controlled eugenics that would strengthen the guardian class. He states,

> The best men must cohabit with the best women in as many cases as possible and the worst with the worst in the fewest and that the offspring of the one must be reared and that of the other not, if the flock is to be as perfect as possible. (5.459d–e)[139]

We thus notice that the goal of this controlled birth and rejection of children of the inferior class aimed to ensure the reproduction of the most perfect offspring. The concern for lineage purity justifies the segregation of people into two classes, including the exposure of infants. Although the practice seems callous, we must keep in mind the assumptions that motivate the behavior—that a mixed lineage would lead to the deterioration of the human race. Infancy exposure was not an inhumane practice from this perspective. It aims to preserve the superiority of the ethnic community by preventing the development of inferior people.

This objective to develop a more perfect ethnic group by avoiding intermingling with inferior people is also noticeable in Plato's *Menexenus*. Again, he proposes,

> But we and we alone, could not bring ourselves either to hand them over or to join in the agreement. So firmly-rooted and so sound is the noble and liberal character of our city, and endowed also with such a hatred of the barbarian, because we are pure-blooded Greeks, unadulterated by barbarian stock. For those who cohabit with us are none of the type of Pelops, or Cadmus, or Aegyptus or Danaus, and numerous others of the kind, who

---

137. Euripides, *Suppl.* 219–25.
138. Plato, *Tim.* 18d–19a.
139. Also *Resp.* 5.415a–c.

> are naturally barbarians though nominally Greeks. But our people are pure Greeks and not a barbarian blend, whence it comes that our city is imbued with a whole-hearted hatred of alien races. (245c–d)

We thus can observe that the Greeks have a "hatred," as Plato describes, toward the "barbarian" simply because they are not pure-blooded people. The presence of the barbarian poses a risk to Greek lineage. Barbarians must be avoided at all costs, including other Greeks who have questionable ancestry of "barbarian blend." Even more, the protection of a pure lineage demands "hatred" toward ethnic groups who are deemed inferior. As such, having a hybrid identity, that is, a mixture of various ethnic groups, would not be highly esteemed in the ancient world.

But why such a segregationist stance against ethnic groups of mixed or uncertain ancestry? Plato's remarks on Athenian Greek identity are revealing. He claims that the Greeks are not immigrants but "born from the soil" and thus surpass all in intelligence, and esteem both justice and the gods.[140] Plato affirms the superiority of Athenian pure linage, unlike some Greeks and barbarians who have a mixed background. The assumption we again find is that through intermixture, the outcome of one's offspring would only lead to a deterioration of one's descendants. Plato argues,

> The intermixture of States with States naturally results in a blending of characters of every kind, as strangers import among strangers novel customs and this result would cause immense damage to people who enjoy a good polity under right laws. (*Leg.* 12.949e–950a)

But Plato does recognize that it is impossible to avoid foreigners. Yet they are welcomed only on the condition that they do not bring innovations or overstay their tourism. After that point they must be expelled.[141]

This concern for genealogical purity continues in the writings of Aristotle. He believes that revolts are caused by an openness to foreigners. He assumes that a lack of shared tribal descent would only lead to ethnic tensions and expulsions.[142] Foreigners are viewed as the cause of social problems. Aristotle also assumes that certain people were natural slaves of a permanently inferior condition. Even if Greeks were ever taken captive and sold into slavery, this would not change their noble birth. Aristotle insists

---

140. Plato, *Menex.* 237b–238b.
141. Plato, *Leg.* 12.953a–b.
142. Aristotle, *Pol.* 5.1303a.

that only barbarians who are slaves by nature are slaves everywhere.[143] In other words, Greeks are distinct from barbarians and superior to them, even when their social conditions change. This superiority is not found in subjective conditions but is due to being born a Greek.

We thus can understand why segregationist attitudes were maintained when dealing with foreigners and offspring. The utilization of infant exposure and avoidance of non-Greeks secured the advancement of one's descendants.[144] This was not solely a practice undertaken by Athenians. Plutarch mentions that the Spartans would regularly reject infants that did not meet their bodily inspection. The Spartans assumed that if the offspring was not well equipped at the very beginning for health and strength, then it was of no advantage either to itself or the state.[145] But was this also applicable to the Romans who had questionable origins? Does their mixed identity suggest that they did not consider lineage important? As mentioned earlier, it was Dionysius of Halicarnassus who regarded the Romans as being Greek in origin. He defends Roman origins by arguing that as descendants from Troy, they too have a pure genealogy. Lineage concerns did not entirely escape the Roman mind.

How then should we assess the views of genealogical purity? Isaac recognizes that in the ancient world there was a common conviction that a pure lineage signified ethnic superiority.[146] He notes that immigrants were treated poorly based on the assumption that mixture among different groups would produce inferior descendants.[147] As Isaac points out, this view also led to other assumptions, actions, and hostile views toward foreigners. That is, since the quality of an entire people is determined by lineage preservation, then the purer ethnic groups need to be protected from foreigners who are considered contaminates to the native people.[148]

Isaac finds the negative perception of a mixed lineage in various Greek and Roman writers. This also includes Diodorus of Sicily, who was writing under Roman rule, admitting that both Greeks and non-Greeks aimed to enhance their dignity with autochthony, that is, indigenous ancestry to the land without foreign contamination.[149] Diodorus states,

---

143. Aristotle, *Pol.* 1.1252b, 1254a–1255a.
144. Aristotle, *Pol.* 5.1335b.
145. Plutarch, *Lyc.* 16.1–2.
146. Isaac, *Invention of Racism*, 109.
147. Isaac, *Invention of Racism*, 133.
148. Isaac, *Invention of Racism*, 148.
149. Isaac, *Invention of Racism*, 135.

> Not only do Greeks put forth their claims but many of the barbarians as well, all holding that it is they who were autochthonous and the first of all men to discover the things which are of use in life, and that it was the events in their own history which were the earliest to have been held worthy of record. (1.9.3)

Tacitus also echoes this similar view of lineage purity in his discussion on the Germans. He describes them as all living in "filth and sloth, and by the intermarriages of the chiefs they are becoming in some degree debased into a resemblance to the Sarmatae."[150] Isaac reads Tacitus's claim as undoubtedly reflecting the belief that Germans who marry non-Germans become something less than Germans.[151]

The belief in a pure, uncontaminated ethnic origin was not a minor point. This was of significant concern for the ancients. And as we have reviewed in Plato and Aristotle, a mixed lineage or intermarriages between ethnic groups was presumed to develop an inferior quality of descendants. This judgment about the ethnic quality of descendants is also exemplified in Livy's discussion about the mixture of foreign offspring. He states,

> Gauls, born in their own land, these now are degenerates, of mixed race, and really Gallogrecians, as they are named, just as, in the case of plants and animals, the seeds have less power to maintain their natural quality than the character of the soil and climate in which they live has power to change it. The Macedonians who hold Alexandria in Egypt, who hold Seleucia and Babylonia and other colonies scattered throughout the world, have degenerated into Syrians, Parthians, Egyptians; Massilia, situated among the Gauls, has acquired something of the disposition of its neighbors. What have the Tarentines retained of that stern and dreadful Spartan discipline? Whatever grows in its own soil, has greater excellence; transplanted to a soil alien to it, its nature changes and it degenerates towards that in which it is nurtured. (*His. rom.* 38.17.9–12)

Livy believes that the Gauls had degenerated into Gallogreceians, Macedonians into Syrians, and that the Tarentines have lost their Spartan discipline. Livy views these ethnic mixtures as generating inferior ethnic groups. He even compares interracial offspring to agricultural practices. Precisely, that seeds can only exceptionally grow in their own soil and become degenerate once they are transplanted to foreign soil. In other words, people should

---

150. Tacitus, *Germ.* 46.
151. Isaac, *Invention of Racism*, 142.

remain in their native lands and not mix with other ethnic groups because it would lead to a deterioration of humanity.

What can we observe from the ancient writers and the arguments of classists above? The ancients assumed that indigenous people who did not have a contaminated genealogy were not only purer, but superior. This claim was based on the view that hybridity or a "mestizo" identity was reflective of an inferior status and gradual decline of humanity. That is, immigration and the mingling of various people with different ethnic groups were believed to lead to an inferior and contaminated ethnic group. Progress or improvement of the human species was not assumed to emerge when different ethnic groups mixed and produced children.

The significance of genealogical connection to an important figure was not lost on early Christians. Buell notes that Christians also used myths of descent to regularly define themselves with a respected pedigree with historical relation to key figures such as Abraham and Jesus.[152] She observes that this enabled them to explain their recent historical emergence, assert superiority, and articulate a universalizing ideal where all people could be reunified.[153] This concern to preserve ethnic purity or reinvent one's lineage was done on the assumption that a mixed ethnic identity would not be well received in the ancient world. And as we have noted in Euripides, Plato, and Aristotle, it was a concern for genealogical lineage purity that shaped ethnic relations, social privileges, and diplomatic relations. The ancients valued a pure genealogical ancestry and as a result, justified hatred toward others who would threaten their future descendants. If Greeks were to mix with barbarians or other foreigners, it was assumed that the offspring would only bring irreparable harm to the State. Thus, in order to preserve one's descendants and the future of the State, an avoidance of foreigners was permissible. As we find with Roman writers, they too recognized the challenges of a mixed ethnic identity. This even compelled Dionysius to reinvent the origins of Roman history in order to give their pedigree a more esteemed origin.

Greek and Roman Attitudes Toward the Jews

The Greeks and Romans knew of ethnic differences and developed a rationalization for their views based upon environmental determinism and genealogical lineage. They were able to observe and make comments on

152. Buell, *Why This New Race*, 75–76; Buell and Hodge, "Politics of Interpretation," 235–51; Rom 4:13–18; 9:8; Gal 3:26–29; 1 John 3:9.
153. Buell, *Why This New Race*, 90–91.

various groups including Ethiopians, Gauls, Germans, Scythians, Persians, Parthians, and Indians to name a few. They also did not fail to notice the Jewish people, their way of life, belief, and history. As the Jews lived and expanded into various parts of the empire, their presence was not always welcomed but brought violent conflict with the Greeks and Romans. Yet our focus is not to trace the history of Jewish relations with the Greeks and Romans. Instead, I will examine how the contact was perceived and how this can inform our understanding of emerging Christianity in which the gospel was written.

Radin believes that the first contact between the Jews and Greeks was either in military conflict or the slave market.[154] He finds that when the Jews were under Greek jurisdiction, they obtained an exemption from participating in cultic activities which created barriers to mutual understanding which resulted in Greek resentment given that the Jews were free from prosecution of impiety.[155] These ethnic contacts, however, did not lead to uniform hostility or admiration.[156] Radin insists that racial friction was relatively rare and Greek attitude varied from enthusiastic veneration to determined antagonism.[157] Balsdon, however, argues that the Greeks had never liked Jews and where large Jewish communities resided in a single city, like Alexandria or Antioch, they were always in conflict.[158] Sherwin-White also claims that Greek racial prejudice manifested itself at full strength toward the Jews. Yet these feelings of dislike were reciprocal. The Greeks disliked the Jews and the Jews disliked the Greeks, as noticed in their rejection of Greek life.[159] He insists that the conflict within the diaspora was possibly racially motivated, especially since the Romans required the Greeks in Asia to grant Jewish colonies the right to free assembly, practice social-religious customs, settle internal legal controversies, and collect money for Jerusalem.[160] Boatwright also agrees that there was a distinct hostility toward the Jews. She notices that more than any other group, the Jews of Judea seem to have resisted assimilation into the Roman provincial system.[161] Peter Schäfer most recently argues that there did exist in antiquity a phenomenon which he describes

---

154. Radin, *Jews Among*, 78; See Joel 3:6.
155. Radin, *Jews Among*, 165.
156. Radin, *Jews Among*, 209.
157. Radin, *Jews Among*, 166.
158. Balsdon, *Romans and Aliens*, 67.
159. Sherwin-White, *Racial Prejudice in Imperial Rome*, 86–87.
160. Sherwin-White, *Racial Prejudice in Imperial Rome*, 89.
161. Boatwright, *Peoples of the Roman World*, 132.

"Judeophobia." He outlines this hatred and fear of Jews as an ancient form of anti-Semitism and anti-Judaism.[162]

Josephus's writings provide evidence of various examples that exemplify the relationship between the Jews and Greeks. His recorded decrees reveal persistent Greek oppression and rejection of Jewish exemptions that they obtained from the Romans. For example, in the Greek island of Delos the Jews were in conflict with the Greek authorities. Josephus publishes Julius Gaius's decree which states,

> The Jews of Delos, and some other Jews that sojourn there, in the presence of your ambassadors, signified to us, that, by a decree of yours, you forbid them to make use of the customs of their forefathers, and their way of sacred worship. Now it does not please me that such decrees should be made against our friends and confederates, whereby they are forbidden to live according to their own customs, or to bring in contributions for common suppers and holy festivals, while they are not forbidden so to do even at Rome itself. For even Gaius Caesar, our imperator and consul, in that decree wherein he forbade the religious societies to meet in the city, did yet permit these Jews, and these only, both to bring in their contributions, and to make their common suppers. Accordingly, when I forbid other religious societies, I permit these Jews to gather themselves together, according to the customs and laws of their forefathers, and to persist therein. It will be therefore good for you, that if you have made any decree against our friends and confederates, to abrogate the same, by reason of their virtue and kind disposition toward us. (*Ant.* 14:213–16)

We notice that the Jewish people in Delos petitioned the Romans, because their right to participate and practice their customs was restricted by those in Delos. The decree also testifies to the privileged exemption that the Jews received under Roman rule, which suggests that not all Jewish experiences were uniform. What we cannot discount is the evidence of aggressive suppression of Jewish customs and religious observations, which also reflects other hostile actions from rulers like Antiochus Epiphanes.

Josephus notes other oppressive activities in Miletus, a coastal city south of Ephesus. The Jewish people were forbidden to celebrate the Sabbath, worship, follow the Torah, and maintain their agricultural food. Josephus asserts that "the Jews should not be prohibited to make use of their

---

162. Schäfer, *Judeophobia*, 6–11.

own customs."¹⁶³ The Jews also had tensions in Sardis. Again, Josephus preserves the decree that was sent to reaffirm their rights as fellow citizens who should have the freedom to assemble and worship according to their ancient customs.¹⁶⁴ A similar issue also occurred in Ephesus. The Jews were impeded from practicing their customs and even fined for keeping the Sabbath.¹⁶⁵ After this oppressive action against them, Josephus notes that the Jews had to petition the Romans in order to have their rights restored. These cities received pressure to conform to Roman law and suspend these tyrannical activities. The decrees Josephus cites bears witness to various forms of ethnic hostility in various cities.¹⁶⁶ Indeed, Sherwin-White believes that in the late Republic period the Greek cities of Asia showed their dislike of Jewish settlements by official persecution, which needed to be checked by the Romans.¹⁶⁷

This experience was not limited to these Greek cities alone. Ethnic oppression also occurred in Alexandria between the Greeks, Egyptians, and the Jews.¹⁶⁸ Undeniably, Schäfer insists that the most violent eruption of anti-Jewish sentiment in antiquity is found in Alexandria.¹⁶⁹ He traces the origin of the hostility to the Jewish support of Rome, which was contrary to the Greek and Egyptian view of the Romans. Josephus writes that when Gaius died and was succeeded by Claudius, the Alexandrian Jews initiated a revolt against their fellow Alexandrians. They used the opportunity of Gaius's death to bring retribution to their oppressors.¹⁷⁰ Why such a reaction? Josephus explains that during Gaius's reign the Jewish people refused to acknowledge Gaius as a god.¹⁷¹ Philo explains the situation and relationship in more detail. He remarks that when Gaius was alive the Greeks of Alexandria invited Flaccus to help them "denounce the Jews" in order to gain Gaius's favor.¹⁷² Philo states that the Jews were forced to have emperor images set up in their synagogues, were stripped of their rights, branded as "foreigners

---

163. Josephus, *Ant.* 14.244–46.
164. Josephus, *Ant.* 14.259–61.
165. Josephus, *Ant.* 14.262–64; 16.172.
166. Josephus, *Ant.* 19.287–91.
167. Sherwin-White, *Racial Prejudice in Imperial Rome*, 90.
168. Josephus, *Ant.* 19.278; Philo, *Flacc.* 1.22.
169. Schäfer, *Judeophobia*, 136.
170. Josephus, *Ant.* 19.278.
171. Josephus, *Ant.* 19.284–86.
172. Philo, *Flacc.* 23.

and aliens," had their homes and synagogues desecrated, and expelled into a corner of Egypt which led them to extreme poverty and death.[173]

Schäfer interprets this Jewish experience in Egypt as a political drama between Flaccus, Gaius, and the Alexandrians. He believes that both the Alexandrian Egyptians and Greeks were able to release their suppressed hatred toward the Jews during this period.[174] Schäfer also notes that this conflict in Alexandria reveals that the source of the tension centered on civil rights. This is supported by the various decrees from Claudius for Jewish protection, which testifies to the desire to restore Jewish privileges that had been restricted.[175] But Schäfer also suggests that we should not view this tense conflict solely through political lens, as if anti-Semitism only belongs to the cultural, religious, or irrational realm.[176] He notes that the Greek leaders of Alexandria relied on the Egyptians for support in their political struggle against the Jews, given that they too held anti-Jewish feelings.[177]

How does one interpret the ethnic violence between Greeks and Jews? Why such an eruption of violence and massive bloodshed in various cities? We know that violence was not limited to Jerusalem alone during the Roman war with the Jews. Extreme violence was directed against the Jews in Caesarea,[178] Damascus,[179] and Syria.[180] Even more, animosity toward the Jews would have led to their final expulsion in Antioch if it had not been for General Titus's intervention.[181] Sherwin-White insists that in the contemporary period, racial prejudice may occur simply because of otherness, the dissimilarity of customs, or exclusiveness. In the Roman period the Jews were disliked because of their refusal to cooperate in the Hellenistic civilization while coexisting in large groups within Greek cities.[182] In other words, ethnic hostility against the Jews was due to their peculiar culture, and this was also intensified when they received legal exemptions and protection.

We find a possible rationale on why this hostility existed when we turn to specific Greek writers such as Diodorus of Sicily. Diodorus remarks that when Antiochus Epiphanes was laying siege of Jerusalem, certain advisors

---

173. Philo, *Flacc.* 41–71.
174. Schäfer, *Judeophobia*, 143.
175. Schäfer, *Judeophobia*, 146.
176. Schäfer, *Judeophobia*, 158.
177. Schäfer, *Judeophobia*, 159–60.
178. Josephus, *J.W.* 2.457.
179. Josephus, *J.W.* 2.559–61.
180. Josephus, *J.W.* 2.462–63.
181. Josephus, *J.W.* 7.100–111.
182. Sherwin-White, *Racial Prejudice in Imperial Rome*, 93–96.

encouraged Antiochus that the Jews as a race should become eradicated because they alone avoid dealings with all nations and look upon non-Jews as enemies.[183] These advisors describe the story of the Jews in Egypt and how they were driven out for being lepers, impious, and hated by the gods.[184] They also explain that some of these expelled Jews landed in Judea and were led by Moses who instituted a mode of life that was based on their experiences in Egypt.[185] In retelling this alternative history, Diodorus explains that when the Jews settled in Jerusalem they organized into a nation and made their "hatred of mankind into a tradition." He credits Moses as the one who "introduced a most unsocial and intolerable mode of life" as the result of their expulsion.[186] He also states that Moses "ordained for the Jews their wicked customs and practices, abounding in hatred" (μισάνθρωπος) and "enmity to all other men."[187] This included the law not to break bread with any other race nor show them good will.[188] In Diodorus's description of Jewish history, Antiochus is portrayed in a positive light. Antiochus is also stunned that the Jewish people would hold hatred toward others and maintain "xenophobic laws." In this retelling of history, Diodorus also adds that the advisors encouraged Antiochus to force the Jews to change their ways. Antiochus, as Diodorus explains to the reader, was too magnanimous and mild-mannered for such requests. Instead, Antiochus took hostages, exacted a tribute, and dismantled the walls of Jerusalem.[189]

Diodorus's understanding of Jewish origins and exodus from Egypt is an alternative interpretation of Jewish history. This view is embedded within the wider Greek perspective that aimed to understand Jewish disdain of foreigners. This also explains why Antiochus emerges as one who attempts to change Jewish anti-social practices. In a sense, Antiochus stands as a liberator who aims to civilize and absorb the Jews within the greater Hellenistic culture. This positive rendering of Antiochus can also serve further aims. It

---

183. Diodorus, 34.1.

184. Diodorus, 34.1. When Diodorus later recounts the history of the Jews from Hecataeus of Abdera he further adds detail about Jewish origins. He retells an earlier alternative history that identifies the cause of the Jewish departure from Egypt as an expulsion by the Egyptians (40.3.1–2).

185. Diodorus, 34.1.3.

186. Diodorus, 34.1.3. See also Diodorus's further descriptions from Hecataeus in 40.3.4; Josephus attempts to rebuttal this charge by pointing out that the Jews admit foreigners and do not expel them, which should be a testimony to their humanity (*Ag. Ap.* 2.258–261).

187. Diodorus, 34.1.3–5.

188. Diodorus, 34.1.2.

189. Diodorus, 34.1.3–5.

may possibly explain why the Greeks are justified in their violence toward the Jews. Simply put, the Greeks try to be friendly, but the Jews are not willing to adapt to the Greek way of life.

Yet one also notices in Diodorus's remarks and description of the Jews that the origins of misanthropic customs are traced to Moses and their "leprous" experiences in Egypt. But what does it mean to be a "misanthropic" and how serious is this charge in the Greco-Roman world? Katell Berthelot remarks that the Jews are the only people or nation ever accused of being misanthropic and inhospitable in Greek literature.[190] She notes that a misanthropic person was a well-known comedy character who runs away from the life of the city and mistrusts their fellow human beings.[191] Plato describes the misanthropic as those whose relational problems eventually lead them to hate all people. Plato explains,

> For misanthropy arises from trusting someone implicitly without sufficient knowledge. You think the man is perfectly true and sound and trustworthy, and afterwards you find him base and false. Then you have the same experience with another person. By the time this has happened to a man a good many times, especially if it happens among those whom he might regard as his nearest and dearest friends, he ends by being in continual quarrels and by hating everybody and thinking there is nothing sound in anyone at all.[192]

Schäfer also finds the charge of misanthropy traced back to a Greek cultural context. He notes that the misanthropic person within a Greek context is unable to distinguish between good and bad people, thus forcing the misanthropic to assume that only bad people exist.[193] This suspicion of people also places the misanthropic on the lowest end of the social scale. Schäfer explains that when applied to the Jews, as in the case of Diodorus's account, it portrays them as holding uncivilized values in their disdain of people.[194]

We thus notice that the Jewish rejection of Greek life was explained in terms of misanthropy. Even Aristotle remarks that those who refuse to fellowship with others do so because they are a god or an animal.[195] Ber-

---

190. Josephus points out that the Spartans were also known for expelling foreigners (*Ag. Ap.* 2.258–61).

191. Berthelot, "Misanthropy," 1:467; "Hecataeus of Abdera and Jewish Misanthropy"; Schäfer, *Judeophobia*, 23.

192. Plato, *Phaed.* 89d–e. See also Plutarch, *Ant.* 69.4.

193. Schäfer, *Judeophobia*, 173.

194. Schäfer, *Judeophobia*, 174–76.

195. Aristotle claims that humanity is by nature a "political animal." This suggests

thelot further holds that what makes a misanthropic character strange and reprehensible stems from the recognition that the person ought to be socially involved but refuses to do so.[196] Thus when Diodorus credits Moses for inventing practices that were in stark contrast to all nations, this was not a minor point. These remarks reflect the wider Greek experience with Jews—a negative perception that included the idea that they lacked a basic friendliness toward strangers.

One may presume that when we turn to Roman experiences the relations were more amicable than Greek ones, especially since Josephus's published decrees describe the Jews as "friends of Rome."[197] Erich Gruen in fact argues that Jewish presence in the city of Rome during the late Republic was thriving, active, and an engaged community. He perceives their urban presence as hardly threatening.[198] But despite a positive portrayal of general assimilation into Roman life, this was neither the case at all times nor does it negate hostile experiences, a point Gruen admits. In fact, Tacitus agrees with Diodorus's claim that Antiochus aimed to change the Jews into a better people by introducing Greek customs.[199] Tacitus also continues the same Greek belief about Jewish antisocial behavior.[200] He claims that the Jews are a "race detested by the gods"[201] who under Moses' leadership created laws that are opposed to those practiced by others.[202] He remarks,

> This worship, however introduced, is upheld by its antiquity; all their other customs, which are at once perverse and disgusting, owe their strength to their very badness. The most degraded out of other races, scorning their national beliefs, brought to them their contributions and presents. This augmented the wealth of the Jews, as also did the fact, that among themselves they are inflexibly honest and ever ready to shew compassion, though they regard the rest of mankind with all the hatred of enemies. They sit apart at meals, they sleep apart, and though, as a nation, they are singularly prone to lust, they abstain from intercourse

---

that those who are not a part of a city-state but live in isolation cannot be fully human, for no person, according to Aristotle, can function without interaction and communication with the other (*Pol.* 1253a).

196. Berthelot, "Hecataeus of Abdera and Jewish Misanthropy."

197. The Roman authorities describe the Jews as "worthy of such a favor, on account of their fidelity and friendship to the Romans" (*Ant.* 19.284–91).

198. Gruen, *Diaspora*, 26.

199. Tacitus, *Hist.* 5.8.

200. Tacitus, *Hist.* 5.2–3.

201. Tacitus, *Hist.* 5.3.

202. Tacitus, *Hist.* 5.4.

with foreign women; among themselves nothing is unlawful. Circumcision was adopted by them as a mark of difference from other men. Those who come over to their religion adopt the practice, and have this lesson first instilled into them, to despise all gods, to disown their country, and set at naught parents, children, and brethren. (*Hist.* 5.5)

The belief that Jews are antisocial and hate all non-Jews is not limited to the Greeks alone. Tacitus's remarks are similar to Diodorus's accusation of misanthropy. Tacitus generalizes, simplifies, and stereotypes Jewish people without qualification. Even more, he adds that the Jews demonstrate this animosity through their relations with women and meals, a very unnecessary description that only flares up the suspicion of Roman males. Quite possibly, Tacitus may find the Jewish people as a threat because of the impact they have with converts who are convinced to "scorn their national beliefs," "disown their country," and participate in similar hostility toward others. Although Gruen finds Tacitus's comments sardonic in nature,[203] he agrees that Tacitus does not have sterling recommendations and reserves fierce comments for those who crossed over to Judaism.[204] But reading Tacitus's remarks about this minority Jewish population within Rome would lead us to assume that the Jews were very inhospitable, uncaring, and an infectious group of people. Suspicion certainly arises, and unjustifiable contempt will occur if people believe in Tacitus's vitriolic comments.

These Greek and Roman writers provide mainstream evidence that the Jews were perceived to be hostile toward foreigners.[205] But was this always the case from a Roman perspective? The Romans certainly preserved the status of the Jews, including their right to worship, gather, and practice their sacred rites. Josephus's preservation of imperial decrees reflects the reality that Jewish privileges would have been revoked without Rome's support. We also find Philo noting that the Jews in Rome who were brought as captives to Italy were never compelled to alter any of their observances including Sabbath worship, Jerusalem offerings, or studying the Torah. This also includes the support of their civil rights and Caesar's refusal to exile them.[206] When we explore the relations between the Jews with the Romans, however, Philo's remarks that the Jews were well regarded seem to obscure the full picture. Philo admits that during the reign of Tiberius the relationship with

---

203. Gruen, *Rethinking the Other*, 190.
204. Gruen, *Diaspora*, 44.
205. Schäfer, *Judeophobia*, 31–33.
206. Philo, *Legat.* 1.155–58.

Rome became hostile,[207] and he defends the Jewish observances which were perceived to be unsociable and inhumane.[208] Gruen interprets these occasional outbreaks and exiles not as an expression of anti-Judaism, but largely Roman performance and ceremonial activities. That is, the actions of Rome by Claudius and Tiberius were done solely to benefit the government's image because they had to portray themselves as guardians of ancient Roman rituals.[209] One must however recognize that solely because deportation was not universally applied to all Jewish people this should not lead us to suggest that anti-Jewish sentiments did not exist. Ceremonial deportation is still deportation.

Moments of desirability and hostility fluctuated toward the Jewish people. Prior to Tacitus, one of Rome's first opponents of Judaism was Cicero. His report challenges Philo's claim that the Jews in Rome were always protected. Cicero praises the Jewish expulsion from Rome, including the proposal that no wealth from Italy or Asia should be sent to Jerusalem. He even asserts that "to resist this barbarous superstition" is an "act of dignity" and to "despise the multitude of Jews . . . was an act of the greatest wisdom."[210] Cicero does not have high regard for the Jewish people. He considers them enemies, especially since they resisted Pompey. He even states that Judaism is at variance with the "splendor of this empire and dignity of our name and the institution of our ancestors."[211]

Truly, what is the Roman racial perspective of the Jews? Although Gruen does not regard Cicero's comments as amounting to anti-Semitism, he admits that the Jewish faith was frequently labeled as superstition.[212] Schäfer finds that Cicero's critiques against the Jews position him as a champion of Rome's values and bolsters the argument that the Jewish religion is incompatible with Rome's ancestral customs and institutions.[213] Radin believes that the Romans viewed the Jews from the perspective of a dominant race over the conquered, which was no different from Roman views of other foreigners.[214] He notes that when tensions arose, the penalty of expulsion was imposed solely for foreign Jews, and may have only included

---

207. Philo, *Legat.* 1.159–60.
208. Philo, *Virt.* 140–41; Berthelot, "Philo's Perception of the Roman Empire," 166–87.
209. Gruen, *Diaspora*, 39–41.
210. Cicero, *Flac.* 67.
211. Cicero, *Flac.* 68–69.
212. Gruen, *Diaspora*, 20–43.
213. Schäfer, *Judeophobia*, 182.
214. Radin, *Jews Among*, 215.

the order not to come within a milestone of the city.²¹⁵ Balsdon claims that the exposition of Jewish scriptures in the synagogue impacted proselytizing activity. It had the attraction of a philosophy lecture which was something unparalleled in other cults.²¹⁶ In addition, he finds that some Romans found the regular rest day an attractive feature of Judaism and adopted it in their own lives.²¹⁷ Balsdon nonetheless admits that Romans who converted to Judaism went no further than studying the Jewish scriptures and observing the Sabbath.²¹⁸ The Romans held the Jews in great contempt for the practice of circumcision, which provides a rationale for the existence of Godfearers. Later in the second century, we find the claim that if a Roman citizen or a slave was circumcised, the doctor was liable to execution and the circumcised person would lose property and become exiled.²¹⁹

Is this hostility toward the Jews evidence that Roman elites were losing influence upon the populace and the Jewish religion was gaining current by Godfearers? Although some Romans converted to Judaism, not all had positive views of the Jews. Isaac comments that the Romans held the belief that the east had a corrupting and degenerating influence that could not be reversed.²²⁰ He finds the Roman historian Lucius Flores claiming that,

> The conquest of Syria first corrupted us, followed by the Asiatic inheritance bequeathed by the king of Pergamon. The resources and wealth thus acquired spoiled the morals of the age and ruined the state, which was engulfed in its own vices as in a common sewer. (*Epit. rom. hist.* 1.47, 7–8)

We also find Juvenal, a contemporary of Tacitus, expressing a similar perspective about Jewish customs and their refusal to participate with non-Jews. He states,

> Some who have had a father who reveres the Sabbath, worship nothing but the clouds, and the divinity of the heavens, and see no difference between eating swine's flesh, from which their father abstained, and that of man; and in time they take to circumcision. Having been wont to flout the laws of Rome, they

215. Radin, *Jews Among*, 314–15.

216. Balsdon, *Romans and Aliens*, 67. Horace states, "Like the Jews, we will force you to come over to our numerous party" (*Sat.* 1.4.143).

217. Balsdon, *Romans and Aliens*, 234.

218. Balsdon, *Romans and Aliens*, 231.

219. Balsdon, *Romans and Aliens*, 232. Justinian quotes second-century Antoninus Pius who decreed that Jews were only permitted to circumcise their own sons in *Dig.* 48.8.11.

220. Isaac, *Invention of Racism*, 306–7.

> learn and practice and revere the Jewish law, and all that Moses committed to his secret tome, forbidding to point out the way to any not worshipping the same rites, and conducting none but the circumcised to the desired fountain or all which the father was to blame, who gave up every seventh day to idleness, keeping it apart from all the concerns of life. (*Sat.* 14.96–104)

Juvenal mocks the Jewish practice of circumcision by comparing it to eating swine. He also believes that the Jews "flout the laws of Rome" which may suggest a complete disdain for Roman law. Juvenal perhaps perceives the Jewish people's way of life as one that fails to fall under the jurisdiction of Roman law. He also assumes that they refuse to share Moses' teachings with non-Jews and use the Sabbath practice as an excuse for idleness. Gruen cautions us from taking Juvenal's comments too seriously. He finds them laughable rather than dangerous.[221] But these derogatory statements are not merely comical. They reflect Roman superiority over the marginalized within their midst. Mocking ethnic groups as entertainment reveals the privileged status of the writer, especially since the Jews are given no opportunity to respond.

What explains such critical attitudes and comments about the Jewish people, their converts, and their way of life? Schäfer believes that in the first and early second century the growing influence of Jews in Rome provoked society. He insists that the attraction to Judaism was viewed as a threat to Rome and all that Rome stood for.[222] Schäfer contends that this is evident in Seneca's concern about foreign influence when he claims, "the vanquished have given their laws to the victors."[223] Roman sentiments were certainly provoked. The elites perceived the corruption of Rome coming from the interaction with Jewish people and other foreigners. And as noted earlier, Livy expresses a similar rejection of ethnic integration when he claims, "whatever grows in its own soil prospers better, transplanted to alien soil it changes, and it degenerates to conform to the soil which feeds it."[224] Livy recognizes that although Rome is diverse, it is best if ethnic groups reside in their own location because to migrate or colonize would inevitably lead to humanity's deterioration.

We thus find Livy, Seneca, Juvenal, and Florus believing that contact with foreigners, including the Jews, was detrimental to Roman life and values. More specifically, in Diodorus's and Tacitus's comments we find that they viewed the Jews as antisocial. They interpret the Jewish social

---

221. Gruen, *Diaspora*, 45.
222. Schäfer, *Judeophobia*, 183.
223. Seneca in Augustinus, *Civ.* 6.11.
224. Livy, *His. rom.* 38.17.9–12.

behaviors in terms of hatred against humanity. They paint the Jews in the most demeaning way and retell their history in order to explain and justify the continual oppression and violence against them. We also notice that Roman writers considered contact with foreigners as having a denigrating effect to the overall vitality and success of the Roman Empire. Isaac even remarks that the Romans feared that if the Roman troops resided too long in foreign land, they would eventually be like foreigners and lose their Roman identity.[225] These Greek and Roman writers admit that colonization and violent integration of the Jewish people were not having the success they hoped. When the Jewish people refused to assimilate, these Roman writers justified their fear, violence, or hatred by blaming it upon their laws and their founder Moses.

The Ethnic Reality of the Greco-Roman World

How then should we assess the racial environment of the ancient world? After exploring the various views, justifications, and rational of diverse ethnic groups, we have a clear portrait of the ethnic context of the gospel. We know that the Greeks and Romans explained, put forth value judgments, and rationalized the existence of different groups within the Greco-Roman world. Their racial ideology aimed to influence and impact relations throughout the empire. We are also more aware of why they perceived various groups as different, inferior, or anti-social. How ubiquitous these views and perceptions of ethnic groups would be difficult to determine. But given the mention of various Greek and Roman writers, we cannot assume that it did not occupy a space within the racial imagination of those within the first century. Nor should we assume that the emergence of early Christianity did not concern itself with these ethnic perspectives and relations.[226] The ethos of the empire was both xenophobic and xenophilic. These traits are not mutually exclusive and as previously mentioned, ethnic relations are not a zero-sum game.

Although the Roman Empire was successful in absorbing many geographical regions, it did so in spite of exhibiting ethnic expressions of superiority, xenophobia, critical attitudes toward immigrants and foreigners, and justification of violence against ethnic groups. There was a range of ethnic views in the ancient world, as there are today. Some Roman writers considered contact with foreigners as having a denigrating effect to the overall

---

225. Isaac, *Invention of Racism*, 315.

226. Buell, "Challenges and Strategies," 44; Cosgrove, "Did Paul Value Ethnicity?," 278–281.

vitality and success of the Roman Empire. Others viewed ethnic groups as inferior if their lineage was impure. Mixture between ethnic groups was believed to only bring irreparable harm to the descendants and future of humanity. They utilized infancy exposure to keep the race pure. They also looked down upon those who would intermarry. Both Romans and Greeks rationalized their views toward those throughout the empire based upon environmental assumptions. They believed that the extreme climate of the northern and southern region impacted both the physical and intellectual development of people. These ethnic judgments enabled them to have a sense of superiority over the conquered. It justified their oppression, expulsion, and political policies that oppressed ethnic groups, foreigners, and immigrants. They believed that they were superior because of the location of their homeland which was the center of the Mediterranean world, a location placed there by the gods.

These are the ethnic scripts embedded in the wider context of the Greco-Roman world of the first century. These ethnic views, as well as one's own ethnic and racial perspectives toward the other, have the potential to unleash the most dehumanizing representation, violence, and oppression. Assuming that ethnic prejudice did not exist or that the early Jewish, Jewish Christianity, and Gentile Christianity did not have to deal with these realities would be misleading. It is within this ethnic reality that the Johannine community engaged and encountered diverse people groups. It was within this context that they started to reimagine what it meant to join a community that was filled with Jews, Greeks, and Samaritans. One can thus imagine the new difficulties that the Johannine community would have in understanding their own race relations and the growing movement of Christianity, especially since it emerged from Judea in the east. How would they interact with their fellow Jews who had expelled them from the synagogue? Would they continue to hold anti-Jewish xenophobia or prejudice? How would they welcome those who once oppressed, colonized, and partaken in the violence against their community in the history of Greek and Roman conquest? Would they welcome Greeks and Romans into the community and on what terms? And how would they perceive one another in light of racial stereotypes of foreigners, immigrants, and people from diverse environmental regions and mixed identities? The Johannine community needed to navigate these issues as they encountered various ethnic groups and found the ever-present need to respond to the growing diversity in their community. It is for this reason, as this monograph argues, that we find a new articulation of the Spirit. An articulation that does not solely concern itself with revealing Jesus but also creating and birthing a community that includes all humanity.

PART II

Ethnicity and the Spirit in Jesus' Public Ministry

4

Study of the Spirit in Context

How should we understand the pneumatic language in the gospel now that we have assessed the Johannine setting and the ethnic environment of the Greco-Roman world? In what ways are the discussions of the Spirit in the gospel articulated for an ethnic context? My focus on the Spirit with these ethnocritical concerns is not dissimilar from previous approaches. We must remember that many scholars draw upon particular Johannine circumstances in order to inform their understanding of the Spirit, whether this includes a context of liturgical issues, polemical strife with the Jewish synagogue, or simply the delay of the Parousia. What distinguishes my approach is that I include the ethnic and racial ideologies of the ancient world as the needed lens for our understanding. Scholars such as Raymond Brown have dismissed this significance in interpreting the gospel. He claims that due to the gospel's universalism all ethnic categories had lost significance.[1] And in studying the Spirit, we find William Loader claiming with surprise that the work of the Spirit in John remains almost entirely at the level of information-giving, acquaintance and confrontation with truth, and the mediation of presence.[2] Thus the goal of this study has been to demonstrate why these views are inadequate. It is not that I find them totally wrong, but I do notice that these approaches lack the critical yet basic component in the study of communities and people groups. That is, any discussion about ancient communities means that we are talking about people who have ethnic identities, not just theological ones.

We will begin with an exegesis of the Spirit discourses in the public ministry of Jesus which will include 1:32–33; 3:1–10; 4:23–24; 6:62–63;

---

1. Brown, *Introduction*, 180–81; *John 1–12*, lxxviii.
2. Loader, *Jesus in John's Gospel*, 432.

7:37–39, followed by the Paraclete sayings 14:15–27; 15:26–27, 16:7–15, and Johannine Pentecost in 20:19–23. Each analysis will incorporate various findings discussed in the previous chapters in order to provide a new synthesis and understanding of the racialized Spirit. I do not assume to discuss all aspects of the Spirit, solely the portions that are relevant to the reality of race in the ancient world. But before we proceed, I also want to examine what πνεῦμα means in the ancient world. That is, how was this term understood and what are its implications? Should we assume that our post-Nicene understanding of the Spirit was employed in the gospel? These are questions that we will first seek to answer.

Πνεῦμα in the Ancient World

John Levison points out that πνεῦμα is a bewildering term that includes diverse meanings that range from subterranean vapors, heavenly winds, human attitudes, ghosts, and a holy spirit.[3] Hermann Kleinknecht notices that within Greek literature and thought, πνεῦμα had a material characteristic and was naturally understood within the realm of the senses.[4] He remarks that there is always a force in πνεῦμα in that power flows and disappears with it.[5] Eberhard Kamlah explains that the root of the term denotes a dynamic movement of the air, such as to blow, breath, or emit a fragrance.[6] The term πνεῦμα was not always understood as a spiritual activity or principality, nor does it always suppose a divine meaning in the Christian sense. Πνεῦμα is also identified and utilized in relation to the physiological sense of "breath" which is inhaled and exhaled by humans or animals.[7] The earliest use of the term in Greek literature understand πνεῦμα as wind or breath. Aetius, in quoting the early pre-Socratic philosopher states, "Anaximenes, son of Eurystratus, of Miletus, declared air to be the source of beings . . . as our soul, he says, which is air, controls us, so do breath (πνεῦμα) and air encompass the whole world order (1.3.4)."[8] We can observe that "breath" or

---

3. Levison, *Spirit in First-Century Judaism*, 1.

4. Kleinknecht, "πνεῦμα, πνευματικος," *TDNT* 6:332–59. See also Kerferd, "Pneuma," *EP* 5:360; Peters, *Greek Philosophical Terms*, 160–62.

5. Kleinknecht, "πνεῦμα, πνευματικος," *TDNT* 6:335.

6. Kamlah, "Spirit, Holy Spirit," *NIDNTT* 3:689.

7. Aeschylus, *Sept.* 464; Thucydides, 2.49.2; Plato, *Tim.* 66e; 91c; Homer, *Il.* 5.696.

8. Drozdek remarks that unlike the human soul, the cosmic air surrounds the world and gives life. Similar roles are found between the of the universe and the of human beings. See Drozdek, *Greek Philosophers as Theologians*, 12–13. See also Plutarch, who criticizes Anaximenes's theory between the relation of cold and hot air with matter (Plutarch, *Prim. frig.* 7).

"πνεῦμα" is perceived to be ubiquitous in the universe and analogous to the breath in human beings. Anaximenes views air and breath synonymously. Πνεῦμα is the source of human life. As "breath" within human beings, it is also a sign, condition, and agent of life. This made πνεῦμα directly related to "life" or "living creature," as found in the literature that describes πνεῦμα as breathing or its absence in reference to dying.[9] We also find that "wind" was a common interpretation for πνεῦμα. It was defined either as a calm or strong blowing wind in a storm.[10] Πνεῦμα was inhaled and exhaled, felt in everyday life, and daily experienced in weather.

In addition, πνεῦμα is related to the psychological concept ψυχή and is often equated with it as we find in Philo's description of the formation of humanity.[11] Yet πνεῦμα is also described as functioning within the human being as a vital force which moves the body.[12] As a substance, it was thought to be the seat and agent of the higher intellectual and spiritual function.[13] The Greek biographer Diogenes Laërtius who explores early Stoic philosophers notes that except for Chrysippus, most held that the soul was an indestructible spirit that resided within humanity and animals. He points to Zeno and Posidonius who define the soul as a "warm breath" that animated humanity and enabled movement.[14] Kleinknecht also explains that πνεῦμα takes on a transferred sense of an invisible force or influence for good or ill. Πνεῦμα was understood as that which inspires, stirs, enthuses, and fills a person. This was believed to be imparted by the gods and prominent in poets, priests, and the ecstatic speech of prophets.[15]

The Stoic use of the term identified πνεῦμα as a cosmic force of divine origin that permeated all the substance in the universe.[16] Stoic philosophy

9. Kleinknecht, "πνεῦμα, πνευματικος," TDNT 6:336; Aeschylus, Pers. 507; Polybius, Histories, 31.10.4; Euripides, Hec. 571.

10. Aeschylus, Prom. 1086; Herodotus, Hist. 6.16a; Xenophon, Hell. 6.2.27; Philo, Gig. 10; Opif. 29.

11. Philo remarks, "For in many places of the law as given by Moses. He pronounces the blood to be the essence of the soul or of life, saying distinctly, 'For the life of all flesh is the blood thereof.' And when the Creator of all living things first began to make man, after the creation of the heaven and the earth, and all the things which are between the two, Moses says, 'And he breathed into his face the breath of life (πνεῦμα ζωῆς), and man became a living soul (ψυχὴν ζῶσαν),' showing again by this expression that it is the breath which is the essence of the life (πνεῦμά ἐστιν ἡ ψυχῆς οὐσία)" (Det. 80).

12. Aristotle, Mot. an. 10.

13. Kleinknecht, "πνεῦμα, πνευματικος," 358.

14. Diogenes Laërtius, Lives of Eminent Philosophers, 7.1.

15. Kleinknecht, "πνεῦμα, πνευματικος," TDNT 6:337–38; Euripides, Iph. aul. 760; Xenophon, Hell. 7.4.32; Homer, Od. 19.138; Il. 5.696; 10.482; 20.110.

16. Alexander of Aphrodisias states, "Chrysippus's theory of mixture is as follows: he

regarded πνεῦμα as a cosmic substance and never a personal divine being with attributes or qualities as we find in biblical literature. They recognized πνεῦμα as a power or deity that permeated the universe, giving it life and unity.[17] Philo also recognized this use of πνεῦμα within scripture and its analogous comparison to air as we find in Greek writers. In examining the Spirit of God in creation he asserts,

> The Spirit of God is spoken of in one manner as being air flowing upon the earth (ἀὴρ ἀπὸ γῆς), bringing a third element in addition to water. . . . Since the air, as it is very light, is raised and borne aloft, having water as it were, for its foundation; and in another manner, unalloyed knowledge is said to be so, which every wise man naturally partakes of. (*Gig.* 1.22)

Yet he also describes πνεῦμα as divine qualities such as wisdom, understanding, and knowledge.[18] Philo describes the Spirit of God that was upon Moses by saying,

> The Spirit which is upon him is the wise, the divine, the indivisible, the undistributable, the good Spirit, the Spirit which is everywhere diffused, so as to fill the universe, which, while it benefits others, it not injured by having a participation in it given to another, and if added to something else, either as to its understanding, or its knowledge, or its wisdom. (*Gig.* 1.27)

Philo portrays the divine Spirit in relation to knowledge but also points to its ubiquitous nature in the entire cosmos, a theme reflected by Greek writers. The Spirit cannot be entirely understood materialistically in relation to air. There is no thinning out of the Spirit and loss of quality when it comes upon various people in different places. Yet Philo does not suppose that the Spirit of God will always remain with humanity.[19]

---

supposes that the whole of nature is united by the *pneuma* which permeates it and by which the world is kept together and made coherent and interconnected" (*Mixt.* 216). In critiquing Stoic views, we find Plutarch quoting Chrysippus, who claimed, "Physical state are nothing else but airs. For bodies are contained by these, and the cause that every one of the bodies contained in any habit is such as it is, is the containing air, which they call in iron hardness, in stone solidness, in silver whiteness" (*De Stoic. Repugn.* 43 [1053f]).

17. See Hager, "Chrysippus's Theory of Pneuma," 97–108; Kleinknecht, "πνεῦμα, πνευματικος," *TDNT* 6:358; Quintilian, *Inst.* 7.3.5.

18. Philo, *Gig.* 1.23.

19. Philo, *Gig.* 1.27–28, 47. Those who have the divine Spirit for a prolonged period are "those who, having put off all the things of creation, and the inmost veil and covering of false opinion, come to God in their unconcealed and naked minds" (*Gig.* 1.53).

In this brief review, we thus find that πνεῦμα had a wide range of meanings due to its use in explaining the wind, breath, life, moral impulses, and the human soul. The Greeks understood πνεῦμα as a natural or psychological phenomenon within the realm of the senses. Most recognize how necessary πνεῦμα was for life, and some identified its role as a powerful energy that could move the body into an inspired state. Philo embraces the diverse understanding of the term. He compares it to the qualities of air, affirms its presence throughout the cosmos, but also recognizes its divine aspect and relation to the knowledge, wisdom, and presence of God. We can thus recognize why Levinson admits that the term πνεῦμα has a range of meanings. From this review thus far, we can notice its diverse usage.

Spirit in the Biblical Tradition

In the Septuagint πνεῦμα was the most frequent translation of the Hebrew רוּחַ (*ruach*) which occurs about 287 times.[20] Although frequently used to describe wind or air, the Septuagint affirms that its source and command ultimately comes from God.[21] Similar to our findings in Greek literature, πνεῦμα refers to the breath of humanity and animals. Even more, God is the one who gives, sends, raises, replaces, and withdrawals πνεῦμα from creation.[22] Strikingly, we also find an anthropomorphic use of πνεῦμα that expresses God's breath, often coming out from his nostrils.[23] This use is however frequently found within contexts of eschatological judgment. One could postulate that there are overlapping understandings between the Greek and Hebrew notion of πνεῦμα. According to Kamlah, πνεῦμα signifies an outward expression of life force inherent in all human behavior rather than the act of breathing. He suggests that this differs from the ordinary, visible, and tangible phenomena of the world.[24]

Nonetheless, within the Septuagint πνεῦμα intimately relates to human function and emotions. It is synonymous with the human spirit, one's heart, or relates to one's breath that is revived, strengthened, released, or

---

20. Werner Beider, "πνεῦμα, πνευματικος," *TDNT* 6:367.

21. Gen 8:1; Exod 15:10; Num 11:31; 1 Kgs 18:45; 19:11; 2 Kgs 3:17; Ps 10:6; 47:8; 77:39; 102:16; 103:4; 106:25; 147:7; 148:8; Eccl 1:6, 14, 17; 2:11, 17, 26; 4:4, 6, 16, 6:9; 8:8; 11:5; Job 1:19; 8:2; 12:10; 15:2; 16:3; 43:8; Hos 4:12; 12:2; Amos 4:13; Jonah 1:4; 4:8; Isa 7:2; Jer 4:11–12; Ezek 1:4; Dan 2:35; Wis 5:11, 23; 13:2; 17:17. See also Sir 43:17.

22. Gen 6:17; 7:15; 1 Kgs 17:17; Ps 103:29; 134:17; 145:4; Eccl 3:19–21; 12:7; Job 7:7; 12:10; 27:3; 32:8; Hag 1:14; Zech 12:1; Isa 42:5; 57:16; Ezek 11:19; 36:26; 37:5–10; Dan 5:23; 10:17; 1 Esd 2:1, 5; 2 Macc 7:22–23; Tob 3:6; Wis 15:11; 16:14; Sus 1:44.

23. Exod 15:8; 2 Sam 22:16; Ps 17:16; 32:6; Job 4:9; Isa 30:28; 33:11; Wis 11:20.

24. Kamlah, "Spirit, Holy Spirit," *NIDNTT* 3:691. See also Jdt 10:13.

downcast.²⁵ Werner Bieder remarks that πνεῦμα was considered the seat of all the functions of the soul.²⁶ The human expression of πνεῦμα is found in the description of the prophet Daniel as having an extraordinary holy spirit, Elisha receiving Elijah's spirit, and its evaporation into non-existence.²⁷ But the human spirit and physical wind was not unrelated to God. God is recognized as the giver and sustainer of human πνεῦμα and Lord over the πνεῦμα experienced in weather, regardless of the material function of the wind or human breath. God is also described as the God of all flesh and spirits²⁸ and having the ability to stir or harden human spirits.²⁹ Human breath as πνεῦμα is essentially of God and returns to its divine origin in God.

Πνεῦμα also refers to God's divine Spirit³⁰ which is holy,³¹ incorruptible (Wis 12:1), and an agent of creation.³² The Spirit also takes an active role in the affairs of humanity. This includes instructing or admonishing (Neh 9:20, 30; Zech 7:12), revealing (Sir 48:24), abiding or entering humanity,³³ judging (Isa 28:6), lifting prophets to transport them into a heavenly realm,³⁴ or acting as an agent of purification (Isa 4:4). Πνεῦμα as a divine agent is also noticeable in the manifestations and involvement with selected people in biblical literature. The πνεῦμα of the Lord comes upon humanity for specific functions such as empowering with physical strength, prophesying, proclaiming, or leading God's people.³⁵

In addition, we also find the use of πνεῦμα in relation to moral virtues, vices, and entities. Wisdom is described as a loving spirit (Wis 1:6; 7:22–23),

---

25. Gen 45:27; Num 14:24; Josh 2:11; Judg 15:19; 1 Sam 30:12; 1 Kgs 20:5; 2 Kgs 2:9, 15; Ps 30:6; 33:19; 50:12, 14, 19; 76:4, 7, 8; 141:4; 142:4, 7; Prov 15:4; Job 10:12; 17:1; 34:14; Mal 2:15–16; Isa 19:3; 65:14; Ezek 21:12; Dan 2:1, 3; 7:15; 10:17; Tob 4:3; Jdt 7:19; 14:6; Wis 5:3; 1 Macc 13:7; Bar 3:1; Sir 9:9; 34:13; 38:23.

26. Beider, "πνεῦμα, πνευματικος," TDNT 6:369. See also Wis 5:3; Pr Azar 3:39, 86; Tob 4:3.

27. Dan 5:12; 6:4; Sus 1:44; Sir 48:12; Wis 2:3.

28. Num 16:22; 27:16; 2 Macc 3:24; 14:46.

29. Deut 2:30; 1 Chr 5:26; 2 Chr 36:22; Ezra 1:1, 5; Jer 28:11.

30. Gen 6:3; Num 23:7; Judg 13:25; 2 Sam 23:2; 1 Kgs 18:12; 22:24; 2 Kgs 2:16; 2 Chr 18:23; Ps 105:33; 138:7; 142:10; Mic 2:7; 3:8; Zech 4:6; Isa 30:1; 48:16; 63:14; Ezek 11:24.

31. Ps 50:13; Isa 63:10–11; Wis 9:17.

32. Gen 1:2; Ps 103:30; Judg 16:14; Ps 32:6; Job 33:4; Jdt 16:14; Wis 1:7; 12:1; Bar 21:4.

33. Hag 2:5; Ezek 2:2; 3:24; 37:14; Dan 4:8–9, 18; 5:11, 14.

34. Ezek 3:12, 14; 8:3; 11:1, 24; 37:1; 43:5.

35. Gen 41:38; Num 11:17, 25–29; 24:2; 27:18; Judg 3:10; 6:34; 11:29; 14:6, 19; 15:14, 1 Sam 10:6, 10; 11:6; 16:13–14; 19:20, 23; 1 Chr 12:18 [LXX 12:19]; 2 Chr 15:1; 2 Chr 20:14; 24:20; Joel 3:1–2; Zech 12:10; Isa 11:2; 32:15; 42:1; 44:3; 59:21; 61:1; Ezek 11:5; 36:27.

discipline is noted to be a holy spirit (Wis 1:5), and God is portrayed as a giver of a spirit of wisdom for special abilities.[36] In terms of vices and entities, God is understood to be in control of a multitude of spirits. This includes a spirit of jealousy (Num 5:14, 30), evil spirits,[37] deceiving spirits that are akin to evil angelic beings,[38] the spirit of harlotry (Hos 4:12; 5:4), unclean spirits (Zech 13:2), vengeful spirits (Sir 39:28), and a spirit that causes deep sleep (Isa 29:10). The moral personification of πνεῦμα is thus noticeable. The term is found in reference to moral impulses or influences, divine entities, and God's activity and presence. With this wide usage, it is not surprising for some like George Johnston to essentially argue that πνεῦμα is a divine power of God and not the third person of the Trinity.[39] We nonetheless observe that humanity not only has a spirit, but God is also a God of spirits and manifests the divine self as πνεῦμα.

Spirit in Qumran Literature

When we turn to Qumran literature, we find many pneumatic references related to purification and prophecy. Craig Keener finds the most common themes including both the idea of the Spirit purifying or empowering God's people and the Spirit inspiring and revealing.[40] When describing the activity of God's Spirit as a purifying agent, the literature often uses the phrase "spirit of holiness." F. F. Bruce notes that although the Christian idea of a "Holy Spirit" is rarely found in the Old Testament, the phrase begins to appear in Qumran literature, yet not as a distinct person within the Godhead.[41] God's spirit of holiness enables humanity to contemplate the "light of life" and become united to the truth.[42] Spirit references to the role of prophecy, knowledge, or revelation are found throughout various Qumran texts.[43] The implications suggests that it is God's divine breath which enables the interpreter to understand truth so that one may live a righteous life.

36. Exod 28:3; 31:3; 35:31; Deut 34:9; Job 32:8; Isa 11:2; Sir 39:6; Wis 7:7.
37. Judg 9:23; 1 Sam 16:14–16, 23; 19:9; Tob 6:8.
38. 1 Kgs 22:21–23; 2 Kgs 19:7; 2 Chr 18:20–22; Isa 19:14; 37:7.
39. Johnston, *Spirit-Paraclete*, 122.
40. Keener, *Spirit in the Gospels*, 9.
41. Bruce, "Holy Spirit in Qumran Texts," 50. See references to God's spirit of holiness or holy spirit in 1QS 8:16; 9:3–5; 1QH 4:25; 6:12; 8:1–5, 10–15; 15:6; 16:10–14; 17:32; 20:11; CD 2:12.
42. Although described as the "spirit of holiness," we also find the "spirit of uprightness and humility" in 1QS 3:7–9. The "spirit of holiness" is contrasted to the "spirit of injustice" in 1QS 4:20–22.
43. 1QS 8:16; 1QH 5:18; 6:12, 25; 17:32; 20:11–13; CD 2:12.

The Qumran literature also affirms that God created humanity with a spirit,[44] often noted to be either good or unjust[45] and related to the volition of a person's will.[46] A person's moral impulses are often defined as spirits. John Pryke observes that the majority of the references within Qumran literature describe a person's spirit. He remarks that one's spirit is the supernatural part of humanity's nature given by God, but not necessarily a synonym for soul.[47] This also includes the belief that people hold a holy spirit that can be morally defiled through sin.[48] Indeed, the *Thanksgiving Hymns* describes a person as a "spirit of flesh" (1QH 4:24; 5:14). Bruce, however, argues that the references to a holy human spirit should only be understood as holy because it is God who has placed the spirit within them.[49]

In rare occasions, angels are also described as spirits but nonetheless created by God (1QH 9:1–14; 18:8). They are "holy ones" who are created to dwell in their dominions. This includes the spirit of light and darkness, or simply the spirit of Belial.[50] Other references to angelic beings include a spirit of evil, perversion, and haughty spirits.[51] But as Pryke argues, the dualism between the spirits of light and darkness are not metaphysical but moral. The angels of darkness attempt to influence humanity's moral behaviors and determine the final outcome of each person.[52]

The Implications

How then do we assess the diverse uses and understandings of πνεῦμα? Levison reminds us that neat boundaries between Jewish texts and their Greco-Roman contexts are difficult to draw. He also contends that even where there are considerable degrees of correspondence between cultures, it is still difficult to determine who influenced or was dependent upon the other.[53]

---

44. 1QS 7:18, 22; 1QH 4:15; 5:15–20; 6:25; 7:10, 20; 8:10–14; 9:15; 12:31.

45. 1QS 4:20–25; 1QH 4:24. See also 1QM 7:5 which describes a "perfect spirit" in reference to the qualities of soldiers. Being "poor in spirit" is found in 1QM 14:7. Evidence of following either the spirit of righteous or falsehood is manifested through moral activities. See 1QS 4:1–25 for full list of practices.

46. CD 3:2, 8.

47. Pryke, "Spirit and Flesh," 346.

48. CD 5:10–14; 7:3–4; See also *Jub.* 1:20–23.

49. Bruce, "Holy Spirit in Qumran Texts," 54.

50. 1QS 3:24; 1QH 5:1–4.

51. 1QH 6:10; 1QH 9:20–24; 1QS 11:1–2. Spirit of falsehood is mentioned in 1QS 4:10–24; 1QH 4:23–24.

52. Pryke, "Spirit and Flesh," 351.

53. Levison, *Spirit*, 5–6.

Kamlah remarks that Judaism was indeed influenced by its Hellenistic environment and identified πνεῦμα as a vital force divinely breathed into humanity, often indistinguishable from the soul but contrasted with the body.[54] John Breck recognizes that the fundamental difference between Greek and Hebrew thought on the Spirit is the ultimate origin.[55] It is true, as he claims, that in Hebrew thought πνεῦμα is never reduced solely to a natural phenomenon subject to the laws and limits of the cosmos.[56] Although we find πνεῦμα used to describe "wind" or "human breath," there are also divine references and uses of the term. We discover in Qumran literature echoes of New Testament ideas on purification, prophecy, and knowledge of God's truth. But the Qumran literature also includes the assumption that spirits are moral impulses and angelic beings. Finally, we also find πνεῦμα commonly used to describe the human spirit. This reminds us that although πνεῦμα was divinely created, it remains distinguished from the creator.

What then are the implications of these diverse usages? Primarily, it should lead us to have contextual sensitivity in our understanding of πνεῦμα. There is no universal understanding of the term, only various contextual expressions and applications. This also should caution us in assuming that πνεῦμα is always in reference to a divine being or divine presence. In Greek literature we find πνεῦμα employed to describe natural phenomenon. With regard to human activity, πνεῦμα also refers to one's breath, life, or soul. But properly understood, πνεῦμα was impersonal within a Greco-Roman context and understood in light of a physical or psychological movement within the realm of the senses.

In Jewish literature there are similar physical and psychological expressions but with additional references to divine origin, activity, and identity. Πνεῦμα describes the breath in living creatures, angelic beings, forces or influences that stir humanity into moral decisions or understanding, and is used in reference to God's own being. Particularly, πνεῦμα as the divine God engages in various activities with humanity and creation. And just as we find humans having a spirit that originates from God, so too we find spirits existing as independent entities under the rule of God.

What about the pneumatic language within the Fourth Gospel? After examining Jewish and Greco-Roman literature, we are more aware of its ranges of meaning. I do not presume that πνεῦμα within the gospel always has a divine reference to the third person of the Trinity as properly understood in a post-Nicene context, nor do I believe that we should

---

54. Kamlah, "Spirit, Holy Spirit," *NIDNTT* 3:692.
55. Breck, *Spirit of Truth*, 100.
56. Breck, *Spirit of Truth*, 100.

automatically interpret the term theologically. This does not mean that I agree with George Johnston's claim that the gospel does not have any usage that permits the translation of the "Holy Spirit" in a full trinitarian way.[57] Πνεῦμα is that one word that encapsulates invisible but experienced activity in natural phenomena, internal human impulses, moral virtues and vices, and incorporeal beings or divine entities. We find this wide application also within the Fourth Gospel. The physical expression of πνεῦμα is found in Jesus' statement to Nicodemus, "The πνεῦμα blows wherever it pleases. You hear its sound, but you cannot tell where it comes from or where it is going" (John 3:8). Jesus is also described as having a human spirit (πνεύματι) that was stirred when news of Lazarus's death reached him (John 11:33). But πνεῦμα does not solely have natural or human connotations, nor is it solely an abstract term. The majority of πνεῦμα expressions in the gospel refer to divine personhood. We find the explicit reference that "God is πνεῦμα" (John 4:24) and the Paraclete is described as the "holy πνεῦμα" from the Father (John 14:27). The gospel utilizes the diverse uses of the term.[58] In fact, Dodd remarks that if we were to use the Trinitarian formula, the gospel speaks not of the Father, Son, and Spirit but of Father, Son, and Paraclete. He insists that πνεῦμα is appropriate to deity and connotes reality or absolute being.[59]

As a result, we must be cautious to not assume that the gospel failed to have a robust theological understanding of the Spirit. Incorporating the theological, material, and human use of the term is vital in our study. We must recognize that the pneumatic language was neither new nor an idea unique to a Jewish context. The environment of the Greco-Roman world would have also provided the readers from a diverse ethnic background with some common language, ideas, resources, and images to draw from in an understanding of the divine πνεῦμα.[60] Our study thus explores how an ethnic and racial context aids our understanding of gospel's pneumatology. Or said differently, our goal should be to observe how ethnicity enables us to theologize the movement, activity, presence, and identity of πνεῦμα. It is within the context of ethnic interaction that we become aware of the activity and identity of the divine πνεῦμα.

57. Johnston, "Spirit-Paraclete," 30.

58. See John 11:33; 13:21; 19:30, where πνεῦμα is utilized to express Jesus' inner emotions and human spirit. In other occasions, the divine πνεῦμα of God is clearly emphasized in 1:32–33; 3:34; 4:24; 6:63; 7:39; 14:17, 26; 15:26; 16:13; 20:22. Crump makes a striking case to view 19:30 in reference to the Holy Spirit in "Who Gets What," 78–89. This would suggest, however, as Bennema points out, that there are two impartations of the Spirit. See Bennema, "Giving of the Spirit," 195–213, esp. 204–5.

59. Dodd, *Interpretation*, 226.

60. See Buch-Hansen, *Spirit that Gives Life*.

5

Interpreting the Anointing of the Spirit

JOHN 1:32-33

THE EARLIEST MENTION OF THE SPIRIT IN THE FOURTH GOSPEL is found in John the Baptist's confession. It is in this confession that John describes the descending presence of the Spirit upon Jesus. Although the Spirit is mentioned twice in John's confession, John is actually describing a revelatory experience. He states,

> I have seen the Spirit come down like a dove from heaven and remain upon him. And I did not know him, but the one who sent me to baptize in water, that one said to me, "The man on whom you see the Spirit come down and remain upon him, this one is the one who will baptize with the Holy Spirit."
>
> Τεθέαμαι τὸ πνεῦμα καταβαῖνον ὡς περιστερὰν ἐξ οὐρανοῦ, καὶ ἔμεινεν ἐπ᾽ αὐτόν. κἀγὼ οὐκ ᾔδειν αὐτόν, ἀλλ᾽ ὁ πέμψας με βαπτίζειν ἐν ὕδατι ἐκεῖνός μοι εἶπεν, Ἐφ᾽ ὃν ἂν ἴδῃς τὸ πνεῦμα καταβαῖνον καὶ μένον ἐπ᾽ αὐτόν, οὗτός ἐστιν ὁ βαπτίζων ἐν πνεύματι ἁγίῳ. (1:32-33)[1]

Craig Koester affirms that the first act of the Spirit is a revelatory one.[2] He suggests that this anticipates the promise that the Spirit will remain upon the community of faith after Jesus departs.[3] Marianne Meye Thompson finds

---

1. All New Testament Greek passages are from the fourth edition of *The Greek New Testament*, edited by Barbara Aland, et al. (Stuttgart: Deutsche Bibelgesellschaft, 2002).

2. Koester, *Word of Life*, 135-36.

3. Koester, *Word of Life*, 136; Keener, *John*, 461; Morris, *John*, 134; Barrett, *St. John*, 148.

the significance of John the Baptist seeing the Spirit upon Jesus in terms of what the Spirit does for the Baptist.[4] Others such as Gary Burge point out that the descent of the Spirit signifies Jesus' anointing and empowerment.[5] As Tricia Brown states, "it legitimizes Jesus as the bearer of the divine benefit of spirit that he will confer to his potential clients."[6] These readings affirm that the role of the Spirit is focused on either identifying, empowering, or affirming Jesus' identity as the dispenser of the Spirit. But is the Spirit solely functioning in this revelatory manner? What does a "descent of the Spirit" mean for both the Jewish religious leaders in the narrative and the ethnic members of the Johannine community? Are there any ethnic views of the ancient world that are being challenged?

In this chapter I will argue that the Spirit does not function as a revealing or empowering manner as commonly described. The Spirit's descent confirms that Jesus' mission is specifically focused for reconciling an ethnically diverse world. But before we uncover this reading, we will first examine the role of John the Baptist in the gospels in order to highlight the narrative's distinguishing focus. Afterwards, we will analyze the ethnic characters within the narrative and meaning of the Spirit's descent. Finally, we will revisit the role of the Spirit and how this reading resonates with the ethnic environment of the Johannine community.

John the Baptist Among the Gospels

John the Baptist is mentioned within all four gospels.[7] In the Fourth Gospel he is interrogated by the Jewish religious leaders and repeatedly denies being the Christ, Elijah, or the prophet (1:19–25). The gospel explicitly mentions that it was the Jews of Jerusalem, later described as the Pharisees, who sent the priests and Levites to question him (1:19, 24).[8] We do not find in the Synoptics such an encounter. In fact, there are substantial differences between the Fourth Gospel's presentation of the Baptist and the

---

4. Thompson, *God of the Gospel of John*, 164.

5. Burge, *Anointed Community*, 52–59; Keener, *John*, 461; Morris, *John*, 133n75; Brown, *John*, 1:66; Millos, *Juan*, 190.

6. Brown, *Spirit in the Gospel of John*, 92; Morris, *John*, 134.

7. For a closer analysis of the differences, see Webb, *John the Baptizer and Prophet*, 70–77.

8. Ἰουδαῖος and Φαρισαῖος is noticed by commentators. See Barrett, *St. John*, 142–45; Brown, *John*, 1:44; Morris, *John*, 122; Keener, *John*, 32–33; Ashton, *Understanding*, 167.

Synoptic account.[9] But from these differences we notice that the Fourth Gospel creates distance between the John the Baptist and Jesus. This clearly distinguishes John's role as a testifier of Jesus' identity, not his baptizer. The Fourth Gospel also emphasizes both a descent (καταβαῖνον) and remaining presence (ἔμεινεν ἐπ᾽ αὐτόν) of the Spirit upon Jesus.[10] Although all gospels agree that the Spirit descends upon Jesus like a dove and that Jesus is a Spirit baptizer, they each describe the decent of the Spirit differently.[11] The Fourth Gospel emphasizes the presence of the Spirit upon Jesus apart from the Baptist's activity. The Baptist states, "I *have seen* the Spirit come down and remain upon him" (v. 32) and "I *have seen* and testify" (v. 34). The descent is described with perfect indicative verbs τεθέαμαι and ἑώρακα which places the activity prior to Jesus' appearance. Even more, when God reveals to John the Baptist how he would identify Jesus, this incident is not described in the narrative (v. 33). It occurs prior to John's testimony and confrontation with the religious leaders. These are but a few of the notable differences and similarities in wording, events, perspectives, and chronology. But contrary to the Synoptics, the Fourth Gospel introduces Jesus as one who already has the Spirit. As previously mentioned, John the Baptist plays no initiating role in the coming presence of the Spirit. He only identifies the Spirit upon Jesus (vv. 32–34).

---

9. For example, the only communication John the Baptist has with religious leaders is found in Matthew, when he criticizes the Pharisees and Sadducees for being a "brood of vipers" (Matt 3:7). In Mark, John the Baptist hears the people of Jerusalem confess their sins (Mark 1:5). Luke records John's use of the phrase "brood of vipers" but pins it as a description of the crowd (Luke 3:7). But the Fourth Gospel presents an interrogative scene which highlights the identity of the Baptist. The Fourth Gospel presents a minimum of three days beginning with the Baptist's conversation with the religious leaders (1:19–28) and final pronouncement of Jesus' identity before his disciples (1:35–42). Strikingly, the only time Jesus speaks within this episode is when he addresses the followers of John the Baptist (1:37–39). This differs from the Synoptic portrait (Matt 3:16; Mark 1:9; Luke 3:21). Matthew adds that Jesus and the Baptist have a conversation in the Jordan river before the baptism (Matt 3:14–15).

10. The use of μένω occurs 40 times in the Fourth Gospel.

11. Matthew 3:11–12 and Luke 3:16–17 describe the Spirit baptizer with the added eschatological imagery of fire, winnowing fork, and separation of wheat from chaff. The language evokes an eschatological judgement theme. This eschatological imagery is absent in both Mark and the Fourth Gospel. See France, *Matthew*, 116; Fitzmyer, *Luke 1–9*, 466. Allison points out that the context for the judgement warning is the Baptist's criticism on Jewish confidence in Abraham's descent. See Allison, *Constructing Jesus*, 215. Only Mark and the Fourth Gospel describe Jesus as one who will baptize solely with the Holy Spirit (Mark 1:8; John 1:33). The Synoptics agree that after the Spirit's descent, a voice from heaven declares Jesus as God's beloved son, a declaration absent in the Fourth Gospel (Matt 3:17; Mark 1:11; Luke 3:22).

The readers and those within the narrative are made aware of the Baptist's identity as a testifier, not as one who is known by his diet, dress, or fiery sermons on repentance.[12] This portrayal has made scholars question the reliability of the Baptist's identity in the Fourth Gospel, especially since it also differs from Josephus's description of the Baptist.[13] The gospel's departure from the Synoptic tradition may explain the particular need to emphasize that John the Baptist was not the messiah, especially since he continued to have followers outside of Judea.[14] However, E. P. Sanders doubts that the gospel presents a reliable tradition.[15] He argues that Jesus was a follower of John the Baptist and this reality led to the Christian need to relegate the Baptist to a subordinate position, something which the gospel clearly does.[16] But Bultmann presents another way at looking at the issue. He proposes that the Johannine narrative may contain a reliable historical tradition reflective of John the Baptist's followers within the Johannine community.[17] There are some similarities that reflect a shared tradition.[18] But the gospel has a different pneumatic emphasis and chronology. The gospel includes God's involvement with John the Baptist prior to Jesus' appearance. There is also a repeated emphasis of the Spirit's presence on Jesus. The gospel certainly takes a different approach by emphasizing John the Baptist's testifying role in identifying Jesus amongst the crowd. This is one of the most distinguishing

---

12. Navarro notices that the manner in which John the Baptist is presented as a testifier also parallel concluding remarks in 21:24, "Nos indican, por tanto, que nos hallamos ante una inclusión que abarca el entero." See Navarro, "Estructura testimonial del Evangelio de Juan," 515–16.

13. Josephus, *Ant.* 18.116–19. However, scholars such as Nir challenge this image and argue that this is a Christian interpolation. See Nir, "Josephus's Account of John the Baptist," 32–62.

14. In Acts 18:25; 19:3 we find the early Jewish Christian missionaries encountering followers of John the Baptist in Ephesus. Justin Martyr also mentions that followers of the Baptist still existed (*Dial.* 80). We also find a strong refutation that John the Baptist was not the Christ but a forerunner of Jesus in *Clem. Recogn.* 1.54, 60. Luke 3:15 mentions that some thought John was the Christ.

15. Sanders, *Historical Figure of Jesus*, 94.

16. Sanders, *Jesus and Judaism*, 91–93.

17. Bultmann, *John*, 108.

18. All Gospel accounts pronounce John the Baptist as a forerunner of Jesus in light of Isaiah 40:3 and depict him as a baptizer in the Jordan. It must be noted that only Luke includes Isaiah 40:4–5. Ferda suggests that John uses the Isaiah text to give his activities eschatological significance. See Ferda, "John the Baptist," 177. Although the Fourth Gospel does not mention John performing the baptismal rite, he is described as such in 1:25–31. Each Gospel also identifies the Spirit on Jesus like a dove and affirms Jesus as a Spirit baptizer.

aspects we find. But who are those in the crowd? And why must they hear John the Baptist's testimony that Jesus already has the Spirit?

John the Baptist's Testimony in Light of Isaiah

When John the Baptist appears in the narrative he is described as a man who was sent from God and commissioned to testify about the coming light so that all may believe (1:6–7). He is mentioned within the prologue as the first one who testifies of Jesus' preexistence (1:15). This reveals that his primary role is to testify about Jesus, not to baptize him. Andrew Lincoln remarks that John the Baptist's mission to testify to "all people" is a desired goal as noted in the prologue.[19] Bultmann finds this expression not reflective of the historical situation of the Baptist's ministry, but a preserved tradition of the goal to reach a wide audience.[20] It must be noted that the use of πάντες in v. 7 clearly evokes a message that goes beyond the ethnic-geographical confines of Judea. Within the prologue, John the Baptist is a testifier of the light that is not solely limited to Judea. The light comes to the world in order to shine upon πάντα ἄνθρωπον (1:9). Indeed, Brown remarks that the imagery of light entering the world echoes the language of Isaiah.[21] The prophet Isaiah asserts, "The people who walk in darkness (σκότει) will see a great light (φῶς), those who live in a dark (σκιᾷ) land, the light (φῶς) will shine on them" (9:2 [9:1 LXX]). This Isaiah passage reflects John 1:5 which describes Jesus' identity and mission with similar vocabulary (τὸ φῶς ἐν τῇ σκοτίᾳ φαίνει). Who are those in the darkness in Isaiah 9? Those in darkness are the people of God who have suffered oppression and await their messianic deliverer.[22] Yet in John 1:5 the darkness refers to all people within the cosmic sphere who do not understand the Logos.[23] But are these two groups of people in Isaiah and the Fourth Gospel radically different?

The imagery of light and darkness found in Isaiah illuminates the narrative movement in the gospel. Throughout Isaiah the light which shines upon the people is not restricted to those in Judea who are awaiting redemption. In Isaiah 42:6 the Servant of the Lord is commissioned to be a "light to the nations" (ἐθνῶν). Brevard Childs remarks that the Servant's mission in 42:6 carries a universal scope by embodying a covenantal relationship with

---

19. Lincoln, *Truth on Trial*, 59.
20. Bultmann, *John*, 51.
21. Brown, *John*, 1:28.
22. Childs, *Isaiah*, 80–81; Kaiser, *Isaiah 1–12*, 125–27.
23. See John 3:19; 8:12; 12:35, 46.

the nations.²⁴ He also finds the Servant's mission to all the nations as the true climax of his divine calling to all creation.²⁵ Joseph Blenkinsopp adds that in 42:1–4 God addresses an audience in order to recommend an individual whom God has chosen, endowed with the divine Spirit, and whose mission it is to establish law and order among the nations without violence or brutality.²⁶ He also adds that although Isaiah 42:1–6 includes no instructions on how the Gentiles become enlightened, it becomes a foundational text that describe Israel's role in bringing salvation to all humanity.²⁷

We also find in Isaiah 49:6 the prophet affirming the universal scope of the Servant's mission. In this passage, God asserts that the Servant is "a light of the nations (ἐθνῶν)" so that "salvation may reach to the end of the earth." Although this text may not explain Gentile salvation, Joel Kaminsky and Anne Steward insists that all nations will recognize God's sovereignty.²⁸ We find similar mission in 60:1–3, which states,

> Arise, shine, for your light has come, and the glory of the Lord has risen upon you. For behold, darkness will cover the earth and deep darkness the peoples. But the Lord will rise upon you and His glory will appear upon you. Nations (ἔθνη) will come to your light, and kings to the brightness of your rising.

Again, demonstrated is an interest in the restoration of God's people. But the "shining light" is not solely benefiting the Jewish exiles alone. The light that shines upon them is also aimed to the Gentiles and kings of distinct nations.²⁹ We must note that the coming light promised by the prophet is an eschatological hope of restoration that will extend beyond the ethnic boundaries of Jewish exiles.³⁰ This restoration will also include a diminishment of

---

24. Childs, *Isaiah*, 326. See also Gelston, "Universalism in Second Isaiah," 393–94; Kaminsky and Steward recognize the impact of the light upon the Gentiles but suggest that this does not necessarily imply that all nations will receive salvation. See Kaminsky and Steward, "God of All the World," 147–50.

25. Childs, *Isaiah*, 385.

26. Blenkinsopp, "Second Isaiah," 88.

27. Blenkinsopp, "Second Isaiah," 90–92. See also Goldingay and Payne, *Isaiah 40–55*, 228.

28. Kaminsky and Steward, "God of All the World," 150–56.

29. In the Septuagint, the term "nations" is ἔθνος, which can also be translated as "Gentiles."

30. According to Blenkinsopp, Jerusalem becomes the political center of the world. The Gentiles are in anguish (60:1–3), bring tribute (60:5–7, 11, 16), supply labor for the temple (60:10, 12–14), led to Jerusalem in a triumphal procession (60:11), and universally acknowledge the supremacy of Israel (60:14). To understand the Gentile motivation behind these activities, he thinks that the nations are being made an offer

ethnic hostility between the Jewish people and their captors. In other words, the anticipated light that will shine upon all not only brings salvation, it brings ethnic reconciliation.

Is the imagery of a "shining light" of ethnic reconciliation in Isaiah being echoed in John the Baptist's pronouncement to the Jews? Yes, and we must notice how this developing universal mission of the light within Isaiah shaped the background of the prologue in the Fourth Gospel and John the Baptist's mission as a testifier. John the Baptist is commissioned by God to indiscriminately testify concerning the light so that all people may believe (1:6-8). This emphasis that John the Baptist is not the light does not solely explain his identity.[31] It explains the Baptist's mission to usher in the global salvation mentioned in Isaiah's pronouncements of the coming "light to the Gentiles." Jesus is indeed the light of the world, or as Isaiah would state, a "light to the Gentiles." The prophetic tradition includes the expectation that the Gentiles would come to faith in God at the end of the age.[32] And in the gospel this expectation was now being fulfilled. What then was the sign of this manifestation and fulfilled promise? It was the Spirit's presence upon Jesus. But if the Spirit is a demonstration of a mission to reach the Gentiles, how does this relate to the Baptist's conflict with the Jews in the narrative? What are the ethnic implications of the discourse, especially between the Baptist and the Jewish leaders who question him?

Interrogating the Baptist

When we turn to 1:19-42 we will notice various temporal breaks. In vv. 29, 35, and v. 43 the recorded activity spans three days. The phrase "the next day"[33] helps us identify the sequence of events accordingly:

vv. 19-28	The First Day: John is Questioned by the Jewish Religious Leaders
vv. 29-34	The Next Day: John Reveals the Identity of Jesus
vv. 35-42	The Next Day: John Reveals the Identity of Jesus to his Disciples

---

that they cannot refuse. See Blenkinsopp, "Second Isaiah," 93. Childs interprets the light in terms of the city of God and the original mission of the Servant to be a light of the nations as noted in 42:6; 49:6 (Childs, *Isaiah*, 499).

31. Bultmann, *John*, 51; Wink, *John the Baptist*, 88.

32. See Schnabel, "Israel, the People of God," 35-57; Oswalt, "Mission of Israel," 85-95.

33. The temporal marker "τῇ ἐπαύριον" is also found in 1:43; 6:22; 12:12.

In vv. 19–28 the ministry of John the Baptist begins with the assertion, "this is the witness of John when the Jews sent priests and Levites" (v. 19). The Jewish religious leadership question the Baptist's identity and purpose for baptizing (v. 25). The first question they ask John the Baptist is, "why are you baptizing?" (v. 19). Lincoln finds a lawsuit motif within this confrontation closely associated with the threat of excommunication from the synagogue and denial of Peter.[34] Samuel Millos puts it more directly. He suggests that the question is a type of accusation. It is as if they were asking John the Baptist, "¿quién te crees que eres?"[35]

But why distinguish the religious leadership within this episode as an ethnic group? The writer mentions in v. 19 that οἱ Ἰουδαῖοι ἐξ Ἱεροσολύμων sent the Levites and priest and also describes them as the Φαρισαῖος in v. 24. The difficulties of reconciling the Ἰουδαῖος with the Φαρισαῖος who sent priests and Levites is noticed by commentators.[36] Historically, priests were not under the authority of the Pharisees in the first century but under the Sadducees, which was a different sect.[37] Brown suggests that by the time the gospel was written, the Judaism that survived the destruction of the Temple was of strongly Pharisaic persuasion. As such, the writer simplifies the Jewish religious authorities as "Pharisees" because it would have been most meaningful to the current situation.[38] John Ashton agrees that the use of "Jews" refers to the authorities in Jerusalem. He also recognizes that during the time of Jesus the Pharisees would not have the authority to initiate the official enquiry as the narrative suggests.[39] Although he admits that throughout the gospel "οἱ Ἰουδαῖοι" carries overtones of mistrust and hostility, he insists that the priests and Levites were conscientiously discharging their duties. Ashton reads the encounter as the Jewish authorities giving the Baptist an opportunity to testify.[40]

Is this encounter then solely an inquisitive one? Or does it convey a hostile tone that is reflective of a trial in which a person is interrogated as Lincoln and Millos would argue? We must note that throughout this first

---

34. Lincoln, *Truth on Trial*, 60–61; Bultmann, *John*, 86; Beasley-Murray, *John*, 29–30; John 9:22; 12:42; 13:38; 18:25, 27.

35. Millos explains, "No cabe duda que el mensaje de Juan y su bautismo resultaban inquietantes para ellos. Nadie se había atrevido a llamar a todos, incluido ellos, al arrepentimiento" (Millos, *Juan*, 162).

36. Lindars, *John*, 105; Barrett, *St. John*, 143–45; Keener, *John*, 431–33.

37. Josephus, *Ant.* 13.171–72; 13.293–98; 17.41; 18.11–17; *J.W.* 2.119, 162–66.

38. Brown, *John*, 1:44.

39. Ashton, *Understanding*, 167.

40. Ashton, *Understanding*, 168.

day John the Baptist is asked a series of questions. There are a total of seven questions which include:

v. 19	Who are you?	Σὺ τίς εἶ;
v. 21	Then who [are you]?	Τί οὖν;
v. 21	Are you Elijah?	Σύ Ἠλίας εἶ;
v. 21	Are you the prophet?	Ὁ προφήτης εἶ σύ;
v. 22	Who are you?	Τίς εἶ;
v. 22	What are you saying about yourself?	τί λέγεις περὶ σεαυτοῦ;
v. 25	Why then are you baptizing if you are not the Christ, nor Elijah, nor the prophet?	ί οὖν βαπτίζεις εἰ σὺ οὐκ εἶ ὁ Χριστὸς οὐδὲ Ἠλίας οὐδὲ ὁ προφήτης;

This dialogue may seem as if the Jewish religious leaders were curious about the Baptist's identity. Yet in each occasion they allow little opportunity for the Baptist to respond to the questions leveled against him. When they press him for a definitive answer in v. 22, he appeals to Isaiah 40:3 and defines himself as the "voice" in the wilderness. When they inquire about his baptismal activity, the Baptist does not answer this final question. Instead, he shifts the focus to the unknown person within their midst (vv. 26–27). And most importantly, the narrator introduces this first day of questioning by describing it as "ἡ μαρτυρία τοῦ Ἰωάννου" (v. 19).

The term "μαρτυρία" is utilized not solely in relation to bearing witness to facts or truths, but also within a legal sphere such as a trial or legal transaction.[41] By describing the Baptist's first day as a "μαρτυρία" it is difficult to avoid the tone of an interrogative trial or those who suffered for the faith. The witness of John the Baptist and the multitude of questions from the Jewish leadership reveals initial confrontation. Should we then read "οἱ Ἰουδαῖοι" negatively within this opening context? Does it suggest that the "Jews" were hostile to the Baptist, thus creating a scene in which his first

---

41. Strathmann, "μάρτυς, μαρτυρία," *TDNT* 4:476. This feminine noun is not common in the Septuagint nor the New Testament. The majority of occurrences are within the Johannine writings and Revelation. The concept of a witness as a martyr takes greater significance in the second century when describing those who risk their lives or suffer death, especially those who died under the reign of Marcus Aurelius. Eusebius mentions that according to Hegesippus, the descendants of Jude were interrogated by the Emperor Domitian in the late first century. They became leaders of the churches because "they had borne testimony and were of the Lord's family" (*Hist. eccl.* 3.20.8). See also 2.25.8; 2.23.18; 3.32.3; 5.1.1–5.2.2; 5.19.3.

opposition came from a particular ethnic group? Is this reference to the "Jews" more reflective of the Johannine community's vocabulary given that John the Baptist was historically a Jew.[42] Or perhaps, as some suggest, we should read this description as a non-ethnic designation?[43]

Shaye Cohen notices the difficulties in defining "Jewishness" in terms of an ethnic group, geographic group, or a religious group.[44] He points out that originally the term was an ethnic-geographic term related to those who inhabited of the land of Judea.[45] Cohen insists that it was only later that the term was applied to people who were neither ethnic nor geographic Judeans but had either come to believe in the Judean God or joined the Judean state as allies or citizens.[46] Despite the ambiguity or lack of universal definition, he admits that the ethnic reference was so strong that both the Judeans themselves and the Greeks and Romans had a sense that all Judeans belonged to a single group.[47] Would this be the case later at the end of the first century when the gospel was written? The readers would immediately recognize the Jews as an ethnic group given its close association with the geographical region of Jerusalem as noted in 1:19. Even with the cultural and religious connotations, central to our understanding of the term is the ethno-geographic designation.

Scholars however point out the ambiguities and polemical use of the "Jews" in the gospel. Brown claims that the term is akin to a technical title for the religious authorities who were hostile to Jesus.[48] He insists that when the gospel was composed the only Judaism of the time was Pharisaic Judaism.[49] Brown argues that passages such as 6:60–66; 8:31–45; and 12:42–43 reveal the existence of various Jews who believed in Jesus but responded differently during the time of the Johannine community. He believes that the Fourth Gospel is attempting to persuade crypto-Christians to leave the synagogue[50] while criticizing other Jews who emphasized physical descent from Abraham, held a low Christology, and rejected the membership of

---

42. Martyn, *History and Theology*, 37n17; Brown, *Community*, 41; Keener, *John*, 227.
43. Bultmann, *John*, 86–87; Padilla, *Juan*, 21.
44. Cohen, *Beginnings of Jewishness*, 14.
45. Cohen, *Beginnings of Jewishness*, 69.
46. Cohen, *Beginnings of Jewishness*, 70, 94–96.
47. Cohen, *Beginnings of Jewishness*, 75.
48. Brown, *John*, 1:lxxi.
49. Brown, *John*, 1:lxxii.
50. Brown, *Community*, 71–73.

Samaritans.[51] His reading assumes that the Jews in the gospel mirror the Jews known by the Johannine community.

Culpepper attempts to resolve the problem from a literary perspective. The various uses of "Jews" in the Fourth Gospel demonstrates to Culpepper that there was no distinction between the Jewish people in general, Judeans, or religious authorities who were hostile toward Jesus.[52] He insists that they are presented in a pattern of increased levels of conflict and opposition with some receptive and others rejecting Jesus' revelation.[53] As a result, he contends that the "Jews" becomes a term by which the gospel characterizes both Jesus' opponents and the community's opponents.[54] In addition, he proposes that they reflect universally applicable characteristics which includes negative categories and images associated with unbelief.[55] This reading also suggests that the Fourth Gospel is anti-Jewish, or at least creates the potential for anti-Semitism. But Culpepper does note that the anti-Jewish polemic is motivated by theological concerns.[56] Regardless of this rhetoric, he also contends that the gospel is pro-Jewish in that the theology is shaped by its Jewish roots and wholly dependent upon it.[57]

James Dunn notices the difficulties of interpreting the gospel's characterization of the Jews. He implores the interpreter to analyze the text in light of the factional polemic of Second Temple Judaism and emerging Christianity.[58] When done accordingly, he believes that we would notice that the gospel is not anti-Jewish, but reflective of an intra-Jewish conflict akin to the conflicts that characterized Judaism during Jesus' time.[59] This view is similar to Paul Anderson who also interprets the gospel as reflecting a set of intra-Jewish engagements.[60] He holds that the gospel cannot be portrayed as anti-Semitic nor anti-Jewish in the general sense. Instead, it reflects an intra-Jewish debate between a radical Jewish messianism and parental Judaism. To those who suggest that the gospel is anti-Jewish, Dunn and Anderson challenge them to consider which Judaism is being criticized.

---

51. Brown, *Community*, 74–81.

52. Culpepper, *Anatomy*, 126. See also Culpepper's "Gospel of John and the Jews," 273–88.

53. Culpepper, *Anatomy*, 128.

54. Culpepper, "Gospel of John and the Jews," 282.

55. Culpepper, *Anatomy*, 129.

56. Culpepper, "Gospel of John and the Jews," 285.

57. Culpepper, "Anti-Judaism," 68–69.

58. Dunn, "Embarrassment of History," 51.

59. Dunn, "Embarrassment of History," 44–45.

60. Anderson, "Anti-Semitism and Religious Violence," 309.

They both agree that the gospel seeks to warn fellow Jews not to follow the dominate view of the Jewish people which was in conflict with Johannine Christianity.[61]

How then are we to interpret οἱ Ἰουδαῖοι within this episode? When we turn to the gospel we will notice that not all references to the "Jews" are hostile. The term Ἰουδαῖος" is found within the gospel 72 times. It is used to describe customs or festivals,[62] the ethnic group,[63] a regal title,[64] and geographic region.[65] When we focus more closely on its ethnic use, we find a diverse characterization. On most occasions, the Jews are introduced in the narrative as those who challenge John the Baptist, his disciples, and debate Jesus' teachings.[66] The Jews are also presented as a group hostile toward Jesus and his teachings. They are described as seeking to kill Jesus for violating the Sabbath or calling God his own Father.[67] They accuse Jesus of having a demon or being a Samaritan (7:20; 8:48, 52; 10:20). But they are not the only one speaking incendiary remarks. It is within these confrontational contexts that we find Jesus recognizing their unbelief (6:36, 64), calling them a child of the devil (8:44), stating that they are not from God (8:47), and describing them as liars (8:55).

On some occasions the Jews are linked with the Pharisees or other religious authorities.[68] This also includes being involved in Jesus' arrest and death.[69] Although we may find Jesus in a hostile confrontation within the narrative, we are also made aware that Jesus is a Jew (4:9) and celebrates the festivals of the Jews (2:13; 5:1). The Jews are also astonished at Jesus' teaching (7:15), believe in him (7:31, 43; 8:30–31; 11:45; 12:9–11), wonder if he is the Christ (10:24), and even console Martha and Mary when Lazarus dies (11:19, 31, 33, 36). These positive portrayals are scattered throughout various episodes. When some Jews openly confront Jesus, the narrative also reminds us that not all were hostile. Some are even noted to avoid speaking

---

61. Dunn, "Embarrassment of History," 41–46; Anderson, "Anti-Semitism," 282.

62. John 2:6, 13; 4:9, 22; 5:1; 6:4; 7:2; 11:55; 19:40, 42.

63. John 1:19; 2:18, 20; 3:1, 25; 4:9 (2 times), 22; 5:10, 15, 16, 18; 6:52; 7:1, 11, 13, 15, 35; 8:22, 31, 48, 52, 57; 9:18, 22 (2 times); 10:19, 24, 31, 33; 11:8, 19, 31, 33, 36, 45, 54; 12:9, 11; 13:33; 18:12, 14, 20, 31, 35, 36, 38; 19:7, 12, 14, 20, 21, 31, 38, 20:19.

64. John 18:33, 39; 19:3, 19, 21 (2 times).

65. John 3:22.

66. John 1:19; 2:18–20; 3:1, 25; 5:10–18; 6:41, 52; 7:35; 8:22; 10:19; 11:37; 13:33; 18:20.

67. John 5:18; 7:1, 19; 8:37, 59; 10:31, 33; 11:8, 53–54.

68. John 1:19; 3:1; 7:32; 9:15–18; 19:21.

69. John 18:12–14, 31, 36–40; 19:7–14, 31.

openly in fear of the Jews (7:13; 9:22; 19:38; 20:19), especially since they were threatened with excommunication (9:22).

We thus find no consistent portrayal of the Jews within the gospel. Although Brown, Culpepper, and Dunn may help us understand the rhetoric of the "Jews" within the gospel, we still cannot avoid noticing the anti-Jewish polemic. Jan van der Watt holds that the anti-Jewish language is vilification rhetoric, motivated also in part from love.[70] But could these ethnic circumstances, tensions, or prejudices toward Jews explain why the gospel is laced with such antipathy and caricature? Is the gospel creating a stereotypical portrayal of the "Jews" and thus becoming the founding seeds of later anti-Jewish sentiment?[71] Some scholars would agree, but not all find the gospel reflective of an anti-Jewish or anti-Judaism tone.

We have already argued that within the Greco-Roman world there existed racial prejudice and hostility toward various groups, including Jews.[72] Millos notes that although the term "Jews" is commonly used to refer to the Jewish authorities, as the narrative proceeds the term becomes synonymous with the enemies of Christ.[73] Janis Leibig explains that the writer establishes a theological vendetta that legitimatizes and even generates ethnic antipathy of the Jewish people.[74] Adel Reinhartz proposes a sympathetic reading where the language can be interpreted as part of the community's move toward self-definition and warning not to return to Judaism,[75] but she also notices that this reading cannot excuse the gospel's harsh utterances about the Jews. She insists our attempt to neutralize the negative rhetoric by explaining it in terms of expulsion does not alleviate the problem.[76]

Must we assume that there is only one way of interpreting οἱ Ἰουδαῖοι in the gospel?[77] The diverse characterization of the Jews makes it difficult to conclude that the gospel is either anti-Jewish or pro-Jewish. Finding positive characterization of the Jews in 4:22 does not negate the hostile tone in 8:44, nor should we assume that the negative remarks about the

70. Watt, "Is Jesus the King of Israel?," 54.

71. See Leibig, "John and the Jews," 209–234; Reinhartz, "Judaism in the Gospel of John," 382–93; *Befriending the Beloved Disciple*; Bennema, "Identity And Composition of Οἱ Ἰουδαῖοι " 239–63; Sheridan, "Issues in Translating οἱ Ἰουδαῖοι," 671–95; Wahlde, "Jews in the Gospel of John," 30–55.

72. Diodorus, 34.1; Tacitus, *Hist.* 5.2-8; Cicero, *Flac.*, 67–69; Juvenal, *Sat.*, 14.96–104.

73. Millos, *Juan*, 159.

74. Leibig, "John and the Jews," 223.

75. Reinhartz, "Judaism in the Gospel of John," 391–92.

76. Reinhartz, *Befriending the Beloved Disciple*, 75–76.

77. Wahlde, "Jews in the Gospel of John," 52.

Jews suggest that the positive portrayals in the gospel were solely a causal mention. As mentioned earlier, positive remarks toward ethnic people on one occasion does not neutralize the negative portrayal of ethnic people on other occasions. We must agree with Culpepper and Reinhartz who notices these elements running throughout the narrative. They find the gospel as both anti-Jewish and pro-Jewish. Tom Thatcher in fact describes this as a paradox in that the gospel seems to be at once both the most Jewish and the most anti-Jewish of the gospels.[78] I would also add that this is not solely evidence of a theological conflict. It includes the reality of an ethnic struggle of anti-Jewish and pro-Jewish attitudes within the Johannine community. The gospel does not state that the characters were afraid of the "Jewish ideas" but of the "Jews," that is, the ethnic people whose ancestral origins point to a particular region. Theology does not exist without a community that upholds and defends the theological claims. And no community is void of an ethnic identity or identities.

When we return to the implications that this has for our reading of 1:19–31, the context echoes a courtroom battle. The οἱ Ἰουδαῖοι in this episode refer to the Jewish authorities who challenge John the Baptist. And at the same time, it also functions as a literary device that enables the Johannine Jews and other ethnic members of the community to recognize that behind their tensions with other non-Johannine Jews stands the real culprits of their confrontation: the Pharisaic religious authorities. The gospel thus serves to embrace their fellow Jewish kin while at the same time making a sharp break with them. The use of οἱ Ἰουδαῖοι in this passage however does not defuse the rising tension with the Jews and religious leaders throughout the gospel. It aims to resonate with the readers who are also facing similar interrogative experiences. In the same way the Baptist was confronted and challenged, so too are Jewish and other ethnic members of the community being confronted and challenged by the religious leaders and Jews of their own time. They, like the Baptist, must stand and be a witness to the authorities.

How then should Baptist-like testifiers of the Johannine community respond? We find that John the Baptist does not engage in an open hostility with the Jewish religious leaders-and neither should the Johannine community. Indeed, John the Baptist answers their questions, a model to the Johannine members on how they should respond under interrogative duress. And their response should include a deliberate effort in pointing the Jewish religious leaders to the one that they should be concerned about: μέσος ὑμῶν ἕστηκεν ὃν ὑμεῖς οὐκ οἴδατε (v. 26).

---

78. Thatcher, "John and the Jews," 3–38.

Rereading the Baptist's Testimony

In vv. 29–31, which is the next day according to the narrative time, the testimony of the Baptist becomes more specific. When the Baptist sees Jesus he asserts,

> Behold, the lamb of God who takes away the sin of the world. This one is whom I said, after me comes a man who has a greater rank than me, because he was before me. And I did not know him, but so that he may be revealed to Israel, because of this I came baptizing in water.

> Ἴδε ὁ ἀμνὸς τοῦ θεοῦ ὁ αἴρων τὴν ἁμαρτίαν τοῦ κόσμου. οὗτός ἐστιν ὑπὲρ οὗ ἐγὼ εἶπον, ὀπίσω μου ἔρχεται ἀνὴρ ὃς ἔμπροσθέν μου γέγονεν, ὅτι πρῶτός μου ἦν. κἀγὼ οὐκ ᾔδειν αὐτόν, ἀλλ᾽ ἵνα φανερωθῇ τῷ Ἰσραὴλ διὰ τοῦτο ἦλθον ἐγὼ ἐν ὕδατι βαπτίζων. (vv. 29–31)

Here John the Baptist identifies Jesus as the Lamb of God who takes away the sin of the world (v. 29).[79] There is an ethnic tone in the claim that Jesus removes τὴν ἁμαρτίαν τοῦ κόσμου.[80] John the Baptist also explains that Jesus was the one whom he referred to when he said, "after me comes a man who was before me" (v. 30). This claim echoes the previous day when he informed the Jewish religious leaders that "the one who comes after me, I am unworthy to unite the thongs of his sandals" (v. 27). By referring to the testimony, John the Baptist assumes that the same Jewish religious leaders remained near the Jordan, although we cannot be certain. Yet on this new day, the Baptist reveals to the audience that Jesus was within their midst as the Lamb of God.

---

79. Barrett and Morris are certain that the phrase has a Hebrew background but doubt the exact reference (Barrett, *St. John*, 146; Morris, *John*, 130). Brown claims that this refers to the Suffering Servant and paschal lamb in Isa 53:7 (*John 1–12*, 62–63). Dodd argues for an apocalyptic warrior lamb. He believes that the Fourth Gospel is drawing upon an image of a powerful Lamb who is divinely appointed as a leader for the people of God as found in the *T. Jos.* 19:8 and Revelation. See Dodd, *Interpretation*, 230–38; 293. Beasley-Murray also follows Dodd's argument in Beasley-Murray, *John*, 24–25.

For possible sacrificial allusions, see Gen 22:8; Exod 12:5; 29:38–46; Lev 4:32; 14:12, 21, 24–25; 16:21; 17:11; Num 6:12; Isa 53:7; Jer 11:19; Mark 14:24; John 18:28; 19:36; Acts 8:32; 1 Cor 5:7; 1 Pet 1:18–19; 2:22–24. Other allusions include a warrior lamb found in Rev 5:6–13; 6:16; 7:14–17; 17:14; *1 En.* 90:9–12; *T. Jos.* 19:8–11; *T. Benj.* 3:8. For allusions to the universal removal of sin, see Isa 53:12. Schipper challenges the claim that the lamb imagery relates the paschal lamb in Leviticus. See Schipper, "Interpreting the Lamb Imagery," 315–25.

80. The singular use of "ἁμαρτία" suggests the totality of sin from all humanity.

We notice that John the Baptist finally answers the question that the Jewish religious leaders had posed on the previous day, regardless if they were present to hear the answer. That is, he answers the question about the reason why he was baptizing. In v. 31 the Baptist explains that his sole mission in performing the water rite was to reveal Jesus to "Israel." There is a striking ethnic limitation in the overall mission of the Baptist in this response. We must remember that the Baptist was previously described as a testifier so that "all people" may believe (v. 7), claimed that Jesus was the Lamb of God for the "world" (v. 29), but now insists that Jesus was being revealed for "Israel" (v. 31). The use of "Ἰσραήλ" makes the revelation of Jesus very ethnocentric. But if John's testifying role was not solely for "Israel" but for "all people" as v. 7 suggests, why use this limited ethnic designation?

The use of Israel here expresses a self-identity that encompasses the historic past of the Jews.[81] Cohen insists that the term as a concrete social reality is first and foremost a function of pedigree, genealogy, and birth, even if applied to converts.[82] We also find the use of "Israel" including nationalistic and ethno-specific overtones within the gospel. Jesus is described as the King of Israel in 1:49 and 12:13. Nathanael is described as a true "Israelite" (1:47) and Nicodemus is described as the "teacher of Israel" (3:10). Although the term is not mentioned frequently, on most occasions throughout the New Testament it is applied to the ethnic Jews. Josephus even explains that the name "Jews" came from the tribe of Judah, and he uses the term interchangeably with "Israel."[83]

Yet scholars agree that the whole point of John the Baptist's mission was to make Jesus manifest to the people of Israel, not lead them to repentance.[84] But Brown detects that underneath this mission to reveal Jesus to Israel is an apocalyptic assumption that a hidden messiah would not be made known until the proper time.[85] We find elements of this expectation in Trypho's response to Justin when he says,

> But Christ—if he has indeed been born, and exists anywhere—
> is unknown, and does not even know himself, and has no power
> until Elijah come to anoint him, and make him manifest to all.
> (*Dia.* 8.4)

---

81. Thiel argues that "Israel" and "Jew" were used as insider and outsider self-designating terms. See Thiel, "'Israel' and 'Jew' as Markers," 80–99; contrary to Tomson, "Jews in the Gospel of John," 211.

82. Cohen, *Beginnings of Jewishness*, 337–38.

83. *Ant.* 11.132–33, 173; cf. 6.29–30.

84. Bultmann, *John*, 91–92; Lindars, *John*, 108; Barrett, *St. John*, 133; Morris, *John*, 132.

85. Brown, *John*, 1:53.

Brown also offers the possibility that the emphasis of the Baptist's role in revealing Jesus to Israel reflects a polemic against the Baptist sectarians. He insists that the text fails to include John baptizing Jesus in order to remove any sectarian argument that would make Jesus subordinate to the Baptist.[86] In other words, so that there would be no confusion about the relationship between John the Baptist and Jesus, the gospel emphasizes the point that the Baptist's only role was to reveal Jesus to Israel.

Our reading cannot avoid the ethnic language, inclusive mission, and confrontation between a Jewish Baptist and the Jewish religious authorities. Perhaps another way to understand this ethnic dynamic is to explore how the specific mention of "Israel" is set alongside Jesus' role in taking away the "sin of the world." That is, Jesus is presented for both the Jewish people and the Gentiles. The use of the terms "Jews," "Israel," and "world" touches the concerns and hopes of all ethnic readers, leaving no one doubting Jesus' aim and mission to each ethnic group, beginning with Israel. As we proceed with John the Baptist's claims, we find additional insights that were presented to the Jewish leadership within the narrative: that Jesus is their awaited Spirit anointed figure who came for an ethnic mission.

The Spirit Upon the Ethnic Savior

As we review the role of the Spirit within the Baptist narrative, several questions arise. First, what does the coming Spirit signify in light of these ethnic overtones? Is the Spirit actually participating in a revelator function as scholars claim?[87] We can agree that the only way that John was able to identify Jesus before the crowd and Jewish religious leaders was due to the Spirit's descent (καταβαῖνον) and presence upon him (μένον ἐπ᾽ αὐτόν). John the Baptist states,

> I saw the Spirit descending like a dove from heaven, and it remained upon him. And I did not know him, but the one who sent me to baptize in water said to me, 'The one on whom you see the Spirit descending and remaining—this is the one who baptizes with the Holy Spirit.' And I have seen and testified that this man is the Son of God.
>
> Τεθέαμαι τὸ πνεῦμα καταβαῖνον ὡς περιστερὰν ἐξ οὐρανοῦ, καὶ ἔμεινεν ἐπ᾽ αὐτόν· κἀγὼ οὐκ ᾔδειν αὐτόν, ἀλλ᾽ ὁ πέμψας με βαπτίζειν ἐν ὕδατι ἐκεῖνός μοι εἶπεν, Ἐφ᾽ ὃν ἂν ἴδῃς τὸ

---

86. Brown, *John*, 1:65; Keener, *John*, 441–42.
87. Bultmann, *John*, 92n4; Beasley-Murray, *John*, 28.

> πνεῦμα καταβαῖνον καὶ μένον ἐπ᾽ αὐτόν, οὗτός ἐστιν ὁ βαπτίζων ἐν πνεύματι ἁγίῳ. κἀγὼ ἑώρακα, καὶ μεμαρτύρηκα ὅτι οὗτός ἐστιν ὁ υἱὸς τοῦ θεοῦ. (vv. 32–34)

Scholars point to a revelatory activity of the Spirit within this narrative. The use of key terms such as βλέπω (v. 29), φανερόω (v. 31), θεάομαι (v. 32), ὁράω (vv. 33–34), and οἶδα (vv. 31, 33) scattered throughout the narrative point to this revelatory emphasis. Johnston remarks that these terms are employed for looking at earthly things and for visions or spiritual perceptions. Contrary to Morris, he insists that the language points to an unusual religious experience such as a vision.[88] Johnston claims that the witness of John the Baptist affirms that Jesus had received his Messianic endowment at his baptism. He suggests that the resting of the Spirit ought to be understood in light of Genesis 8:8 and Isaiah 11:2 which combine the imagery of the dove with the Spirit upon the messianic figure.[89] Burge also interprets the descent of the Spirit as having revelatory significance that points to Jesus' anointing.[90] The Spirit, as he argues, serves as the sole signal of the Messiah's identity and holds the revelatory key that tells the Baptist when his expectation has been fulfilled. But most importantly, Burge insists that narrative's focus is on the Spirit's empowerment which includes Jesus' ability to be the distributor of the Spirit.[91] He agrees that the Spirit's presence reflects messianic texts.[92] This, as he argues, stresses the anointing and dwelling of the Spirit on Jesus which signifies a messianic status.[93] Tricia Brown suggests that the pneumatic presence upon Jesus signifies that he is a bearer of the "spirit" and one who gives the "spirit" to potential clients. Analyzing the narrative through patron-client relations leads her to argue that Jesus is being singled out as one who will proffer divine benefits, especially since he is the only figure able to broker access to the "spirit realm" of God.[94]

Although these readings aptly point out the messianic anointing, the emphasis generally turns to the Spirit's revelatory activity. The main activity of Spirit however is not a revelatory one. We are not informed within

---

88. Johnston, *Spirit-Paraclete*, 18. Morris proposes that John is not talking about a vision but a real experience in seeing the Holy Spirit come down upon Jesus. See Morris, *John*, 133.

89. Johnston, *Spirit-Paraclete*, 18–21.

90. Burge, *Anointed Community*, 52.

91. Burge, *Anointed Community*, 53–55.

92. Burge, *Anointed Community*, 56. See Num 11:26–29; Isa 11:2; 42:1; 48:16; 61:1; 1 En. 49:3; 62:2; T. Jud. 24.2; T. Levi 18; Sir 48:12, 24; Jub. 14.

93. Burge, *Anointed Community*, 62. See also Keener, *John*, 461; Millos, *Juan*, 190.

94. Brown, *Spirit in the Writings of John*, 90–93.

the narrative when the Spirit descends upon Jesus. Instead, we are made aware that Jesus has the Spirit. The true revealer within the narrative is not the Spirit, but John the Baptist. It is the Baptist who reveals to the Jewish leaders that Jesus has the Spirit. It is the Baptist who has been testifying and responding to the interrogative questions of the Jewish authorities that he is not the one they should be expecting. In fact, the Baptist's revelatory activity is vital because the Jewish authorities could not identify Jesus who was within their midst. As John the Baptist states, "among you stands one whom you do not know" (v. 26). By pointing out their inability to know the one within their midst, the readers are also drawn back to the prologue where Jesus is also described as the Logos who came to his own people but was not received (v. 11). Now, these Jewish religious leaders and the people in the crowd are given an opportunity to identify Jesus. They are made aware through the Baptist's testimony that Jesus has emerged into the scene and comes with the Spirit upon him. As a result, our focus should not be on when or what initiated the Spirit's descent, but what it means to hear John the Baptist proclaim that Jesus bears the Spirit. What then does the descent and presence of the Spirit upon Jesus signify to Jewish religious leaders and people within the narrative? What does the Spirit's coming presence signify in light of the Isaianic hope of the coming light?

The Spirit's presence upon people is reflective of various encounters within the Old Testament. We find the activity of prophecy strongly associated with the coming Spirit. During the exodus from Egypt, seventy elders of Israel were given the Spirit that was upon Moses in order to assist the leading of the Israelites. This experience with the Spirit resulted in the elders prophesying upon the camp (Num 11:17, 25–29). Other instances of prophesying activity include Balaam (Num 24:2), King Saul (1 Sam 10:6), and Saul's messengers (19:20–23).[95] The Spirit of God also comes upon people to fulfill specific activities such as empowering Israel's judges.[96] Even more, when David is anointed as Israel's next king, the Spirit of the Lord came upon him, which was the same Spirit that left Saul (1 Sam 16:13–14). This transfer motif is also found between Moses and Joshua (Deut 34:9) and Elijah with Elisha (2 Kgs 2:9–15).

Scholars however have pointed out that the descent of the Spirit in John 1:29–33 is most reflective of the description of the Spirit in Isaiah 11:2. Indeed, there are other literary allusions between John the Baptist's testimony in John 1:29–33 and Isaiah's description of the anointed one in 11:1–10 that makes the connection convincing. In the gospel the Spirit is

---

95. See also 1 Chr 12:19 [LXX 12:18]; 2 Chr 15:1; 20:14; 24:20.
96. Judg 3:10; 6:34; 11:29; 14:6, 19; 15:14.

described as coming down (τὸ πνεῦμα καταβαῖνον) and remaining upon Jesus (μένον ἐπ' αὐτὸν). This echoes the promise of the Spirit's (πνεῦμα τοῦ θεοῦ) rest upon God's anointed (ἐπ' αὐτὸν) in Isaiah 11:2. Other allusions include similar animal imagery and narrative time. We find the mention of a lamb (ἀρνός/ἀμνὸς) and the emphasis that the events within the narrative occur on a particular day (ἡμέρᾳ/ἐπαύριον) in both Isaiah and the gospel. The lamb (ἀρνός) in Isaiah however is described in relation to a restoration of creation's harmony, whereas in the gospel Jesus is described as the lamb (ἀμνὸς) of God who takes away the sin of the world. The two words are not identical and are certainly used differently within their contexts. But when combined with the emphasis that the coming of the Spirit would occur on a particular day, the notion that we are to think about Isaiah 11 in light of John the Baptist's testimony is more persuasive. How then would the Jewish religious leaders understand the descent of the Spirit upon Jesus in light of the wider context of Isaiah 11:1–10? And, as John Christopher Thomas asks, why would Jesus need such an anointing?[97]

In Isaiah 11:1–10 we find a new hope of a promised descendant of Jesse who will not only be marked by the Spirit[98] and rule with justice, but whose very presence will inaugurate the extended rule to all ethnic people. Jim Roberts also notices that this text conveys the recognition that God's rule will extend to the whole earth, a promise that echoes the description of nations going up to the mountain of God in order to receive instruction and knowledge in Isaiah 2:2–5.[99] In Isaiah 2:2 the prophet proclaims that the mountain of God will be the highest amongst the world and all nations (ἔθνος) will come to it.[100] Oswalt agrees that within this text the focus is upon Israel's glorious destiny as a lighthouse to the nations for truth and peace.[101] As previously noted, within the Septuagint the term "nations" is translated from ἔθνος which can also be translated as "people" or "Gentile."

It is difficult to avoid the wider ethnic impact of the anointed one's mission in Isaiah. This promise conveys an inclusion of ethnic groups who will participate in the messianic age. When the Spirit thus comes upon the anointed one in Isaiah, included is a broader mission to reach all the diverse people of the world. This ethnic mission is not only found in Isaiah 11, also in Isaiah 42:1 we find God proclaiming, "Behold, my Servant, whom

---

97. Thomas, *Spirit of the New Testament*, 159.

98. Oswalt asserts that his leadership will have a supernatural endowment. See Oswalt, *Isaiah 1–39*, 279–86.

99. Roberts, *First Isaiah*, 177–82.

100. Roberts, *First Isaiah*, 41.

101. Oswalt, *Isaiah 1–39*, 114–15.

I uphold, my chosen one in whom my soul delights. I have put my Spirit upon Him. He will bring forth justice to the nations." Although Childs recognizes the difficulties in identifying the Servant, he insists that this figure is equipped with the traditional attributes associated with Israel's charismatic deliverers and whose task is to restore order in the world.[102] John Goldingay and David Payne, who do not believe that this passage conveys a missionary activity, nonetheless admit that the Servant has the commission to bring justice to the nations.[103] Goldingay suggests that in many ways the destinies of the nations is no different from the destiny of Israel. They are expected to live in the light of the knowledge of God, are liable for their shortcomings, and are destined to turn to God who lives in Zion.[104]

What then are the ethnic scripts that the Spirit language in Isaiah and the Baptist's testimony is provoking? Even more, why does the gospel note that Jesus has the anointing of the Spirit promised by Isaiah? These Isaiah scholars recognize the wider ethnic reach of the Servant who is anointed by the Spirit and the future hope for the ἔθνος. And what is most important is that these texts, Isaiah 42:1 and 11:2 also echo John 1:32–34 with the similar pneumatic phrase "Spirit upon him."[105] Millos suggests that the descent of the Spirit upon Jesus was an anointing that equipped him for a ministry he was about to realize. He finds Jesus as "el profeta por excelencia" whose words were similar to the prophets, words enabled by the power of the Spirit.[106] But when we read the descent of the Spirit upon Jesus in light of the Isaiah's hope, a new reading emerges. The descent of the Spirit signaled to the Jews that a mission for the future redemption of all ethnic people, beginning with the Jews, has been initiated.

Descent of the Spirit Through Ethnic Eyes

What I aim to challenge is the assumption that the Spirit solely functions within this opening section in a revelatory, empowering, or confirming role. While it is true that the Spirit had come upon Jesus and this helped the

---

102. Childs, *Isaiah*, 324–25; Lindsey, "Isaiah's Songs of the Servant," 16. Wilson notices that in Isaiah the nations are included within the Servants' Spirit-empowered activity. They are meant to recognize God, reject idolatry, and serve God's purpose to restore and glorify the temple in Zion. See Wilson, *Nations in Deutero-Isaiah*, 325.

103. Goldingay and Payne, *Isaiah 40–55*, 216. See also Baltzer, *Deutero-Isaiah*, 128; Oswalt, *Isaiah 40–66*, 108–110; *Isaiah 1–39*, 49–52; 58–59; Marcus, "'Plain Meaning' of Isaiah," 249–59.

104. Goldingay, *Theology of the Book of Isaiah*, 123–26.

105. See also Isa 61:1–5; 32:15; 44:3; 59:21.

106. Millos, *Juan*, 192.

Baptist identify him as the Lamb of God, Spirit-Baptizer, and Son of God, there is more to the Spirit's role within the narrative. While these themes can be included, if we focus upon them alone we miss the wider ethnic implications that were presented to the Jewish religious leaders within the narrative. In addition, John the Baptist is primarily identified as a testifier. He points to Jesus as the light who enters the world to redeem and baptize all people in the Holy Spirit. The Baptist's mission also concerned itself with revealing Jesus to the ethnic members of Israel, especially the Jewish religious leaders. These were Jewish leaders who confronted and challenged John the Baptist with questions about the purpose of his activity, but they were also unaware that the one whom they needed to focus upon was already in their midst. This is what John the Baptist aims to reveal to the Jewish Pharisaic religious leaders, that the true light and anointed one with the Spirit for all people has emerged. Hearing John the Baptist proclaim that the Spirit had descended upon Jesus reveals to the Jewish religious leaders a vital aspect about Jesus; that the expected Messiah for Israel and savior of Gentiles was now present.

The ethnic members within the Johannine community are also made aware that the mission of Jesus was not solely limited to Israel or regulated to an ethnocentric focus alone. Jesus' identity as the bearer of the Spirit has a wider ethnic reach that was foretold by the prophet Isaiah. This mission to the Gentiles was not secondary, accidental, or an aberration to his mission. It was indispensable for his entrance and introduction to the Jewish religious leaders and world. Not knowing this wider ethnic mission was also the critical failure of the Jewish religious authorities who could not recognize Jesus within their midst. The fact that the narrative has emphasized Jesus' identity as the light within the prologue would have also signaled to the readers that the ethnic mission had commenced. The Spirit within this context functions as more than a simple revelation of Jesus' identity. The Spirit signifies to all the Jews that the eschatological ethnic mission has now been initiated. This not only marks Jesus as a bearer of the Spirit, it alerts all that what Isaiah promised is now being fulfilled.

As a result, the ethnic members of the Johannine community must respond to the interrogation, pressure, and challenge of the Jewish religious authorities of their time. They ought not to respond with ethnic suppression or violence against them. Instead, they can mirror John the Baptist's testimony by proclaiming that Jesus is the one whom the exiles have been waiting for—he is the promised Servant of God who delivers Israel and brings all the nations to a knowledge of God and baptismal immersion in the Spirit. This also means that Jesus comes as the one who bears the Spirit with a mission to the diverse ethnic communities of the Greco-Roman world. The ethnic members of the Johannine community are certain of this because from this first mention of the Spirit, no one is beyond the reach of Jesus' Spirit-anointed mission.

6

Creating and Subverting Genealogical Relations

JOHN 3:1–10

THE DIALOGUE BETWEEN JESUS AND NICODEMUS IN JOHN 3 has created a literary riddle for interpreters.[1] Scholars notice that Nicodemus appears to serve as a foil to introduce the larger themes of spiritual birth and membership into the kingdom of God. Nicodemus meets Jesus in the night and greets him by saying, "Rabbi, we know that you are a teacher who has come from God" (3:2). In an unprovoked manner, Jesus responds to Nicodemus's greeting with an immediate discussion about being born again. Why such a move? What was of such grave importance that Jesus preferred to discuss with a "ruler of the Jews" (3:1) the role of the Spirit as an entrance requirement into the kingdom? Brown views the discussion about entering into the kingdom of God prompted by Nicodemus's description

---

1. Brown notices that Nicodemus makes three statements in verses 2, 4, and 9. Brown, Dodd, and Lindars notice that the dialogue turns into a monologue from verses 11–21. See Brown, *John*, 1:144–45; Dodd, *Interpretation*, 303; Lindars, *John*, 146. Beasley-Murray contends that it is doubtful that the Evangelist intended the readers to hear verses 13–21 and 31–36 as the voice of Christ (Beasley-Murray, *John*, 46). Morris admits that there are meditations of the Evangelist, but it is difficult to know where they begin (Morris, *John*, 202). Millos, however, prefers to view a unity within the chapter. He asserts that it is "un relato histórico homogéneo y no una redacción resultante de unificar distintas fuentes." In fact, he suggests that when we compare verses 1–21 and 22–36 we can notice that "la parte segunda recoge y amplia pensamientos que están en la primera" (Millos, *Juan*, 290). Mateos and Barreto prefer to view the dialogue with Nicodemus continuing from 2:23. They suggest that 3:22 should be read with the following episode with the Samaritan woman (Mateos and Barreto, *Juan*, 181–82, 207).

of Jesus as one who comes from God.² Lindars claims that because of Jesus' special insight, he knew the question before Nicodemus had a chance to ask.³ And we find Millos noting that Jesus' response was not a natural transition, but stems from a desire to understand Nicodemus's true motivations for the visit.⁴ But we must notice that Nicodemus does not ask a question in the opening greeting. He only affirms Jesus' identity based on his knowledge of Jesus' miraculous activity.

Regardless of the motivation, we find Nicodemus entering into the narrative but then gradually disappearing as Jesus commences a lengthy monologue. We are nonetheless left with an unclear reason that motived Jesus' response. We only know that Jesus does respond. Jesus gives a lengthy dialogue about being born again (ἄνωθεν), being born of water and Spirit (γεννηθῇ ἐξ ὕδατος καὶ πνεύματος), and a comparison of those who are born of the Spirit with the wind.⁵ There is a concern about birth (γεννάω) given that the term appears within this dialogue 8 times. With such a focus on this concept, what does it mean to suggest that being born of the divine Spirit is necessary to see the kingdom? As previously asked, why does Jesus bring up this topic? These two questions will be the focus of our attention.

Various scholars have addressed these issues in distinct ways. They recognize that between these words we may be hearing the Johannine community deal with issues of the sacraments,⁶ believing Jews,⁷ or a developed view of salvation defined in terms of rebirth.⁸ While these views are not mutually exclusive, scholars have rightly observed the implications for the Johannine community. What has not been explored is how the discussion addresses the realities of ethnicity in the ancient world. If we read the dialogue with ethnic concerns, we can gain further insight on a possible reason why this conversation occurred and its implications for the Johannine community. In fact, I argue that this dialogue is an ethnic argument for

---

2. Brown, *John*, 1:138. Grese suggests that this affirmation that Jesus has come from God is a request for more revelation (Grese, "Unless One Is Born Again," 677–93). Tricia Brown finds Nicodemus's greeting including an inadequate estimation of Jesus which triggered a response (Brown, *Spirit in the Writings of John*, 118).

3. Lindars, *John*, 150.

4. Millos, *Juan*, 299.

5. Within this dialogue, the use of πνεῦμα is translated as both wind and Spirit. There is both a divine and material use of the term.

6. Barrett, *St. John*, 174; Beasley-Murray, *John*, 55; Dodd, *Interpretation*, 308; Lindars, *John*, 152; Burge, *Anointed Community*, 150–58.

7. Barrett, *St. John*, 169–76; Beasley-Murray, *John*, 55; Lindars, *John*, 149.

8. Barrett, *St. John*, 170–74; Brown, *John*, 1:144–45; Beasley-Murray, *John*, 55; Belleville, "Born of Water and Spirit," 140; Grese, "Unless One Is Born Again," 677–93.

the inclusion of non-Jewish ethnic members, those who sought to justify their place within the family of God without Jewish genealogical lineage or heritage. This dialogue was necessary because some Jewish leaders like Nicodemus were hesitant about the incorporation of Gentile members. This is not to suppose that all were resistant. The emergence of new ethnic members within the community challenged the establishment to rethink what it means to consider non-ethnic Jews as children of God. We are therefore not only hearing a dialogue about the Spirit's role in birthing new members into the kingdom of God, but an argument of ethnic inclusion based on the Spirit.

In order to demonstrate this reading, we will first examine Nicodemus's role and historic identity. We will then proceed to reread the Spirit language and how claims of genealogical descent are being challenged with the birthing language. Together, this reading will not only help us understand why the conversation occurred, but how the Spirit's involvement in rebirth was an argument that justified the inclusion of ethnic members within the community. This conversation between Jesus and Nicodemus not only articulates the Spirit's participation in the incorporation of both Jews and non-Jews into the kingdom of God; it is also reflective of the struggle that various members of the Johannine community experienced in their admittance into the faith.

Nicodemus and Pharisaic Identity

The discussion between Nicodemus and Jesus is introduced as a secretive meeting held at night.[9] Nicodemus is noted to be a Pharisee and "ruler of the Jews" (v. 1) while Jesus is described as a rabbi (v. 2).[10] By portraying Nicodemus as a ruler of the Jews, one is drawn back to the story when the Jewish priest and the Levites questioned John the Baptist (1:19).[11] The read-

---

9. Scholars recognize the imagery of the night and its symbolic meaning. Although rabbis were known to study late into the night, within the Fourth Gospel, the night is also reflective of an ominous theme (9:4; 11:10; 13:30). See Barrett, *St. John*, 170; Beasley-Murray, *John*, 47; Brown, *John*, 1:130; Lindars, *John*, 149. Keener believes that this foreshadows his ultimate discipleship in 19:39–42 (Keener, *John*, 536). Morris agrees that there may be more than one meaning in mind, but concludes that Nicodemus came to Jesus at night because of fear (Morris, *John*, 186–87).

10. The term is also used in 1:38, 49; 4:31; 6:25; 9:2; 11:8, and in reference to the Baptist in 3:26.

11. Vrede argues that the Baptist is crucial to understanding the character of Nicodemus. He proposes that the reader is expected to compare the two characters as opposites. See Vrede, "Contrast Between Nicodemus and John the Baptist," 724–25; Lingad, *Problems of Jewish Christians*, 273–74.

ers were then made aware that it was the Pharisees who sent this delegation to John the Baptist in order to question him (1:24). In this scene with Jesus, no delegation is sent. The "ruler of the Jews" comes to Jesus.

As this conversation commences, Nicodemus confesses that Jesus has the ability to do miracles. He states, "we know that you come from God" (v. 2). While we are made aware of Nicodemus's presence in the narrative, in actuality he stands for a larger group of devout Jewish leaders. The use of the plural οἴδαμεν reveals that other Jews are aware of Jesus' miraculous activities and identity. This is a critical point in our understanding of Nicodemus's role. Indeed, Millos notes that this represents a collective knowledge from religious leaders.[12] There were Pharisees who were divided over the identity of Jesus and their minority presence is presumed as the narrative continues. We are also not sure which miracles led Nicodemus and the other Jewish religious leaders to believe in Jesus. Thus far, Jesus had performed miracles in Cana of Galilee (2:1–10) and in Jerusalem (2:23–25). These miracles led several people to faith, including his disciples (2:24–25). It is certainly possible that Jesus' presence in Jerusalem and the report of his miracles captured the attention of Nicodemus and other Pharisees.[13] However, we also discover that Jesus did not trust anyone who came to faith as a result of this miraculous activity (2:24).

How then are we to understand the Nicodemus character? Those who hold a positive view of Nicodemus include Sandra Schneiders. She views Nicodemus as a hero of the Johannine community who progresses in faith from seeing signs to acting on the truth at the end of the narrative.[14] Martyn regards Nicodemus as one of those in the Sanhedrin who secretly believed. He finds Nicodemus's visit reflective of an earnest inquirer. Martyn also notices the positive portrayal of Nicodemus when he later defends Jesus before the Sanhedrin and joins Joseph of Arimathea in burying Jesus' body.[15] Bultmann finds that Jesus' miracles made an impression on Nicodemus, but it may not have moved him to faith.[16] Keener agrees that Nicodemus is more open than other Pharisees. He notices that he has yet to cross over the threshold into discipleship and is at most a representative of some open-minded dialogue partners in the synagogue.[17]

12. Millos, *Juan*, 296.
13. Brown, *John*, 1:135; Morris, *John*, 188.
14. Schneiders, "Born Anew," 191. Munro considers Nicodemus not only reflective of a believer but also comparable to the Samaritan woman in John 4. See "Pharisee and the Samaritan," 710–28.
15. Martyn, *History and Theology*, 88.
16. Bultmann, *John*, 133.
17. Keener, *John*, 533. Lingad perceives Nicodemus as a type of Jewish Christian who

The more critical views include Tricia Brown's analysis, which regards Nicodemus as one who is immediately presented as an untrustworthy figure.[18] She finds his role within the narrative reflecting that of an important broker figure in Palestine during the first century.[19] With this social context in mind, she suggests that Nicodemus is representative of all earthly brokers who cannot conceive of a spiritual birth that lies out of human control.[20] Barrett understands Nicodemus as someone who is uncomprehending and incredulous despite his professional knowledge. He doubts the authenticity of the Nicodemus figure and thus reads the dialogue as one that is also occurring between the church and synagogue.[21] He insists that Nicodemus represents half-believing Jews who were impressed by Jesus' signs but had not reached adequate faith in him.[22] Lindars, Beasley-Murray, and Michael Goulder also view Nicodemus as a figure who represents Judaism at the time of the Johannine community. They agree that this dialogue links the events between the historic ministry of Jesus with the events of the contemporary Johannine church.[23]

How then are we to assess Nicodemus's identity and role within the narrative? Is Nicodemus an unbelieving Jewish Pharisee, half-believing Jew, or earnest Jewish Christian? The more critical views are those that tend to view Nicodemus as a figure who was reflective of an unbelieving Jewish group outside the Johannine community. Those who hold a positive estimation are more likely to perceive him as a sympathetic Jew or Jewish Christian related to the Johannine community. When we focus on Nicodemus within the gospel we will notice the difficulty in interpreting his identity. He not only appears within this discourse but again in a more favorable light in 7:50 and 19:39.

The second appearance of Nicodemus occurs when certain people (ὄχλος) were claiming that Jesus is the prophet while others believing that

---

was attracted to Christianity but stopped short of becoming baptized. He argues that Nicodemus is a type of Jewish Christian who symbolizes partial faith. In this sense, Jesus and Nicodemus stand for very distinct groups that represent the Johannine Christians. See Lingad, *Problem of Jewish Christians*, 294–97.

18. Brown, *Spirit in the Writings of John*, 113.
19. Brown, *Spirit in the Writings of John*, 117.
20. Brown, *Spirit in the Writings of John*, 124.
21. Barrett, *St. John*, 169–70; Beasley-Murray, *John*, 55. Brown finds it difficult to believe in the historicity of Jesus' encounter with Nicodemus. However, he believes that it reflects a solid tradition with homiletical developments. See Brown, *John*, 1:136.
22. Barrett, *St. John*, 176.
23. Beasley-Murray, *John*, 55; Lindars, *John*, 149; Meeks, "Man from Heaven," 63–64. Goulder regards Nicodemus as a typical Jewish Christian who never belonged properly to the disciples or orthodox Johannine church (Goulder, "Nicodemus," 156).

he is the Messiah (7:40–41). Once they realize that Jesus is from Galilee, a debate ensues over Jesus' origins. During this debate, some wanted to seize Jesus but were unsuccessful (v. 44). Then the temple servants, who were previously ordered to arrest Jesus, return to the chief priest and Pharisees without apprehending him. The Pharisees disapprove of the temple servants' failure to arrest Jesus. They question the servants if the failure is due to their belief in Jesus (v. 47). It is during this discussion that Nicodemus exposes his fellow Pharisees for attempting to arrest Jesus without first bringing charges against him. At this moment the reader is also reminded of Nicodemus's role in the gospel. He is described as "one who earlier came to [Jesus], he was one of them" (v. 50). Nicodemus thus emerges from the hostile group of Pharisees but is immediately met with suspicion. The Pharisees reply to Nicodemus, asking, "You are not from Galilee, are you?" Nicodemus does not respond. He does not defend himself from the suspicion that was leveled against him. He simply exits the narrative and we do not hear of him until the end of the gospel.

In 19:38–42, we are introduced to a secret disciple named Joseph of Arimathea who asks Pilate for the body of Jesus. The motivation that led to Joseph's secret allegiance to Jesus is explained in terms of a "fear of the Jews" (v. 38). We are not sure how hostile Joseph's experience with "the Jews" is throughout the narrative given that this is the only mention of his role within the gospel. Although we do find Josephus of Arimathea appearing in Mark 15:43, he is not described as a "secret disciple." Instead, he is presented as a prominent member of the Jewish council and buries Jesus' body without assistance. The gospel however mentions that he is accompanied by Nicodemus who brings myrrh and aloes. Are we then to understand Nicodemus's commitment to Jesus in light of Joseph's identity as a secret disciple? The narrative again explains that Nicodemus was the "one who came to [Jesus] by night" (v. 39), just in case the readers forgot that Nicodemus had first approached Jesus at the beginning of the gospel.

We can thus notice the difficulties in assessing Nicodemus's role within the Fourth Gospel. Culpepper finds Nicodemus's association with Joseph of Arimathea as evidence that he was truly another secret disciple. He suggests that they represent those who believe but do not confess Jesus openly due to the fear of being excommunicated from the synagogue,[24] but Schneiders's analysis notes something else. She concludes that Nicodemus is a type of true Israelite who progresses from seeing signs to acting upon the truth and

---

24. Culpepper, *Anatomy*, 136. Brown does not regard Nicodemus as a Crypto-Christian but rather one who begins as someone who was attracted to Jesus and later made his faith public. See Brown, *Community*, 72n128.

finally confessing Jesus.[25] Undoubtedly, Millos notes that Nicodemus knew and admitted from the beginning that Jesus was sent from God and came as a teacher.[26] He agrees that we may not know when Nicodemus recognized that Jesus was the messiah, but at least he was present when the disciples had fled.[27]

In as much as we may criticize Nicodemus for misreading Jesus' origins (3:2) or refusing to admit his allegiance to Jesus when confronted (7:52), we can at least agree that he is positively portrayed in the final moments of the narrative when all the other disciples were absent.[28] We cannot deny the significance of giving Jesus' body all the dignity that an innocent person deserves (19:40).[29] Most importantly, it is Nicodemus's final association with Joseph and willingness to give Jesus a proper Jewish burial that reveals who he really was: A Jewish Pharisee who was curious, gripped by fear, but became devoted to Jesus with a public embrace of his crucified body.

As a Jewish Pharisee, this secretive identity would have been conflictive with his Pharisaic colleagues given that many, but not all, were openly hostile to Jesus within the narrative,[30] but this also provides evidence that not all Pharisees rejected Jesus. Nicodemus holds both identities, contradictory as they were at times, but also reflective of the reality that the case was still being made on Jesus' identity within the religious establishment. How in other ways, if any, is he also reflective of the contradicting acceptance

25. Schneiders, "Born Anew," 191.

26. Millos, *Juan*, 1734.

27. Millos states, "Sin duda, hay algunos que no se hacen visibles en servicio y con su presencia, pero siendo hijos de Dios, estarán en disposición de hacer Su obra cuando sea necesario" (Millos, *Juan*, 1735).

28. Morris insists that Nicodemus was not only performing a normal courtesy. The excessive provision of myrrh and aloes suggests that Nicodemus was a wealthy man who was trying to make reparation for his failure to do more. Morris finds Nicodemus gaining nothing by affirming his connection with Jesus. This large quantity of spices was also used in royal burials which may signify an affirmation of Jesus' kingship. See Morris, *John*, 729–30; Keener, *John*, 1161–64; 2 Chr 16:14; Ps 45:8 [44:9 LXX]; Jer 34:5; Josephus, *Ant.* 17.199.

29. Chapman points to rabbinic text that requires criminals to be buried in separate plots. He, however, finds Joseph of Arimathea not concurring with the Sanhedrin's will but instead burying Jesus honorably in his own family tomb. See Chapman, "Burial of Jesus," 99; *m. Sanh.* 6:5; *t. Sanh.* 9:8; Josephus, *Ant.* 4.202.

30. In the Fourth Gospel the Pharisees are mentioned 19 times but not all occurrences are hostile to Jesus, especially in 9:17; 12:42. Culpepper notices a development of their role within the narrative. They are first distant observers (1:19, 24; 4:1; 7:32) and then become more active in their opposition to Jesus (7:32). He notes that they eventually blend with the Jews in their official action against Jesus (9:16, 18; 9:40; 10:19). See Culpepper, *Anatomy*, 131. Including Paul, the Pharisees were also believers who were present at the Jerusalem council in Acts 15:5; 23:6.

and rejection of those within Pharisaic Judaism who emerged alongside and within the Johannine community during late first century? We must remember that Christianity as a separate religion did not exist within the first century. As we have surveyed thus far, scholars agree that the story of Jesus and Nicodemus possibly reflects a relationship between the Johannine believers and the Jewish religious leaders. We may also consider if the narrative aims to present Nicodemus as a symbolic figure. And if so, in what way does his identity reflect the larger narrative of ethnic differentiation, separation, and tension between the diverse Johannine community and emerging rabbinic Judaism?

Our exploration of Pharisees must nonetheless avoid caricatures that are not reflective of their historic identity in the ancient world. Josephus mentions that within Judea there were three sects among the Jews which include the Pharisees, Sadducees, and the Essenes.[31] With regard to the Pharisees he proposes that they had "so great a power over the multitude, that when they say anything against the king, or against the high priest, they are presently believed."[32] He also confirms their popularity and sway over the masses by comparing their role to that of the Sadducees. He states,

> The Pharisees have delivered to the people a great many observances by succession from their fathers, which are not written in the laws of Moses. For that reason the Sadducees reject them, and say that we are to esteem those observances to be obligatory which are in the written word, but are not to observe what are derived from the tradition of our forefathers. And concerning these things it is that great disputes and differences have arisen among them, while the Sadducees are able to persuade none but the rich, and have not the populace favorable to them, but the Pharisees have the multitude on their side. (*Ant.* 13.297–98)

Josephus believes that the Jewish people favorably viewed the Pharisees. Elsewhere, he asserts that they are better interpreters of their religious tradition,[33] friendly to one another and the public,[34] and even admits that he was a Pharisee.[35]

Yet this portrayal of the Pharisees in Josephus's writing is rightly met with suspicion. E. P. Sanders agrees with Josephus that the Pharisees were

31. Josephus, *Ant.* 13.171.

32. Josephus, *Ant.* 13.288; 18.15. For Josephus's summary of their views see *Ant.* 18:11–15.

33. Josephus, *J.W.* 1.110; 2.162; *Life*, 1.191.

34. Josephus, *J.W.* 2.166.

35. Josephus, *Life*, 1.12.

not aristocrats but were committed to interpreting the law and observing it correctly,[36] yet he points out that during Herod's reign they were impotent in comparison to the native aristocracy backed by Rome. Although Josephus regards them as having power over the people, Sanders disputes this claim. Sanders proposes that they were ineffective in plotting, protesting, or joining an uprising.[37] He thus views Josephus's summaries as exaggerated descriptions that aim to separate the Pharisees from sedition and revolt in the Jewish War.[38]

Although the Pharisees are portrayed in Josephus's writing as controlling the masses, they did not have such influence.[39] Sanders finds the Pharisees' lack of power confirmed by their limited role in the accounts of Jesus' trial in all four gospels.[40] He also doubts their influence over the people and their role in administering the synagogues during Jesus' ministry.[41] Sanders thus concludes that despite Josephus's statement, they were a moderate group that was an ineffective opposition.[42] But this does not suggest that the Pharisees were rejected or in tension with their own people. James Dunn cautions our analysis by asserting that even if the depiction of Pharisaic influence in Josephus is exaggerated, we cannot discount the Pharisees as a quietist and purity sect without significant influence beyond their own circles.[43] Even Sanders suggests that most Jews would agree with the Pharisees' views and way of life. He regards the Pharisees as the "heart and soul of the nation" regardless if the people were persuaded by them. Sanders insists that many people respected their piety, learning, and desire to faithfully live out the law, and many applauded them for their relative political independence.[44]

How then are we to understand Nicodemus in light of this historic Pharisaic identity? Primarily, we cannot assume that the Pharisees held total power as portrayed in the gospel. Despite Josephus's views, they did not control the people nor were powerful aristocrats or priests. Instead, they were skilled interpreters who had gained enough influence to be respected by the people. Even more, this influence and authority increased after the

---

36. Sanders, *Judaism*, 383.
37. Sanders, *Judaism*, 389.
38. Sanders, *Judaism*, 410.
39. Sanders, *Judaism*, 393–98.
40. Sanders, *Judaism*, 394.
41. Sanders, *Judaism*, 398–401. See Matt 5:21–24; Luke 13:14; Mark 3:1–6.
42. Sanders, *Judaism*, 395.
43. Dunn, *Jesus, Paul, and the Law*, 66.
44. Sanders, *Judaism*, 404–7.

Jewish War. Sanders finds that there is a substantial link and continuity between the Pharisees and emerging Rabbinic Judaism. He asserts that the rabbis of the late first century and the second century regarded themselves as heirs of the Pharisees and took the titles "rabbis" and "teachers."[45]

The Fourth Gospel deliberately portrays the Pharisees as having a more significant role during Jesus' ministry. In many ways, Nicodemus is reflective of a historic Pharisee who desires to learn and be an expert on the things concerning the kingdom of God. His questions throughout the dialogue with Jesus would resonate with many Jews who turned to the Pharisees as the bearers of the tradition and interpreters of the Law. In actuality, Raymond Brown asserts that Nicodemus could have caught the concept of divine begetting from the scripture.[46] Thus, when Nicodemus asks, "how can these things be?" (v. 9), we must also hear within his question the confusion, curiosity, and desire to comprehend how being born again by the Spirit provides entrance into the kingdom of God. But at the same time, Nicodemus is not solely serving as a foil to set up Jesus' lengthy monologue that follows. As an authority figure, he stands on behalf of the people, Jews and Jewish Christians, who are earnestly seeking clarification on a very pertinent issue of Spirit regeneration that was obscure within scripture, not fully understood, but experienced by many. Spirit begetting would not have been a new idea for the Johannine readers, nor should we assume that they would not have any first-hand experience with the concept. They were having questions about the nature and role of the Spirit in granting ethnic people membership into the kingdom of God. This is a significant inquiry, especially since questions about Gentile conversion were an important issue even until the second century.[47] Most importantly, it should have been the emerging rabbinic leadership at the end of the first century who would have been most concerned about finding answers and clarification. This does not assume that all Pharisees were hostile to either the Johannine movement or ethnic members seeking membership in the kingdom of God. Some perhaps were, but those like Nicodemus were more confused and caught

---

45. Sanders, *Judaism*, 412–13; Ashton also notices that the Pharisees within the Fourth Gospel appear to be credited with much more moral authority than they had throughout their history. See Ashton, *Gospel of John and Christian Origins*, 45–46.

46. Brown, *John*, 1:139. See also Belleville, "Born of Water and Spirit," 139–40; Exod 4:22; Deut 32:6; 2 Sam 7:14; Hos 11:1; Ps 2:7.

47. Cohen argues that in the second century the rabbis created the conversion ceremony that is preserved in *B. Yebamot* 47a–b. He argues that this ceremony brought order to a situation where chaos had previously reigned and where there was no standard that distinguished a Gentile who had converted from one who did not. See Cohen, *Beginning of Jewishness*, 218–38.

Γεννάω and the Spirit

What then are the ethnic implications of being born of the Spirit? As previously mentioned, Jesus informs Nicodemus that he must be born ἄνωθεν (v. 3).[48] Nicodemus naturally understands the birthing implication of ἄνωθεν and asks how it is possible for a man to enter into his mother's womb (3:4). Jesus responds by saying that he must be "born of water and Spirit" (3:4). He continues to state that unless one is born of water and Spirit (γεννηθῇ ἐξ ὕδατος καὶ πνεύματος), one cannot enter into the kingdom of God (v. 5). Jesus also asserts that since flesh gives birth to flesh, it is also the same with those born of the Spirit (v. 6). Jesus insists that he should not be amazed about these requirements. He explains that just like the wind, so are those born of the Spirit, moving and operating apart from human control (v. 8).[49]

In reviewing this dialogue, we can notice that it is highly laced with birthing imagery. The term γεννάω can be translated as "begetting," "bearing" or "born." It is used to describe when a child is begotten of a father, women who bear children, or figuratively that which is brought forth, produced, or caused.[50] We find the notion of being "begotten" akin to the idea of a divine begetting.[51] Even more, this language is later utilized within rabbinic literature to describe converts.[52] Maartin Menken rejects the notion that the language conveys a female principle when applied to God.[53] However, Schneiders strongly insists that this passage is one of the clearest New Testament images of the femininity of God.[54] She argues that Nicodemus's literalism allows the evangelist to emphasize Jesus' use of the birthing metaphor to describe our new birth in the Spirit. She points out that this

---

48. The ambiguity of ἄνωθεν is noticed by scholars. It can be translated as "from above" (John 19:11; Jas 1:17; 3:15, 17), "from the beginning" (Luke 1:3; John 19:23; Acts 26:5), or "from the top" (Matt 27:51; Mark 15:38). In this translation, "again" is preferred given that this is what prompted Nicodemus's reaction and the ensuing clarification (Gal 4:9).

49. Within this dialogue, the use of πνεῦμά is translated as both wind and Spirit. There is both a divine and material use of the term.

50. Büchsel, "γεννάω," *TDNT* 1:665; BAGD, 55b–d.

51. Menken, "Born of God or Begotten by God," 366.

52. *b. Yeb.*, 22a "a proselyte just converted is like a child just born." See also 62a; 97b; *b. Ber.*, 47a.

53. Menken, "Born of God or Begotten by God," 366.

54. Schneiders, "Born Anew," 194. See also Weissenrieder, "Spirit and Rebirth," 77.

CREATING AND SUBVERTING GENEALOGICAL RELATIONS   141

female imagery also occurs in the juxtaposition of the male and female parental metaphors in Deuteronomy 32:18 where God is also described with feminine imagery to give birth to Israel.⁵⁵

When we explore the use of the term throughout the gospel, we find various γεννάω references that give attention to both human and divine begetting. Below are the following uses in the Fourth Gospel:

Divine Birth		Human Birth	
1:13	ἐκ θεοῦ ἐγεννήθησαν	3:4	ἄνθρωπος γεννηθῆναι
3:3	γεννηθῇ ἄνωθεν	3:4	κοιλίαν τῆς μητρὸς καὶ γεννηθῆναι
3:5	γεννηθῇ ἐξ ὕδατος καὶ πνεύματος	3:6	γεγεννημένον ἐκ τῆς σαρκὸς
3:6	γεγεννημένον ἐκ τοῦ πνεύματος	8:41	ἐκ πορνείας οὐ γεγεννήμεθα
3:7	ὑμᾶς γεννηθῆναι ἄνωθεν	9:2	τυφλὸς γεννηθῇ
3:8	ὁ γεγεννημένος ἐκ τοῦ πνεύματος	9:19	τυφλὸς ἐγεννήθη
		9:20	τυφλὸς ἐγεννήθη
		9:32	τυφλοῦ γεγεννημένου
		9:34	Ἐν ἁμαρτίαις σὺ ἐγεννήθης
		16:21	γεννήσῃ τὸ παιδίον
		16:21	ἐγεννήθη ἄνθρωπος
		18:37	εἰς τοῦτο γεγέννημαι

The majority of γεννάω occurrences in the Fourth Gospel are in reference to human birth. Most of the references to divine birth are mentioned in Nicodemus's dialogue and in the prologue. Annette Weissenrieder argues that in John 1:12–13 and 3:3–8 are references to ancient family imagery that are being applied to believers. However, she insists that the reader has to wait until the resurrection before the disciples experience this link to God as children.⁵⁶ This is an important insight that cannot be lost in our

---

55. Schneiders, "Born Anew," 194. See also Ps 2:7; Prov 8:25; Hos 5:7; Isa 1:2; 66:9. Philo describes God as the begetter of all things including humanity (*Leg.* 3.219; *Conf.*, 1.63; *Mut.* 1.29). Paul also utilizes this feminine birthing imagery when describing communities and individuals (1 Cor 4:15; Gal 4:19; Phlm 1:10).

56. Weissenrieder, "Spirit and Rebirth," 79.

attempt to understand what it means to be born of the Spirit. Before we proceed on these implications, how have scholars understood the "born of the Spirit," "born again," and "born of water and Spirit" phraseology within this dialogue?

Reinhartz reads this birthing language in terms of ancient medical embryology.[57] She argues that Jesus' begottenness from God resembles the human procreation process which was influenced by Aristotle's theory of epigenesis.[58] She points out that according to Aristotle, seminal fluid was understood as both "water and spirit."[59] This reading is similar to those of Ben Witherington and other scholars who argue that behind the notion of being "born of water" in John 3:5 is the human notion of procreation.[60] This view is contrary to Morris's, who takes this phrase in reference to being born of spiritual water.[61] Reinhartz's view holds that a child of God is one who is begotten of the divine seed that originates in the upper cosmos.[62] While this reading would resonate with those who argue for an allusion to the natural birthing functions and procreation, others suggest that the "water" language is more reflective of a sacramental view of baptism.

Burge suggests that the "water and Spirit" phraseology stems from Old Testament ritual cleansing.[63] He thus proposes that rebirth through water and Spirit implies that Nicodemus needs to submit to the baptism of John.[64] As the dialogue continues with Nicodemus, Burge also insists that Jesus' discussion suggests to the readers that water baptism is theologically

---

57. Reinhartz, "And the Word Was Begotten," 83–103. See Aristotle, *Gen. an.* 716a1–15; 731b25; 735b10; 766b15–769a22.

58. Reinhartz, "And the Word Was Begotten," 86.

59. Reinhartz, "And the Word Was Begotten," 89–92. Aristotle inquires about the cause that generates every person and animal. He points to seminal fluid as composed of water and *pneuma* and explains the reasons for his deduction by comparing it to the properties of oil (*Gen. an.* 735b–736a).

60. Witherington argues against a sacramental reading of "water" within John 3:5 in Witherington, "Waters of Birth," 155–60. He points out that "water" can be and is used as a "terminus technicus" for matters involving procreation, childbearing capacity, or the act of giving birth itself. See Spriggs, "Meaning of Water in John 3:5," 149–50; Fowler, "Born of Water and Spirit (John 3:5)," 159; Prov 5:15–18; Song 4:12–15; 1 John 3:5; 4 *Ezra* 8:8.

61. Morris, *John*, 192–93.

62. Reinhartz, "And the Word Was Begotten," 96. First Peter 1:23 and 1 John 3:9 also utilizes this metaphor.

63. Burge, *Anointed Community*, 162; Ps 51:7; Isa 4:4; Jer 33:8; Ezek 36:25–26; Philo, *Mos.* 2.138.

64. Burge, *Anointed Community*, 163.

meaningful only if it is accompanied by the Spirit.[65] Burge believes that the baptismal language is being reworked because sacramental literalism was being abused and the community was not stressing their identification in the Spirit.[66] This reading is similar to Dodd, Lindars, and Barrett who find the Christian baptism motif in the background of this dialogue.[67] But contrary to Barrett,[68] Dodd and Lindars reject any Hellenistic mythological explanation for the ideas of divine regeneration.[69] Dodd believes that the instructed Christian reader would catch the baptismal language while the Gentile reader would understand it more elusively.[70] Or as Lindars claims, "it is more reasonable to suppose that this is Jewish and Christian teaching in words that are meaningful to a Gentile audience familiar with Hellenistic religious aspirations."[71] These views propose that Christian baptism or ritual cleansing imagery is being woven into the language of being born of water and Spirit.

Bultmann, Morris, and Johnston propose that the phrase "born of Spirit," "born from above," and "born of water and Spirit" refers to the divine will and power of God that is beyond human control and comprehension.[72] This is in reference to God's ability to generate which is a power reflective of the *ruach* of God. This power motif is also found in Tricia Brown's analysis which points out that Nicodemus is powerless to bring about the spiritual birth.[73] She interprets the birthing language in terms of access to God's patronage, something that Nicodemus lacked.[74] To be born into God's family through the Spirit, as she argues, would result in bearing the honor status of God that is commensurate with the status of being a child of God.[75]

---

65. Burge, *Anointed Community*, 169.

66. Burge, *Anointed Community*, 170–75.

67. Dodd, *Interpretation*, 309; Lindars, *John*, 152; Barrett, *St. John*, 174–76. Along similar lines of thought, Beasley-Murray interprets the language of being born again an adaptation of Jewish new creation imagery. He believes this new creation is through water baptism. See Beasley-Murray, *John*, 47–49; Jer 31:33–34; Ezek 11:19–20; 36:25–27; *Jub.* 1:23–25; 2 Cor 5:17; Gal 6:15.

68. Barrett, *St. John*, 174.

69. Dodd, *Interpretation*, 305.

70. Dodd, *Interpretation*, 309–310.

71. Lindars, *John*, 148–52. Grese compares the rebirth language to a journey into heaven found in Persian, Jewish, and Greek literature in Grese, "Unless One Is Born Again," 680–84.

72. Bultmann, *John*, 139n1; Morris, *John*, 188; Johnston, *Spirit-Paraclete*, 10.

73. Brown, *Spirit in the Writings of John*, 122.

74. Brown, *Spirit in the Writings of John*, 120–22.

75. Brown, *Spirit in the Writings of John*, 125.

The views above all agree that the notion of being born by the Spirit is a divine act beyond human control. They differ on the significance of the birthing language, whether it refers to birth through a divine seed, baptism, echoes a ritual cleansing imagery, or reflects God's divine power. Raymond Brown agrees that the dialogue could have been interpreted in light of Christian baptism.[76] He finds it difficult to suggest that Jesus would advocate a sacramental interpretation. Instead, he proposes that being born of the Spirit is primarily the communication of the Holy Spirit.[77] Brown argues that Nicodemus is hearing about the entrance into the kingdom of God as being dependent upon the eschatological outpouring of the Spirit,[78] one that only comes after the resurrection of Jesus.[79] Brown also explains that the imagery of begetting, regeneration, and divine seed of the Johannine literature aims to explain how believers are considered sons of God. He finds this similar to how Paul utilized adoption language.[80] Brown however does not discuss the implications of his claim. In fact, Schneiders, Weissenrieder, Reinhartz, and Tricia Brown also notice the family imagery within the birthing language. But why use this birthing metaphor in a dialogue with Nicodemus? Asked differently, what concrete reality lies at the base of this language?

Γεννάω, the Spirit, and Ethnic Relations

People who are born are "γεννάω" into kinship groups—tribes, clans, and most importantly—ethnic communities. They are placed in relation not only to their immediate family, but also their historic ancestors which shapes their present identity.[81] Johannine scholars rightly recognize the theological implications of γεννάω and the difficulties of interpreting the

---

76. Brown, *John*, 1:142.

77. Brown, *John*, 1:144.

78. Brown, *John*, 1:140–41. See also Isa 32:15; 44:3; Joel 2:28–29; Ezek 36:25–26; 1QS 4.19–21.

79. Brown, *John*, 1:144–45.

80. Brown, *John*, 1:144. See Gal 4:5; Rom 8:23; Titus 3:5.

81. Malina explains this as a "collective personality." He finds that in the Mediterranean worldview people are born into extended families that protect them in exchange for loyalty, commitment, and solidarity. The person's identity is thus dependent on and emerges from the kinship community which includes a tribe, clan, or ethnic identity. Malina insists that this starkly differs from western preferences in which the individual is independent of organizations and institution, with identity based in the individual. See Malina, *New Testament World*, 58–69.

phrase "water and Spirit."[82] We must however not fail to recognize that the birthing language also holds ethnic meaning. To be "γεννάω" also assumes that one is born with an identity derived from one's ethnic ancestors.

Although genealogies have various functions, they establish one's membership and right to be within a group.[83] In regard to ethnicity, Jonathan Hall notices that one of its criteria was whether or not a person could claim to be a descendant.[84] Hall states that what separates ethnic groups from social groups is that ethnic groups share a myth of common descent and an association with territory. He claims that common descent is one of the most distinguishing characteristics of an ethnic group especially since social groups do not presume to share genealogical relations.[85] Even though some genealogical relations are fabricated or exaggerated, there is still an assumption that a person can justify their right to be included within the ethnic community by the nature of birth.

In Greek literature γεννάω is employed to describe one's relationship and responsibility to the wider ethnic-polis. In Plato's *Crito*, we find Socrates debating how one should respond to the unjust verdict of a judge. He concludes that one is still obligated to receive the judgment regardless of the outcome. Socrates puts forth this claim because he recognizes that the individual is indebted to the Greek city on the grounds of birth. He assumes that if one would reject the verdict of the judge, the Greek polis would say,

> What fault do you find with us and the city (πόλιν), that you are trying to destroy us? In the first place, did we not bring you forth (οὐ ἐγεννήσαμεν ἡμεῖς)? Is it not through us that your father married your mother and begat (ἐφύτευσέν) you? (*Crito*, 50b)

Here we find that it was the collective city as well as a father and mother who birthed Socrates. Later we also find this similar birthing language in describing Socrates's relationship with the wider Greek community. He

---

82. The phrase "water and Spirit" can also be understood as an epexegetical phrase, but as the previous scholars mention, it may also have baptismal echoes.

83. Hanson points out that genealogies do not have one simple meaning, function or compositional form but are social constructs. He asserts that they establish a significant kinship group to which one belongs (2 Sam 9:6), embody the honor of the family in a list of names (1 Sam 9:1), identify potential marriage partners (Josephus, *Ant.* 17.12–16), identify outsiders (Josephus, *Ant.* 18.130–141), make a political claim to leadership (1 Kgs 13:2), assert an inheritance or family rights (2 Sam 3:2–5; 5:13–16), establish membership in the religious group (1 Chr 9:1; Ezra 2:59–63; 10:18–44), and establish the right to hereditary offices (Exod 28:1; Lev 16:32). See Hanson, "All in the Family," 30–31.

84. Hall, *Ethnic Identity*, 24–25.

85. Hall, *Ethnic Identity*, 25.

assumes that the Greeks will claim, "we gave birth to you" (ἡμεῖς γάρ σε γεννήσαντες), and explain that it nurtured and gave him a share of all the good things.[86] Yet the Greeks did not only express their relation to their ethnic community with birthing language, they also held the notion that their original ancestors were born from the land and thus originated from the earth.[87]

Again, Socrates explains the earth's relation to the Greeks through birthing imagery. He states,

> The whole earth was putting forth and producing animals of every kind, wild and tame, our country showed herself barren and void of wild animals, but chose for herself and gave birth (ἐγέννησεν) to man, who surpasses all other animals in intelligence and alone of animals regards justice and the gods. And we have a signal proof of this statement in that this land of ours has given birth (ἔτεκεν) to the forefathers, both of these men and of ourselves.... It is not the country that imitates the woman in the matter of conception and birth (γεννησαμένη), but the woman the country. (*Menex.* 237d–238a)

We thus notice that a Greek's relation to the land and wider ethno-polis is expressed through γεννάω imagery. Women's birthing function is presumed to reflect the land's activity of birthing humanity and not vice versa. The land gives birth to their ancestors, and as a result, the descendants are responsible for keeping civic polity and the traditions of the gods.[88] Knowing one's ancestors was vital to one's self-understanding and relation to others. According to Herodotus, King Xerxes appeals to genealogical relations in order

---

86. Plato, *Crito*, 51c.

87. Plato remarks, "But then, stranger, how did animals come into existence in those days? How were they begotten of one another? Socrates, that being begotten of one another was no part of the natural order of that time, but the earth-born race which, according to tradition, once existed, was the race which returned at that time out of the earth; and the memory of it was preserved by our earliest ancestors, who were born in the beginning of our period and therefore were next neighbors to the end of the previous period of the world's revolution" (*St.* 271a).

88. Socrates also continues, "But this her produce of grain she did not begrudge to the rest of men, but dispensed it to them also. And after it, she brought to birth for her children the olive, sore labor's balm. And when she had nurtured and reared them up to man's estate, she introduced gods to be their governors and tutors, the names of whom it behooves us to pass over in this discourse, since we know them, and they set in order our mode of life, not only in respect of daily business, by instructing us before all others in the arts, but also in respect of the guardianship of our country, by teaching us how to acquire and handle arms. Such being the manner of their birth and of their education, the ancestors of these men framed for themselves and lived under a civic polity (*Menex.* 238a–b).

to mitigate conflict with the Argives (*Hist.* 7.150). Likewise, Thucydides remarks that the Athenians claimed to be in genealogical relation to several Greeks in Sicily. They justified their expedition and expansion to the region on the pretense of coming to the aid of their kin (6.2–6.6). Even more, Dionysius of Halicarnassus asserts that the Romans are not barbarian in origin. He points to Rome's genealogy that claims relation with Greek ancestors who came from Arcadia, Peloponnese, and Troy (*Ant. rom.* 1.89–90).

Through γεννάω relations, the ancients were able to define the boundaries of their ethnic group membership, explain their relationship to the community, and justify their presence on the land. This not only led them to justify hostile views or oppression toward those with whom they had no genealogical relations, it enabled them to define the boundaries and rights of their members. Hall insists that the concern to preserve the memory of one's ancestors was done, not solely to define one's ethnic identity, but in order to demonstrate that one shares a common relation with the group.[89] Yet to concern ourselves with "birth" in the ancient world also implies that we are locating and understanding identity in light of a wider ethnic community and ancestors. This is not solely a Greek idea, we find the concern to trace one's lineage also found with Hebrew patriarchs, Israelite kings, and in the gospel's record of Jesus' lineage. The term γεννάω appears frequently to describe sons who were begotten by their fathers, a lineage which is traced to the apical ancestor.[90]

Even though Gentiles were known to convert to Judaism, this did not mean that Gentile genealogical relations became irrelevant. Scot McKnight finds hints of this issue with the status of Gentile converts. Although there is a positive attitude toward Gentiles who desire to convert, he notes that they may have never been seen as fully Jewish, including female proselytes.[91] They may have been officially recognized and socially integrated, but they always remain Gentiles.[92] In other words, the convert, although equally

89. Hall, *Ethnic Identity*, 28.

90. Gen 5:3–32; 10:8–11:27; 25:19; 46:20–21; Ruth 4:18–22; 1 Chr 1:1–9:44; Matt 1:2–16. Luke, however, avoids using γεννάω and explains Jesus' ancestry in terms of sonship (3:23–38).

91. McKnight, *Light Among the Gentiles*, 38–45. See also Collins, *Between Athens and Jerusalem*, 262. Goodman agrees that in the first century there was no active Jewish mission to the Gentiles. He notes that we find Judaism in the second century seeking to redefine the role and status of Gentiles who were seeking to be morally good but not choosing to become Jews. He argues that scholars who turn to Matthew 23:15 to justify Pharisaic missionary activity fail to observe that the text is really discussing how Pharisees gain other Jewish adherents to follow their ways. See Goodman, *Judaism in the Roman World*, 98–100; Feldman, *Judaism and Hellenism Reconsidered*, 243–51.

92. McKnight, *Light Among the Gentiles*, 101. See also Philo's remarks about the

loved and welcomed, is always recognized as a convert and thus inferior to ethnic Jews.

Shaye Cohen argues this point when he traces the conversion ceremony and status of Gentiles in rabbinic literature. He points to *M. Bikkurim* 1:4–5 which states,

> The convert brings but does not recite, because he cannot say (the land) which God has sworn to our fathers to give us. But if his mother was of Israel, he brings and recites. And when he prays by himself, he says, 'God of the fathers of Israel.' And when he is in the synagogue he says 'God of your fathers.'

As the above quote notes, only native Jews are recognized to have Abraham, Isaac, and Jacob as their ancestors. Cohen regards this text as evidence that the convert suffers legal disability because of their non-Jewish lineage.[93] As Cohen argues, this suggests that although the Gentile has changed religious allegiance it does not mean that they gained Jewish ancestry. He notices that they constitute a separate lineage or caste within Jewish society because they lack a Jewish father.[94] He thus finds the Mishnah placing much value on the pedigree and the purity of genealogical descent. Therefore, converts will never be fully equal with the native Jews on the grounds of Jewish lineage.[95]

To be γεννάω of Spirit must therefore be read through this ethnic perspective which includes the dynamics of lineage, genealogy, and relations with one's fellow kin. It was possible for Gentiles to convert to Judaism and even join a Jewish Christian community. We find Philo and Josephus open to Gentile converts. On converts Josephus remarks that "it is not family ties alone which constitute relegation, but agreement in the principles of conduct."[96] Philo even notices the risk that converts take, especially since they "abandon their kinsfolk by blood."[97] He also suggests,

---

admittance of converts and their treatment (*Mos.* 1.147; 2.17–25; *Virt.* 102–108; *Legat.* 211).

93. Cohen, *Beginning of Jewishness*, 309.

94. Cohen, *Beginning of Jewishness*, 324.

95. Cohen, *Beginning of Jewishness*, 325.

96. Josephus, *Ag. Ap.* 2.210. Earlier, he states, "For as to the Greeks, we were rather remote from them in place, than different from them in our institutions, insomuch that we have no enmity with them, nor any jealousy of them. On the contrary, it has so happened, that many of them have come over to our laws, and some of them have continued in their observation, although others of them had not courage enough to persevere, and so departed from them again" (*Ag. Ap.* 2.123).

97. Philo, *Virt.* 1.102–4.

We must look upon as our friends and kinsmen, since they display that greatest of all bonds with which to cement friendship and kindred, namely, a pious and God-loving disposition, and we ought to sympathize in joy with and to congratulate them, since even if they were blind previously they have now received their sight, beholding the most brilliant of all lights instead of the most profound darkness. (*Virt.* 1.179)

But these positive views of converts were not universal. In rabbinic thought, the convert is still ethnically different because they lack genealogical relation with Jewish ancestry. The convert may have the same legal status, and social acceptance, but the convert is not regarded on equal terms with someone who is Jewish by birth.

Genealogical Subversion by the Spirit

Genealogical relations with a community was an important privilege in the ancient world. It defined boundaries, justified certain rights, placed one in relation to the land, and was also used as a pretense for war, expulsion, and even right to rule. Rosalind Thomas remarks that prestige, status, and even moral character was believed to derive from being in genealogical relation to an original progenitor, especially if the person was legendary, heroic or divine.[98] Thus Odysseus was considered the Zeus-sired son of Laertes,[99] Alexander the Great was the son of god Zeus-Ammon,[100] and Augustus was believed to be the son of the god Apollo.[101] Philo also argued that the priests and prophets were "born of God" in order to contrast them to the cosmopolitans of the world.[102] And Buell notes that later in early Christianity, myths of descent were regularly utilized to define oneself with a respected pedigree by placing one in a historical relation to key figures such as Abraham and Jesus.[103] The ancients knew the importance of genealogical association. As we observe with Greek and Roman writers, genealogical myths were vital for the construction of an ethnic identity. They demarcated and influenced how the individual perceived one's identity and responsibilities to the wider ethnic community.

98. Thomas, "Genealogy," 329.
99. Homer, *Il.* 10.144.
100. Plutarch *Alex.* 2.1–3.2.
101. Suetonius, *Aug.* 94.4.
102. Philo, *Gig.* 1.161.
103. Buell, *Why This New Race*, 75–76; Buell and Hodge, "Politics of Interpretation," 235–51. See also Rom 4:13–18; 9:8; Gal 3:26–29; 1 John 3:9.

What then does it mean to be born of the Spirit? When Jesus tells Nicodemus that it is necessary for him to be "born again," "born of water and Spirit," and "born of Spirit," the repeated emphasis on being "born" aims to challenge his understanding of ethnic relations, including the rights and privileges that came with being born into a Jewish ancestry. The exhortation to be "born again" is a pneumatic ethnic argument. Jesus challenges Nicodemus that the Spirit is granting new genealogical lineage that destabilizes all privileged ethnic relations, kinship groups, and ethnic origins. Respected ethnic lineages become insignificant in comparison to the new lineage that is granted through the birthing activity of the Spirit. This is not to eradicate and consider ethnic identity superfluous. Instead, our disparate ethnic identities are bonded through the common birthing experience of the Spirit. By rooting one's origins within the divine Spirit, all human ethnic privileges that come as a result of being born into a particular ancestry become neutralized. Even more, all hostile perceptions of foreigners are to be rejected and viewed as anti-pneumatic.

For the Johannine readers who are observing, and still debating their relationship with the Jews and Jewish Christian communities in the late first century, the pneumatic argument for being "born of the Spirit" had major ethnic significance. Converts were recognized as members of inferior status because of their lack of genealogical relations to the Jewish ancestry. They could not fabricate their genealogy as King Herod did by tracing his ancestry to the Babylonian exiles.[104] They thus hear Jesus challenging Nicodemus to rediscover what it means to ethnically join oneself to a Jewish community in which one has no genealogical relation, ancestry, or heritage. In the ancient world, not having genealogical relations to a community meant that one neither held the territorial right to the common space such as the kingdom of God, nor the ability to justify one's inclusion as an equal member on all terms.

After exploring these implications, we are made aware that "being born again" is ethnic language. This helps us recognize that an appeal to being born of the Spirit is a challenge to those who held genealogical values and boundaries. To champion the need to be "born again" by the Spirit is a direct assault to those in power who uphold and maintain systems of genealogical privileged and ethnic superiority. Since membership in the kingdom of God is not based upon ethnic lineage, the Johannine community needs to be one that has an ever-expansive and inclusive understanding of what it means to be and call one another a child of God. This also means that members should not have trepidation in admitting those who have questionable

---

104. Josephus, *Ant.* 13.257–58; 14.9; 14.403.

ethnic identities—such as the mestizo or hybrid foreigner. Membership into the kingdom of God through the Spirit eradicates the privileges and pride of being a descendant of Abraham. Since we hear Jesus confronting and commencing an unprovoked dialogue with the Jewish religious leaders of his time, the Johannine community is also challenged to recognize that to be born of the Spirit means that one's inclusion into the community is no longer based on genealogical relations. This pneumatic argument of inclusion justifies all non-Jewish members into the kingdom of God and rejects ethnocentric genealogical privilege. More specifically, nationalism and ethnocentric patriotism that maintains and fosters xenophobia and racial hostility because of the foreign location of one's birth are practices that are contrary to the Spirit's birthing activity of inclusion. Xenophobia, racism, and exclusion are not merely wrong for morality's sake. They are the anti-pneumatic spirits that roam the earth and bring about division and animosity toward those whom the Spirit has embraced through a new birth.

7

Advocating for a Pneumatic Non-Violent and Non-Segregation Worship

JOHN 4:23–24

JESUS' ENCOUNTER WITH THE SAMARITAN WOMAN IN JOHN 4 is intriguing for many reasons. The encounter reflects the pattern of a betrothal narrative, given that Jesus was alone with a woman in a public setting.[1] The dynamics of the narrative also include a crossing of gender boundaries that were upheld in the ancient world.[2] It was not typical for Jewish men and Samaritan women to socialize. Yet this is not solely a male-female encounter, it ventures into discussions about the coming prophet, reveals their distinct identities, and deals with issues that stem from their contrasting claims to temple worship. In Jesus' discussion about worship in vv. 23–24, he responds to the Samaritan woman's remark about the legitimacy of Mount Gerizim. The Samaritan woman initiates the topic by making a statement about her ancestors' contention that Mount Gerizim is the proper place to worship, a claim that runs counter to the Jewish emphasis on Jerusalem. Upon closer analysis of Jesus' response, Jesus appears to be

---

1. See Eslinger, "Wooing of the Woman," 166–68. Allusions to betrothal scenes include Gen 24:10–61; 29:1–20; Exod 2:15–21.

2. Philo reflects the ancient gender stereotype and division in public and private spaces when he remarks that the woman is most suitable for the indoor life. In *Spec. Laws* 3.169–71, 178, we find the notion that males and females have two different types of souls. See also Xenophon, *Oeconomicus* 7.19–21; Hierocles, *On Duties* 4.28.21. Ben Sira also warns males of spending time with women alone, especially if they are married (9:9; 42:12). Hanson remarks that women were to remain within the parameters set by the males and constantly guarded. See Hanson, "All in the Family," 28–29.

indifferent to all temple worship and even posits the notion of a God who is actively seeking worshippers outside a temple complex.³

This Samaritan-Jewish dialogue on "worship in the Spirit" has been interpreted in various ways. Some scholars read this to help explain the essence of true worship and the outward cultic inadequacies of a temple. Thus we find Morris claiming that Jesus is concerned with the essential nature of worship, between external worship which has material manifestations and internal worship which is done with one's own spirit.⁴ Millos continues this reading when he states that the focus of the passage refers to those worshippers who are defined by "la condición de su adoración, y no por el lugar desde donde adoran, o por la forma en que lo hacen."⁵ Other readings that follow Bultmann argue that this passage points to an eschatological worship done by redeemed believers. As Bultmann claims, this discussion on worship refers to an age in which every local cult will cease to be important.⁶ Recent readings combine the emphasis of temple displacement but highlight the gender, ethnic, and geographic boundaries that are being eradicated. Keener thus observes that Jesus is calling for a worship that transcends these particularities. As a result, one's experience with the Spirit replace the magnificent temple that was destroyed by the Romans.⁷

These interpretations all agree that Jesus' view on worship makes mountains and temple locations unnecessary for the true worshippers. Where they disagree is on the nature of worship that Jesus advocates, whether it is an internal worship that is spirit-inspired, or one that continues in the realm of the Spirit.⁸ What has yet to be sufficiently elaborated in these

---

3. Jesus' statement includes a critical rejection of both the Samaritan and the Jewish views that affirm mountains. It would have been doubly offensive to the religiously devotee who insisted that proper cultic worship was tied to sacred spaces. Jesus' statement in the Fourth Gospel reflects a Synoptic anti-temple attitude that regards the Jerusalem temple as the improper place of worship because of its corruption (Mark 14:58; 15:29; Matt 26:59–62).

4. Morris, *John*, 238–39; Barrett, *St. John*, 199–200.

5. Millos, *Juan*, 437.

6. Bultmann, *John*, 189–91; Dodd, *Interpretation*, 314; Haenchen, *John 1*, 223; Beasley-Murray, *John*, 61–62; Brown, *John*, 1:180; Lindars, *John*, 188–89; Neyrey, "Jacob Traditions," 433. See also Guiding, who emphasizes the replacement motif in Guiding, *Fourth Gospel and Jewish Worship*, 58–68.

7. Keener, *John*, 608–615; Keener, "One New Temple in Christ," 75–92; Malina and Rohrbaugh, *John*, 98–100; Schneiders, *Revelatory Text*, 180–99. Lee explores the role of the Spirit as the locus of worship in Lee, "In the Spirit of Truth," 277–97. See also Dube, "Reading for Decolonization," 69.

8. The identity of the Spirit depends on how one reads πνεῦμα within these passages. But, as Bruner notes, it is a mistake to read the Spirit in a lower case and suggest that the worshipping is inward. See Bruner, *John*, 263.

discussions is the role of the Spirit with the material identity and practices of these worshippers within the immediate Jewish-Samaritan ethnic context. The focus of this analysis is not to describe the nature of worship, thus involving myself in the debate on whether worship is external or internal, but the deeper ethnic tensions of this dialogue that Jesus attempts to resolve.

The questions that I seek to answer are the following: What does the Spirit have to do with the worship that Jesus advocates? Does a "worship in the Spirit" concern itself with the ethnic identity or sacred spaces of the worshipping community? Along with emerging readings of John 4:23–24, I will argue that Jesus' response is not minimizing Samaritan ethnic identity and tradition through his insistence that worship on mountains will not matter. Jesus urges Jewish and Samaritan communities to understand that worship in the Spirit is primarily characterized by the rejection of violence and antisocial behavior that their mountains symbolize and ethnic ideologies foster. In other words, worship in the Spirit and truth does not transcend ethnic identities or disregard sacred space. It eschews the violent practices and stereotypical ethnic perspectives that sacred spaces have generated.

This particular reading is, what I argue, woven within Jesus' response to the Samaritan woman. It not only provides a challenge to her ancestral claims, but urges Samaritans, Jews, and the readers to reject violent forms of oppression within their worshipping communities. This chapter will thus proceed by demonstrating how the text is presenting two contrasting ethnic communities in tension over worship. Second, I will seek to understand Jesus' statements on worship by exploring Samaritan history within the context of temple-violence within the Roman Empire. We will critically read the language on worship in the Spirit in light of the ethnic context of the readers and Jewish-Samaritan communities.

Reading the Worship Dialogue in Context

In reading the worship dialogue within its ethnic context we notice Jesus' concern with the true worshipper, both in the present and future (vv. 21–23). But this call for true worshippers does not necessarily mean that they are void of ethnicity. Jesus is talking about real people in real locations with their particular histories and layered identities. Although some may see the woman as a symbolic figure, the text reveals attention to the Samaritan woman's personal life, the community she represents, and readers who are in tension with Jews.[9] The reader is made aware of the distinct gender,

---

9. Schneiders views the woman as a symbolic figure representing the Samaritan element in the Johannine community. See Schneiders, *Revelatory Text*, 180–99. See also

ethnic, liturgical, and religious identities and practices. This is set before the reader at the commencement of the dialogue when the Samaritan woman reminds Jesus of his "Jewish" identity and practice of segregation (v. 9).[10] Throughout the text the reader hears the differences between Jesus and the woman, not only in terms of gender and ethnicity, but with respect to their theological traditions.

Yet the conversation gets personal between them. The Samaritan woman comes to know Jesus' identity as a prophet when he reveals her marriage history. However, after Jesus calls the woman to bring her husband, she does not leave the well as Jesus bids. Instead, she draws Jesus' attention to Mount Gerizim (v. 20). This reference to Mount Gerizim, as some suppose, may appear as an attempt to defer further discussions about her marriage history.[11] But we can also entertain the possibility that this discussion arises due to Jesus' amicable address to a Samaritan woman. Contrary to the view of some scholars, the amicable dialogue reveals the possibility that the Samaritan woman sensed the liberty to bring to Jesus' attention a point of bitter conflict between their ethnic communities, especially since she has perceived his identity as the prophet.[12] She presents Jesus this dilemma, given that Samaritan tradition awaited the coming prophet as promised in Deut 18:18. According to Samaritan tradition, they believed that the prophet would arrive at Mount Gerizim and restore the worship of God in the tradition of a priest like Moses.[13] Samaritan hopes anticipated not a Da-

---

Bowman, *Samaritan Problem*; Freed, "Samaritan Converts," 241–56.

10. Scholars note that the enmity between the two groups would have been common knowledge for the first-century reader. See Bultmann, *John*, 178; Brown, *John*, 1:170; Barrett, *St. John*, 194–95. Morris is unsure of how the Jews viewed each other given that the disciples venture into the city to buy food and thus show no reservation with Samaritans. See Morris, *John*, 229.

11. Morris, *John*, 236; Beasley-Murray, *John*, 61.

12. Kim insists that the Samaritan woman has been stereotyped as an immoral woman without the reading knowing why she had many husbands. She points out the role of colonization and victimization within the text, especially since the woman is also used to reveal Jesus' identity and disciple's mission. See Kim, "Korean Feminist Reading of John 4:1–42," 109–119. Lim, however, does not read her presence in the narrative as a victim but rather a creative agent who resists colonization. See Lim, "Speak My Name," 35–51. Likewise, Maccini notes that Samaritans did not make a distinction between the sexes when it came to the obligations of the Law and were even less rigid with woman entering the public sphere. See Maccini, "Reassessment of the Woman," 39–41. Neyrey believes the rhetorical exchange reflects greater mutuality and self-revelation, which are proper to kinship networks. See Neyrey, "What's Wrong with This Picture?," 98–125, esp. 114–15.

13. Deut 27:1–7; Bowman, *Samaritan Problem*, 31; Freed, "Did John Write His Gospel," 250.

vidic Messiah, but a prophet who would have a priestly role and restore the tabernacle worship.[14] This was the essential characteristic of Samaritanism: its concept of a priestly religion founded on the Pentateuch with its focus on Mount Gerizim.[15] Since Jesus was a prophet, then he alone would have been the most qualified person to address this problem that plagued the relations between Jews and Samaritans throughout the decades.

Jesus' response to the Samaritan woman provides a solution, not by denying his Jewish identity or Jewish perspective, but by insisting that the true worshipers will also worship in the Spirit and truth.[16] Yet what is often absent in the readings of this dialogue is that Jesus does not minimize the Samaritan's ethnic identity when he points to a worship in the Spirit. Although he holds that the Samaritans are uninformed in their worship, he concedes that they, both the woman and her ethnic community, could be the new worshippers that the Father is seeking.

This concern for her ethnic community is made evident in the plural forms of the verbs and pronouns which refer to the wider Samaritan and Jewish community.[17] In the passages below, we can observe the wider audience involved that is implied:

> Our (ἡμῶν) fathers worshiped on this mountain, and you all (ὑμεῖς) say that in Jerusalem is the place where worship is necessary. Jesus says to her, Woman, believe me, the hour is coming

---

14. Samaritan claims stem from their reading of Deut 27:3 which mentions Mount Gerizim as the place where the altar is to be built. The Samaritan Pentateuch includes an expansion to the Tenth Commandment (Exod 20:17). It focuses upon the command to engrave within stones all the words of the Law and build a stone altar on Mount Gerizim. Although Deut 12:5 also mentions that there can only be one place to worship God, references to Jerusalem are mentioned in 2 Chr 6:6 and Ps 78:68, which would not have been viewed authoritative since the Pentateuch was the Samaritan's only authoritative scripture. The Jews countered this view by pointing to Exod 20:24 which would make the altar at Mount Gerizim a type of altar mandated in every place, as noted in *Ant.* 4.307–308.

15. Bowman, *Samaritan Problem*, 42.

16. Jesus points to the true worshippers that the father seeks. These worshippers are those whose worship is done ἐν πνεύματι καὶ ἀληθείᾳ. The repeated phrase "Spirit and truth" (ἐν πνεύματι καὶ ἀληθείᾳ) in verses 23–24 points not to a "true spirit" but both the realm of the Spirit and the moral behaviors of the worshipper. Within Qumran literature God gave his Spirit so that interpreters of scripture would understand truth and live a righteous life. See 1QS 8:16; 1QH 5:18; 6:12, 25; 17:32; 20:11–13; CD 2:12.

17. The plural forms often do not get translated in our English versions. The NASB, NRSV, NKJ, NJB, and ESV all translate the plural pronoun ὑμεῖς and plural verb προσκυνήσετε in the singular when the Greek does not necessarily demand this. The NLT, NET, CSB, and NIV try to tease out a proper translation ὑμεῖς in verse 22 but maintain the singular verb "you worship" which is a translation of the plural προσκυνήσετε in verse 21.

when neither on this mountain nor in Jerusalem will you all worship (προσκυνήσετε) the Father. You all (ὑμεῖς) worship what you do not know. We (ἡμεῖς) worship what we know (οἴδαμεν) for salvation is from the Jews. But the hour is coming, and now is, when the true worshipers will worship the Father in Spirit and truth, for such the Father seeks to worship him. God is Spirit, and those who worship (τοὺς προσκυνοῦντας) him must worship in Spirit and truth.

οἱ πατέρες ἡμῶν ἐν τῷ ὄρει τούτῳ προσεκύνησαν: καὶ ὑμεῖς λέγετε ὅτι ἐν Ἱεροσολύμοις ἐστὶν ὁ τόπος ὅπου προσκυνεῖν δεῖ. λέγει αὐτῇ ὁ Ἰησοῦς, Πίστευέ μοι, γύναι, ὅτι ἔρχεται ὥρα ὅτε οὔτε ἐν τῷ ὄρει τούτῳ οὔτε ἐν Ἱεροσολύμοις προσκυνήσετε τῷ πατρί. ὑμεῖς προσκυνεῖτε ὃ οὐκ οἴδατε: ἡμεῖς προσκυνοῦμεν ὃ οἴδαμεν, ὅτι ἡ σωτηρία ἐκ τῶν Ἰουδαίων ἐστίν. ἀλλὰ ἔρχεται ὥρα καὶ νῦν ἐστιν, ὅτε οἱ ἀληθινοὶ προσκυνηταὶ προσκυνήσουσιν τῷ πατρὶ ἐν πνεύματι καὶ ἀληθείᾳ: καὶ γὰρ ὁ πατὴρ τοιούτους ζητεῖ τοὺς προσκυνοῦντας αὐτόν. πνεῦμα ὁ θεός, καὶ τοὺς προσκυνοῦντας αὐτὸν ἐν πνεύματι καὶ ἀληθείᾳ δεῖ προσκυνεῖν. (4:20–24)

When the Samaritan woman states, "Our fathers worshipped on this mountain" (v. 20), she contrasts this ancestral practice with her Jewish contemporaries who insist that Jerusalem is the proper place of worship. Jesus responds with the plural verb "worship" (προσκυνήσετε) which refers to the woman and the wider Samaritan community. He points to a time in which the mountain in Gerizim and Jerusalem will no longer be a place of worship. But when Jesus states in v. 22 that "you worship what you do not know," the plural pronoun (ὑμεῖς) is used to point to all Samaritans who insist they worship the God of Israel. Jesus' response defends the Jews by noting that they (ἡμεῖς) properly worship given that salvation is from them.[18] Again, the plural pronouns and verbs within vv. 20–24 are best understood not only between two individuals, but between distinct communities who hold contrasting claims about worship. Jesus points both to the ignorance of Samaritan worship and the possibility of their future inclusion which will not be limited to a particular mountain.

In closer analysis of Jesus' statement about the ignorance of Samaritans we can notice that he refers to an anti-Samaritan tradition that emerges

18. Bultmann raises the possibility that the plural refers to the Johannine community who understands how to give true worship in Bultmann, *John*, 189–90n6. Morris agrees that the "we" is emphatic and Jesus' siding with the Jewish claims that contrast with Samaritan perspectives. See Morris, *John*, 238.

from 2 Kgs 17:24–41.[19] But it must be noted that the conversation on worship began when the Samaritan woman challenged Jesus as a Jewish prophet. She makes a claim which stands in stark contrast and conflict with the one Jesus represented. She presents the current state of affairs and reminds Jesus about the social and political history between Jews and Samaritans. There is an element of defense in recalling where her fathers worshipped. One cannot help but recognize that embedded within her statement is a memory of violence that has resulted in the formation of a different worshipping community separated by geography. Even more, in bringing this to Jesus' attention she points not to a standing temple, but its ruins, the scars that Jesus' Jewish ancestors had inflicted upon her community.

Before turning to Jesus' response, it is important to understand the tension between Jews and Samaritans, but not from a Jewish perspective which is repeated by many commentaries. To understand the Samaritan woman's boldness to confront Jesus about Mount Gerizim, we must do justice to the violence and segregation experienced by the Samaritans. In our review of Samaritan history, we will highlight the importance of Mount Gerizim to a Samaritan identity that emerged in bitter tension with the Jews.

Samaritan Identity and Mount Gerizim

The people who lived in Samaria did not consider themselves Samaritans. Gary Knoppers makes this point when he insists that the designation "Samaritan" is largely shunned given that the people in this region prefer to call themselves northern Israelites or Samarian Israelites.[20] The story of the Samaritan people as a distinct group emerged after the Assyrian exile. Josephus remarks that the term "Samaritan" is a Greek translation of the settlers' name who were known in the Hebrew tongue as Cutheans.[21] However, Robert Anderson and Terry Giles mention that the name "Cuthean" was one the Jews gave the Samaritans as a reminder of their contempt and belief that they were racially and religiously impure.[22] Josephus himself did not regard the Samaritans as a sect within Judaism,[23] they were ethnically

---

19. Hakola, *Identity Matters*, 105–6.

20. Knoppers, *Jews and the Samaritans*, 15. A Samaritan inscription found on the Island of Delos reads, "The Israelites on Delos who make offerings on the hallowed Mount Gerizim." See Kraabel, "New Evidence of a Samaritan Diaspora," 44–46.

21. Josephus, *Ant.* 9.290.

22. Anderson and Giles, *Keepers*, 15–17; Novakovic, "Jews and Samaritans," 215.

23. Josephus, *Life*, 10.

different.[24] But from a Samaritan point of view, the Cutheans are simply the inhabitants of the northern area of Samaria. They are not directly associated with the Samaritan sect recognized in the first century.[25]

Nonetheless, Josephus's insistence that the Samaritans were distinct from the Jews repeats the stereotypical narrative that they were ethnically impure and thus inferior to Jews.[26] We know that in antiquity there was an assumption that groups of people were either inferior or superior to others based upon influences such as lineage or belonging to particular ethnic groups. The idea that people of superior quality should be of pure lineage without a mixture of foreign elements among their ancestors was an extremely common conviction throughout the ages.[27] As we have observed in Plato's *Menexenus*, the myth of pure lineage and national identity is taken to justify a love of freedom and hatred toward foreigners.[28] Plato assumed that a mixed population would bring immense deterioration to the native people of the land.[29] When the Romans were charged for having a barbarian lineage, it was Dionysius of Halicarnassus who argued that Romans were descendants of the "most ancient Greek people."[30] He attempted to eradicate the Roman stigma that they were descendants of immigrants with questionable ancestral backgrounds.[31] It was however observed that the Romans were different from Greeks and intermingled with other ethnic groups. But he gave a positive spin to this interracial activity and claims,

> The language spoken by the Romans is neither utterly barbarous nor absolutely Greek, but a mixture, as it were, of both, the

24. Josephus, *Ant.* 9.288–91; 10.183–84.
25. Anderson and Giles, *Keepers*, 17; Bowman, *Samaritan Problem*, 2.
26. Josephus, *Ant.* 11.341; 9:288–91.
27. Isaac, *Invention of Racism*, 109.
28. Plato remarks, "But we, and we alone, could not bring ourselves either to hand them over or to join in the agreement. So firmly-rooted and so sound is the noble and liberal character of our city, and endowed also with such a hatred of the barbarian, because we are pure-blooded Greeks, unadulterated by barbarian stock. For those who cohabit with us are none of the type of Pelops, or Cadmus, or Aegyptus or Danaus, and numerous others of the kind, who are naturally barbarians though nominally Greeks; but our people are pure Greeks and not a barbarian blend; whence it comes that our city is imbued with a whole-hearted hatred of alien races" (*Menex.* 245c–d).
29. Plato, *Leg.* 12.949e–950a.
30. Dionysius of Halicarnassus, *Ant. rom.* 1.89.
31. He asserts, "Rome did not become entirely barbarized after receiving the Opicans, the Marsians, the Samnites, the Tyrrhenians, the Bruttians and many thousands of Umbrians, Ligurians, Iberians and Gauls, besides innumerable other nations, some of whom came from Italy itself and some from other regions and differed from one another both in their language and habits" (*Ant. rom.* 1.89).

greater part of which is Aeolic; and the only disadvantage they have experienced from their intermingling with these various nations is that they do not pronounce all their sounds properly. But all other indications of a Greek origin they preserve beyond any other colonists. (*Ant. rom.* 1.90)

From Dionysius's perspective, the only detriment the Romans experience in their contact with foreigners is the inability to properly preserve the pronunciation of their native tongue.

Maintaining a pure linage was an important duty for ethnic groups. This view of maintaining pure lineage also shaped marriage preferences and the control of offspring. When the king of Argos gave his daughter in marriage to a foreign man, it was Theseus, the king and founder of Athens, who said, "you have mingled your clear line with a muddy one and sorely wounded your house."[32] Socrates believed that in order for humanity to reach its full potential, inferior people and noble people should not produce children.[33] This controlled eugenic was necessary in order to improve humanity and ensure the continuance of the most perfect offspring. The assumption within the wider Greco-Roman world was that a mixed lineage was a deterioration of humanity.[34] Even Herod, aware of the suspicion of his ethnic background, fabricates his genealogical lineage in order to locate his identity within the Jewish pedigree of exiles from Babylon.[35]

Strikingly, Josephus refers to Plato's claim when he defends the Jewish conviction that they should not intermarry or socialize with Gentiles. He draws from Plato in stating that he "also ordained that they should not admit of foreigners intermixing with their own people at random."[36] Josephus uses this argument of lineage purity to justify the anti-social behavior that is charged against the Jews, while at the same time trying to propose that Jews are amicable toward foreigners.[37] Nonetheless, this is not to deny the various settlements and migration of foreign people into Samaria. But what we cannot deny is that this migration contributed to the Jewish assumption that the Samaritans were of a mixed lineage and thus held no true ethnic relationship. A mixed lineage fostered the assumption that the Samaritans were inferior, polluted, and should be avoided since they did not preserve their

---

32. Euripides, *Suppl.* 219–225.
33. See Plato, *Tim.* 18d–19a; *Resp.* 5.415a–c, 459d–e.
34. See also Diodorus, 1.9.3; Tacitus, *Germ.* 46; Livy, *His. rom.* 38.17.9–12.
35. Josephus remarks that Nicholas of Damascus reinvented Herod's genealogy (*Ant.* 14.9).
36. Josephus, *Ag. Ap.* 2:257.
37. Josephus, *Ag. Ap.* 2:258–59.

genealogy from Manasseh. This not only explains the anti-social behavior against Samaritans but justifies the ethnic segregation, rejection, and any claim or right to be the legitimate worshippers who descended from Israel. It is a negative perception of the ethnically other, one that also emerges in the gospel narratives.[38]

The Samaritans however would dispute this perception. The people of Samaria viewed themselves as the true Israel and worshiped the Hebrew God as their national deity. They even held similar theology and festivals.[39] They also would contend that they preserved their ancestral traditions, lineage, and even remained faithful to the Torah. Samaritans would not deny presence of foreigners, but point out that they have gradually received a minor foreign presence over the course of several generations.[40] In other words, Josephus does not give us the full story of Samaritan identity. In his writings he has a particular bias toward the Jews and paints the Samaritans as opportunists who only claim to be related to Jews when it benefits them.[41] But if the Samaritans were at odds with the Jews and faced the consistent reputation of being racially impure and thus inferior, was this sufficient to be liturgically at odds with the Jerusalem temple? Certainly not. What led to the eventual division and segregation between two communities was temple violence, a practice that was embraced in ancient Rome against political adversaries.

The violent history that the Samarians experienced during the Hellenistic and Hasmonean periods exacerbated the fragile relationship with the Jews. It led to the emergence of two distinct temples which became sources of division and boundaries of segregation. Josephus remarks that when the Jewish exiles were rebuilding the foundations of the Jerusalem temple it was the Samaritans who besought the governor in order to "interrupt the

---

38. See Matt 10:5; Luke 9:51–56; John 8:48. Sirach also expresses his attitude toward the inhabitants of Samaria by calling them a "foolish nation that lives in Shechem" (50:25–26).

39. Bowman, *Samaritan Problem*, 30–31. Knoppers points out that, according to material culture, the Jews and Samaritans were almost indistinguishable except for the selection of motifs on coins, a cosmopolitan focus, stronger connection to the Phoenician coast, and wealth. See Knoppers, *Jews and Samaritans*, 119.

40. Knoppers points to the archeological remains that suggest a more complex situation than narrated in 2 Kings 17. Major sites such as Megiddo and Samaria show only limited or minimal signs of Assyrian destruction. There is no clear evidence that the Assyrian siege was fatal to the native culture. The destruction of Israel was discriminate, not systemic. See Knoppers, *Jews and Samaritans*, 18–44, 68.

41. Josephus, *Ant.* 12.258–61. See 13.72–73, which describes the Samaritan temple as smaller and poorer. See also Feldman, "Josephus's Attitude," 23–45.

Jews."[42] But from a Samaritan perspective the opposition to the rebuilding of the Jerusalem temple that is chronicled in Ezra 4 did not begin in this manner. The people of Samaria approached the Jewish exiles and desired to help them given that they worshipped the same God. John Bowman agrees with this point when he remarks that the schism was not caused by the Samaritans but by returning Jews.[43] In the *Samaritan Chronicle*[44] the original Jewish exiles wanted to rebuild the temple in Mount Gerizim, but others argued for the location of Jerusalem. Although there was a frequent request for unity, eventually Sanballat and Zerubbabel had to petition to the Persian king in order to settle the dispute.[45] According to Samaritan tradition there was a desire for the reunification of the tribes[46] but certain Jewish priests rejected their assistance, which added to the evolving distrust as we find in Ezra when the Jews were forbidden to intermarry with the Samaritans.

Scholars agree that on the eve of Alexander's entry into Palestine, a Samaritan temple that resembled the Jerusalem temple was built on Mount Gerizim.[47] Knoppers explains that there was a massive expansion of the Gerizim temple during this period, a project rooted in a spirit of competitive emulation.[48] Nonetheless, the Samaritan temple was an expression of national identity that began to emerge in importance as the Samaritans responded to the difficulties they had with the Jerusalem Jews.[49] In other words, the Gerizim temple not only became a place of worship but a symbol of national identity, constructed in response to division and bitter enmity toward Jerusalem. However, the political fortunes of the Samaritans changed especially when the Samaritans violently opposed Alexander's new ruler over Syria.[50] The Jewish people in Jerusalem during this period had no such reaction but watched them revolt against the Greeks.

---

42. Josephus, *Ant.* 11.19; Ezra 4:24.

43. Bowman, *Samaritan Problem*, 20.

44. Earliest manuscript dates to the medieval period (1300–1500 CE).

45. The Jewish exiles insisted, "We will unite all of us and go to el-Quds, and build it up, and we will be one word and one soul." But the offspring of Aaron and Joseph responded, "No, but, on the contrary, we will go up to the Mount of Blessing, and build up the holy place, and we will be one soul and one word" (*Samaritan Chronicle*, 45).

46. This was a hope not lost by other Jews. See 2 *Bar.* 77:19; 78:1; 4 *Ezra* 13:40–48.

47. Meyers and Chancey, *Alexander to Constantine*, 9; Magness, *Archaeology*, 52. Josephus was incorrect in his timing when he claimed that the Samaritan temple was built under Sanballat III in *Ant.* 13.254–56.

48. Knoppers, *Jews and Samaritans*, 125, 191.

49. Meyers and Chancey, *Alexander to Constantine*, 9.

50. Anderson and Giles, *Keepers*, 25; Knoppers, *Jews and Samaritans*, 169; Magness, *Archaeology*, 70; Meyers and Chancey, *Alexander to Constantine*, 13–14.

After the death of Alexander the Great, the bond between the Jews and Samaritans severely deteriorated. When the Jewish Maccabees revolted against Seleucid oppression the Samaritans did not participate, despite the fact that they had a common enemy and experienced the desecration of Mount Gerizim.[51] Anderson and Giles claim that this is explained by the fact that the Maccabees were not fighting for Samaritan religious freedom but their own.[52] The decision not to participate with the Jews proved to be a tragic mistake. The success of the Maccabees led to the emergence of the Hasmoneans who extended their rule over the region of Samaria.

Under the Hasmonean leadership of John Hyrcanus, an assault against Shechem, Mount Gerizim, the city of Samaria, and an enslavement of its Samaritan citizens ensued.[53] The archeological evidence demonstrates that Hyrcanus completely destroyed the settlement overlooking Shechem and left the Gerizim temple buried under a massive layer of ashes.[54] The violence experienced by the Samaritans was so severe that recent excavations have uncovered many weapons—arrowheads, projectiles, spearheads, and daggers—which reflect the brutal battle that was waged. The temple at Gerizim was never rebuilt and has remained a mound of ruins until recent exploration.[55] These same ruins were also laid bare on Mount Gerizim when the Samaritan woman spoke with Jesus. When she thus presses the claim that her fathers worshipped on Mount Gerizim, she is not only reminding Jesus about a point of disagreement, she is bringing forth into the conversation the traumatic experiences of violence that impacted her community. Temple destruction was a potent act of aggression that legitimized power while serving as a symbolic destruction of the community's identity. The Hasmonean destruction of Mount Gerizim must be understood within this wider Roman context of temple destruction. It was an act that not only interrupted the worship of God but was the most brutal way of telling a people who were already considered inferior that they had no identity or right to be worshippers of God.

During the Roman conquest, destroying temples was an important part of the strategy against foreign enemies even though some Roman military commanders and writers had reluctance to support this aggression.[56] The Romans destroyed various temples throughout their conquest

---

51. Magness, *Archaeology*, 94–95.
52. Anderson and Giles, *Keepers*, 28.
53. See Josephus, *J.W.* 1.63–65; *Ant.* 13.254–58, 275–80.
54. Meyers and Chancey, *Alexander to Constantine*, 33.
55. Magen, "Bells, Pendants, Snakes & Stones," 26–35.
56. Roman respect for sacred sites was more of an ideal rather than a reality. See

of Thebes, Corinth, and Carthage.[57] Temples that were destroyed included those dedicated to Bacchus,[58] Isis,[59] and the German temple of Tamfana.[60] When the Jerusalem temple was destroyed, it not only impacted rabbinic thought, it also disrupted Jewish ideological foundations.[61] This violent act against sacred spaces communicated to the conquered a new definition of reality: that they were powerless to define their sacred space and were aliens with no claim to possess it.[62] When a temple was demolished, it was done to wipe out the political center of the rebellion, serve as an example to other cities, and even diminish the sanctity of the land.[63] Thus, violence against buildings was not only an act of eradicating any aspiration to those who would challenge Roman authority, it was done on the assumption that the building was not sacred.[64] This was not only experienced by the Samaritans from the Hasmoneans, or Jews from the Romans,[65] but also continued in the late Christian Roman Empire toward pagan temples.[66]

When we hear Jesus' statements about worship from within this perspective, we must incorporate the wider ethnic tension, lineage ideology, and violence of the Greco-Roman world. Jesus' response to the Samaritan woman about the irrelevance of sacred mountains is not to disregard the ethnic identity, trauma, or violence that the Samaritans experienced when Mount Gerizim was desecrated by the Greeks and destroyed by the Hasmoneans. Jesus is pointing to new attitudes and practices that shape how the Jews and Samaritans view each other, especially since the deteriorating

---

Rutledge, "Roman Destruction," 179–95; Wells, "Impiety in the Middle Republic," 229–43.

57. Rutledge, "Roman Destruction," 185.

58. Livy, 39.18.

59. Cassius Dio, *Roman History*, 40.47.3–4.

60. Tacitus, *Ann*. 1.51.

61. Stein, "Collapsing Structures," 1–28.

62. Friedland and Hecht, "Politics of Sacred Place," 21–61, esp. 56.

63. Rutledge, "Roman Destruction," 179–95.

64. Trajan states, "The soil of an alien country is not capable of being consecrated according to our laws" (Pliny, *Ep*., 10.50). Cicero remarks that a place or temple can only be sacred according to Roman law in Cicero, *Dem*. 127–28.

65. The Roman army did not often consider the looting of temples sacrilegious. See Polanski, "Destruction of Cultural Heritage," 239–52.

66. The troops of emperor Theodosius destroyed the temple of Zeus Belos at the request of the bishop Marcellus of Apamea in 384–85 CE. Likewise, bishop Porphyry petitioned the emperor to destroy the temple of Zeus Marnas at Gaza. The destruction of pagan temples was tantamount to wiping out demonic powers. See Busine, "From Stones to Myth," 325–46.

relations between the Samaritans and Jews continued well outside of Judea under Roman rule and etched in the Rabbinic tradition.[67]

We must note that the Samaritans were no longer able to rebuild their temple[68] and even entered Jerusalem to scatter human bones before the temple colonnades.[69] The Samaritans killed and attacked Galileans who were on their way to worship in Jerusalem only to have the Judeans retaliate by setting nearby villages on fire and killing many who lived within the vicinity of Samaria.[70] Josephus reminds us that there were contentions between Jews and Samaritans over worship in Egypt on several occasions,[71] with one event leading to the execution of Samaritans.[72] Eventually the Samaritans were not permitted to enter the Jerusalem temple[73] and left to mourn the ruins of their sacred mountain with the aspiration to once again worship God. The place of worship was a focal point of contention and at the same time was related to one's ethnic identity. What was a symbol of national ethnic identity emerged into a central point of violence and segregation between the Jews and Samaritans. The ethnic division between Jews and Samaritans is a breach that was developed through the decades of violence, ethnic suspicion, segregation, and religious disagreement on worship. One must thus notice that the conversation between Jesus and the Samaritan woman was not an insignificant point. It had ramifications that could continue violence and ethnic attitudes of superiority or it could reduce those prospects.

Worship in the Spirit in Light of Temple Violence and Ethnic Identity

When the gospel was being composed, the Jewish and Samaritan temples were destroyed but aspirations toward rebuilding the temple did not diminish.[74] Thus, when Jesus insists that worship will be in the Spirit, he is not merely suggesting that geographical locations of worship do not matter

---

67. See *m. Ber* 7.1; 8.8; *m. Seb.* 8.10; *m. Nid.* 4.1.
68. Knoppers, *Jews and Samaritans*, 219.
69. Josephus, *Ant.* 18.29–30.
70. Josephus, *J.W.* 2.234–38; *Ant.* 20.118.
71. Josephus, *Ant.* 12.10.
72. Josephus, *Ant.* 13:74–79.
73. Josephus, *Ant.* 18.30.
74. As noticed during the Bar Kokhba Revolt (132–135 CE). Fuglseth argues that positive attitudes of the temple by the first Christians indicates that the temple was not abandoned even if it was theologically surpassed. See Fuglseth, *Johannine Sectarianism*, 117–85.

for Samaritans, Jews, or the emerging Johannine community. Nor is Jesus solely suggesting that the whole temple apparatus and cult are insufficient to help one worship God.[75] Instead, his statements include larger implications toward ethnic identity and temple violence that the Samaritan woman and the Johannine readers would have identified and felt, especially in light of temple destruction throughout Jewish and Roman history. To gloss over these implications and propose an eschatological reading of the text that minimizes the issues of racial superiority and violence is to miss the full effect of Jesus' statement.

How then should we understand Jesus' dialogue on worship in the Spirit in light of the history of violence, ethnic perceptions of lineage purity, and ethnic tension reviewed? The implications brought forth in this argument suggest that reading Jesus' statement on worship impacts the practices and perspectives that the true worshippers have toward one another. Although Musa Dube believes that the mountain discourse between Jesus and the Samaritan woman included cultural values that were being devalued, replaced, and suppressed,[76] my reading of Jesus' statement on worship is not pointing to a new form of colonialism. In other words, Jesus is not advocating a transcendence of identity or mountains in worship. He is pointing to the uselessness of upholding segregationist claims and ethnic boundaries that the mountains have come to symbolize. Claiming that Mount Gerizim is important, or the temple in Jerusalem, has only led to destruction and the prohibition of the other through violence and attitudes of racial superiority.

When the worship of God is grounded in the Spirit, it does not suggest that worship in a sacred space or one's ethnic identity is irrelevant. Jesus and the apostles continued to travel to the temple for worship and the priority of Jerusalem was still maintained. Worship never occurs in a non-spatial location or by people with no ethnic identities. The response Jesus gives the Samaritan woman should not be viewed in this manner. Instead, what we are reading is a powerful argument that points to the fact that since the worship of God is done in the Spirit, this means that the realm of the Spirit is the most important location of our worship. To enter into this realm means that one has rejected practices and perspectives that have only resulted in ethno-political animosity and violence. This also means that destroying temples has no place within the practices of the worshipping community. Those who insist that mountains matter are those who are bent on destroying one another's temples. Those who believe that they are racially pure

---

75. As noticed with Jesus, Paul, and the Apostles, the Jerusalem temple still played an important role in the early Christian community. See Fuglseth, *Johannine Sectarianism*, 128–36; Acts 2:46; 3:1; 5:42; 21:26–30; 24:17, 18; 25:8; 26:21; Heb 8:5; 9:8–10.

76. Dube, "Reading for Decolonization," 69.

are the ones who justify practices of exclusion and discrimination through temple boundaries and segregation. As a result, there is no justification for the prejudicial views that have characterized Jewish and Samaritan ethnic relations. Jesus' insistence that worship is in the Spirit challenges those who have used ethnicity to segregate, exclude, and condone temple violence. By pointing to the realm of the Spirit in which worship must occur, Jesus also reveals the uselessness of discriminatory practices, perspectives, and symbols that are based on ethnic ideologies.

The Ethnic Implications of Worshipping in the Spirit

Jesus' insistence that worship must be in the Spirit suggests that believers must recognize that institutions of national identity which cause alienate hold no place within the worshipping community. Central to this thesis is the claim that Jesus' dialogue about worship can only be understood when the historical factors of racial hostility, lineage purity, and competing religious temples shape how we read Jesus' response to the Samaritan woman. Jesus' dialogue with the Samaritan woman makes sense to those who understand that the Samaritan woman is not an ignorant worshipper because of her focus upon the temple in Gerizim. She has merely not been made aware that the Spirit will bring about a greater unity and inclusion, one that does not need an appeal to her tradition. As I have attempted to demonstrate, Jesus' dialogue with the Samaritan woman on worship is an attempt to maintain diverse ethnic identities and worshipping traditions through a pneumatic perspective. Jesus' response to the Samaritan woman and her community includes the fact that they no longer need violence and oppression to consider themselves as upholding the true form of worship the Father seeks. Without the Spirit, there is no worship of God and since worship of God is done in the Spirit, this then means that only the Spirit has the right to reject its worshippers and is free to inhabit the realms of the worshipper.

Instead of viewing this discourse on the Jerusalem and Gerizim temple as a rejection of sacred space, the fact that worship of God must be done in the Spirit means that no group can enter the realm of the Spirit and still hold onto claims of racial superiority or violence toward the other's geographical location. For one to reject both Gerizim and Jerusalem is to reject the symbols that have alienated and fomented violence between two communities. The worshippers that the Father seeks are those whose worship includes elements of non-violence and embrace of the other because God is Spirit, and he seeks worshippers who worship him in the Spirit. This is what it means to "worship in the Spirit and truth." Ethnic inclusiveness manifests itself in true worship.

This now points us to think about how the Johannine community may have heard these passages in light of an ever-growing rift between Jews, Greeks, and Samaritans in emerging Christianity.[77] Jesus' discussion on the Spirit presents the ethnic Johannine community with a new way of looking at worship and the temples held by privileged groups. Jesus' insistence that worship is in the Spirit moves the Samaritan woman and readers into another realm that shapes relationships and competing claims. Since God is Spirit and acts toward humanity in Spirit, then all worship toward God and relationship with each other must no longer be bent on the destruction of temples or maintenance of ethnic segregation. This new way of worshipping God will not just replace the temple cult and make it obsolete, it challenges the practices of violence and exclusion that have been used to justify the places of worship. It is not just that temples will not matter, thus moving the issue to synagogues or churches. This dialogue on worship challenges the readers with the fact that the worship the Father seeks in the Spirit must be ethno-inclusive and never justify violence toward sacred spaces.

---

77. Thomas points out that the Fourth Gospel seems to reflect an accurate knowledge of emerging attitudes toward the Samaritans. For an explanation of the rabbinic perspectives and attitudes toward Samaritans, see Thomas, *Spirit of the New Testament*, 137–41.

8

Arguing Against Ethnic Kinship

JOHN 6:62–63

JOHN 6 COMMENCES WITH THE MIRACULOUS FEEDING OF 5,000 people and ventures into a dialogue on the true bread that God provides. The narrative evokes a eucharistic theme of eating Jesus' flesh and drinking his blood. It is within this bread of life discourse that we hear Jesus asserting to his disciples,

> Then what if you were to see the Son of Man ascending to where he was before? The Spirit gives life, the flesh benefits nothing. The words I have spoken are spirit and life.
>
> ἐὰν οὖν θεωρῆτε τὸν υἱὸν τοῦ ἀνθρώπου ἀναβαίνοντα ὅπου ἦν τὸ πρότερον; τὸ πνεῦμά ἐστιν τὸ ζῳοποιοῦν, ἡ σὰρξ οὐκ ὠφελεῖ οὐδέν· τὰ ῥήματα ἃ ἐγὼ λελάληκα ὑμῖν πνεῦμά ἐστιν καὶ ζωή ἐστιν. (6:62–63)

Johnston recognizes the difficulties this text has created for interpreters. He asks, "in a book that insists on the enfleshment of the Logos, how can it be asserted that the flesh has no value?"[1] He wonders if the evangelist was quoting the claims of gnostic spiritualist and agreeing that the flesh has no redemptive medium.[2] He does not find it necessary to conclude that σάρξ refers to the eucharist. Instead, he suggests that this statement is an acknowledgment that even the fleshliness of the Son of Man is not able

---

1. Johnston, *Spirit-Paraclete*, 22.
2. Johnston, *Spirit-Paraclete*, 23.

to release humanity from the grip of evil and sin.³ Yet we must notice that the Spirit within this overall discussion is mentioned in response to the disciples' grumbling and offence of Jesus' teachings. How then should the Spirit be understood within this context? How is the Spirit and flesh compared? And what part of Jesus' teaching did the disciples misunderstand?

Many scholars believe that the mention of the Spirit in this passage serves to emphasize the inability of the flesh to impart life.⁴ Barrett suggests that Jesus, as the Spirit-bearer, is the vehicle of the Spirit and therefore gives life through his crucifixion.⁵ Burge argues that the life-giving focus of the Spirit aims to correct sacramental abuses by revealing that the flesh is of no avail.⁶ Other scholarly readings focus on the dualistic implications of the language. Dodd reads the phrase as a maximum which sums up the whole dialogue that compares the true bread from heaven and material food.⁷ Bultmann finds Jesus' statement as an invitation to make a decision of faith and see what is truly πνεῦμά and σάρξ.⁸ While these readings are not mutually exclusive, there is a tendency to regard the Spirit and flesh as opposing natures that provide different benefits.

The focus of this section revisits the role of the Spirit within this dialogue of 6:62–63. We can agree that the Spirit functions in a life-giving role and is compared to the flesh. But none have yet to discuss the implications that this language has in light of the ethnic kinship which cradles the context of the discourse. In fact, I contend that the comparison between the Spirit and flesh is not a comparison between spiritual and material substance such as food, but a comparison between the Spirit's life-giving activity and the provisions of mortal death from ancestral kinships. That is, with the mention of the Spirit we hear Jesus challenging the disciples to recognize that they must have a proper orientation to the benefits of kinship relations. The σάρξ provides no benefits to descendants in comparison to the life-giving activity of the Spirit.

---

3. Johnston, *Spirit-Paraclete*, 25.

4. Brown, *John*, 1:300. Lindars finds that the flesh refers to the earthly and unillumined part of humanity which is in contrast to the Spirit that gives life and revelation. See Lindars, *John*, 273–74.

5. Barrett suggests that the discourse is incomprehensible except from the standpoint of the complete work of Christ, which includes the ascension and gift of the Spirit See Barrett, *St. John*, 48–51.

6. Burge, *Anointed Community*, 185–87.

7. Dodd, *Interpretation*, 341; Johnston, *Spirit-Paraclete*, 22. Tricia Brown also reads the discourse as a contrast between what is representative of the earthly realm and what is representative of the God realm. See Brown, *Spirit in the Writings of John*, 149.

8. Bultmann, *John*, 446–47.

In order to substantiate this reading, we will focus on the contentious challenge to Jesus' reputation and relationship with the Father, a literary aspect that surrounds the context of the Spirit statement. This will first include a literary review of the bread of life discourse and second, a comparison of the πατήρ statements. In the third part of this study, we will explore how the context of ethnic kinship informs our reading. This will enable us to perceive the impact that doubt had regarding Jesus' identity and relation with the Father.

Bread of Life Discourse in Context

The discourse in John 6 is challenging on many levels given its redundancy, parallel with the Synoptic tradition, and evidence of literary development.[9] The various scenes in John 6 can be outlined in the following:

vv. 1–15	Multiplication of Loaves
vv. 16–21	Walking on the Sea
vv. 22–34	The Crowd Searches for Jesus
vv. 35–50	Bread of Life Discourse
vv. 51–59	Bread of Life Discourse Continued
vv. 60–71	Disciples' Reaction

The opening episode describes Jesus' miraculous feeding of 5,000 during the time of the Passover (vv. 1–15).[10] The crowd that witnesses this event

---

9. Bultmann believes that verse 4, 6, 14, 23, and 27–59 are editorial insertions and contends that chapter 6 follows chapter 4 (Bultmann, *John*, 209–10). Dodd reads that John 6 is a single discourse which draws out the symbolic significance of bread as it progresses (Dodd, *Interpretation*, 333). Keener also regards the entire chapter as a narrative unit (Keener, *John*, 663, 675). Anderson reads the chapter as a Christian homily (Anderson, "Sitz im Leben of the Johannine Bread," 24).

10. In this miraculous multiplication, it is Jesus who was concerned about the people's nourishment which differs from the Synoptic account (Matt 14:15; Mark 6:35–36; Luke 9:12). Jesus instructs the disciples to have the people sit down and takes the bread, gives thanks, and distributes the food (v. 11). The "giving thanks" (εὐχαριστήσας) term is Eucharistic language that echoes Didache 9. The Synoptics prefer the word "blessed" (εὐλόγησεν). See Matt 14:19; Mark 6:41; Luke 9:16. Bultmann does not believe that the language is intending to prefigure the eucharist. See Bultmann, *John*, 213n2. Barrett claims that there is nothing that would be out of place or unusual in any Jewish meal but admits that eucharist associations would be detected in the narrative. See Barrett, *St. John*, 230.

identify Jesus as the "prophet who has come into the world" (v. 14),[11] but Jesus withdraws to the mountain when they attempt to seize him and the disciples sail across the sea of Galilee.[12] While the disciples are on their voyage, the wind becomes violent and they observe Jesus walking on the sea (v. 19–21).[13] Although this miraculous water-walking scene is only witnessed by the disciples, it becomes pivotal for the plot in the next episode, which differs from Matthew and Mark who move onto general descriptions of additional healings (Matt 14:34–36; Mark 6:53–56).

The next day the crowd cannot locate Jesus (vv. 22–24). When they find him at Capernaum, they inquire on his arrival by asking, "Rabbi, when did you get here?" (v. 25). Jesus however recognizes that they search for him because they were satisfied from the bread that was miraculously provided. Brown points out that this crowd that considered him a prophet on the previous day may be different.[14] Yet Keener insists that their response would

---

11. The people draw a connection between Jesus' multiplication of loaves with the miraculous provision of manna in the wilderness. See Deut 18:18; 1 Macc 4:41–50; 14:41; 2 *Bar.* 29:8. This also echoes the Samaritan woman's claim that Jesus is a prophet in 4:19. Other examples of miraculous provision of food by prophets include Elijah (1 Kgs 17:14–16; 2 Kgs 4:3–6) and Elisha (2 Kgs 4:42–44).

12. The disciples in the Fourth Gospel travel across the sea of Galilee to Capernaum on their own initiative. This is contrary to Mark who notes that the disciples were on their way to Bethsaida (6:45).

13. This scene is also sequentially linked in Matthew and Mark (Matt 14:13–33; Mark 6:32–52) but absent in Luke's gospel. Mark adds that Jesus intended to pass them by (Mark 6:48). The disciples in Matthew and Mark believe that they see a ghost (Matt 14:26; Mark 6:49). Matthew adds the scene in which Peter walks on water (Matt 14:28–32). In the Fourth Gospel, however, they are only frightened and reassured with Jesus' words Ἐγώ εἰμι (6:20). Even more, the language that describes Jesus walking "ἐπὶ τῆς θαλάσσης" in verse 19 is ambiguous. Lindars notes that the genitive "ἐπὶ" could be translated "by the sea" which would negate the miracle (Lindars, *John*, 246). Barrett however points out that this should not lead us to assume that a miracle was not intended (Barrett, *St. John*, 233). Beasley-Murry suggests that the phrase "ἐπὶ τῆς θαλάσσης" in verse 19 is also found in Mark 6:47 and Matt 14:25. He finds that if the writer wanted to correct a misunderstanding he could have written that Jesus was walking παρὰ τὴν θάλασσαν (Beasley-Murry, *John*, 89). Bultmann observes that the miracle of walking on the lake should be added with the miracle of immediately arriving at their destination (Bultmann, *John*, 216). It should be noted that there would be no reason for the disciples to be afraid if Jesus was merely walking by the lake (vv. 19–20).

For possible OT allusions, see Ps 29:3; 77:19; 107:29; For background in Greco-Roman mythology, see Homer, *Il.* 24.340–42; Vergil, *Aen.* 4.239–41; Seneca, *Herc. Fur.* 317–24; Apollonius, *Argon.* 1.182–84; Hyginus, *Poet. Astr.* 2.34; Pindar, *Pyth.* 4.61. McPhee argues that the phenomenon of Jesus' walking on the sea remains unparalleled. See McPhee, "Walk, Don't Run," 763–77.

14. Brown, *John*, 1:263. Beasley-Murry suggests that they may not have seen the miracle but only experienced the results (Beasley-Murry, *John*, 91). Kiley suggests that the two-part sea-journey of the crowd (6:22–25) is to be perceived as a narrative

have been natural within the ancient world, given that Roman emperors and politicians pacified people with free food.¹⁵ Although it is difficult to assess if the crowd (ὄχλος) was different,¹⁶ Jesus exhorts them to work for eternal food by having faith in him (vv. 27–29). He reveals that the food he provides is that which the "Son of man" will give them because the Father has sealed him (v. 27). Yet the crowd does not believe Jesus' words. They point out that their ancestral fathers ate manna in the wilderness and ask Jesus for another sign (vv. 30–31).¹⁷ The crowd even claims, "it is written, he gave them bread from heaven to eat" (v. 31).¹⁸ In other words, God's seal of approval is not enough, and they ask Jesus for proof.¹⁹

The emerging debate between Jesus and the crowd focuses on the nature and divine source of bread. Although the origin of the crowd's citation is unclear, Jesus claims that Moses was not the giver of the bread but God, whom he describes as his "Father" (v. 32). It is telling that Jesus does not respond to their request but insists that it was his Father who now gives them the true bread. This claim leads to an ongoing discussion about bread. Jesus even insists that the bread that God now gives is not narrowly concerned

---

elaboration of an Amos 8 prediction of the people searching for the word of the Lord (Kiley, "Geography of Famine," 226–30).

15. Keener, *John*, 676; Livy, 4.13.3; Tacitus, *Ann.* 14.51; Pliny, *Pan.* 1–5.

16. ὄχλος is the focus between 6:2–24. From 6:35–59, the crowd become defined as "οἱ Ἰουδαῖοι."

17. This request for a sign may reflect the assumption that a prophet would again provide bread from heaven akin to Moses' miracle in Exodus. In Exodus 7:9 and in John 6:30 there is a demand for a sign. Josephus also mentions messianic pretenders such as Theudas who convinced the people that he would grant signs akin to those done in the wilderness (*Ant.* 20:97, 169–170); Although Jesus had just multiplied the loaves the previous day, Morris observes that Jesus' miracle was a provision of ordinary bread and not manna from heaven. He notes that it occurred only once and for a limited amount of people which differed from Moses' provision of bread for all the Israelites and for many days. See Morris, *John*, 321; Beasley-Murray, *John*, 91.

18. There are several possible references to this citation (Exod 16:4, 15; Ps 78:24; Wis 16:20).

19. The term σφραγίζω can be translated as "seal of approval" (Matt 27:66; Rev 20:3), "mark with a seal" (John 3:33; Eph 1:13; 4:30; Rev 7:3), or "sanctify" (John 10:36). Keener suggests that this refers to the signs by which God had attested (Keener, *John*, 678); Morris reads this as a mark of ownership which shows that the Father has approved Jesus (Morris, *John*, 318); and Barrett suggests that this seal refers to the descent of the Spirit in John 1:33 especially since the term was also used to describe Christian baptism in 2 Cor 1:22; Eph 1:13; 2 Clem. 7:6 (Barrett, *St. John*, 238). This term is also understood by Burge as a technical word for the Spirit. He suggests that this follows Paul's specialized use of the Spirit on believers (2 Cor 1:22; Eph 1:13; 4:30) and is applied in the gospel in reference to the Spirit's seal on Jesus (Burge, *Anointed Community*, 84–85). It must be noted that the verb is an aorist which points to a past event and can refer to the incarnation or anointing of the Spirit.

with them alone but the entire world (v. 33). At this point, the crowd asks Jesus to provide this bread, but they fail to understand the significance of his words (v. 34).[20]

The first bread of life discourse begins after the crowd's request for bread (vv. 35–50). Lindars points out that when Jesus claims to be the bread of life (v. 35), he is designating himself as the wisdom and word of God coming to humanity, thus being the fulfillment of the law that was given on Mount Sinai.[21] Though the Jews respond by grumbling (v. 41), we can observe why they would assume physical bread. Jesus was previously concerned about their physical needs (v. 5), they followed him for more bread (v. 26), and Jesus informed them that God provides real bread from heaven, thus creating the anticipation for another miracle akin to the wilderness provision in Exodus (vv. 31–32).

But this does not excuse the negative reaction. Their grumbling echoes the grumbling of the Israelites in the wilderness.[22] Even more, for the first time in the dialogue the crowd is described as "Jews."[23] They ask, "Is not this Jesus, the son of Joseph, whose father and mother we know?" (v. 45). Brown observes an element of disparagement in their question about his origins.[24] Morris finds that they point to Jesus' parentage because they can show that Jesus' statement is false.[25] By appealing to Jesus' known father and mother, they call into question his claim to be a descendant of the Father. But Jesus also responds to their challenge. Jesus again points to the activities of his divine Father. He notes that it is the Father who sent him (v. 44), draws people to him (v. 44), teaches people (v. 45), and is never seen (v. 46). After these descriptions, Jesus again claims that he is the bread from heaven whose flesh imparts eternal life (v. 48, 50–51) and that the Jewish people's fathers ate manna in the wilderness and died (v. 49).

---

20. Strikingly, this request echoes the Samaritan woman's request for the water in 4:15. Compare κύριε δός μοι τοῦτο τὸ ὕδωρ (4:15) with κύριε πάντοτε δὸς ἡμῖν τὸν ἄρτον τοῦτον (6:34).

21. Lindars, *John*, 250. Bread was viewed as Torah and wisdom. See Deut 8:3; Amos 8:11–13; Prov 9:5; Sir 15:3; 24:21; Philo, *Decal.* 1.15–17; *Mut.* 1.259–260; *Leg.* 3.162.

22. Beasley-Murray explains that grumbling is a rejection of the Lord's voice, which is expressed here as a rejection of Jesus himself. See Beasley-Murray, *John*, 93. See also Exod 15:24; 16:2; 17:3; Num 11:1; 14:1–3, 27–29; 17:6, 20; 1 Cor 10:10.

23. Lindars suggests that the writer has slipped back into his usual ways of designating Jesus' opponents in Lindars, *John*, 262.

24. Brown, *John*, 1:270–71; Barrett, *St. John*, 244; Lindars, *John*, 263; cf. Matt 13:55; Mark 6:3; Luke 4:22.

25. Morris, *John*, 328.

We find vv. 51-58 repeating similar teachings that describe Jesus as the living bread from heaven that provides life for the world.[26] And as in previous experiences, when Jesus describes himself as the bread from heaven the Jews resist his offer, especially since he asserts that the bread is his "flesh" (v. 51). Jesus' description of his flesh as the "bread of life" leads the Jews to argue with one another about his teaching. Yet this is more than mere grumbling (γογγύζω), they now began to fight (μάχομαι) with one another (v. 52).[27] Jesus does nothing to mitigate their confusion but continues to insist that without partaking of his flesh and blood they will have no life nor remain with him (vv. 53-57). He insists that the Father sent him (v. 57) and reminds them that he is the bread that came down from heaven, which differs from the bread that "their fathers ate and died" (v. 58).[28]

It is after this discussion that the disciples too have difficulties with Jesus' claims. But they not only grumble (γογγύζω) with one another like the Jews (vv. 41, 43). They are scandalized (σκανδαλίζω).[29] Jesus' teaching

26. Bultmann finds the terminology of verses 51b-58 different from verses 27-51a, which gives possible evidence of an editor (Bultmann, *John*, 219). Brown finds that the discourse of verses 51-58 is an addition which breaks up the unity that once existed between verses 35-50 and verses 60-71. He believes that verses 51-58 were inserted to bring out the eucharistic motifs in verses 35-50 (Brown, *John*, 1:302). Although Lindars finds the entire chapter as having a clear unity and self-consistency, he believes that it was an independent composition inserted by John in the second edition of his work (Lindars, *John*, 234). Barrett suggests that the thought of the discourse is coherent and it is not necessary to regard verses 51-58 as an interpolation in the interest of eucharistic doctrine (Barrett, *St. John*, 236). Beutler considers the entire chapter as a coherent, well-structured literary unit. See Beutler, "Structure of John 6," 115-27; Keener, *John*, 687; Burge, *Anointed Community*, 183-84; Beasley-Murray, *John*, 86.

27. See Acts 7:26; 2 Tim 2:24; Jas 4:2.

28. Although the Eucharistic themes are prominent, we also notice various allusions to the Exodus wilderness experience. The mention of the Passover in verse 4 not only locates the setting of the miracle, it situates the story in light of the Israelite's wilderness experience. The bread-breaking experience echoes Moses' miracle of providing manna from heaven (John 6:1-15; cf. Exod 16:4-36; Deut 8:3). Jesus' ascent to the mountain evokes Moses' climb to Mount Sinai (John 6:15; cf. Exod 19:12, 14, 20, 23; 24:1-2, 9, 12-13, 15, 18; 32:1, 15; 34:2-4, 29). Although Barrett suggests that there seems to be no symbolic interest in the mountain, he does not dismiss the allusion to Moses and Mt. Sinai (Barrett, *St. John*, 228). Jesus' claims that no one has seen God seems to challenge Moses' experience of seeing God's glory (John 6:46; cf. Exod 24:10; 33:11-23; Num 12:8). Jesus' walk across the Sea of Galilee draws comparison to God's power in parting the Red Sea (John 6:16-21; cf. Exod 14:21; Isa 51:10). These allusions are aptly noticed by Hylen, who argues that the events in John 6 reinforce rather than undermine the Exodus story. She notes that in order to understand Jesus' identity in these dialogues, one is compelled to understand Moses—given that they were both prophets sent by God to perform signs. See Hylen, *Allusion and Meaning*, 176-78.

29. The term σκανδαλίζω, which can be translated as "stumbling," is also found in 16:1.

about the necessity of eating his flesh and drinking his blood is graphic. Morris believes that these words primarily refer to spiritual realities and may secondarily refer to the sacrament.[30] On the other hand, Bultmann claims that Jesus has his death in mind when he describes his flesh as life to the world. Yet he also suggests that the editor added a secondary interpretation to Jesus' words in terms of the eucharist.[31] Likewise, Barrett believes that the language echoes the eucharist but insists that Jesus is also alluding to the crucifixion.[32] Brown notes that to understand Jesus' words with a favorable meaning they must refer to the eucharist.[33] Scholars observe the eucharistic imagery, but we must note that just like the Jews grumbled when Jesus claimed relation to the divine Father, the disciples are also grumbling and thus inviting Jesus to again reassert his divine origin from above. Indeed, it is within the context of doubting Jesus' origin and relation with the Father that he explains the Spirit's life-giving activity and the inability of the flesh to benefit anyone (v. 63).

The difficulties of Jesus' teaching thus hinge on two aspects: his proper relation with the Father and the meaning of his words. We can notice these elements in the reactions to Jesus' words. The Jewish crowd in John 6 assumes that Jesus was talking about literal bread and his ability to provide manna from heaven. Even more, their scriptures and heritage had shaped their understanding and expectations. As a result, they appeal to the bread experiences of their fathers and challenge Jesus to do the same. And within this challenge, we also find another remarkable claim. Jesus responds to the Jews by pointing out that it was God, his Father, who provides bread and was now providing new bread through him. These claims lead to grumbling

---

30. Morris claims that this refers to a spiritual appropriation of Christ which can takes place through the sacraments. See Morris, *John*, 313, 332–35. Burge and Tricia Brown read the ingestion language in reference to believing or accepting Jesus. See Burge, *Anointed Community*, 180; Brown, *Spirit in the Writings of John*, 143.

31. Bultmann, *John*, 234–35.

32. Barrett, *St. John*, 246–47. Beasley-Murray suggests that "flesh" refers to Jesus' body that is sacrificed for others and appropriately fits the Passover setting. He does not find it necessary to interpret the statement exclusively in terms of the body and blood of the eucharist but admits that it would have been difficult for early Christians to avoid this reading. See Beasley-Murray, *John*, 93–95. Tricia Brown also reads the "flesh and blood" language referring to Jesus' violent death. She insists that the graphic language of eating and drinking Jesus' body refers to the same interpersonal experiences characterized by acceptance and loyalty to Jesus. See Brown, *Spirit in the Writings of John*, 145.

33. Brown, *John*, 1:284–85. Burge agrees that the "flesh and blood" discussion refers to the eucharist (Burge, *Anointed Community*, 182). See the prohibition of eating and drinking blood in Gen 9:4; Lev 3:17; Deut 12:23; Acts 15:20. Ignatius of Antioch utilizes the term "flesh" for the Eucharist in *Rom.* 7:3; *Phld.* 4:1; *Smyrn.* 7:1. See also Justin, *1 Apol.* 66.

and fighting. They not only eschew his identity as the divine bread from heaven, they also point out its impossibility by reminding one another that they know his real father and mother (v. 42).

The Πατήρ Statements

Although bread is a focal topic in the discourse, the contentious nature of the dialogue includes a challenge to Jesus' identity and honor. The Jewish crowd appeals to their ancestral fathers who ate manna and also question Jesus' relation with the Father. The term πατὴρ is mentioned throughout the dialogue fifteen times, which is slightly less than the word ἄρτος which has twenty one occurrences. We can observe that when the term πατὴρ is mentioned, it emerges in order to contrast Jesus' divine Father, his earthly father Joseph, and the Jewish people's fathers. The statements are scattered throughout the dialogue which heightens the conflict between them. The πατήρ statements can be observed in the following chart:

	Jesus' Πατήρ Statements		Crowd/Jews' Πατήρ Statements
6:27	ὁ υἱὸς τοῦ ἀνθρώπου ὑμῖν δώσει· τοῦτον γὰρ ὁ πατὴρ ἐσφράγισεν ὁ θεός.		
		6:31	οἱ πατέρες ἡμῶν τὸ μάννα ἔφαγον ἐν τῇ ἐρήμῳ
6:32	οὐ Μωϋσῆς δέδωκεν ὑμῖν τὸν ἄρτον ἐκ τοῦ οὐρανοῦ, ἀλλ' ὁ πατήρ μου		
6:37	Πᾶν ὃ δίδωσίν μοι ὁ πατὴρ πρὸς ἐμὲ ἥξει		
6:40	τοῦτο ἐστιν τὸ θέλημα τοῦ πατρός μου, ἵνα πᾶς ὁ θεωρῶν τὸν υἱὸν καὶ πιστεύων εἰς αὐτὸν ἔχῃ ζωὴν αἰώνιον		
		6:42	ἔλεγον, Οὐχ οὗτός ἐστιν Ἰησοῦς ὁ υἱὸς Ἰωσήφ, οὗ ἡμεῖς οἴδαμεν τὸν πατέρα καὶ τὴν μητέρα;

6:44	οὐδεὶς δύναται ἐλθεῖν πρός με ἐὰν μὴ ὁ πατὴρ ὁ πέμψας με ἑλκύσῃ αὐτόν
6:45	πᾶς ὁ ἀκούσας παρὰ τοῦ πατρὸς καὶ μαθὼν ἔρχεται πρὸς ἐμέ
6:46	οὐχ ὅτι τὸν πατέρα ἑώρακέν τις εἰ μὴ ὁ ὢν παρὰ τοῦ θεοῦ, οὗτος ἑώρακεν τὸν πατέρα
6:49	οἱ πατέρες ὑμῶν ἔφαγον ἐν τῇ ἐρήμῳ τὸ μάννα καὶ ἀπέθανον
6:57	καθὼς ἀπέστειλέν με ὁ ζῶν πατὴρ κἀγὼ ζῶ διὰ τὸν πατέρα, καὶ ὁ τρώγων με κἀκεῖνος ζήσει δι' ἐμέ.
6:58	οὗτός ἐστιν ὁ ἄρτος ὁ ἐξ οὐρανοῦ καταβάς, οὐ καθὼς ἔφαγον οἱ πατέρες καὶ ἀπέθανον.

The above chart reveals a back and forth appeal to the πατὴρ. Jesus reveals that the Father has set his seal upon him, the Son of Man, who will give them bread (v. 27). In response, the Jewish crowd claims that their πατέρες ate manna in the desert (v. 31). This is a reaction to Jesus' claim to have the approval of the πατήρ. In a veiled manner, the crowd is also challenging Jesus to perform the same miracle that their ancestral fathers experienced. That is, they aim to point to their privileged relation to the experience of their ancestors in order to leverage Jesus to act. This combative dialogue is further noticeable in Jesus' following response when he says that it was not Moses who gave their ancestors bread but πατήρ μου (v. 32). Jesus' response agrees they may have a special claim and privilege as descendants of the Israelites who ate manna in the wilderness, but now Jesus has a distinct relation to God who provides manna, not for one privileged ethnic group, but for the entire world. When Jesus later points out that they do not believe, he does so by explaining that the πατὴρ draws all to him and thus challenges their relationship with the divine father (v. 37). Jesus also asserts that the will of the πατὴρ is for him to eschatologically raise from the dead all who believe, which places him in a superior status to Moses who could not do this for those who died in the wilderness (v. 40).

These πατὴρ statements that affirm Jesus' relationship with God are received with suspicion by the Jewish crowd. This suspicion is noticeable when they publicly ask one another if Jesus is the son of Joseph, a πατέρα whom they know (v. 42). But why would they appeal to Jesus' earthly father whom they knew? Within the context of the dialogue, it is noticeable that when Jesus shuns their ethnic privilege, they respond by attempting to challenge Jesus' honor. The Jews call into question Jesus' relationship with the divine Father and undercut his claim to provide bread. Jesus thus responds by explaining that the Father sent him, has taught those who draw to him, and insists that no one has seen Father (vv. 44–46). Jesus reveals his relationship with the Father with the assertion that he is the "bread of life" and reminds them that their πατέρες ate bread but died (v. 49). Jesus continues to claim that as the "living bread from heaven" he will give his flesh for the entire world. The Jews again question the significance of his words (v. 52). Jesus responds by insisting that they must eat his flesh or have no life in them (vv. 53–56). It is at this point that he furthermore claims that the living πατὴρ sent him, he lives because of the πατὴρ, and all who eat his flesh will live (v. 57). This focus on life starkly differs from the results of death from eating the manna provided by the Jewish people's fathers. For the second time, Jesus makes this comparison by pointing to the reality that their πατέρες are dead, thus revealing that their appeal to their ancestral privilege cannot grant anything but the certainty of death (v. 58).

As we notice throughout the dialogue, when Jesus asserts his relationship with the Father, the Jews challenge him with an appeal to their fathers and point out that they know his real father—Joseph. In other words, they utilize their ancestry in order to leverage Jesus to act and embarrass him. When this fails, they question Jesus' identity by pointing out that his divine claims are unfounded. Why is this significant? And why a focus on πατὴρ and Jesus' reminder that their πατέρες had died? Morris insists that when Jesus describes God as "his Father" Jesus is indicating a consciousness that reveals a relation to the God which his hearers did not have.[34] But from an ethnocritical perspective, the focus on ethnic kinship with an appeal to πατὴρ reflects a realization to the limitations that ethnic benefits and privileges provide. In order to understand the implications of this πατὴρ language, we also need to recognize two important values in the ancient Mediterranean world. First, how one's relationship within a kinship impacts one's identity and second, how public perception and affirmation of this

---

34. Morris, *John*, 322.

identity was to be valued above all. Jesus navigates through these issues as he responds to the challenge and rejection of his identity as the living bread from heaven that is sent by the Father.

Ethnic Kinship and Honor in the Ancient World

People in the ancient world lived, interacted, and related to one another within a context of kinship. This centered on the immediate relations of the family with the father as the head of the household and extended to other related kinship groups who in whole made up one's ethnic group. Cicero delineates the degrees of human relations beginning with common humanity and ending with one's kin. He states,

> To proceed beyond the universal bond of our common humanity, there is the closer one of belonging to the same people, tribe, and tongue, by which men are very closely bound together. It is a still closer relation to be citizens of the same city-state; for fellow-citizens have much in common. . . . But a still closer social union exists between kindred. Kinship, starting with that infinite bond of union of the human race in general, the conception is now confined to a small and narrow circle. For since the reproductive instinct is by nature's gift the common possession of all living creatures, the first bond of union is that between husband and wife; the next, that between parents and children; then we find one home, with everything in common. And this is the foundation of civil government, the nursery, as it were, of the state. . . . The bonds of common blood hold men fast through good-will and affection, for it means much to share in common the same family traditions, the same forms of domestic worship, and the same ancestral tombs. (*Off.* 1.53–55)

According to Cicero, the family was foundational to society and was prized above all relations given the exclusive bonds through blood relations, traditions, worship, and ancestral tombs.[35] K. C. Hanson asserts that kinship during the first century was the primary social domain given that no relation, institution, or value was untouched by the family and its concerns.[36] As a central institution in the ancient world, it absorbed all aspects of family life. Bruce Malina also notes that it is through one's kin that the family's practices, values, and the ancestral gods are inherited.[37] Sally Humphreys

---

35. See also Aristotle, *Pol.* 1.1252b.
36. Hanson, "All in the Family," 27.
37. Malina, *New Testament World*, 82–83; Hanson, "All in the Family," 27–28.

explains that kinship on a smaller scale was the nuclear household, also known as οἶκος in Greek and *familia* in Latin. It also extended to a network of social relationships constructed through marriage and legitimate filiation which stretched beyond the household into corporate descent groups.[38] As the above definitions reveal, kinship language is family language.[39] But even more, kinship language is also ethnic language given that it emerges from the basic family unit and extends to blood relatives and genealogical descendants.[40]

Within a kinship institution the household was primarily patriarchal. This meant that the older males held a prominent position within the family, including sway over the younger males. This esteemed position of the older males also included the power of life and death over children and slaves, especially within a Roman household.[41] In addition, Hanson asserts that the father who was a person of power and dominance also communicated this honor, reputation, vocation, and social standing to his son and descendants. And since the communication of honor was passed to descendants, there is a heightened concern with genealogies given that they reveal one's connection to a family group and inheritance.[42]

When a person is described in terms of their kinship and his or her genealogy is traced, the individual's identity is to be considered in terms of the family's honor and corporate reputation. Indeed, Hanson points out that one of the key ways in which a genealogy expresses a claim to honor is by

---

38. Humphreys, "Kinship," 430.

39. See Miller, "Greek Kinship Terminology," 46–52.

40. Hall, *Ethnic Identity*, 36–37. Patterson points out that kinship was also meant to be seen as a device for political diplomacy. It articulated a bond between states that existed between members of a family or between citizens of the same polis. But he also notes that the concept of kinship was regarded as a subcategory of intimacy—that is, kinship denoted consanguinity while intimacy could denote consanguinity but also a variety of other kinds of relationships. See Patterson, *Kinship Myth in Ancient Greece*, 14–15; Jones, *Kinship Diplomacy*.

41. The Roman writer Gaius claims, "There are virtually no other peoples who have such power over their children as we have" (*Inst.* 1.55). Dionysius of Halicarnassus says, "The lawgivers of the Romans gave virtually full power to the father over his sons, even during the whole life, whether the thought proper to imprison him, to scourge him, to put him in chains and keep him at work in the fields, or to put him to death, and this even though the son were already engaged in public affairs, though he were numbered among the highest magistrates, and though he were celebrated for his zeal for the commonwealth" (*Ant. rom.* 2.26.4). Hanson explains that this was based on the assumption that the male's seed was responsible for the creation of a child (Hanson, "All in the Family," 28). See Gen 2:7–23; Wis 7:1–2; 1 Cor 11:7–9.

42. Hanson, "All in the Family," 39.

the choice of the apical ancestor, such as David, Moses, or Abraham.[43] Thus when Jesus calls God his πατήρ, he was not solely establishing a distinct relationship with God, he was revealing his status and honor as a son. By embedding his identity within a divine relationship with God, Jesus circumvents his local kinship and even ethnic identity to establish a direct genealogical relation with God. It is at this point that the Jews grumble (vv. 41, 43) and remind Jesus that his real kinship is not divine but grounded in his earthly kin with his father named Joseph, a man whom they know (v. 42).

What then are the implications of challenging Jesus' relation with the Father? In the ancient world, the most significant social commodity was honor. Since people participated and derived their identity from their immediate kinship group and ethnic community, what someone said or how one was perceived by others was of prime importance. Again, we find Cicero describing the role in public admiration and praise when he states,

> While people admire in general everything that is great or better than they expect, they admire in particular the good qualities that they find unexpectedly in individuals. And so they reverence and extol with the highest praises those men in whom they see certain pre-eminent and extraordinary talents, and they look down with contempt upon those who they think have no ability, no spirit, no energy. (*Off.* 2.36)[44]

From Cicero we can notice that the bestowal of honor is a public activity. It is a reputation that is given by others. We also find Xenophon claiming that what makes extraordinary people different from animals is that they crave honor and praise.[45] Similarly, Plutarch, in quoting Thucydides, affirms that

---

43. Hanson, "All in the Family," 40.

44. Cicero also explains the motive of bestowing honor. He claims, "Whenever, then, people bestow anything upon a fellow-man to raise his estate or his dignity, it may be from any one of several motives: it may be out of good-will, when for some reason they are fond of him; it may be from esteem, if they look up to his worth and think him deserving of the most splendid fortune a man can have; they may have confidence in him and think that they are thus acting for their own interests; or they may fear his power; they may, on the contrary, hope for some favor—as, for example, when princes or demagogues bestow gifts of money; or, finally, they may be moved by the promise of payment or reward. This last is, I admit, the meanest and most sordid motive of all, both for those who are swayed by it and for those who venture to resort to it" (*Off.* 2.21). See also 2.31.

45. Xenophon, "For indeed it seems to me, Hiero, that in this man differs from other animals—I mean, in this craving for honor. In meat and drink and sleep and sex all creatures alike seem to take pleasure; but love of honor is rooted neither in the brute beasts nor in every human being. But they in whom is implanted a passion for honor and praise, these are they who differ most from the beasts of the field, these are accounted men and not mere human beings" (*Hier.* 7.3).

this craving extends even until death.[46] Aristotle maintains that honor is the most esteemed good given to the gods and humanity. He claims,

> Now the greatest external good we should assume to be the thing which we offer as a tribute to the gods, and which is most coveted by men of high station, and is the prize awarded for the noblest deeds; and such a thing is honor, for honor is clearly the greatest of external goods. Therefore, the great-souled man is he who has the right disposition in relation to honors and disgraces. And even without argument it is evident that honor is the object with which the great-souled are concerned, since it is honor above all else which great men claim and deserve. (*Eth. nic.* 1123b)[47]

Malina also explains that to honor someone is to socially acknowledge a person's reputation, worth, and identity in a public manner.[48] Jerome Neyrey adds that honor is not honor unless it is publicly claimed, displayed, and acknowledged. It expresses one's social standing and although one can acquire it, it normally is gained through one's participation and association with a family.[49]

We can agree that in the ancient world honor is dependent upon how one is perceived. It is a public image that is given by others as a result of deeds, actions, or individual qualities. Also, since honor is a public acclamation, one's reputation can be marred, challenged, or despised by others. That is, to dishonor someone is to reject or call into question the person's reputation, including the person's status within the family, and membership to the kinship group or ethnic community in which one is embedded. Hanson even observes that a person who makes an honor claim and is rebuffed by the community is akin to being humiliated, labeled as ridiculous or contemptuous, and treated with disdain.[50] Yet honor is not solely social aggrandizement, it is a status claim that needs to be affirmed by one's social group or kin. To have it called into question and rejected is a public disgrace.

---

46. Plutarch, "It is not the desire of honor only that never grows old, but much more also the inclinations to society and affection to the state, which continue even in ants and bees to the very last" (*An seni.* 783f; Thucydides, 2.44.4).

47. Aristotle states, "Men's motive in pursuing honor seems to be to assure themselves of their own merit, at least they seek to be honored by men of judgement and by people who know them, that is, they desire to be honored on the ground of virtue" (*Eth. nic.* 1095b).

48. Malina, *New Testament World*, 29–31.

49. Neyrey, "Loss of Wealth," 88. See also Neyrey, *Honor and Shame*, 5–6.

50. Hanson, "How Honorable," 83.

These social dynamics of kinship and honor give the bread of life discourse a tangible ethnic context. It shapes our reading of the dialogue between Jesus, the Jewish crowd, and the disciples in various ways. First, when Jesus claims "πατήρ μου" he reveals his identity as God's son, thus aligning his social status and identity in relation to God. Jesus claims a relation with the Father which also assumes an honor communicated from father to son. Second, this claim leads to a response from the crowd. They challenge Jesus' divine identity by pointing to his real ethnic father—Joseph.[51] By questioning Jesus' identity, they also publicly challenging his divine honor. They remind Jesus that he is not who he claims and ground his identity in his proper ethnic kin. By calling into question this status, they not only publicly humiliate him, they reject his identity as the bread from heaven. Third, Jesus avoids this public shaming by reasserting his relationship with the Father and thus creating an ethnic distance with their fathers. We can observe a degree of separation between Jesus' Father and their fathers. Jesus states, "*your* fathers ate bread and died," not "*our* fathers ate bread and died."[52] Jesus reasserts his claim of honor that is ascribed to him as God's divine son, the divine bread from heaven, and one who has God's approval. He does so by asserting a degree of ethnic separation from the Jewish crowd's ancestral appeal to their fathers and his ethnic father Joseph. Yet in his appeal to his living Father from above, he reminds them that their fathers are dead and thus exposes the reality that their privileges have provided. That is, the common benefit that ancestral fathers have given all descendants is death.

Spirit and Flesh Revisited

As we are drawn through the various claims and appeals to the πατήρ statements within the chapter, we now realize that the issue is not merely the meaning of Jesus' graphic language. People are also being confronted with the divine claims Jesus makes by asserting a unique relation with the Father which also circumvents his earthly relation with Joseph. It is this entire dialogue between Jesus and the Jews that the disciples overhear and have difficulties, not only with the meaning of Jesus' words, but with his claim to be in relation with the divine Father. In addition, the grumbling of the Jews is not limited to the crowd alone. Jesus also perceives that the disciples were grumbling amongst themselves (v. 62). By doing so, the disciples respond

---

51. Matt 1:2–16; Luke 3:23–38. Jesus' honor is questioned by referring to his family or origins in Mark 6:3; Matt 13:54–57; Luke 4:22; John 4:44; 6:42; 7:40–42. See how Paul turns to his ancestors to describe his honor in Rom 11:1; Phil 3:5.

52. See also John 8:17, 56; 15:25.

in the same way that the Jewish crowds had when they questioned Jesus' identity as the divine bread from heaven, his status as God's son, and the honor derived from his relation to God the Father. The difference, however, between the grumbling of the Jews and the grumbling of the disciples is that the Jews publicly call into question Jesus' relation with the Father. They publicly point out that Joseph is his real father. The disciples do not do this. However, this does not mean that they were not doubtful of Jesus' claim to have a divine status and relation with the Father. We find evidence that the disciples were seriously doubting Jesus' identity which resulted in many leaving and one eventually betraying him as noted in the concluding verses of the dialogue (vv. 64–66).

What role does the Spirit have within this discourse? How should we understand the flesh and Spirit comparison? And in what way does the ethnic context inform our understanding of the terms? We have noticed that scholars find it difficult to conclude that the "flesh" in v. 63 refers to either eucharistic or crucifixion language. It seems strange that Jesus would insist that the life of the world is his "flesh" or urge his hearers that they must "eat the flesh of the Son of Man" but then discredit the flesh by insisting that it has no benefits. Some rightly attempt to solve this dilemma by pointing out that the reference to flesh within vv. 60–71 and the previous discussions are different.[53] Other readings articulate the implications of a consistent understanding of the "flesh" within the dialogue and underscore the difficulties this has in our understanding of v. 63.[54] But what has yet to be considered

---

53. Bultmann notices the ambiguity of σάρξ within this discourse (Bultmann, *John*, 446). Brown finds the exaltation of the Spirit and depreciation of the flesh not about the Eucharist. Instead, the passage compares the Spirit's life-giving role with humanity's inability to grant eternal life. He finds similar language in Paul's writings (Rom 8:4; Gal 5:16; 6:8). See Brown, *John*, 1:299–300. Lindars also notices the difficulties of the gospel's use of the term flesh in verses 51–58, 63. He claims that verses 60–71 were originally a homily that was added to the chapter to give it a narrative framework. Flesh in verse 63 refers to the earthly part of humanity which is unilluminated by the revelation of God and unable to give life. See Lindars, *John*, 271–73. Morris also admits that the thought of verse 63 is very complex. He believes that the mention of the Spirit is unquestionably a reference to the Holy Spirit and the flesh refers to the limitations of "fleshly life" (Morris, *John*, 340). Tricia Brown notices the dualistic use of the terms. She suggests that "flesh" in verses 51–58 refers to Jesus' body and in verse 63 takes a different meaning that does not negate Jesus' flesh. See Brown, *Spirit in the Writings of John*, 139, 150. Millos asserts that the flesh must not only refer to the limitations "del ser humano, sino también en relación con el impedimento de entender las cosas de Dios" (Millos, *Juan*, 698).

54. Dodd finds that the comparison between the Spirit and flesh aims to draw a distinction between the sphere of absolute reality and the phenomenal order (Dodd, *Interpretation*, 341). Burge reads this language in reference to the eucharist and the inability of the rite to communicate life (Burge, *Anointed Community*, 106, 185–86).

is how the Spirit-flesh comparison can also be read in light of the privileges and benefits of ethnic relations within kinship groups and the challenge to Jesus' identity and status with the Father.

We notice that prior to Jesus asserting that the "Spirit gives life" and that the "flesh provides no benefits," he draws the disciple's attention to his identity from above. Jesus asks, "what then if you see the Son of Man ascending to where He was before? (v. 62). This appeal to his divine relation with the Father and status from above continues the previous πατήρ statements throughout the bread of life discourse. This suggest that Jesus' disciples were not only having difficulties with Jesus' graphic language, but also with his distinct claim to be in relation to God as his Father.

Scholars recognize that Jesus is again referring to his divine identity and presence with the Father prior to the incarnation and affirmed at the cross.[55] But Wayne Meeks points out that the motif of Jesus ascending and descending from the heavens is one that occurs exclusively to identify Jesus as a stranger amongst the Jewish people.[56] He argues that this theme marks Jesus as the alien from all people of the world, which includes a progressive alienation of Jesus from the Jews.[57] More specifically, it serves to contrast Jesus from his own ethnic Jewish community by uniting his origin with God who is from above. Meeks finds this motif in episodes where the primary point of the story is the inability of the people, including the "Jews," to understand and accept Jesus' identity.[58] Within the bread of life discourse, this situation occurs not only with the Jews, but also with the disciples. That is, Jesus' assertion to have descended from heaven emerges in a situation where both the Jews and his own disciples question his divine relation with the divine Father. Within the context of the bread of life discourse this claim

---

Beasley-Murray also argues that "what profits" nothing is the recognition that the flesh alone, including the crucified body of Jesus, does not achieve the end purpose of God. On the other hand, the life that is given to the world is also bound up with the sending of the Spirit for the union of God and humanity in Christ. See Beasley-Murray, *John*, 96. Keener finds the comparison between the Spirit and flesh aiming to clarify Jesus' metaphorical language. He asserts that it is Jesus' words rather than his literal flesh that communicates life that is promised through bread. See Keener, *John*, 694–95.

55. Brown notices that this response is part of the complaint against Jesus (Brown, *John*, 1:299). Morris agrees that this statement refer to Jesus' preexistence (Morris, *John*, 339–40). See also Barrett, *St. John*, 250; Bultmann, *John*, 445; Lindars, *John*, 273; Keener, *John*, 694.

56. Meeks argues that the "ascent and descent" motif serves as an expression of Jesus' unique self-knowledge, a key to his identity, as well as Jesus' foreignness to humanity. See Meeks "Man from Heaven," 60–68. See also John 1:51; 3:13; 6:33, 38, 41–42, 50–51, 58, 62; 8:14; 9:29; 19:9; 20:17.

57. Meeks, "Man from Heaven," 76–77.

58. Meeks, "Man from Heaven," 66.

emerges at a significant point of contention. That is, both the Jewish crowd and disciples are failing to observe Jesus' divine relation with the Father and his identity as the bread of life. And as we have observed, this is a key point that is challenged with the πατήρ statements throughout the discourse.

How then does this inform our understanding of the Spirit which immediately follows Jesus' statement to ascend to the Father? We must observe that Jesus' need in v. 62 to reaffirm his identity from above reveals that doubts of his relationship with the divine Father had trickled into the internal discourse of the disciples. When Jesus responds with the assertion that the Spirit is a life-giver "ζωοποιέω" and that the flesh has "οὐκ ὠφελεῖ οὐδέν," we must read this in light of Jesus' aim to reorient the disciples' understanding of his kinship relation with their Jewish fathers and his earthly father Joseph. If the disciples resort to Jesus' earthly kinship, they will fail to observe his true origin from above and the honorable status that is communicated to him from the divine Father. In other words, the "flesh" in this context is not material or bodily substance. It refers to human kinship relations that no longer hold sway over Jesus' divine identity. In addition, we notice that in comparison to the life-giving activity of the Spirit, the flesh has only benefited death to its descendants. This statement about the Spirit and flesh is another way of saying that ethnic flesh relations have not privileged anyone in contrast to the life-giving activity of the Spirit. And we certainly know that they have not benefited anyone because their ancestors ate manna and died, a point that Jesus expressively makes throughout the discourse (vv. 49–50, 58).

This reading also contends that we need to consider another way of reading the ambiguous term σάρξ within the dialogue. Within this context, σάρξ does not refer to physical substance, epistemological limitations, or bodily flesh. It refers to an ethnic understanding of kinship. Besides the occurrences of σάρξ within John 6, the term is found within five locations in the Fourth Gospel. It first appears to describe those who are born of God and not from the will of the σάρξ (1:13). This use of σάρξ euphemistically refers to the procreation of human beings from male-female relations. The singular use of σάρξ evokes the imagery of a family with a child, which is distinct from the divine begetting of God's children. And as we have previously reviewed, family language is also ethnic language. The "will of the σάρξ" is the will of ethnic fathers who have power of life and death over their children and thus their descendants.

The second use of the term σάρξ describes the Logos becoming σάρξ and dwelling amongst the early witnesses of Jesus' ministry (1:14). Yet the Logos which became σάρξ is noted to come to his own people, that is, his own ethnic group (1:11). In other words, the incarnation of the Logos is not solely an incarnation of the divine word into a non-ethnic human body. It is an incarnation that includes an understanding of becoming ethnic σὰρξ amongst a particular ethnic group that observed (1:14) and rejected the Logos' entrance into the world (1:11). Σὰρξ in the singular continues to have a broader understanding of male-female kinship relations. Later in 3:3 we hear Jesus describing to Nicodemus that the Spirit gives birth to Spirit, and σὰρξ gives birth to σὰρξ. In this context, σὰρξ is again a euphemistic way of evoking an imagery of biological procreation of ethnic and kinship groups. Another use is found in 8:15 when Jesus responds to the Pharisees who were judging him according to the σὰρξ. This is not to be understood as a judgement based upon Jesus' physical appearance. The Pharisees were challenging Jesus' claim that assumed a divine relation with the Father. They even asked, "where is your father?" (8:19). Eduard Schweizer finds that the people were assessing his identity based upon his genealogy and descendants, a type of judgement according to the σὰρξ which Jesus was rejecting.[59] Within this context, σὰρξ again refers to Jesus' kinship group. It is not solely a human physical body; it includes a corporate understanding of an ethnic σὰρξ. Lastly, the final use of σὰρξ is found in Jesus' prayer for the disciples in 17:2. Within Jesus' prayer to the Father, he asserts that God had given him authority over all σὰρξ. This is not solely a general statement that asserts Jesus' authority over all human beings. It also alludes to the upcoming experience of being crucified by the Romans. This prepares the reader to recognize that although Jesus will undergo Roman execution, his authority over all flesh includes authority over foreigners and their foreign governments.

However, within 6:51–58 σὰρξ indeed refers to the body.[60] But it must be noted that translating "body" in every appearance where σὰρξ is mentioned fails to take into account how the term also evokes a corporate understanding and relation to ethnic kinship. In other words, σὰρξ is not just human flesh or a general anthropological term. It is a term that also includes the wider concept of a flesh rooted in an ethnoracial kinship identity and status. Paul himself utilizes this use of σὰρξ in explaining Jesus' identity as a descendant from David and relation to the Jewish people in Romans 1:3 and 9:5.[61]

---

59. Schweizer, "σὰρξ," *TDNT* 7:138.

60. Menken argues that "flesh and blood" refers to Jesus' crucified flesh and not Eucharistic elements. He also finds that the language does not necessarily point to anti-docetic tendencies. He regards the use of σὰρξ in verse 63, however, as a general anthropological term. See Menken, "John 6:51c–58," 183–204.

61. Paul also describes the Jewish people as his kinsmen according to the σὰρξ (Rom 9:3; 11:14). He likewise describes Israel according to σὰρξ (1 Cor 10:18). In Luke

Like many scholars reviewed, Tricia Brown aptly notices this distinct use of σάρξ within the dialogue.⁶² Although she focuses on the inadequacy of all those in the "realm of the flesh" as incapable of brokering life,⁶³ I, however, contend that this inadequacy also extends to ethnic and kinship groups that define the "realm of the flesh." Within 6:63 σάρξ refers to family relations, ethnic heritage, and ancestral relations which were viewed as the foundation of human life. It is the life-giving activity of the Spirit that is set in contrast to the results of death which comes from all σάρξ relations and to all σάρξ descendants.

The Spirit as a life-giver must also be viewed in light of those who aim to leverage their privileges based upon their ethnic and kinship group, family kinship relations, and heritage. We also notice that the contentious debate on Jesus' identity and relation to the Father first began with the crowd (vv. 2–34), then the Jews (vv. 35–59), and now includes the disciples (vv. 60–66). On the first two occasions, they tried to leverage their ethnic heritage in order to compel Jesus to act. They appealed to the experience of their fathers in order to move Jesus to provide bread from heaven. When this ethnic appeal to their fathers did not work, the Jews focused on Jesus' kinship identity in order to rebuff his divine claims and relation with the divine Father.⁶⁴ The appeal to their ancestors leads Jesus to point out the reality—that their ancestors are dead and are incapable of granting any life-giving sustenance today. Or said another way, it is true that the Jewish fathers ate manna in the wilderness, but this point of pride and attempt to use this ethnic heritage to leverage Jesus to action will fail. No one can leverage God for the benefit of their own ethnic group. Jesus' provision of bread cannot be narrowly leveraged for the benefit for one ethnic group alone because the bread from heaven is food for the entire world.

The Spirit of Life and Benefits of the Flesh

The bread of life discourse begins with a comparison between the living bread that Jesus offers and the perishable food that the Jewish people seek. It is this comparison which leads the crowd to lay claim to their ancestral

---

3:6 and Acts 2:17, σάρξ refers not solely to humanity but rather a humanity that includes distinct ethnoracial corporate identities.

62. Brown, *Spirit in the Writings of John*, 140–41.

63. Brown, *Spirit in the Writings of John*, 149.

64. We can notice this repetitive assertion of Jesus' relation with the Father throughout the dialogue. He informs the crowd (vv. 27, 32), Jews (vv. 37, 40, 44–46, 57), and disciples (vv. 57, 62, 65).

memory of their fathers who ate manna in the wilderness. In response, Jesus reminds them of his relationship with the living Father and the Jewish crowd's relation with their dead fathers. In the bread of life discourse Jesus asserts that he is the "bread of life," a claim that includes the divine relation with the Father. It is this claim that the Jewish crowd rejects because they know the kinship relation that Jesus has with his earthly father—Joseph. Who is Jesus? Is he truly making a claim to have a divine relationship and origin with the Father? The Jewish people grumble because Jesus claims to have come down from heaven (vv. 33, 38, 41–42, 50–51, 58). They challenged him by pointing out that they knew his real father (vv. 41–42). And now, doubt about the identity of Jesus has also spread amongst the disciples who are also grumbling amongst themselves (vv. 60–61). How then do the disciples manage these ancestral claims? Simply put, too much of a focus on rooting one's life and identity to one's ancestors will bring about no added privileges or benefits. The flesh profits nothing.

We therefore can notice that Jesus claims to be in relation to the divine Father, and this is also made in comparison to the benefits of the Jewish people's fathers and Jesus' earthly father named Joseph. Even more, it is in the discourse that the benefits of the "flesh" are revealed to only result in death. How then are we to understand the statement, "the Spirit gives life, the flesh benefits no one" within this context? My reading of σὰρξ does not concern itself with material substance or human body. As I pointed out, σὰρξ is term that encompasses kinship, which within this context refers to the identity, benefits, privileges of their ethnic ancestors. These are privileges that have only resulted in death to their descendants. Even more, presuming that since Jesus had an earthly father name Joseph means that he cannot make the divine claim to be the "bread from heaven" or relation with the divine Father is misguided.

In comparison to the life-giving activity of the Spirit, the flesh's benefits to descendants, that is, kinship status and identity, hold no source of privilege in them. These benefits cannot be utilized to posture oneself, or even place one within a superior position over someone whose ancestry is questionable or unknown. Only the Spirit grants life and is the source of all life—spiritual and physical. The activity of the Spirit as a life-giving force also suggests that earthly kinship status and identity cannot hold sway over the newly birthed people of the Spirit. Ancestral fathers hold no power or authority over the maternal life-giving activity of the Spirit

9

Native Resistance to the Greeks?

JOHN 7:37-39

OUR FINAL EXPLORATION OF THE SPIRIT WITHIN THE PUBLIC ministry of Jesus is found during the Feast of Tabernacles. On the last day of the festival Jesus states,

> If anyone is thirsty, let him come to me and drink.[1] The one who believes in me, as the scripture said, from his innermost being will flow rivers of living water.
>
> Ἐάν τις διψᾷ ἐρχέσθω πρός με καὶ πινέτω. ὁ πιστεύων εἰς ἐμέ, καθὼς εἶπεν ἡ γραφή, ποταμοὶ ἐκ τῆς κοιλίας αὐτοῦ ῥεύσουσιν ὕδατος ζῶντος. (7:37-38)

---

1. The punctuation follows the ASV, ESV, KJV, NIV, NASB, RSV, and P66, P75. This reading differs from the NRSV, NET, NLT, which begins a new sentence at καθώς. The debate over the punctuation centers on whether the phrase "he who believes in me" should be taken with the preceding verse. For a review on the punctuation, see Cortes, "Yet Another Look at John," 79-86, esp. 81-83; Kilpatrick, "Punctuation of John," 340-42. Scholars who support Jesus as the source of the living water propose that the phrase "the one who believes in me" describes the one who comes to Jesus. They punctuate the passage: "If anyone is thirsty, let him come to me and the one who believes in me drink. Just as scripture says, out of [Jesus'] innermost being rivers of living water will flow." Arguments point out that throughout the gospel Jesus is described as the source of living water in 4:14 and 19:34. See Bultmann, *John*, 305; Brown, *John*, 1:320-23; Beasley-Murray, *John*, 115-16; Keener, *John*, 728-30; Burge, *Anointed Community*, 93; Brown, *Spirit in the Writings of John*, 158. Scholars who prefer the traditional punctuation, which views the believer as the source of living water, include Barrett, *St. John*, 271; Lindars, *John*, 301; Morris, *John*, 347, 373-76; Millos, *Juan*, 773-74. Thomas prefers to identify the ambiguity of the text and does not find it impossible that both meanings could be identified. See Thomas, *Spirit of the New Testament*, 164.

In this passage, Jesus invites those who were attending the final day of the festival to approach him in order to receive satisfaction from their thirst. This invitation however was not for literal water. The writer elaborates the meaning of Jesus' statement by clarifying,

> He said this about the Spirit, whom those who believed in him were to receive, for the Spirit was not yet, because Jesus had not been glorified.
>
> τοῦτο δὲ εἶπεν περὶ τοῦ πνεύματος ὃ ἔμελλον λαμβάνειν οἱ πιστεύσαντες εἰς αὐτόν· οὔπω γὰρ ἦν πνεῦμα,[2] ὅτι Ἰησοῦς οὐδέπω ἐδοξάσθη. (7:39)

This statement on the Spirit explains to the reader what Jesus really meant with his invitation. But what specifically does water and Spirit signify within this dialogue? The imagery and relationship of the water and Spirit is attested throughout biblical literature.[3] Bultmann interprets the water imagery as a symbolic representation of an eschatological blessing which anticipates the giving of the Spirit.[4] Brown further adds that the imagery is a symbol of the revelation that Jesus gives to those who believe in him.[5] Morris explains that Jesus takes the water symbolism of the feast and orients it to a proclamation on the satisfaction of the soul in terms of the Spirit. Although he agrees that the living water has its source in Christ, he insists that it also becomes a source for others through the believer.[6] Johnston likewise

---

2. Copyist attempts to make corrections mitigate a possible misreading by adding "δεδομένον" in manuscript B, 1230, it1, b, c, e, vg, syr. Other witnesses such as D* and itd, f add the phrase "ἐπ᾽ αὐτοῖς." See Metzger, *Textual Commentary*, 186.

3. The imagery of Spirit as poured (ἐκχέω) is found in Joel 2:28 [LXX 3:1]; Zech 12:10. The imagery of water (ὕδωρ) and Spirit (πνεῦμα) is mentioned in Neh 9:20; Isa 44:3; Ezek 36:25–27. On water (ὕδωρ) and temple imagery, see Ezek 47:1–12; Joel 3:18 [LXX 4:18]; Zech 13:1; 14:8; Rev 22:1. On echoes of general thirst (διψάω) and drinking (πίνω) imagery, see Ps 42:1–2 [LXX 41:1–2]; Prov 5:15; Isa 29:8; 55:1. The theme of water (ὕδωρ) and salvation or thirst (διψάω) is found in Isa 12:3; 49:10; 58:11. Associations of water, wisdom, or the law is found in Sir 24:30–31; 2 Bar. 77:13–16. Water is also associated with the rock Moses struck in the wilderness in Num 20:8; Deut 8:15; 1 Cor 10:4.

4. Bultmann, *John*, 303–5. Burge's eschatological reading proposes that Jesus viewed himself as the fulfillment of all tabernacles expectations (Burge, *Anointed Community*, 93). See Barrett, *St. John*, 271; Lindars, *John*, 297–301; Keener, *John*, 728–30; Brown, *Spirit in the Writings of John*, 158.

5. Brown, *John*, 1:328; Other readings view Jesus as the rock of the wilderness which provides the water-Spirit. See Beasley-Murray, *John*, 116–17; Badcock, "Feast of Tabernacles," 172; 1 Cor 10:4; Justin, *Dia*. 131; Tertullian, *Adv. Jud*. 13.

6. Morris, *John*, 373–75. Tricia Brown reads the text as a messianic fulfillment but interprets the language in terms of brokering the satisfaction of spiritual thirst (Brown,

views the water-Spirit association in reference to the disciples who become a source of life. He suggests that the divine power of Spirit is expressed in terms of "water inexhaustibly gushing up" within believers in order to continue Jesus' mission.[7]

These various readings aim to reconcile the writer's comments on the Spirit with Jesus' invitation to the thirsty, either in terms of revelation, the fulfillment of an eschatological hope, spiritual satisfaction, or divine power. How we interpret the water-Spirit imagery depends on the biblical texts we assume are echoed within the narrative. In the writer's comments, we also hear for the first time that the Spirit had "not yet been given" because Jesus "had not been glorified" (v. 39). From the writer's perspective, the giving of Spirit is a post-glorification experience.[8] This explanation however creates an inconsistent scenario. Why would Jesus invite the thirsty to drink if the Spirit could only be received after his glorification? Did Jesus' invitation draw an embarrassing non-response from his own ethnic community which led the writer to reinterpret the true meaning of the invitation? Although we find the association of water and Spirit attested throughout biblical literature, we must remember that this association is primarily the writer's interpretation. Without the writer's explanation of Jesus' words, we are left wondering if anyone truly responded to Jesus' invitation. But if the writer aims to compel the reader to think about Jesus' invitation from a post-glorification perspective, this must also include post-glorification readers who, as I argue, are ethnically diverse. In other words, the real question we must ask ourselves is the following: how would the diverse post-glorification ethnic readers in the Johannine community hear the invitation to come and drink? Even more, are there any clues in the narrative that point us to an ethnic audience that is being addressed with this invitation?

This analysis of the Spirit within the public ministry of Jesus will explore how the invitation compels the readers to envision the partaking of the Spirit within the midst of ethnic hostility. From the narrative, we will

---

Spirit in the Writings of John, 152-65).

7. Johnston, *Spirit-Paraclete*, 48. Millos likewise views the believer as the source of living water. He states that they are not "agentes de salvación, pero proclaman la salvación e invitan a los perdidos a creer en Cristo" (Millos, *Juan*, 772-73).

8. Bultmann suggests that the evangelist does not see the Spirit as a special gift, such as speaking in tongues. Instead, the Spirit is another Paraclete who takes Jesus' place (Bultmann, *John*, 304). Dodd finds the conception of the Spirit after the resurrection different from the farewell discourse. He asserts that the insufflation came from a different tradition (Dodd, *Interpretation*, 430). Barrett remarks that this is not to deny the existence of the Spirit nor that the Spirit was active but rather to show that the Holy Spirit was not given in the characteristically Christian manner until the close of the ministry (Barrett, *St. John*, 272).

notice that the invitation is rooted in intra-ethnic Jewish tension and kinship rejection. When Jesus invites the people to come and drink on the last day of the festival, the invitation includes Jesus' openness to receive the Greeks. Second, since this analysis stems from an awareness of a Greek mission, I will also explore the implications of this invitation in light of Greek-Jewish ethnic relations. Lastly, I will incorporate our findings and determine how ethnic Greek readers within the Johannine community would hear this pneumatic language and invitation. We will observe that the giving of the Spirit must be understood as an invitation that is given in spite of ethnic hostility and cross-cultural suspicion. Through this analysis of the narrative, we find that racial resistance and rejection are never impassable boundaries that prohibit the giving of the Spirit.

Ethnic Hostility and Rejection as the Context of the Invitation

The setting of Jesus' invitation to the thirsty is during the Feasts of Tabernacles in Jerusalem (7:2–9). Although the festival's origins are attributed to Abraham in Jubilees (16:21–31),[9] it emerges as a celebration of the Hebrew wilderness experience when they lived in temporary shelters (Lev 23:33–43). Granted that agricultural thanksgiving festivals were practiced by Canaanite pagans, George MacRae does not find enough evidence to attribute the source of the festival to them.[10] We find within the Pentateuch various details about the harvest feast. It lasted for eight days (Lev 23:36), reenacted the wilderness experience through the construction of and dwelling in temporary shelters (Lev 23:42), involved a public reading of the law (Deut 31:10–13), included daily sacrifices (Lev 23:36; Num 29:12–28), and required rest from labor (Lev 23:35). This festival of votive offerings and sacrifices was the most important celebration according to Josephus.[11] It was celebrated in order to remind future generations of the Lord's deliverance of the Hebrews from Egypt.[12] Philo also remarks that the festival provided a time to "remember one's poverty, and in an hour of glory to

---

9. The phrase "set wreaths upon their heads" in Jubilees 16:30 has Hellenistic influence.

10. See Judg 8:33; 9:27; MacRae, "Meaning and Evolution," 251–76, esp. 267.

11. Josephus states, "The Feast of Tabernacles ... was celebrated by the Hebrews as a most holy and most eminent feast" (*Ant.* 8.100).

12. Josephus describes the celebration on the fifteenth day of the seventh month when the "season of the year is changing to winter" (*Ant.* 3.244). The Jewish people would come to the courts of the temple to hear the Torah read by the high priest who stood on a high desk (*Ant.* 3.245; 4.209).

recollect the days of one's disgrace, and at a season of peace to think upon the dangers that are past."[13]

The celebration of this festival continued after the Babylonian exile (Neh 8:13–18).[14] We find the prophet Zechariah warning those who did not celebrate the feast that God would withhold rain from their fields, even if they lived in Egypt or other distant locations (Zech 14:16–19).[15] As MacRae points out, we hear for the first time in Zechariah the association of rain with the festival.[16] Further references to this festival in rabbinic literature enhances our understanding of the water and wine pouring libations. Water was drawn from the pool of Siloam in a golden pitcher and brought to the temple by the priests. The people would follow the priests who drew the water to the entrance of the temple courtyard in celebration (*m. Sukkot* 4:1). This procession was a joyful experience with music and the reading of Isaiah 12:3 which states, "you will joyously draw water from the springs of salvation" (*m. Sukkot* 4:9–10; 5.1).[17]

Although this joyful week-long festival serves as the ceremonial context, Jesus' experience with those in Jerusalem is nowhere near celebratory. The tone of the chapter, as Dodd suggests, is noticeably polemical with

---

13. Philo, *Spec.* 2.208. He also explains that this festival was celebrated in tents because there was either no necessity for remaining in the open air laboring the land, or due to the injuries from the burning of the sun and violence of the rains (*Spec.* 2.206); He also describes the eighth day as a "crowing feast" that brought a fitting conclusion to all the other feasts throughout the year. This additional day was an appropriate conclusion given that the time of the harvest ended (*Spec.* 2.211).

14. Josephus mentions that after the Babylonian exile both Jeshua the high priest and Zerubbabel the governor invited all the exiles to celebrate the Feast of Tabernacles in Jerusalem (*Ant.* 11.75). He describes the festivity occurring at the eastern gate of the temple. They heard Ezra read the laws of Moses (*Ant.* 11.154–57). This festival was also celebrated by the Hasmoneans and their descendants which includes Jonathan the high priest (*Ant.* 13.46), Hyrcanus (*Ant.* 13.241–42), Antigonus (*Ant.* 13.304), Alexander (*Ant.* 13.372), and Aristobulus (*Ant.* 15.50).

15. Keener remarks that the ancient purpose of the water-drawing ritual was to secure rain, given that it was essential for agriculture (Keener, *John*, 723). God was understood as the source of rain and having the power to withhold it because of disobedience (Deut 11:14, 17; 28:12; 1 Sam 12:17; 1 Kgs 8:35–36; Ps 147:8; Jer 5:24; Amos 4:7; Zech 10:1; 14:17–18).

16. MacRae, "Meaning and Evolution," 269.

17. Dodd notes that rabbinic exposition frequently applied Zech 13:1 and Ezek 47:1 to the libation ceremony (Dodd, *Interpretion*, 350). Grigsby points to further rabbinic texts that add a fuller understanding of the celebration. This includes the expectations of rain upon those who are spiritually dry (*Pesiq. Rab.* 52) and the eschatological hope for water flowing from the temple (*t. Sukkah* 3.3–12). See Grigsby, "'If Any Man Thirsts,'" 101–8.

various hostile characters moving in and out of the scenes.[18] Furthermore, we find that the chapter begins and ends in ethnic conflict which includes division within Jesus' own kinship and ethnic community. An overview of the chapter can be visualized according to the following succinct and interconnected episodes:

vv. 1–9	Jesus Rejected by his Ethnic Kin
vv. 10–13	Jesus Secretly Arrives in Jerusalem
vv. 14–24	Jesus Teaches in the Temple
vv. 25–27	The Crowd Debates Jesus' Kinship Origins and Identity
vv. 28–36	Jesus Teaches and Discusses his Departure
vv. 37–39	Jesus Invites the Thirsty
vv. 40–44	The Crowd debates Jesus' Kinship Origin and Identity
vv. 45–53	The Pharisees Debate Jesus' Identity

The chapter begins with the writer explaining that Jesus was intentionally avoiding Judea because his own Jewish people desired to kill him (7:1).[19] This avoidance could not be maintained for long because the Festival of Tabernacles was approaching. As the festival drew near, Jesus' brothers urged him to leave Galilee with his disciples in order to reveal himself to the world (vv. 2–9). This request in v. 4 to leave Galilee and emerge in the "public" (παρρησία) scene was not prompted with Jesus' benefit in mind. The writer explains that they "did not believe in him" and assumed that he wanted to regain his disciples (v. 5).[20] Jesus rejected his family's request and continued to remain in Galilee until they left (v. 9).

When Jesus finally arrives in Jerusalem to celebrate the festival, he did not want his presence known (v. 10). The writer explains that the Jews were looking for him and, in a murmuring (γογγυσμός) fashion, debating

18. Dodd, *Interpretation*, 346. Tensions first emerge with Jesus' brothers (vv. 2–9), crowd (vv. 12–13, 20–24, 31, 40–44), Jews (vv. 1, 11, 15–19, 35–36), Jerusalemites (vv. 25–30), chief priests (vv. 32, 45), Pharisees (vv. 32, 45–53), and officers (vv. 32, 45–46). The various characters demonstrate an escalating tension and division amongst them.

19. The statement "the Jews seek to kill him" (ἐζήτουν αὐτὸν οἱ Ἰουδαῖοι ἀποκτεῖναι) identically parallels 5:18 when Jesus healed a man and considered himself equal to God.

20. In this sense, Galilee must be viewed as a secretive place. Keener points out that like Mary, Jesus' brothers were challenging him to act. However, he notes that they did not believe in him which would have been disconcerting from family members. See Keener, *John*, 704–5. The basis of the taunt, as Lindars suggests, is Jesus' words which occur in Mark 4:22; 10:26; Luke 8:17; 12:12; *Gos. Thom.* 5 (Lindars, *John*, 283).

amongst themselves if he was a good man or leading the people astray (v. 12). Martyn suggests that the phrase "leading the people astray" reflects a legal charge of enticing others to worship foreign gods.[21] These comments may refer to Jesus' previous divine claims, but the writer adds that no one desired to publicly expose themselves as Jesus' defender because there was a "fear of the Jews" (v. 13).[22]

About halfway through the celebration week, Jesus finally makes his presence known to the people by teaching in the temple (vv. 14–31). It is during his teaching that a confrontational dialogue occurs with the Jews. The Jews question the source of his teachings which, as Morris claims, may suggest that they had never heard him speak (v. 15).[23] Jesus appeals to a praxis hermeneutic to defend his teachings. That is, only those who resolve to do the will of God can discern the source of Jesus' teachings (v. 17). He makes it known that they not only fail to know the law, but are also attempting to kill him (vv. 17–19).[24] The Jews find this claim and his accusation absurd. They accuse him to be demonically possessed and ask him to expose those who want to kill him (v. 20). Their desire for clarification does not mollify the tense dialogue. Jesus explains that some seek his death due to a miracle he previously performed on the Sabbath (vv. 21–24).[25] Perhaps some in the crowd were present at that miracle event, or at least aware of Jesus' healing of the paralytic man the last time he was in Jerusalem.

The writer then turns to another group called the "Jerusalemites" (Ἱεροσολυμιτῶν)[26] who were not pilgrims of the festival but native Jews.

---

21. Martyn suggests that this charge against Jesus reflects excommunication experience with the synagogue. See Martyn, *History and Theology*, 80–83. Jesus is called a deceiver in rabbinic literature (*b. Sanh.* 43a; *b. Sotah* 47a). See Deut 13:1–6 [LXX]; Justin, *Dial.* 69.

22. This phrase "fear of the Jews" appears in the gospel for the first time. It emerges later in 9:22; 19:38; 20:19. Ashton notes that the phrase "the Jews" has a religious component and adversarial function throughout the gospel. See Ashton, *Understanding*, 67–68.

23. Morris, *John*, 359.

24. Scholars find Jesus is distancing himself from the Jews with the phrase "did not Moses give to you (ὑμῖν)." They believe this expression to be historically unlikely but reflective of a later debate between the church and synagogue. See Barrett, *St. John*, 263; Brown, *John*, 1:312. The use of ὑμῖν also echoes ὑμετέρῳ in 8:17 and ὑμῶν in 10:34.

25. Jesus is alluding to 5:2–9, when he healed a man who was paralyzed for thirty-eight years. Jesus was criticized by the Jews who saw the healed man carry his mat on the Sabbath (vv. 10–16). The writer explains that the Jews sought to kill Jesus for violating the Sabbath and calling God his equal (v. 18).

26. This rare term is found only here in the Fourth Gospel and in Mark 1:5; 4 Macc 4:22; 18:5; Sir 50:27. Beasley-Murray contends that these "Jerusalemites" were inhabitants of Jerusalem who would have been better informed about the hostile intentions of

They identify Jesus and recognize that his public appearance was placing his life in danger (vv. 25–27). Yet for these Jerusalemites, his ethnic kinship was on their minds. Although they question amongst themselves whether Jesus was truly the Messiah, they conclude that since they know where he is from, he could not possibly be the expected one. They assume that the Messiah's origins would be a mystery (v. 27).[27] Following their discussion, Jesus continues to teach in temple and responds to the rumors about his kinship (vv. 28–29). This time, he informs them that they do not know his origin because they do not know who sent him. The crowd immediately reacts by attempting to arrest him (v. 30). Although they fail, we also find that some actually believe in him, and the Pharisees who overhear the discussion respond by sending officers to arrest Jesus (vv. 31–32).

In the midst of this escalating drama and grave threats, Jesus explains that he will no longer be present (vv. 33–34). The Jews are confused with his statement. Some interpret Jesus' claim as a desire to go amongst the dispersion (τὴν διασπορὰν τῶν Ἑλλήνων) and teach the Greeks.[28] They are unaware of what he means about "going to a place where they cannot find him" and wonder why he would venture to another region (vv. 35–36). But why would some assume that Jesus is leaving to the Greeks when he discusses his departure? What could have prompted their assumption that a Jew would desire to travel to a Greek region?

Dodd explains that when we examine Jesus' experience during the Feast of Tabernacles there is a "vivid impression of the constant presence, and urgency of the opposition."[29] The narrative reveals to the reader that Jesus' life was in danger with circumstances occurring in the background

---

the Sanhedrin (Beasley-Murray, *John*, 110).

27. Although Jesus was known to be from Nazareth (1:45; 18:5, 7; 19:19), the messianic secret of the Synoptic tradition is also within the gospel. Barrett points out that the messiahship of Jesus was both hidden and revealed, which differs from the Markan perspective (Barrett, *St. John*, 59). Lindars notes that one strand in the Jewish messianic expectations was that Messiah's origins would be unknown (Lindars, *John*, 293). Keener, however, finds that this contradicts known tradition of the Messiah's origins in Bethlehem (Keener, *John*, 718). For possible origin of the secret messiah tradition, see Justin, *Dial.* 8.4; 110.1; *1 En.* 48:6; 62:7; *2 Esd* 13:52. Other passages that point to the sudden appearance of the Messiah include Dan 9:25; Mal 3:1; *4 Ezra* 7:28; 13:32; *2 Bar.* 29:3.

28. The Ἕλλην are not Greek speaking Jews. They are ethnic Greeks which may include proselytes as we find in John 12:20 and Acts 17:4. Greek-speaking Jews are described as Ἑλληνιστής (Acts 6:1; 9:29; 11:20). In Acts, the Greeks are placed in comparison to the Jews in 14:1; 16:1, 3; 17:4; 18:4; 19:10, 17; 20:21; 21:28. See also Paul's juxtaposing of Jews and Greeks in Rom 1:16; 2:9, 10; 3:9; 10:12; 1 Cor 1:22, 24; 10:32; 12:13; Gal 3:28; Col 3:11.

29. Dodd, *Interpretation*, 346; Beasley-Murray, *John*, 104.

of the narrative. Thus far, Jesus' journey is motivated in part by the looming threat of death from his own ethnic community. The scene begins with the writer informing the reader that the Jesus did not want to go to Judea because the Jews were plotting his death (v. 1). While in Galilee, Jesus' unbelieving brothers taunt his reclusive presence (v. 5). They assume that Jesus needs to reveal himself, ironically, to the broader ethnic world (v. 7). Although Jesus desires to remain in safety (vv. 1–9), he eventually ventures to Jerusalem on his own terms (vv. 5, 8). While in the temple, the readers are made aware that other Jews are talking about him with trepidation (vv. 10–13). Some believe in him, while others think he is a threat to the worship of God. Regardless of this hazardous environment, Jesus boldly reveals himself to the public by teaching in the temple, knowing that this appearance would put his life in danger (vv. 14–24). This disclosure generates a fierce reaction from the Jews. They question the source of his teaching (v. 15), plot his death (v. 19), become angry with him (v. 23), question his ethnic kinship (v. 27), and attempt to apprehend him (v. 30). All the while, the threat of his life continues while his own ethnic religious leaders devise a plan to arrest him (vv. 32, 45–46).

Ethnic hostility and kinship rejection permeate the dialogue and context of the Feast of Tabernacles. This was supposed to be a celebratory week. But for Jesus, going to Jerusalem had only accelerated his imminent death and fomented a rejection from his own ethnic community. Those within the narrative who hear Jesus' statement recognize that in light of the various rumors about his teaching, origin, and awareness of a desire to kill him, leaving Jerusalem for the Greeks seems like a possible safe alternative. For the readers of the narrative, they become aware that Jesus' own ethnic community in Jerusalem had turned against him. Jesus' own ethnic kin in Galilee had also rejected him. Jesus' option is either to remain in Jerusalem and die, or leave for another ethnic community and region, which ironically would fulfill the brothers' request to "reveal himself to the world" (v. 4).

We can thus notice why Jesus' enigmatic statement about "going away" would lead the Jews to wonder if Jesus intends to teach the Greeks in the diaspora (v. 35). Venturing to the diaspora to teach the Greeks would be the safest route given the constant threat and attempt to arrest Jesus. However, these questions that the Jews present are left unanswered. Jesus does not clarify the confusion caused by his words even though he has no problem doing so on other occasions.[30] Although we later find in the narrative what

---

30. Jesus had previously responded to murmurings in the crowd (vv. 15–17) and defended his own origins (vv. 25–29). Jesus also interjected himself into conversations in order to clarify statements or murmurings. In John 4:33, the disciples wondered amongst each other if someone brought Jesus food. He interrupts their discussion and

Jesus meant (16:28), Bultmann hears within the Jewish response an element of irony which becomes a prophetic reference to the later Christian mission.[31] Scholars rightly notice the prophetic irony within the Jewish crowd's statement. This accusation to venture into Greek regions does not make sense when we observe the overall plot of the gospel, especially for a Johannine Jesus who never traverses in Gentile regions.[32] But for irony to succeed, as Gail O'Day contends, the writer must establish a relationship with the audience and share some knowledge or perceptions.[33] That is, the readers of the dialogue must find the real meaning of the statement in and through the expressed meaning, not removed from it.[34] This suggests that they would neither dismiss the Jewish charge that Jesus intends to go to the Greeks nor fail to observe Jesus' refusal to clarify the record. The ironic statement is successful because although the readers know that Jesus does not end up going to the Greeks within his public ministry, he is doing so through the Johannine community and their openness to receive them.

Greek-Jewish Ethnic Relations

What then are the implications in knowing that a Jewish teacher such as Jesus has an openness to teach the Greeks? How would a Greek audience perceive Jesus' silence when he is accused of desiring to venture into their region? When we explore the relations between Jews and Greeks, the experiences range from amicable and mutual interest to hostile and violent

---

explains what he meant by "food" (v. 34). In 6:43 Jesus responds to the grumbling of the Jews who were debating his origin and meaning of his statements (vv. 41–42). In 6:61, Jesus becomes aware of his disciples' misunderstanding and clarifies his teaching (vv. 62–65). Later, in 16:17–18, the disciples are puzzled by his comments about "going away," but Jesus explains in vv. 19–28.

31. Bultmann suggests that, like Caiaphas, they unwittingly prophecy the future activity among the Mediterranean (Bultmann, *John*, 309). See Barrett, *St. John*, 269; Lindars, *John*, 296; Beasley-Murray, *John*, 11–113; Keener, *John*, 721; Millos, *Juan*, 767. Brown suggests that the Jews thought Jesus would find a better hearing among Gentiles (Brown, *John*, 1:314). Morris proposes that they may believe Jesus wanted to go to the Jewish synagogues as a springboard for a Greek mission (Morris, *John*, 371).

32. Unlike the Synoptics, Jesus does not venture into Gentile regions but mostly remains in Galilee and Jerusalem. Segovia notices that Jesus' public life revolves around Jerusalem in four major cycles (1:19–3:36; 4:1–5:47; 6:1–10:42; 11:1–17:26). Jesus' journey fluctuates between Jerusalem and Galilee (1:35–2:12; 4:1–3, 43–54; 6:1–7:9), Bethany (1:19–34; 11:1–12:12), and Samaria (4:4–42). See Segovia, "Journey(s) of the Word," 23–54; "Gospel of John," 156–93, esp. 174–93.

33. O'Day, *Revelation*, 29.

34. O'Day, *Revelation*, 8.

encounters. Radin explains the source of the hostile relationship in terms of impiety. The Jews were a living reminder that their presence was a danger to the state, given that they received exemptions from participating in the cultic life of the city.³⁵ In the second century, the Greek orator Aelius Aristides in Asia Minor charges the Jews with impiety for not worshipping the gods. He accuses them of this impious behavior and claims that they have "seceded from the Greeks" and all the "better people."³⁶ This is not to suggest that the Greeks believed the Jews did not worship any gods at all. Mnaseas of Patara, another Greek historian, suggests that the Jews worshipped a donkey. This account is cited by Josephus in his response to Apion who retells an incident in which an Idumaean entered into the temple and stole a golden head of a donkey.³⁷ Josephus also notices Apion's claim that Antiochus Epiphanes found the head of a donkey within the Jewish temple.³⁸ The donkey is not the only animal that the Greeks assumed the Jews worshipped. Plutarch assumes that the Jews do not eat pigs because pigs taught them how to cultivate the land.³⁹ Although Plutarch recognizes that various people worship different gods, the assumption behind these suspicions is that the Jews were truly animal worshippers. Indeed, Schäfer regards these stories as anti-Jewish legends which were an expression of hostility that aimed to depreciate them in the eyes of Egyptians and Greeks.⁴⁰

Sherwin-White also recognizes that the Greeks participated in hostile suppression of Jewish rights. He finds Greek racial prejudice exhibited toward the Jews at full strength in certain Greek cities of the eastern provinces.⁴¹ Similar to Radin's observations, he concludes that the source of the dislike was due to the Jewish community's refusal of the Greek life.⁴² The Jews were known for their exclusive behaviors in the ancient world. Isaac also contends that the main objection against them was that they were

35. Radin, *Jews Among*, 163–65.
36. Aelius, *Ora.* 46.
37. Josephus, *Ag. Ap.* 2.112–13.
38. Josephus, *Ag. Ap.* 2.80. Also found in Tacitus, who claims that "Moses introduced new religious practices, quite opposed to those of all other religions. The Jews regard as profane all that we hold sacred; on the other hand, they permit all that we abhor. They dedicated, in a shrine, a statue of that creature whose guidance enabled them to put an end to their wandering and thirst (donkey), sacrificing a ram, apparently in derision of Ammon" (*His.* 5.4.2).
39. Plutarch, *Quaest. conv.* 4.4–5.3.
40. Schäfer, *Judeophobia*, 57–58.
41. Sherwin-White, *Racial Prejudice in Imperial Rome*, 86. See especially Josephus, *Ant.* 14.213–16, 14.244–46; 14.259–64; 16.172; 19.278; 19.284–91.
42. Sherwin-White, *Racial Prejudice in Imperial Rome*, 87–91.

perceived as anti-social.[43] This practice, as Isaac identifies, was akin to barbarianism, especially since the Jews lived among civilized people and would not share meals with non-Jews.[44]

One of the earliest Greek records of Jewish anti-social behavior is preserved by Diodorus of Sicily. He retells the encounter of the Greeks with the Jews in the siege of Jerusalem by Antiochus Epiphanes. In one instance, Antiochus's advisors claimed that the Jews should become ethnically eradicated because "they alone avoid dealings with all nations and looked upon them as their enemies."[45] These advisors explain the origins of Jewish anti-social behavior by tracing the practice to their exile experience in Egypt.[46] Diodorus claims that in the Jewish state's early formation they turned their "hatred of mankind into a tradition." Diodorus points to Moses and the "leprous" experiences in Egypt as the origins of Jewish misanthropic customs. He credits Moses as the founding figure who "introduced a most unsocial and intolerable mode of life."[47] He also views Antiochus as a liberator who attempted to incorporate the Jews into the civilized Greek world. Diodorus states that Antiochus attempted to force the Jews to change their ways but failed to help them become more civilized.[48] This Greek view of Jewish history and antisocial behavior explains the rationale of their peculiar customs and lack of social interaction.

Another Greek critic was Apollonius Molon who was a rhetorician in Rhodes. He likewise condemned the Jews for holding anti-social practices. According to Josephus, he claims that the Jews refuse "admission to persons with other preconceived ideas about God, and for declining to associate with those who have chosen to adopt a different mode of life."[49] Another Greek sophist of the Roman era was Philostratus. He details the constant trouble that the Romans had with the Jews, even suggesting that it was impossible to change their ways. He states that the Jews

> have long been in revolt not only against the Romans but against humanity; and a race that has made its own life apart

---

43. Isaac, *Invention of Racism*, 479.

44. Isaac, *Invention of Racism*, 479.

45. Diodorus, 34.1.

46. Diodorus, 34.1. Diodorus later recounts the history of the Jews from Hecataeus of Abdera who has a more positive perspective (40.3.1–2).

47. Diodorus, 34.1.3. Josephus attempts to rebuttal this charge by pointing out that the Jews admit foreigners and do not expel them, which should be a testimony to their humanity (*Ag. Ap.* 2.258–261).

48. Diodorus, 34.1.3–5.

49. Josephus, *Ag. Ap.* 2.58.

and irreconcilable, that cannot share with the rest of mankind in the pleasures of the table nor join in their libations or prayers or sacrifices, are separated from ourselves by a greater gulf than divides us from Susa or Bactra or the more distant Indies. What sense then or reason was there in chastising them for revolting from us, whom we had better have never annexed? (*Vit. Apoll.* 5.33)

While these views emerge from Greek writers, we also find that they reflect Roman thought.[50] The Jews were widely known for separating themselves from non-Jews, a practice viewed as a form of Greek social hatred.

These misanthropic charges led Josephus to respond to Apion's claims that the Jews swore an oath "to show no good will to a single alien, above all to Greeks."[51] In fact, Josephus emphatically defends the Jewish view of the Greeks. He states,

> We neither hate nor envy them. On the contrary, many of them have agreed to adopt our laws, of whom some have remained faithful, while others, lacking the necessary endurance, have again seceded. (*Ag. Ap.* 2.123–24)

The Jews certainly had social problems with the Greeks. The relationship was at times rancorous. And out of all the ethnic communities in the ancient world, only the Greeks are rumored to be annually murdered within the Jerusalem temple.[52]

Even though the Greeks express disaffected views, this did not suggest that all interactions reflected such experience. There were also positive experiences and perceptions between the two ethnic communities. Although it is difficult to pin down the first encounter between Greeks and Jews, we know that since the time of Herodotus the Greeks were aware of Jewish

50. We later find Tacitus, a Roman historian, also agreeing that Antiochus of Epiphanies wanted to improve the Jewish people as a civilization. Tacitus remarks, "The Jews are extremely loyal toward one another, and always ready to show compassion, but toward every other people they feel only hate and enmity" (*Hist.* 5.5.1; 5.8). Pompeius Trogus, a Roman historian from Gaul, is quoted by Justin saying, "They remembered that they had been driven from Egypt for fear of spreading infection, they took care, in order that they might not become odious, from the same cause, to the inhabitants of the country, to have no communication with strangers; a rule which, from having been adopted on that particular occasion, gradually became a custom and part of their religion" (*Epit.* 36.2).

51. Josephus, *Ag. Ap.* 2.121.

52. Josephus, *Ag. Ap.* 2.91–96. Damocritus also states, "On the Jews; in which [latter] he says that they used to bow down to the golden head of an ass, and every seven years hunted a stranger and attacked him and tore his flesh into thin strips and thus killed him" (Δαμόκριτος, *Suda*).

presence in the east. Herodotus mistakes them for "Syrian Palestinians" when he describes them as a group of people who learned the custom of circumcision from the Egyptians.[53] We also discover in Josephus's writings further testimony of contact and Greek admiration. Josephus believes that the Greeks were acquainted and utilized Jewish writings in their works.[54] This includes Pythagoras, a man "ranked above all the philosophers," who was an admirer of Jewish institutions.[55] Josephus even submits that Pythagoras "introduced many points of Jewish law into his philosophy."[56] From Josephus's perspective, the Greeks were not only acquainted with the Jews but also had cross-cultural interactions that were beneficial.

Josephus also retells an encounter between Aristotle and a Jewish man. In this encounter, Aristotle states,

> There were features in that man's character, at once strangely marvelous and philosophical, which merit description. . . . The man was a Jew of Coele-Syria. These people are descendants from the Indian philosophers. The philosophers they say are in India called Calani, in Syria by the territorial name of Jews, for the district which they inhabit is known as Judea. Their city has a remarkable odd name, they call it Hierusaleme. Now this man, who was entertained by a large circle of friends and was on his way down from the interior to the coast, not only spoke Greek but had the soul of a Greek. During my stay in Asia, he visited the same places as I did, and came to converse with me and some other scholars, to test our learning. But as one who had been intimate with many cultivated persons, it was rather he who imparted to us something of his own. (*Ag. Ap.* 1.177–81)

From Aristotle's perspective, the Jews were considered descendants of philosophers. The Jewish man he encounters had the soul of a Greek and was bilingual. He not only impressed Aristotle but is described in such a way that his identity was reflective of a Greek identity. This esteemed view of the Jews as philosophers is also found in Porphyry who quotes a disciple of Aristotle named Theophrastus. Although Theophrastus criticizes the Jews for their cultic sacrifices and mistakenly believes that they sacrifice humans, he nonetheless describes them as, "a race of philosophers [who] converse with

---

53. Herodotus, 2.104.

54. Josephus, *Ag. Ap.* 1.161.

55. Josephus, *Ag. Ap.* 1.162–63; Porphyry also quotes Antonius Diogenes, who claims that Pythagoras borrowed his knowledge of dreams from the Jews (*Vit. Pyth.* 1.11).

56. Josephus, *Ag. Ap.* 1.165–66.

each other about divinity, and during the night they view the stars, turning their eyes to them and invoking God with prayers."[57] And although we find Hecataeus of Abdera describing the Jews as antisocial, we must point out that he also praises Moses for his outstanding wisdom and courage.[58]

The Jewish people are portrayed as having an esteemed intellectual honor in the writings of Aristotle, Porphyry, and others. The Greeks recognized the Jews for their intellectual wisdom that was comparable to Greek philosophy. Some writers also admit that Greek philosophy was dependent upon, or at least consulted, the Jewish intellectual tradition. Erich Gruen in fact argues that the Greeks were comfortable in ascribing to Jews conceptualizations that coincided with their own and including them within the Greek philosophical tradition.[59] He suggests that the mutual appropriations of cultures between the Jews and Greeks was not a diminution of their identity but an enhancement of it.[60] The claim that the Jews were to be regarded along the same philosophical intellectual heritage would have been an acclamation for the Jewish people who lived amongst the Greeks in the Roman world. This also further points out that relationship was not always hostile. We do find elements of mutual interest and openness to share and gain wisdom from one another.

Rereading the Invitation to Receive the Spirit through Greek Eyes

John Collins reminds us that the Jews in the diaspora setting were not reluctant exiles but open to Hellenistic influences and culture, and aspired to gain respect from the Greeks.[61] This Jewish openness to Greek culture does not suggest that resistance and tensions were absent. In the history of Greek-Jewish relations, we find ethnic hostility and ethnic admiration alongside one another. Collins admits that Judaism appeared as a strange religion and they experienced occasional hostility due to social tensions and the distinctiveness of the Jewish religion.[62] Yet Collins points out that the conflicting tensions between positive and negative estimations of Judaism led to some

57. Porphyry, *Abst.* 2.26.
58. Diodorus, 40.3. See also Hecataeus's remarks about a Jewish solider, named Mosollamus, who accompanied Alexander the Great. He is described as intelligent, robust, and a good bowman (Josephus, *Ag. Ap.* 1.200–204).
59. Gruen, *Rethinking the Other*, 314.
60. Gruen, *Rethinking the Other*, 325.
61. Collins, *Between Athens and Jerusalem*, 5.
62. Collins, *Between Athens and Jerusalem*, 8–12.

measure of accommodation and acculturation.[63] Ethnic boundaries were certainly crossed in the diaspora setting. When these dividing walls were traversed there was a sharing of intellectual capital and improved relations. This shows us that regardless of suspicious views, ethnic boundaries were not impassible. And while ethnic suspicion and seclusion developed, ethnic understanding and appreciation also emerged.

When this ethnic context of Greek-Jewish relations is applied to vv. 33–36, the charge that Jesus desired to "go to the Greeks" could have been viewed in at least two ways. The Jewish crowd realizes that this would be the one place where Jesus could hide from the looming threat of death. Where else could Jesus go and not be found by the Jews if not amongst the Greeks, a place where Jerusalem Jews would neither dare to venture nor seek him out? But from another perspective, this also could have been viewed as an opportunity for Jesus as a "Jewish philosopher" to share wisdom with hospitable Greeks. In the midst of an ethnically hostile context, Jesus entertains the embrace of Greek pupils by failing to clarify the record. The Jerusalem Jews are left in suspense, wondering if his statement of going to a place where he could not be found is an enigmatic way of hiding from them. In Jesus' reticence, we implicitly find that he is not like others who express non-association with Greeks. Jesus is ethnically open to reach the Greeks and does not mind being accused of venturing to them.

Then on the final day of the festival Jesus states, "If anyone (τις) is thirsty, let him come to me and drink. The one who believes in me, as the scripture said, from his innermost being will flow rivers of living water (v. 37)." The call for "τις" to approach him on this final day of the festival must be read within the context of intra-Jewish conflict and Jewish-Greek relations. The previous day Jesus had insisted that no one would be able to "come" (ἐλθεῖν) to him (v. 34) and the Jews wondered what he meant by his "ἐλθεῖν" statement (v. 36). Then on the following day, after failing to clarify what he meant about not being found, he now opens the invitation for anyone who thirsts to "come" (ἐρχέσθω) to him (v. 37).[64] This "anyone" includes any person from within Jesus' own ethnic community and potential Greek pupils who are also perceived as being Jesus' new mission. We are unaware if anyone actually does take Jesus' offer. The Jews react and question the implications of his statements on messianic and prophetic terms (vv. 40–44). And like Jesus' previous statement about leaving, they are also unaware of what he means about approaching him if they are thirsty.

63. Collins, *Between Athens and Jerusalem*, 25.

64. Daise notes that the use of ἔρχομαι in John 7:37 is likely a narrative carryover of a theme begun in the immediately preceding passage of 7:33–36. See Daise, "If Anyone Thirsts," 687–99.

Yet between Jesus' invitation to approach him and the reaction of the Jews, there lies the writer's interpretation of Jesus' words. The writer explains, "He said this about the Spirit, whom those who believed in him were to receive, for the Spirit was not yet, because Jesus had not been glorified" (v. 39). As mentioned earlier, why would Jesus invite the thirsty to drink if the Spirit could only be received after his glorification? Jesus' invitation certainly cannot be understood from the perspective of the characters in the narrative. They struggle to find the meaning of Jesus' statement because they are confounded by his kinship origins and possible desire to go to the Greeks. We notice that the invitation is only properly realized from the perspective of the readers who live in a post-glorification period. Only they find the true meaning of Jesus' invitation through the writer's comments. And this meaning is cradled within a context of ethnic boundary crossing and the mounting pressure of ethnic hostility and rejection from one's own kin. These ethnic aspects are easily discernable to the diaspora readers, because as ethnic members within the Johannine community, they too are familiar with the hostility and amicability that abounds between Greeks and Jews. As listeners of Jesus' words, observers of the ironic charge of going to the Greeks, and with the writer's explanation, they actually become the real people Jesus is inviting to come to him. What then does Jesus' statement on the Spirit mean for these ethnic readers?

Notwithstanding, whether the source of the living water emerges from within the believer or from within Jesus' own being, the promise still stands. Jesus invites the parched of the land to be refreshed by approaching him with faith. These soon to be satisfied ones are assured with a boundless supply of water, which the writer interprets in terms of the Spirit. Although there is no direct source to the scriptural reference, there are at least three possible scriptural themes or catchwords[65] that Jesus utilizes in describing the giving of the Spirit. The first possible allusion is Exodus 17:1–6 when the Hebrews were in the desert and grumbled over the lack of water.[66] They voraciously complained and threatened to kill Moses. In response, God instructs Moses to strike the rock at Horeb with his staff. Water flowed from the rock in the presence of all the people which mitigated the death threat. This divine intervention is described in Psalm 78:15–16 [LXX 77:15–16][67] and 105:41 [LXX 104:41] as God giving the people abundant water like streams running down like a river. Although Brown recognizes the possible

65. For an review on John's use of scripture, see Williams, "John, Judaism," 77–100.
66. Also found in 1 Cor 10:4.
67. Menken argues that the source of the quotation is Psalms 78:15 [LXX 77:15]. He suggests that κοιλίας in verse 38 is a substitute of the πέτρα that gushed out water in the wilderness. See Menken, "Origin of the Old Testament," 160–75.

temple imagery, he also points out that it closely echoes the desert wandering experience. He finds that just as the manna given to their ancestors was not the real bread, so the water from the rock that Moses struck was only a foreshadowing of the true water of life that flows from the Lamb.[68] As the readers will observe later in the narrative, water and blood emerge from Jesus' side when the Romans strike him with a spear in 19:34. Applied to the gospel's context, Jesus' call to all those who are thirsty would resonate with the wilderness theme of the festival and the pending death that was being plotted by his own ethnic kin. In addition, the readers would find in Jesus' experience a similar rejection motif that Moses encountered with his own people. This demonstrates to the readers that the opportunity to receive the Spirit is never abolished through ethnic divisions and hostilities. Even in the midst of intra-Jewish conflict or ethnic suspicion, partaking the Spirit is an invitation that Jesus opens to all, including those who are ethnically suspicious of others.

The second allusion is found in prophetic literature which associates the water imagery with the temple in the eschatological age. In Ezekiel 47:1–12 the prophet is presented with a vision of the temple with water flowing from its foundation and bringing life to all the creatures within its water, nourishing the vegetation of the land, and filling the oceans. The water flowing from the temple indiscriminately gives life to the earth. This water-temple imagery also emerges in Zechariah 14:8 and Joel 3:18. Similar to Ezekiel, these prophetic passages also describe water flowing from the temple to different parts of the world.[69] Bultmann finds in this literary echo the notion that Jesus is putting an end to the Jewish cult, including the ceremonial water libation that occurred during the festival.[70] But these prophetic passages hold an ethnocentric view of Jerusalem as the center of God's flowing water.[71] As Barrett points out, the Johannine reference trans-

---

68. Brown, *John*, 1:327. Tricia Brown also suggests that in the festive context where the Israelites are celebrating and recalling Moses' water miracle, Jesus sets himself as the replacement of Moses and the fulfillment of Israel's thirst and longing (Brown, *Spirit in the Writing of John*, 164).

69. Freed remarks that in post-exilic and rabbinic Judaism, Jerusalem was thought of as the center of the earth and held an eschatological expectation that a great stream of water would flow from the temple and bless the land. See Freed, *Old Testament Quotations*, 28–30.

70. Bultmann, *John*, 304–6. See also Beasley-Murray, *John*, 116; Lindars, *John*, 301; Burge, *Anointed Community*, 93; Keener, *John*, 730; Greene, "Integrating Interpretations," 333–53. Millos perceives the temple imagery in the background but holds the believer as the source of the living water (Millos, *Juan*, 773–74).

71. Jerusalem is viewed as the navel of the earth according to *Jub.* 8:19; Ezek 38:12; *B. Sahn.* 37a.

fers the fulfillment of the prophecy from a temple in the city to a person.[72] The hope for water flowing from the temple is subverted with the claim that the Spirit will come upon all who dwell in various lands. The Spirit does not erupt from a Jerusalem temple but from within various ethnic people who have faith in Jesus. For the ethnic readers in the diaspora who hold no legitimate claim or access to the Jewish temple, they now become the center of God's overflowing Spirit. In a sense, anyone who approaches Jesus, including Greeks, become what Millos describes as the "santuario de Dios."[73] No temple is sufficient to contain the erupting wells of the Spirit that burst upon ethnic people who dwell in various geographical locations throughout the empire.

Finally, the invitation to the thirsty echoes the salvific promises of the prophet Isaiah. The redeemed draw water from the spring of salvation with joy (12:3).[74] The prophet reminds the people that they will no longer thirst, because God will lead them to springs of water (49:10). Isaiah also has a similar invitation to the thirsty who lack the resources to become nourished (55:1). Drinking water and experiencing a satisfaction from thirst physically expresses the reception of God's salvation and restoration. This water-Spirit imagery is also noted to be poured upon thirsty and dry lands (44:3). As such, Morris suggests that Jesus' statement takes the water symbolism of the feast, hope for rain, and bodily needs, in order to turn their attention to the deep need of the soul.[75] Thus, when Jesus cries out if "anyone" was thirsty, his invitation assumes that people in an arid condition were deeply in need of the Spirit. Yet those who thirst and live within a barren land are no longer assumed to be solely the Jews in exile or Jews in Jerusalem. The invitation given to all who hear includes the Jews and Greeks who live in the ethnically hostile parched lands of racial suspicion. But most of all, it also includes those who await the coming nourishment of the Spirit that would bring an end to the fear and trepidation of ethnic association and crossing of boundaries.

---

72. Barrett, *St. John*, 271.

73. Millos, *Juan*, 774.

74. Marcus proposes that the image of drawing water from Isaiah 12:3 was taken over by John and reinterpreted it in a Christological manner. See Marcus, "Rivers of Living Water," 328–30.

75. Morris, *John*, 373.

Overcoming Ethnic Suspicion through the Spirit

As we can observe above, there are various interpretations of Jesus' statement on the Spirit. Yet these allusions are not merely echoed, they are transposed for a new ethnic audience that understands the struggles and challenges between Greeks and Jews. The ethnic readers would associate Jesus' statement on the Spirit in light of their own diaspora region and race relations. The giving of the Spirit is akin to the water that delivered Moses from an intra-ethnic confrontation. The Spirit subverts an ethnocentric, eschatological temple in exchange for an indiscriminate flowing of the Spirit in all parts of the world. And finally, the language reflects images of God's satisfying salvation through the pouring of the Spirit upon anyone living in lands that suffer from ethnic hostility and spiritual drought. Jesus draws upon a multitude of water metaphors, and the writer reinterprets these historic images of intra-ethnic tension, ethnocentric temples, and hope for renewal in terms of the Spirit.

This chapter begins with kinship rejection in Galilee and concludes with the religious leaders debating Jesus' identity in Jerusalem. The invitation to receive the Spirit is spoken in a context of ethnic suspicion and outreach. What prompted the invitation to receive the Spirit was the charge that Jesus would dare to venture to the Greeks in the diaspora. Within Jesus' enigmatic invitation for the thirsty, the writer reconfigures a Jewish understanding and expectations of water with the giving of the Spirit to any person, including non-ethnic Jews. Jesus' invitation to the thirsty is a kaleidoscope of multifarious images that embraces the assumption that the Spirit will indiscriminately flow within people who dare to approach Jesus. While the water-Spirit imagery may allude to various scriptural themes, our reading includes another contextual dynamic: the recognition that the dialogue is ethnically hostile and that the true interpreters of Jesus' invitation include ethnic readers—especially Greeks. We can detect this possible reading because the context includes the accusation that Jesus desires to flee to the Greeks. Jesus' inability to clarify this misunderstanding has major implications for the readers who hear this dialogue within their diaspora context. And since Jesus does not refuse this Greek outreach, this also provides a justification for the Johannine community's mission which inhabits the diaspora of Asia.

PART III

Ethnicity and the Spirit-Παράκλητος in the Farewell Discourse and Conclusion of the Gospel

10

Discussion on Παράκλητος and Πνεῦμα τῆς Ἀληθείας in the Farewell Discourse

THE FOURTH GOSPEL DOES NOT LIMIT ITS PNEUMATOLOGICAL language to the term πνεῦμα. We find further language παράκλητος to describe the Spirit in key passages of the Farewell Discourse (14:16, 26; 15:26; 16:7) and Johannine letter (1 John 2:1). Scholars notice the difficulties in translating the term παράκλητος.[1] Otto Betz remarks that the term originates from a forensic context, even though it is not akin to the Latin *advocatus*.[2] Kenneth Grayston notices that παράκλητος is often translated as an advocate, helper, or counselor, and appears in a legal context. He insists that it is to be understood as a supporter or sponsor.[3] Grayston suggests that since the term is not used in reference to a legal title or official, the forensic meaning should be dismissed.[4] Frederick Harm observes that παράκλητος is used to describe an advocate in a court of law, an intercessor or defender, and a person who pleads another's cause. He, however, does not find that this meaning is crucial to the gospel's perspective of the Spirit and prefers to explore how παράκλητος throughout the gospel is characterized as a

---

1. For example, the NRSV, NET, NLT, and NAB translate the term as "advocate." The NASB, NKJ, and ESV prefer "helper." The NIV and CSB translate παράκλητος as "counselor." The NJB prefers the transliteration "Paraclete," although the term is not an English word.

2. Betz, *Der Paraklet*, 1. He insists that it "stammt aus der forensischen Sphäre" and is in reference to "den herbeigerufenen, Mann, der vor dem Richter für den Angeklagten spricht, den Fürsprecher, den Anwalt."

3. Grayston, "Parakletos," 82.

4. Grayston, "Parakletos," 71. See Dionysius of Halicarnassus, *Anti rom.* 11.37.1.

helper, teacher, witness, and judge.⁵ Although Grayston and Harm explore non-forensic and literary meanings for παράκλητος, Johannes Behm finds that the history and concept of παράκλητος show that all subsidiary meanings were interwoven into the primary sense of advocate.⁶ He agrees that παράκλητος is not used as a title for a professional legal adviser. Yet this should not suggest that the forensic meaning is absent. Behm thus proposes that the non-forensic meanings are to be understood in light of the primary legal understanding of the term. A παράκλητος should thus be understood as a "person called in to help, summoned to give assistance," or "helper in court."⁷

We notice this legal meaning in the writings of Philo. When Philo retells the story of Joseph's experience with his brothers who sold him into slavery, παράκλητος terminology is used to alleviate fears of retribution. Joseph states, "do not be downcast, I give you complete forgiveness for all the things which you have done to me. Do not think that you want anyone else as a παρακλήτου" (*Ios.* 1.239). Philo also utilizes an advocacy meaning to describe the priests and people who come before the temple. The son of a priest is considered a παράκλητος just in case the priest is unable to make himself worthy and consecrated when he enters the temple (*Mos.* 2.134–35). A sinner who needs to make appeasement is also encouraged to have a "conviction" of the soul, described as a παράκλητος, who will help the individual stand with confidence in the temple as sacrifices are made (*Spec.* 1.237).⁸ And reconciliation with God is described as being brought forth through the intervention of a παράκλητος (*Praem.* 1.166).

Philo also uses παράκλητος to describe key figures who intervene in punishments and act on behalf of others. Marco is described as a παράκλητος and chief advisor to the emperor Tiberius (*Flacc.* 1.13, 22). The Egyptian people reminded Flaccus that the city of Alexandria itself would be a παράκλητος on his behalf to Gaius (*Flacc.* 1.23). And when Flaccus was exiled, it was Lepidus who interceded as a παράκλητος to help alleviate his banishment (*Flacc.* 1.151, 181). The advocacy use of the term is also found in describing God and humanity. Παράκλητος metaphorically conveys the notion that God has no need for someone to remind him to provide for creation (*Opif.* 1:23). Humanity, on the other hand, does need

---

5. Harm, "Distinctive Titles," 119–35. Hoeck makes a similar observation but proposes a Christocentric Paraclete who clarifies the truth of Christ. See Hoeck, "Johannine Paraclete," 23–37.

6. Behm, "παράκλητος," TDNT 5:814. See also Nel, "Notion of the Holy Spirit," 1–8.

7. Behm, "παράκλητος," TDNT 5:801–3.

8. Klauch, "Accuser, Judge, and Paraclete," 107–118, esp. 113.

and experiences a παράκλητος when it comes to the physical senses. That is, the physical senses such as tasting, seeing, and smelling confront us with a variety of experiences, trying to captivate or persuade us like an advocate or παράκλητος for pleasure (*Opif.* 1:165).

According to Philo, παράκλητος takes a legal and advocacy meaning. Primarily, the language is found to describe those who are in need of help and require assistance, whether the individual is in the temple, politics, under judgement, or in dire need for reconciliation. This advocacy meaning runs throughout Philo's writings. One who needs a παράκλητος is one who stands in need of an advocate. When we explore παράκλητος in early Christian literature the advocacy meaning also appears. We find in the Didache 5.5 a warning about the "advocates of the wealthy" (πλουσίων παράκλητοι) who are mentioned alongside oppressors of the afflicted and unjust judges.[9] Eusebius recounts the experiences of Christians in Gaul who were unmercifully persecuted for the faith. In one occasion, a young man by the name of Vettius Epagathus approached the governor at the tribunal in order to defend the Christians. Eusebius describes him as a "Christian advocate" (παράκλητος Χριστιανῶν) who had in himself the "advocate" (ἔχων δὲ τὸν παράκλητον ἐν ἑαυτῷ) when he gladly laid down his life in defense of his fellow Christians.[10]

Exploring the significance of the παράκλητος expression therefore requires that we take into account the legal nuances of the term. This term primarily refers to an advocate in court. In fact, Lochlan Shelfer argues that the term was develop as a precise equivalent to the Latin term *advocatus*, contrary to Betz's claim.[11] Shelfer finds that in pagan literature the term is exclusively used for defenders, never prosecutors. A παράκλητος is thus someone of an elevated status who speaks and acts on behalf of someone who is in danger before a judge.[12] Shelfer agrees that the legal terminology and background of the term is not exhaustive, but a judicial context is woven throughout the Farewell discourse.[13] Strikingly, Morris, who also agrees that the term has forensic meaning, defines παράκλητος as a "legal friend."[14] As Behm also points out, the only difference is that the Spirit in

---

9. Reference to the "πλουσίων παράκλητοι" is also found in Barnabas 20:2.
10. Eusebius, *Hist. eccl.* 5.1.10.
11. Shelfer, "Legal Precision," 131.
12. Shelfer, "Legal Precision," 141.
13. Shelfer, "Legal Precision," 146–47.
14. Morris, *John*, 576.

Johannine literature is not the defender of the disciples before God, but their counsel in relation to the world.[15]

When we turn to the Farewell discourse this does not mean that we should exclude the different nuances and additional activities of the παράκλητος. The Spirit as παράκλητος is promised to be with the disciples forever, abiding with and in them (14:16–17). The παράκλητος will also teach and remind the disciples (14:26), testify (15:26–27), and convict the world (16:7). These communicatory activities and movement of the Spirit-παράκλητος are not limited to the disciples. The world is also a recipient of the παράκλητος activity. But this forensic meaning also positions us to further explore how we are to understand all the communicatory activities of the Spirit and the reason why such an advocate activity would emerge. In other words, when the Spirit-παράκλητος is presented within the Johannine narrative, why utilize this forensic meaning to describe the Spirit's movement to the disciples and the world? What pressing need led Jesus to reimagine and articulate the Spirit as an advocate for the disciples?

Although this study does not assume that we should exclude the different nuances and additional communicatory activities such as teaching and revealing, we cannot ignore the guiding description of the Spirit as advocate nor assume that παράκλητος holds no meaning. The Spirit as παράκλητος carries an advocacy connotation as we find in 1 John 2:1.[16] In the Johannine letter the meaning is undoubtedly an advocate. To thus explore the use of παράκλητος in the Farewell Discourse the legal background of the term must bear weight in our interpretation and shape how we understand the related pneumatic activities. These implications must be drawn out in our analysis of the Johannine narrative.

The Spirit as the Πνεῦμα τῆς Ἀληθείας

Lastly, the Fourth Gospel also uses the phrase πνεῦμα τῆς ἀληθείας as an expression for the Spirit. Although absent from the Old Testament, this particular Johannine phrase has a strong Jewish background. Alfred Leaney notes that the discovery of the scrolls at Qumran have shed light on its meaning. He insists that the "Spirit of Truth" was not a mere description of an entity but an opposing and personal or quasi-personal principle in the universe which influenced the characters and destinies of people.[17] Leaney believes that according to Qumran convictions, the Spirit of Truth

15. Behm, "παράκλητος," *TDNT* 5:803–4.
16. See also *2 Clem.* 3:9.
17. Leaney, "Historical Background," 151.

is that persona who controls and inspires the proper actions of the children of light.[18] Leaney insists that the writer adapts and takes over the Spirit of Truth as another figure identified with the Paraclete.[19] Applied to the Fourth Gospel, the Spirit of Truth comes from the Father to teach and lead the disciples into truth. But John Breck further points out that Iranian and early Jewish literature also held to the view of a "spirit of truth" and "spirit of error" as inspirational agents which led people toward good or evil. This also reveals that the emergence of the "Spirit of Truth" in Johannine literature is not unique.[20] Breck holds that this view of the Spirit was shaped by Iranian dualistic worldview of Zoroastrianism in its description of the struggle between good and evil.[21]

Within the Testaments of the Twelve Patriarchs we also find an ethical dualism that distinguishes the "spirit of truth" from the "spirit of error." Evil actions and various impulses within humans are attributed to various spirits who hold sway over humanity.[22] This includes the spirit of fornication, hatred, trickery, injustice, lying, insatiateness, jealousy, deceit, arrogance, and the spirit of Beliar.[23] In particular, we find the mention of the "spirit of truth" in terms of judgment and testifying:

> two spirits await an opportunity with humanity, the spirit of truth and the spirit of error. In between is the conscience of the mind which inclines as it will. The things of truth and the things of error are written in the affections of man, each one of whom the Lord knows. There is no moment in which man's works can be concealed, because they are written on the heart in the Lord's sight. And the spirit of truth testifies to all things and brings all accusations. He who has sinned is consumed in his own heart and cannot raise his head to face the judge. (*T. Jud.* 20:1–5)

We thus notice that the spirit of truth is not the only spirit that confronts humanity. Both the spirit of truth and error attempt to lead humanity toward moral actions. But the spirit of truth not only attempts to persuade all humanity; it also convicts humanity of wrongdoing. Breck asserts that this didactic and forensic role is also characteristic of the Spirit in the

---

18. See 1QS 3.13–4.26.
19. Leaney, "Historical Background," 152.
20. Breck, *Spirit of Truth*, 86–87.
21. Breck, *Spirit of Truth*, 112–14.
22. *T. Sim.* 2:7; *T. Jud.* 19:4; 20:1–5; *T. Dan* 5:11.
23. *T. Rub.* 3:1–8; 5:3; *T. Sim.* 2:7; 3:1–2; 4:7; *T. Levi* 4:9; *T. Jud.* 14:1–8; 26:3; *T. Iss.* 7:7; *T. Zeb.* 9:8; *T. Dan.* 1:6–8.

Johannine tradition.[24] He also finds that although the spirits of truth and error are sometimes indistinguishable from human inclinations, it would be an oversimplification to suggest that they are identical as if human sins are the working of appropriate evil spirits.[25] Breck thus maintains that the authors of the Twelve Patriarchs integrate an older tradition of the two spirits and two inclinations into a metaphysical dualism with moral and eschatological themes.[26] Strikingly, in the Testament of Judah the coming Messiah will have the "spirit of understanding and sanctification" and will give the saints the spirit of holiness and authority to trample upon wicked spirits (*T. Jud.* 18:7–12). Breck interprets this passage as the role of the Spirit in defending the elect against the forces of evil and inspiring them to actions of moral rectitude.[27]

The "spirit of truth" and "spirit of error" must be understood from the vantage point of Jewish ethical dualism. This is not an abstract understanding of the spirits. Instead, it refers to the active guidance of the spirits toward goodness or evil, as expressed in one's moral lifestyle and actions. This theme also emerges in Qumran literature. For the Qumran sectarians, Breck finds that the "spirit of truth" had a dual function in revealing truth and sanctifying the remnant in preparation for the eschaton, especially as noted in 1QS 4.20–25 which states,

> God will then purify every deed of man with his truth. He will refine for himself the human frame by rooting out all spirit of injustice from the founds of his flesh. He will cleanse him of all wicked deeds with the spirit of holiness, like purifying waters. He will shed upon him the spirit of truth (to cleanse him) of all abomination and injustice. And he shall be plunged in to the spirit of purification, that he may instruct the upright in the knowledge of the Most High and teach the wisdom of the sons of heaven to the perfect of way. . . . Until now the spirits of truth and injustice struggle in the hearts of men and they walk in both wisdom and follow. . . . For God has established the two spirits in equal measure until the determined end, and until the renewal, and he knows the reward of their deeds from all eternity.

The Johannine Spirit's identity and activity is akin to the "spirit of truth" in 1QS 3:13–4:26. In the above passage, the principal agent of evil is the "spirit of deception" or "spirit of error." Again, these spirits were not inclinations or

---

24. Breck, *Spirit of Truth*, 117.
25. Breck, *Spirit of Truth*, 118–19. See also *T. Ash.* 1:3–9; 3:2; *T. Benj.* 6:1–7.
26. Breck, *Spirit of Truth*, 120.
27. Breck, *Spirit of Truth*, 124.

impulses within humanity. As Breck argues, they are spiritual powers that dwell within humanity, created by God, and are fundamentally opposed to one another.[28] Both spirits struggle against one another for mastery of the human will. The person's ethical conduct thus manifests which spirit one has obeyed. Or more specifically, the spirit of truth not only inspires correct interpretations and brings wisdom, but aids one toward the proper ethical conduct and response to the truth.[29] No one was exempt from having portions or under the influence of either spirit.

It must be pointed out that Breck's insightful analysis brings to light the moral role of the "Spirit of Truth" in Johannine literature. Breck remarks that in the theology of the Qumran Covenanters, those who undergo ritual washing are symbolically experiencing in their flesh the Spirit's inner cleansing.[30] Even more, Breck finds that within Qumran literature the "spirit of truth" is created by God and called the "prince of lights," the "angel of truth," and "spirit of holiness." This spirit is promised to guide and assist the righteous. The spirit has dominion over all the children of righteousness, and the spirit's function is to illumine the minds of the righteous, purify, and inspire them to just conduct.[31]

In addition, Qumran teaching on the "spirit of truth" and "spirit of error" also divides humanity into two classes, each of which is under the lordship of one of these spirits.[32] Breck observes that there is a cosmic struggle between the spirits within individuals and not only divides the person, but divides people from one another.[33] However, he cautions us from assuming that the flesh is the source of evil, as in gnostic teaching. Instead, the flesh is the sphere of conflict where the one experiences the influences of these spirits.[34] As such, Breck finds that the phrase "spirit of truth" within Hebrew thought should not be understood as a rational category. He contends that the Spirit may be described as the "spirit of truth" insofar as it proclaims the true word of the Lord, especially since it was an expression of the divine will and purpose.[35]

The Johannine expression "Spirit of Truth" does not emerge in a vacuum. The early Qumran community had already utilized this description of

28. Breck, *Spirit of Truth*, 111–45; 160–61; 1QS 3:17–21; 4:16–18, 23–25.
29. 1QS 4:2–14, 16–18.
30. Breck, *Spirit of Truth*, 126.
31. Breck, *Spirit of Truth*, 136. See also 1QH 9:32; 12:11; 14:25; 16:6–11.
32. Breck, *Spirit of Truth*, 131.
33. Breck, *Spirit of Truth*, 133.
34. Breck, *Spirit of Truth*, 132.
35. Breck, *Spirit of Truth*, 141.

God's spirit. The spirit of truth according to the Qumran community was actively present in the world, leading, cleansing, purifying, and guiding the community. We also become aware that the spirit of truth was not alone, but there was an equally created and opposing spirit called the spirit of error. Both these spirits were under God's control, created by God, and given to all humanity. Indeed, humanity was consistently in tension with these spirits that not only resided within, but externally influenced and guided their moral decisions. The similarities are apparent, as noticed by Breck. But the difference in the Johannine literature is that the Spirit of Truth is not described as given to all people, only to the disciples. Only the disciples are promised to have the Spirit of Truth, which suggests that the Spirit is with no one else. Why is this so? Tricia Brown proposes that the reason why the writer found it necessary to align the Paraclete with truth was due to other Paracletes who supposedly represent falsehood.[36] But who are these other Paracletes that Brown supposes?

Conclusion

After examining this pneumatic language and how it may have been understood by Jewish and Greco-Roman readers, we are provided with ranges of meanings that are vital to our study of the Spirit-Paraclete within the Farewell Discourse. But finding definitions is only a preliminary step. It may help us understand how the Fourth Gospel's pneumatic language reflects or differs from its emerging context, but we still need a social, cultural, and literary analysis of the gospel to further enlighten our knowledge of the Spirit's activity and identity. Nonetheless, we are able to stake out some primary definitions. First, we can identify that there are certainly ethical connotations to the pneumatic phrase "πνεῦμα τῆς ἀληθείας."[37] This should lead us to recognize that the "Spirit of Truth" in the Fourth Gospel is not solely a description of the Spirit as beholder of abstract truth, but the activity of the Spirit that reveals God's divine will and influences the disciples toward a godly life. This also leads us to have a qualifying understanding of the Spirit-παράκλητος. Given that the "Spirit of Truth" appears on only three occasions and after the mention of the παράκλητος (14:17; 15:26; 16:13), this further elaborates how we ought to understand the Spirit's activity as advocacy. In other words, the Spirit as Paraclete and Truth suggest that the Spirit not only

---

36. Brown, *Spirit in the Writings of John*, 181.

37. 1QS 1:5–7; 4:19; 8:2; *T. Iss.* 7:1–5; *T. Ash.* 5:3; *T. Dan* 1:3; 6:8–10; *T. Rub.* 3:8; 6:9. *T. Ben* 10:3.

engages in advocacy activities, but also reveals, sanctifies, and guides one toward righteousness.

What then are the ethnic implications? Or should our understanding of the Spirit be based solely on moral or theological grounds? Although the pneumatic identity and activity of the Spirit as Paraclete and Spirit of Truth may solely appear to have theological implications, this is not so. As we will notice in the following sections, it is within the context of ethnic rejection, fear, loss of kinship, and oppression, that this activity and identity of the Spirit as Paraclete emerges.

11

Responding to the Orphaned

JOHN 14:16–17, 26

THE SPIRIT IS DESCRIBED AS THE PARACLETE AND SPIRIT OF Truth on four occasions within the Farewell Discourse. We also find the rare use of the phrase "Holy Spirit" mentioned for the second time.[1] In this section, we will focus on the first two Paraclete sayings in 14:16–17 and 14:26 given their proximity and literary unity.[2] The texts state:

> And I will ask the Father, and another Paraclete he will give to you, so that he may be with you forever, the Spirit of truth, whom the world is not able to receive, because it does not see him nor know him, you know him because he remains with you and will be in you.
>
> κἀγὼ ἐρωτήσω τὸν πατέρα καὶ ἄλλον παράκλητον δώσει ὑμῖν ἵνα μεθ᾽ ὑμῶν εἰς τὸν αἰῶνα ᾖ, τὸ πνεῦμα τῆς ἀληθείας, ὃ ὁ κόσμος οὐ δύναται λαβεῖν, ὅτι οὐ θεωρεῖ αὐτὸ οὐδὲ γινώσκει·

---

1. John 1:33; 20:22.
2. For instance, Jesus remarks that he will not speak much longer and commands the disciples to get up and leave with him (14:30–31), but the dialogue continues several more chapters. Segovia holds that 18:1 continues where 14:31 ends. He also holds that 15:1–17 was an independent discourse and the addition of 15:18–16:4a was motivated in part by an attempt to provide further teaching concerning the disciples. For further analysis on the independence and literary relationship of the discourse, see Segovia, "John 15:18–16:4a," 210–30. Barrett also claims that 13:31–14:31 and 15–17 are alternative versions of the discourse (Barrett, *St. John*, 379); Brown notices that 13:31–14:31 parallels 16:4b–33 (Brown, *John*, 2:589); and Keener also affirms the literary unity of the first two Paraclete sayings (Keener, *John*, 953).

ὑμεῖς γινώσκετε αὐτό, ὅτι παρ᾽ ὑμῖν μένει καὶ ἐν ὑμῖν ἔσται.³ (14:16-17)

> But the Paraclete, the Holy Spirit, whom the Father will send in my name, this one will teach you all things, and bring to your remembrance all that I said to you.

ὁ δὲ παράκλητος, τὸ πνεῦμα τὸ ἅγιον ὃ πέμψει ὁ πατὴρ ἐν τῷ ὀνόματί μου, ἐκεῖνος ὑμᾶς διδάξει πάντα καὶ ὑπομνήσει ὑμᾶς πάντα ἃ εἶπον ὑμῖν [ἐγώ]. (14:26)

In these verses we find Jesus informing the disciples that he will ask the Father for another advocate (v. 16), which presumes that Jesus is the first advocate.⁴ In addition, for the first time the world is mentioned as not being able to receive the Paraclete, or the Spirit in general (v. 17). This marks the disciples as special recipients of the Paraclete because of their knowledge and relationship with the Paraclete. The Paraclete has an abiding presence with the disciples, described in terms of being "with" and "in" them (v. 17). And lastly, the Paraclete is portrayed as the "Holy Spirit" who will teach and remind the disciples of Jesus' words (v. 26).

The pneumatic activities seem very straightforward and uncomplicated, perhaps unrelated to any ethnic discourse or racial ideologies. Bultmann finds that the promise of the Paraclete is a promise for the continuation of revelation. He states, "the Spirit is the power of the proclamation of the word in the community."⁵ In reference to v. 26, he remarks that the promise of the Paraclete ensures that the revelatory work of Jesus will continue.⁶ He thus understands the role and function of the Paraclete in terms of a revelatory activity in and through the church.⁷ Similar to Bultmann, Barrett suggests that the Paraclete is the "Spirit of Christian paraclesis" that is joined and made manifest in the activity of the church. He interprets the revelatory activity of the Paraclete not in terms of providing new revelation but in

---

3. There is textual uncertainty over this verb. Early manuscripts, such as P66 B D* W, prefer the present tense verb, ἐστιν. Metzger suggests, however, that the preferred reading is ἔσται given substantial support from P66c, 75vid ℵ A Θ Ψ 28 33vid 700 syrs, h (Metzger, *Textual Commentary*, 208).

4. This is also supported by 1 John 2:1, where Jesus is described as a παράκλητος before the Father. Tricia Brown suggests that this passage does not presume that Jesus ceased being a Paraclete but rather that another Paraclete joins him by providing access to the Father through him (Brown, *Spirit in the Writings of John*, 212).

5. Bultmann, *John*, 615; Barrett, *St. John*, 386; Johnston, *Spirit-Paraclete*, 123; Domeris, "Paraclete as an Ideological," 17-23, esp. 20; Keener, *John*, 980.

6. Bultmann, *John*, 626; Brown, *John*, 2:644.

7. Bultmann, *Theology of the New Testament*, 2:50.

reference to its "application" in Jesus.[8] Tricia Brown, however, proposes that the Paraclete brokers access to Jesus. This brokerage is not primarily aimed to perpetuate Jesus' revelation but continue it, including that which has yet to be revealed.[9] Michaels and Millos further propose that the promise of the Paraclete's revelatory activity has implications in the authority and composition of the gospel.[10] That is, the Paraclete is active in the reading and hearing of Jesus' words through the gospel text.

There is an agreement that the activity of the Paraclete is Christologically focused and ensures continuity with the activity of Jesus. Since the Father sends another "Paraclete," this suggests that we ought to understand the Spirit-Paraclete in terms of Jesus' mission. The parallels between the mission of Jesus and the mission of the Paraclete are aptly noticed.[11] Scholars differ on the primary role of the Spirit-Paraclete. This includes activities such as reminding, mediating, advancing, or replacing Jesus' presence.[12] But what is the relationship between the Spirit-Paraclete and ethnicity? How does the Spirit-Paraclete's interaction and activity also address the ethnic ideologies and racial scripts of the Greco-Roman world? Does the Spirit-Paraclete have anything to say about ethnic identity, relations, or ideologies? Bultmann agrees that the Spirit-Paraclete is continuing Jesus' revelatory activity in the church. But who is this "church" and why should we assume that they were of all one monocultural and monoethnic identity? Throughout all the various discussion on the Paraclete, what has not been discussed is how the Spirit-Paraclete sayings also contributes to a reimaging of ethnic identity and relations. In fact, I argue that the presence of the Paraclete makes it possible for the disciples and Johannine community to develop a new racialized identity as "children of God." How do we know that the Paraclete's presence makes this divine ethnic identity possible? When Jesus states that he will ask the Father for another Paraclete, he does this so that they would not be left as orphans (14:18). This orphan imagery is not accidental. We

---

8. Barrett, *St. John*, 77, 386–90; Beasley-Murray, *John*, 264; Burge, *Anointed Community*, 212–13; Morris, *John*, 582–83.

9. Brown, *Spirit in the Writings of John*, 210.

10. Millos: "Tales cosas, son ampliadas por la obra de enseñanza del Espíritu en la mente de los apóstoles que las trasladan a los escritos bíblicos del Nuevo Testamento. En el momento actual, sigue enseñando el verdadero sentido y significado de las verdades reveladas en la Escritura, de modo que podamos comprender, discernir y enseñar la Palabra como fuimos enseñados" (Millos, *Juan*, 1375). See also Michaels, *John*, 792.

11. Burge, *Anointed Community*, 140–42.

12. Brown, *John*, 2:643, 653; Lindars, *John*, 478; Keener, *John*, 951–71; Burge, *Anointed Community*, 138–47; Mateos and Barreto, *Juan*, 639–40, 645; Brown, *Spirit in the Writings of John*, 191; Ashton, *Understanding*, 450–51; Sheridan, "Paraclete and Jesus," 125–41.

must notice that to be orphaned also means to be fatherless—a relation that was vital for the construction of one's ethnic identity and social standing in the ancient world. And as I argue, the orphan metaphor is also racialized language. It provides a new lens in understanding how ethnic identity and ethnic relations are reimagined and developed as a result of the Spirit-Paraclete's presence.

This chapter will thus seek to provide a compelling reason why we must reconsider our understanding of the Paraclete's presence from this ethnocritical perspective. But first, we will explore the Farewell Discourse and the ethnic implications of the "children" and "orphan" imagery. Second, we will examine how the orphan imagery is related to ethnic identity and relations in the ancient world by reviewing Greek and biblical literature. And lastly, we will incorporate these views in order to reimagine how the presence of the Spirit-Paraclete as an advocate, revealer, teacher, and ultimately, the Holy Spirit, creates a new racialized understanding of the disciples and Johannine community.

The Farewell Discourse and Kinship Language

The Paraclete sayings are all located in the Farewell Discourse (John 13–17). John Stube describes this portion of the gospel as the hinge on which the narrative turns.[13] It contains literary difficulties, given the repeated themes, new teachings, and chronological arrangement.[14] Bultmann finds that although the Farewell Discourse brings a radical division of the gospel, he believes that it ends in 14:31 and chapters 15–17 are either secondary insertions or not in their right place.[15] Brown proposes that the Farewell Discourse includes topics that were preached from different periods and traditions of the Johannine community.[16] But today, scholars such as Stube and Fernando Segovia find a literary unity within the discourse. In this analysis, I agree with Stube and Segovia that the discourse has a strategic unity with no need

---

13. Stube, *Graeco-Roman Rhetorical Reading*, 1.

14. The literary difficulties not only include the apparent ending in 14:31, but also Peter's question in 13:36 which does not reconcile with Jesus' statement in 16:5. New material not found in the Synoptic tradition includes the foot washing of the disciples (13:1–20) and the Paraclete sayings (14:16–17, 26; 15:26–27; 16:7–15). The Farewell Discourse also does not contain a Passover meal. Barrett finds that the gospel is weaving together Synoptic material (Barrett, *St. John*, 363). See Brown, *John*, 2:582–603; Dodd, *Interpretation*, 390–423, esp. 399; Ashton, *Understanding*, 422; Keener, *John*, 893–94.

15. Bultmann, *John*, 458–59.

16. Brown, *John*, 2:594.

to posit a variety of authors in the composition or construction of the text.[17] As such, my focus in this analysis will highlight the ethnic imagery in the dialogue and its implications to our understanding of the Paraclete sayings.

But first, what is a Farewell Discourse? This is a literary genre found in antiquity that incorporates the final sayings of a beloved figure, generally before death. Ruth Sheridan recognizes that these discourses were characterized by a motif of succession. This is most evident in how the discourse highlights the final words of a prominent figure and the provision of a legitimate successor.[18] We find farewell speeches throughout biblical literature which include Jacob's blessing of his children before his death (Gen 47:29–49:33), Joshua's speech to Israel (Josh 22–24), and David's final speech (1 Chr 28–29). Deuteronomy in its entirety is also considered as Moses' farewell address to the Hebrew people. Other patriarchal figures who give farewell addresses include Enoch, Noah, Abraham, Isaac, Rebecca, Ezra, and Baruch.[19] Besides Jesus' farewell address to the disciples within the gospels, another most prominent farewell address is Paul's message to the elders of the Ephesian church in Acts 20:17–38.

Yet Sheridan asserts that the Testament of the Twelve Patriarchs is the most fully developed example of a Farewell Discourse. She notes that this includes the patriarch's narration of past events to gathered kin, an exhortation toward ethical behavior, and a prophecy of events that will befall the kin after the death of the patriarch.[20] The literary discourse, in sum, functions to

> provide a place of transition in the overall narrative of God's people at which point continuity will be ensured between the traditions embodied by the dying patriarch or king and the future of the successors and later generations.[21]

John Ashton also observes similarities between the Johannine Farewell Discourse and both Moses' farewell in Deuteronomy 31–34 and the Testament of Moses.[22] He not only identifies the concern for succession but also the theme of commission. Other scholars recognize how the discourse

---

17. Segovia, *Farewell to the Word*, vii–viii; Stube, *Graeco-Roman Rhetorical Reading*, 81.

18. Sheridan, "Paraclete as Successor," 129–30.

19. *1 En.* 91–108; *Jub.* 10:1–15; 20:1–23:1; 35:1–36:18; *4 Ezra* 14:27–48; *2 Bar.* 77–87.

20. Sheridan, "Paraclete as Successor," 131–32. See specifically *T. Dan* 2:1; 5:7–8; *T. Gad* 4:1–7; *T. Jos.* 1:1; *T. Levi* 1:2; 4:1; 13:5–7; *T. Naph.* 1:2–5; 4:1–5; 9:2; *T. Reu.* 1:2–4; *T. Sim* 1:2; 3:1–2; 5:1–5; *T. Mos.* 1:15.

21. Sheridan, "Paraclete as Successor," 132.

22. Ashton, *Understanding*, 445–51.

aims to strengthen discipleship, affirm the disciples' calling and vocation, draw a sharp distinction in rank and succession, and ward off the threat of those who inappropriately claim succession.[23] The Farewell Discourse is not a unique literary genre but reflective of other discourses that preserve a patriarch's final words. It is, as Brown describes, "Jesus' last testament" in which he speaks to his own before he is on his way to the Father.[24]

There is, however, an ethnic motif that is critical to our understanding of the discourse. Sheridan states that some Farewell Discourses focus on the proper successor who is not related kin, as in the case between Moses and Joshua or Elijah and Elisha. But she finds that on most occasions the successor is another kinship member, as in the example of Jacob and Joseph, David and Solomon, and the figures in the Twelve Patriarchs.[25] Although Sheridan does not elaborate on the implications this has for the formation of ethnic identity, she suggests that this is an area to further explore in the Johannine discourse.[26] J. A. Draper also finds that the Farewell Discourse shapes how the community understood itself. He points out that when the Paraclete is discussed, it takes place within the context of boundary maintenance and distinction from the world.[27] Though he describes the community as an "introversionist sect," he argues that the Paraclete sayings have the goal of disassociating the community members from the world, given that they alone have the Spirit who guides them into all truth.[28]

Both Sheridan and Draper find that the discourse concerns itself with identity formation and distinction. Bruce Malina and Richard Rohrbaugh also notice that there is an element of "fictive kinship" within the discourse.[29] Tricia Brown hints at this idea when she notes that familial imagery and concerns lie at the heart of the indwelling language of John 14–17, not concerns about mystical unity.[30] Undeniably, Jesus' final words are given to his disciple in the same manner that a patriarchal figure would give his final words to his own flesh and blood kin. We cannot ignore how the farewell address, which is generally given to kinship members, must also shape how we are to understand ethnic identity and relations. Is Jesus' promise

---

23. Stube, *Graeco-Roman Rhetorical Reading*, 2; Rand, "Story and a Community," 31–45, esp. 33–34; Woll, "Departure," 225–39.
24. Brown, *John*, 2:582; Beasley-Murray, *John*, 263.
25. Sheridan, "Paraclete as Successor," 133–34.
26. Sheridan, "Paraclete as Successor," 139.
27. Draper, "Sociological Function," 13–29.
28. Draper, "Sociological Function," 27.
29. Malina and Rohrbaugh, *John*, 228.
30. Brown, *Spirit in the Writings of John*, 204–5.

of the Spirit-Paraclete providing the opportunity for the disciples to view themselves as newly formed ethnic kin, joined and united to one another, and awaiting the coming of the Spirit-Paraclete who will continue Jesus' mission? Most certainly. And what is the evidence that there is a reimagining and forming of an ethnic community? It is the use of child and orphan imagery that permeates the Farewell Discourse and gospel. This imagery, as I argue, is the narrative's way of reimagining one's ethnic kin.

In order to identify this child/orphan imagery, I also want to point out how this develops throughout the narrative. But first, let us recall that when we are talking about kinship, we are essentially discussing the family. Kinship groups are the basic family units that make up society, colonies, tribes and city-states. Malina describes kinship as being concerned with naturing and nurturing human beings who are interpreted as family members.[31] This is important because within the Mediterranean world, a person's identity is dependent and emerges from the kinship group. This means that a member's identity is also derived from the tribe, clan, or ethnic community in which one resides. Since a kinship member is also a member of an ethnic community, any child born within a family is thus placed in relation not only with their immediate kin, but their historic ethnic ancestors whose reputation also plays a formative role for the child. We thus can notice the significance of genealogies in the ancient world and their role in establishing relations and identity.

The relation between a child and his or her ethnic community is evident in Cicero's description of human relations. As previously mentioned, Cicero identifies the close degree of human relations from kinship to general humanity. He states,

> To proceed beyond the universal bond of our common humanity, there is the closer one of belonging to the same people, tribe, and tongue, by which men are very closely bound together. It is a still closer relation to be citizens of the same city-state; for fellow-citizens have much in common. . . . But a still closer social union exists between kindred. Kinship, starting with that infinite bond of union of the human race in general, the conception is now confined to a small and narrow circle. For since the reproductive instinct is by nature's gift the common possession of all living creatures, the first bond of union is that between husband and wife; the next, that between parents and children; then we find one home, with everything in common. (*Off.* 1.53–55)

---

31. Malina, *New Testament World*, 82; Hanson, "All in the Family," 27.

Unquestionably, the bonds between kinship groups are closer than the bonds between ethnic groups. But Aristotle puts it another way by arguing that the city-state is prior to the individual and no individual can exist without the state. He asserts,

> The state is also prior by nature to the individual; for if each individual when separate is not self-sufficient, he must be related to the whole state as other parts are to their whole, while a man who is incapable of entering into partnership, or who is so self-sufficing that he has no need to do so, is no part of a state, so that he must be either a lower animal or a god. (*Pol.* 1.1253a)

The point thus remains: kinship is the essential web of relations that a child enters. Cicero finds kinship as the basic element of humanity. Aristotle notices the state's role in forming the child. In both cases, a child is not only related to their kin but is also placed in a social and political relationship with their ethnic community, the state, and humanity in general.[32] Or said another way, a child is not only placed in relationship to their kinship group, but also with their ethnic ancestors. No child exists without some relation to a kinship group, and all kinship groups are in some relation to an apical ancestor.

Is this kinship imagery evident in the Farwell Discourse? Unquestionably. At the beginning of the Farewell Discourse in 13:1, Jesus is aware that his departure from the world was at hand and that he was going to return to the Father. This departure has grave consequences for the disciples. Jesus knows that he is going to leave the disciples. He washes their feet and predicts a betrayal, prompting Judas to depart from the group (13:2–30). Afterward, Jesus again states that the time for his "glorification" had come, which creates anticipation of Jesus' death (vv. 31–32).[33] After cryptically warning the disciples about his glorification, Jesus describes them as "little children" (τεκνία) who will no longer experience his presence (v. 33). The disciples do not understand what this means. And we find here for the first time the disciples being called "little children," which is not new language used to describe the believers in the gospel. Nonetheless, Jesus continues to inform them that they will not be able to find him, thus ensuring the reality of their inability to be with him. Peter responds to this news with the bold assertion that he would follow Jesus wherever he goes. But he does not know that he would soon deny Jesus (vv. 34–38).

This state of pending abandonment—not knowing where Jesus is going, what Jesus means about his moment of glorification, and the sudden realization that the disciples would no longer see Jesus—sets the tone for

---

32. See Humphreys, "Kinship," 430; Miller, "Greek Kinship Terminology," 46–52.
33. John 7:39; 12:16, 23.

chapter 14. Jesus exhorts the disciples to not be troubled but to believe in the Father and in him (14:1). He again explains his departure and return in terms of going away to his "Father's house" to prepare a place for them (vv. 2–6). This description of going to his "Father's house" includes the declaration that if they know Jesus, then they would know the Father and thus have already seen him (v. 7). At this point Philip asks Jesus to reveal the Father. Jesus replies, "he who has seen me has seen the Father" (v. 9) and claims, "I am in the Father and the Father is in Me" (v. 11). The unity and distinction between the Father and Jesus are emphasized in this response to Philip and the disciples. In fact, the mention of the "Father" is found 23 times within this chapter alone. William Loader suggests that in these passages Jesus stands for the Father in the world, not as an unconscious mouthpiece but in Jesus' willingness for the Father to work and speak through him.[34] Or as Bultmann also states, Jesus redirects the attention of the disciples to the indirect vision of God in himself.[35] But since Jesus stands for the Father in the world, we must notice that this imagery is also coupled with a portrayal of the disciples as "children." Since 13:33 the disciples are also described as "little children" (τεκνία) who are about to experience the most drastic event that can happen to a child: becoming orphaned. And although Jesus is not the Father, the narrative is woven in kinship imagery that portrays Jesus as a father who speaks to his children, warning them about his coming death and the responsibilities thereafter.

Stube remarks that calling the disciples "children" in 13:33 is affectionate language.[36] But this language is not a new metaphor for believers or the Johannine community. Since the prologue in 1:12, those who believe in Jesus are given the right to be a "child of God" (τέκνα θεοῦ). Although the prologue is a hymn that retells the story of Jesus' activity in creation, it also foreshadows major theological themes that will be developed within the narrative.[37] In particular, by stating that those who believe will be authorized to be God's children, it emphatically pronounces that Jesus holds the singular power to determine who is a member of the family of God. The prologue rejects the limitations that genealogical lineages have in the construction and maintenance of ethnic identity, relations, and inheritance. It rejects the assumption that one is a child of God solely due to birthing and ancestry relations (1:13). And as argued in the previous chapters, these

---

34. Loader, *Jesus in John's Gospel*, 345.

35. Bultmann, *John*, 608.

36. Stube, *Graeco-Roman Rhetorical Reading*, 98.

37. Gordley, "Johannine Prologue," 781–802; Need, "Re-Reading the Prologue," 397–404.

are also themes and issues that the Spirit deals with throughout Jesus' public ministry.

How does one become a child in God's family? One must be "born of God," an expression that also emerges in the narrative as "born of the Spirit" (3:8). Lineage with God is thus created through divine means. And this "child" imagery is also ethnic imagery. It is a type of racial language that seeks to also challenge notions of ethnic inheritance, privilege, superiority, and genealogical relations. This idea is announced in the prologue. It proclaims that the creation of a new divine family will no longer be restricted to "blood, the will of flesh, or the will of man" (1:13), key aspects that set the parameters of ethnic and genealogical lineage. In other words, the phrase "children of God" or "little children" in the prologue and Farewell Discourse is racialized language.

Later in 8:33-44 we read sharp language that identifies Jesus' Jewish opponents with the children of Satan. George Beasley-Murray points out that in this case, Jesus is distinguishing between Abraham's descendants (σπέρμα) in 8:33-37 and Abraham's children (τέκνον) in 8:39, which suggests that the latter category is more important than the former.[38] When we trace σπέρμα throughout biblical literature we will notice that it is used in relation to covenantal promises. God made a covenant with the σπέρμα or "descendants" of Noah (Gen 9:9), Abraham (Gen 12:7; 13:15,16, 18; Ps 104:6-8), Aaron (Num 18:19), Phineas (Num 25:12-13; Sir 45:24), and David (Ps 89:3-4, 29-30, 35-37; Sir 45:25). Even Nehemiah reminds God of the covenant that was made to the σπέρμα of the Israelites (Neh 9:8). In particular, Sirach 44:11-13 suggests that the Jewish people were eternally inheritors of the covenant because of their genealogical relations to the patriarchs. Sirach states,

> With their seed (σπέρματος) shall continually remain a good inheritance, and their children (ἔκγονα) are within the covenant. Their seed (σπέρμα) stand fast, and their children (τέκνα) for their sakes. Their seed (σπέρμα) shall remain forever, and their glory shall not be blotted out (KJA).[39]

God's promises are granted explicitly to the descendants (σπέρμα) of the patriarchs, descendants who are also known as "children." Thus, to make a distinction between the τέκνον and σπέρμα in John 8:33-44 not only evokes God's covenant with the patriarchs and their descendants, it also creates a new racial lineage. It delineates those who can rightfully call themselves a

---

38. Beasley-Murray, *John*, 134.
39. Sir 44:21.

"child" within the family of God and claim the privileges that were given to the patriarchs. This also sets the "children of God" in distinction and in a contested relation to those who are ethnically related to the patriarchs through genealogical relations.

But if we are to identify the notion of τέκνον as racial language, how does one become incorporated into this group? The Fourth Gospel has already provided a solution to this problem by revealing that God is now bringing "children" into the covenant through Jesus' authorization (1:12) and the Spirit's begetting (3:8). And within 8:33–44 we find Jesus challenging those who consider themselves "children of Abraham," which is a challenge to their racial privileges of the covenant based upon their ethnic relations of genealogical lineage.

The next time that τέκνον is used is in John 11:52 when the writer explains how the death of Jesus would gather all the "children" who are scattered throughout the Diaspora. Leon Morris argues that while this language would suggest that this is referring to the Jews of the Diaspora, it is arguably referring to Gentile Christians.[40] We must however note that this comment about the "children of God" being gathered as a result of Jesus' death is the narrator's comment for the readers. The comment reflects on Caiaphas's statement that rationalizes the death of Jesus. Caiaphas states that it is preferable to allow the execution of Jesus than for the whole nation to perish by the hands of the Romans (11:50). The narrator interprets these words as an unintended prophecy about the impact that Jesus' death would have for the Jews and "children of God who are scattered abroad" (11:52). In other words, the "children" imagery is an additional explanation of Caiaphas's statement, given from the standpoint of the Johannine community. This also suggests that this racialized understanding of the community as "children of God" was already familiar to the readers, as noticeable in the Johannine letters.[41]

Throughout the Johannine letters the recipients are called "children of God" because they have been granted this new identity through their faith in Jesus and birth in the Spirit. This new identity within the family of God is coded racial language, a type of ethnic reimagining that centers oneself in relationship to a progenitor. Just as the Greeks and Romans ethnically distinguished themselves from the barbarians and the Jews ethnically distinguished themselves from the Gentiles, so too we find the Johannine writer making this same racial distinction and categorization. But for the writer of the Johannine letters, the language utilized to draw sharp boundaries

---

40. Morris, *John*, 505; Michaels, *John*, 654; Brown, *John*, 1:440.
41. 1 John 2:1, 12, 28; 3:1–2, 7, 10, 18; 4:4; 5:2, 21; 2 John 1:1, 4, 13; 3 John 1:4.

between ethnic groups includes the new categories of the "world" and "children of the devil" (1 John 3:1, 10; 4:5). Either one is a "child of God" within the community or "child of the devil" who is in the world. All racial and ethnic categories are subsumed with this new τέκνον ethnic language.

The use of the "child" (τέκνον) imagery from the prologue to the Johannine letters expands our imagination of what it means to be a member of God's household. This racial language is provoking the Johannine community to understand its ethnic identity, not solely in terms of Jewish, Greek, or Samaritan ideologies and privileges, but also as newly born children of God who have another divine racial identity because of the activity of Jesus and the Spirit-Paraclete. And as stated within the prologue, membership into this new family of God are no longer restricted to the boundaries of ethnic formation and identity in the Greco-Roman world. To be a "child of God" means that one has been granted membership into a divine ethnic group by the authorization of Jesus, begetting of the Spirit, and confirmation through the presence of the Paraclete. This imagery within the discourse is therefore playing a formative role upon the Johannine community's understanding of their ethnic identity in light of the Paraclete.

We cannot fail to notice the kinship imagery running throughout the dialogue when we turn to the Farewell Discourse. The discourse uses kinship language such as "Father," "children," and "orphan" within the context of the Spirit-Paraclete's anticipated activity and presence. The discourse is weaving together this imagery in the announcement and anticipation of the coming loss of Jesus who is akin to a beloved father figure. Bultmann rightly notices that this language is simply a portrait and that Jesus is not to be thought of as a father of the believers nor along the same view that Philo describes the Logos as the father.[42] But this should not lead us to reject the kinship imagery altogether. Even more, we cannot fail to notice, as previously pointed out, that the disciples are called children within the gospel and the Johannine community also viewed itself as the children of God. This is a racial argument that aims not only to bind together the disciples, but also the diverse ethnic Johannine community who was experiencing challenges by those who barred and doubted their presence and membership within the family of God. The very promise that the Paraclete will come to the disciples should dispel all notions of abandonment from Jesus and their heavenly Father. Jesus promises to send the παράκλητος to the disciples so that they would not identify themselves as fatherless children (14:16–17). He states, "I will not leave you orphaned (ὀρφανούς), I will come to you"

---

42. Bultmann, *John*, 618n1.

(14:18). Undeniably, without the Paraclete the disciples would indeed be orphans, lost and ostracized from their own kin and ethnic community.

Orphans in Antiquity

The status of orphans was a visible reality in the ancient world. Although today we identify orphans with those who lost both parents, this was not always so. The term ὀρφανός in Roman patriarchal culture was identified with someone who had lost their father. Only later in the sixth century (CE) did the term refer to a child who lost both parents.[43] The gospel's use of the vivid metaphor not only refers to the most vulnerable and defenseless in Greco-Roman antiquity, but it also portrays how many would have viewed the disciples and the Johannine community after Jesus' death and departure. In fact, Paul uses this orphan expression to express his own separation from and longing to be with the Thessalonians (1 Thess 2:17). He also describes the Galatians as children under a guardian, which implies that the Gentiles were metaphorically orphaned (Gal 4:1–5). But what was the reality of orphans in the ancient world? And how do the realities and experiences of orphans also shape how we are to view the Spirit-Paraclete's presence and activity? In this section we will review the status of orphans in Greek and biblical literature in order to understand the literary usage of the term in the Farewell Discourse.

First, to think about orphans is to come to terms with the reality of a father's death. Sabine Hübner and David Ratzan point out that ancient fatherlessness was rooted in this pervasive and endemic reality. They find that there were many fatherless children, given the high mortality rate of men and their tendency to marry late in life.[44] Walter Scheidel also notices that about one-third of all children within the Greco-Roman period would have lost their father by the age of fifteen.[45] J. T. Fitzgerald points to further conditions that would have contributed to early paternal death such as disease, short life expectancy, and war.[46] Scholars agree that the loss of a father brought serious economic disruption, especially since fathers were the head of the household and the economic provider. This is the most common difficult situation that would befall all orphans, regardless of social status. Related to economic disruption that resulted from a father's death includes the risk posed to a child's inheritance, undue hardship and grief for

43. Fitzgerald, "Orphans in Mediterranean Antiquity," 30.
44. Hübner and Ratzan, "Fatherless Antiquity," 9.
45. Scheidel, "Demographic Background," 31–40.
46. Fitzgerald, "Orphans in Mediterranean Antiquity," 30–34.

the mother, and the possibility of becoming susceptible to oppression and exploitation.⁴⁷ The situation was even worse for orphaned girls who would have difficulties raising the required dowry for marriage.⁴⁸ These economic challenges certainly motivated many widows to immediately remarry, but this did not always solve the problem. Hübner finds that in Roman law the stepfathers were depicted as legacy hunters who aimed to embezzle their stepchildren's inheritance.⁴⁹ They actively sought out widows in order to take advantage of their situation and gain immediate wealth. Although guardians were appointed to safeguard the inheritance of orphans, Hübner remarks that the laws issued to safeguard the orphan's inheritance only applied to Roman citizens.⁵⁰ This left most non-Roman orphans without legal protection. Even more, orphans were at the mercy of stepfathers who were not legally obligated to provide for them.⁵¹ Certainly, the widow was now taken care of through remarriage. But the situation of an orphan was not guaranteed to become ameliorated with a stepfather.

In response to the problem, Scheidel notices that parental death included a wide range of family responses such as older siblings being called to assume responsibility for younger siblings, being fostered by related kin, or coming under the control of an appointed guardian.⁵² The orphan's extended kin was the most important support group. But even though guardians, older siblings, and extended kin often took it upon themselves to care for orphans, the harsh consequences of being orphaned were difficult to alleviate.

Within the Homeric epics, Georg Wöhrle finds that an orphaned child was often put in a precarious and sometimes fatal situation.⁵³ When Hector of Troy died in his fight with Achilles, his wife Andromache was not immediately aware of the situation. She assumed that Hector was going to defeat Achilles. But when she hears cries from the hallways she runs to the walls of Troy only to find her husband's body dragged through the dirt. She bursts into tears at the realization of Hector's death. And in her lament, the impact that his death would have on their son emerges. She states,

> And your son, the child of doomed parents, our child, a mere babe, can no longer give you joy, dead Hector: nor can you give

47. Hübner and Ratzan, "Fatherless Antiquity," 10–13.
48. Hübner and Ratzan, "Fatherless Antiquity," 11.
49. Hübner, "Callirhoe's Dilemma," 64–67.
50. Hübner, "Remarriage and Stepfathers," 67.
51. Hübner, "Remarriage and Stepfathers," 81.
52. Scheidel, "Demographic Background," 40.
53. Wöhrle, "Sons (and Daughters) without Fathers," 174.

joy to him. Even if he survives this dreadful war against the Greeks, toil and suffering will be his fate, bereft of all his lands. An orphaned child is severed from his playmates. He goes about with downcast looks and tear-stained cheeks, plucks his father's friends by the cloak or tunic, till one, from pity, holds the wine-cup to his lips, but only for a moment, enough to wet his lips but not his palate. And some lad with both parents alive strikes him with his fist and drives him from the feast, jeering at him in reproach: 'Away with you, now! You've no father here.' So my child will run in tears to his widowed mother, my son Astyanax, who sat on his father's knee eating the rich fat and the sheep's marrow, and when he was sleepy and tired of play, slept in his nurse's arms in a soft bed, his dreams sweet. Now, with his dear father gone, ills will crowd on him." (Homer, *Ill*. 22.484–505)

The dire fate of Hector's son is not lost in Andromache's words. She realizes that her son's life has drastically changed because of Hector's death. Her son who was once eating in luxury will be cast out from the table, beaten by strangers with no one to protect him, ridiculed, deprived of his land, and socially ostracized from his friends. Wöhrle finds that in Andromache's lament there is a genuine danger that Hector's son would encounter, especially since as an orphan he would be deposed of his inheritance.[54] And if Andromache's speech reveals a situation that could happen to the powerful, how much more dire a situation for orphans who did not have access to the privileges of royalty? The death of a father places a child's economic, social, and inheritance in jeopardy.

Although not all orphans were neglected, all of them, both the wealthy and poor, faced economic and social challenges.[55] In Greek mythology, Zeus was known to be a god who watched over orphans.[56] And as we find in the case of Euripides's Ion, Apollo commissions Hermes to bring the orphan child, Ion, to the temple at Delphi where he could be raised by a priestess.[57] But further comments on Euripides's Ion deserve mention. Although this Greek story weaves together various themes and issues related to identity, deception, vengeance, and trust in the gods,[58] it also explores how an or-

---

54. Wöhrle, "Sons (and Daughters) without Fathers," 163–64.

55. Hübner remarks that it was the wealthy aristocrats who were able to provide guardians that served as father figures over the orphan's property. In other occasions, stepfathers would adopt orphans, welcome them into their homes, and protect them. See Hübner, "Remarriage and Stepfathers," 80–81.

56. Hesiod, *Op*. 327–34.

57. Euripides, *Ion*, 25–35.

58. Rehm, *Greek Tragic Theater*, 131–45; Radding, "Paeanic Crises," 393–434;

phan came to an awareness of his ancestral origins. Specifically, the view of orphans in the Greek world, their role and status, and how they would have been received even though adopted. While Euripides's Ion was written in the early fifth century (BCE),[59] it is important to point out that Ion eventually becomes the ancestral founder of the Greek cities in Asia Minor. His descendants possessed the coastal regions of both Europe and Asia.[60] Asia Minor was considered in the Greek tradition to have been founded by an orphan who eventually was revealed to have divine origins as a begotten child of Apollo.

Euripides begins the narrative by first providing a background of Ion's life. The Greek god, Hermes, explains the circumstances that led to Ion's orphaned state. He admits that the god Apollo forcibly took a woman named Creusa to a cave near the northern cliffs of Athens and impregnated her. When the time came for the baby to be born, Creusa returned to the same cave and abandoned the boy. The baby was left to die, but Apollo knew that the baby was there. He commissioned Hermes to bring the baby to the temple at Delphi where he could be raised by a priestess. Ion thus grew up as a temple servant, unaware that his father was Apollo and that his mother was an Athenian woman. In retelling this narrative background, Hermes insists that Ion will eventually receive what belongs to him and that Apollo would cause his name to be great, and he would be the founder of the cities of Asia.[61]

The story starts when a woman was named Creusa came to the temple of Apollo. She traveled with her husband to seek a petition from Apollo because of her barrenness. Creusa meets the temple servant, Ion, and asks about his identity and family. Ion reveals that he has no inheritance or claim to land. His home is, as Ion states, "wherever I fall asleep" and his food comes from the cultic altars and gift of foreigners.[62] But this unawareness of his identity and family did not last. Unbeknownst, he was literally talking to his mother who had abandoned him many years earlier. He had spent his entire life in the temple, raised by a priestess and unaware of the true identity of his mother and father.

Later Creusa's husband named Xuthus comes with a word from the oracle. He is told that the first person he meets when he leaves the temple would be his son and that they would no longer be childless. It happens that

---

Weiss, "Psychoanalytical Reading of Euripides," 39–50.
   59. See Martin, "On the Date of Euripides's Ion," 647–51.
   60. Euripides, Ion, 70–74; 1575–90.
   61. Euripides, Ion, 1–75.
   62. Euripides, Ion, 314–25.

Ion was the first person Xuthus met while leaving the temple. Xuthus adopts him and asserts that Ion is his son and no other (οὐκ ἄλλῳ, τέκνον).[63] Although Ion is now adopted, he still laments and desires to know his mother. He recognizes that while he has received a father and been given an inheritance, the reality of his orphan experiences was not erased. While talking to Xuthus, Ion expresses his deep desire to know his mother, but Xuthus encourages him with the benefits of his new life and the new status of being his son. Xuthus states,

> My son, the god has acted well in causing you to be found. He has brought you to me and you for your part have found a beloved father. What you naturally long for, I too desire, my son, that you should find your mother and I should learn who it was that gave me you as my son. . . . So leave the god's precincts and your homeless life, join purposes with your father and come to Athens. There your father's prosperous power and great wealth await you. You will suffer from neither of two disabilities by being called ignobly born and poor. You will be called high-born and rich. (*Ion*, 570–80)

Xuthus attempted to reassure Ion that he would no longer be an orphan but now hold a new status. Having a father meant that Ion had a home, power, honorable reputation, status, and wealth. Even though Ion was a temple servant, he had been an orphan without the benefits that were being granted by Xuthus. This should have caused Ion to rejoice because his fortunes had turned. Ion, however, reflects upon the reality of his situation, regardless of his new status as a son. Ion recognizes that although he has a new father, he has a foreigner as a father and still does not know his real mother or father. He considers this reality a "blot upon my name" which will keep him powerless—a "nobody and the son of nobodies" as he describes.[64] Ion recognizes that he is nonetheless a foreigner and that the Athenians prided themselves on not being associated with foreigners. He not only prefers to live a humble life, away from all the wealth and power, but also recognizes that Creusa would become bitter because his presence would remind her of her inability to have a child.[65]

Within Euripides's Ion the reader is made aware that the Greeks shunned foreign marriage. Athenians claimed to have been born from the earth and avoided the possibility of polluting their lineage.[66] Cresusa was an

---

63. Euripides, *Ion*, 535.
64. Euripides, *Ion*, 585–90.
65. Euripides, *Ion*, 605–645.
66. Euripides, *Ion*, 265–70.

Athenian and her husband, Xuthus, was an Acheaean. They were married because Xuthus won her as a dowry after fighting for the Athenians in a war.[67] But Xuthus's lineage is a respectable one which traces its ancestry to the son of Aeolus, who was Zeus's son.[68] Lineage was central to the role of identity. It not only placed one in relation to one's family, but also in relation to the land, inheritance, and ethnic community. Since Ion was an orphan, he did not know the true identity of his father or mother. Regardless of his adopted status, he still considered himself a perpetual foreigner until he finds his mother. He states,

> I pray that my mother may be Athenian, so that I may have free speech as my maternal inheritance! For if a foreigner, even though nominally a citizen, comes into that purebred city, his tongue is enslaved and he has no freedom of speech. (*Ion*, 670–75)

Ethnic identity, citizenship status, and questionable ancestry—these were the issues that plagued Ion. He knew that he would encounter several challenges in Athens, even though he now had a father to cling to for a new identity. The reality of his orphaned conditioned had permanently left him without a mother or father and therefore without a secure place within the Athenian community. We also become aware that the Athenians rejected foreigners, even though foreigners did what they could to be like them. Not even Xuthus's adoption of Ion would assuage Ion's concerns regarding this situation.

How then does Ion become accepted into the Athenian community? His father can only do so much given that his father was a foreigner. Euripides conveys the presumption that true incorporation in Athens required an Athenian mother, a requirement that an orphan would not be able to fulfill, regardless of adoption. Genealogical relation to the land was vital for any association to its rights and privileges. It is only later that Euripides's reveals Ion's true identity, that he was certainly of the Athenian race and had an Athenian mother. Even more, Ion becomes aware that his father was the god Apollo, bolstering the legitimacy of his lineage and status. No longer is Ion an orphan, but the son of a god.

Although the story of Ion is a story of an orphan who comes to an awareness that he is born of the god Apollo and has an Athenian mother, this story also reveals the tragedy that orphans experience without divine intervention. Truly, without Apollo's attempt to ameliorate the harm he

---

67. Euripides, *Ion*, 295.
68. Euripides, *Ion*, 63, 290.

caused to Cresusa, Ion would have died in the cave where he was exposed. And without Xuthus's attempt to adopt Ion, Ion would have remained without an inheritance, power, wealth, and privilege. This also demonstrates the reality of orphans when they have no association or awareness of their ethnic origins and kin. Like Ion, orphans are landless and homeless, utterly dependent upon the offerings of foreigners for sustenance. Without adoption, orphans would have no claim to an inheritance nor grafted into a kinship community with a name and recognition.

When we turn to biblical literature, the dire situation for orphans also emerges. Marcus Sigismund notes that the central characteristic of orphans in the Old Testament is the lack of rights and their defenseless position in society.[69] This is notable in the various injunctions to care and protect orphans, especially since they are most susceptible to being oppressed, murdered, sold as slaves, experiencing theft and financial distress, and denied justice.[70] Due to these harsh experiences, God emerges as their surrogate father and protector. God promises to hear the cries of orphans and avenge them (Exod 22:22–27). God is described as executing justice for orphans (Deut 10:18). The Psalmist also portrays God as a "helper of the orphan . . . who inclines his ear to vindicate the orphan and oppressed" (Ps 10:14, 17–18). Or as more poignantly described, "He is a father to the fatherless" (Ps 68:5). And in Hosea the prophet claims, "For in you the orphan finds mercy" (14:3). God in the Old Testament is deeply concerned about the status and welfare of orphans and is depicted as their defender. Even more, the Israelite community is given an injunction to protect and provide for them, not causing them any more undue hardship.

Although the New Testament rarely mentions orphans, the same command to care for orphans is assumed. In particular, Jesus demonstrates his ability to raise a dead orphan boy who was the only son of a widow in a town called Nain. This miracle led many to affirm that God has come to help his people, thus truly caring for orphans (Luke 7:11–16). James describes true religion as "caring for the orphans and widows in their misfortune" (Jas 1:27). This same exhortation to care for orphans also emerges within the context of caring for widows in Paul's letter to Timothy. Paul exhorts Timothy to make sure that the real widows who need assistance are taken care of, which presumes that these widows have orphan children and no extended kin to help care for them (1 Tim 5:1–16). In the Fourth Gospel the mention of orphans aims to metaphorically describe the pending situation of

---

69. Sigismund, "'Without Father, without Mother,'" 87.

70. Exod 22:22; Deut 10:18; 14:28–29; 24:17–22; 26:12–13; 27:19; 2 Kgs 4:1; Job 24:9; 29:12; 31:17–22; Ps 94:6; Prov 23:10; Isa 1:17, 23; Jer 5:28; 7:6; 22:3; Ezek 22:7; Zech 7:10; Mal 3:5.

the disciples after Jesus' death. Tricia Brown notices that within the Farewell Discourse, the concern is for group cohesion which is described in family imagery.[71]

In light of the above exploration of orphans in antiquity, we notice that they were truly the most vulnerable in antiquity. Without divine advocacy, as in the case of Euripides's Ion and in biblical literature, orphans would be in an utterly disastrous situation, totally dependent upon extended kin. We are also more aware that the death of a father was the death of a significant member that brought devastating consequences to children, not only socially and economically, but it left them utterly dependent upon the care of their own kinship community. We find in this fourth century (CE) papyri an orphan girl revealing the realities of her condition. The experience of abandonment is most evident in her plea. She writes,

> Before all, I pray God that my letter finds you healthy and happy. This is my prayer. Please be informed, dear aunt, that my mother, your sister, has been dead since Easter. While my mother was with me, she was my whole family. Since her death, I have remained here alone in a strange land with no one to help. Please remember me, dear aunt, as if my mother were still alive, and if you find someone to help, please send him to me. Please give my greetings to all our relatives. May the Lord protect you and keep you in good health for many peaceful years. (P. Bour. 25)

Notice that since the death of her mother she has been alone and abandoned. We do not know what happened to her father, her extended kin, nor religious community.[72] As an orphan she views herself alone in a strange land and at the mercy of family members who were far away.

The threat of social and economic instability caused by losing one's father was a problem for children. Being orphaned left children defenseless and vulnerable to oppression and exploitation, thus in need of not only their family, but also an advocate. As we can notice in the above letter, not all orphans and widows were immediately taken care of by their extended kin. There were no orphanages during antiquity until the mid-fourth century.[73]

Turning back to the Fourth Gospel, the reality of being orphaned would have been a vivid metaphor that illustrated the grave consequences of abandonment that would befall the disciples. The death of Jesus was not only going to disassociate them from him, but also from one another and

---

71. Brown, *Spirit in the Writings of John*, 204–5.

72. The closing of the letter echoes Numbers 6:24–26, which may suggest an orphan with a Christian background.

73. Fitzgerald, "Orphans in Mediterranean Antiquity," 44.

their own kinship community. How then does Jesus mitigate the pending orphaning caused by his death? How does Jesus assuage the fear of total abandonment that will result from his departure and return to the Father? Or asked another way, how can the disciples and Johannine community view themselves as "children of God," although it may appear that they have been abandoned by Jesus—the only person who made visible the Father on earth? Simply put, it is the presence of the Paraclete.

Rereading the Revelatory Activities of the Paraclete

The sending of the Spirit as Paraclete therefore compels us to bring to the forefront of our pneumatological imagination the role of advocacy for the fatherless, including the newly born children of God who are also known as the disciples and Johannine community. The παράκλητος imagery thus communicates a pneumatological advocacy for the children of God, those who are orphaned and abandoned, excommunicated, on the verge of poverty, with their land and inheritance in jeopardy, but nonetheless born of the Spirit. The forensic terminology to describe the Spirit does not emerge by accident in the Johannine discourse. The distressing experiences of the metaphorically orphaned believers, their fear of abandonment, and imminent disassociation from their kinship and one another is mitigated by the sending of the Spirit-advocate. This was the situation of the disciples and Johannine community that prompted such a need for a new image for the Spirit.

What then are the ethnic implications of the sending of the Paraclete? Or as asked earlier, what is the relationship between the Spirit-Paraclete and ethnicity? Primarily, without the Paraclete, the disciples are indeed orphaned. They are disassociated from their ethnic kin and in perpetual destabilizing ethnic relationships not only with their family, but also with each other. And for the Johannine community, without the Paraclete they would be forever spiritually orphaned—without rights, privileges, and access to the family of God. But since they truly have the Paraclete with them, the diverse ethnic Johannine community is held together and secure as God's newly born children—children who are no longer bound to ethnic and kinship relations. Even more, because of the Paraclete the disciples and Johannine community are united together to one another as newly formed ethnic kinship members, a divine family birthed by the activity of the Spirit, and all joined in a divine lineage to the Father through the authorization of Jesus.

It is within this context that we can now understand the revelatory benefits of the Paraclete's presence. This includes experiencing the teachings of Jesus because the Paraclete comes in the authority of Jesus (14:26). The Paraclete will engage in the continual pedagogical activity on Jesus' behalf, because Jesus is no longer physically on earth. Remembrance of Jesus' words certainly includes the words of Jesus found within the gospel, but also points to a future time in which the teachings of Jesus will need to be recalled and applied. As such, we must also notice that divine revelation is mediated for the disciples and Johannine community through the Paraclete. There are no teachings or remembrance of Jesus' words apart from the revelatory activity of the Spirit. This divine revelation of Jesus' words and teachings does not come to the world, for the world is incapable of knowing the Paraclete. The Father does not send the Spirit-Paraclete's revelatory benefits to the world, nor does Jesus request that the Father send the Spirit-Paraclete benefits to whomever. The world cannot experience the revelatory activities of the Spirit-Paraclete because the world is not presumed to yet be within the divine family of God. This also suggests that to experience the revelation of the Spirit presumes that one is also included within the divine family of God. The promise that Jesus gives the disciples—that the Spirit-Paraclete will be with them forever—is one of comfort and promise of continual revelation. Yet the Spirit-Paraclete is unlike a fatherly figure who will die, leave his household, or abandon his children. This presence of the Spirit-Paraclete is one that is not susceptible to the limitations of kinship families. The presence of the Spirit-Paraclete communicates the eternal presence of the Father and the Son in a divine kinship community.

The Paraclete of the Orphaned

We therefore can observe that the discussion of the Paraclete in the Farwell Discourse includes words that are spoken to disciples who are being portrayed as children and potential orphans. It is within this context of Jesus' coming death, a sense of physical abandonment and departure, that Jesus promises to send another παράκλητος who will remain with the disciples forever. The Paraclete will teach, remind, and be with the disciples. The final words of Jesus are thus given so that the disciples would not despair—they will have a Paraclete. But more specifically, the παράκλητος is one who comes to the disciples so that they would not presume that their experiences—the loss of their rabbi—would be akin to an orphan's loss of a mother or father. The gospel utilizes this child/orphan imagery on several occasions. This is no accident. And within the context of the discourse the child/orphan imagery emerges even further to describe the Spirit-Paraclete's presence in a racialized reality.

As a result, this imagery must shape how we understand the activity and presence of the Paraclete in the construction, subversion, and creation of ethnic identity as "children of God." Regardless of the dominant view that the Spirit-Paraclete is solely concerned about revelation, we notice that the Spirit-Paraclete is also concerned about understanding one's ethnic identity and kinship relations. The Spirit-Paraclete is not just the successor of Jesus, but defender of those who have been disassociated from their kinship and ethnic communities. How then can the emerging Johannine community justify any exclusion and rejection of Jewish or non-Jewish members? How can the community continue to uphold the dominance of patriarchy in the formative construction of its identity? It cannot. The promise of the Spirit is a promise to always have a legal defender who resides within and with the ethnic children of God. This is a subversive and decentralizing movement that challenges the patriarchal culture of the Johannine community. Members of the community need to be made aware that they are divine children of God because of the presence of the Paraclete. They are not just abandoned believers. All Jewish and non-Jewish believers are also "children" who are orphaned by their ethnic kin but grafted as members of the family of God through the presence and activity of the Spirit-Paraclete.

This also suggests that the Spirit-Paraclete's presence will subvert all patriarchal figures who attempt to define and determine the rights and inheritance of the ethnic children of God. Since the Spirit-Paraclete abides and resides within each member, no one patriarchal representative on earth holds the formative power over individual community members. The hegemony that patriarchal figures once held is rejected by the Spirit-Paraclete. If one is a newly born member by the Spirit, then one is a child of God. And as a child, one is a member of a community where family relations with patriarchal figures no longer hold a dominating power. What once separated ethnic members from one another—issues such as lineage and inheritance—are no more because of the Spirit. The children of God are now united together as a family of God through the indwelling presence of the Spirit-Paraclete. And again, this is not to suggest that one's cultural or ethnic identity is discarded or becomes superfluous. Instead, it is joined and fashioned along with other ethnic members because of the Spirit-Paraclete's presence and activity in continuing the mission of Jesus. Where the children of God are located, so is the presence of the Paraclete—a presence that was promised by Jesus and commissioned by the Father to be with the disciples.

12

Understanding the Paraclete in an Ethnically Hostile World

JOHN 15:26–27; 16:7–15

IN JOHN 15:26–27 AND 16:7–15 THE SPIRIT-PARACLETE IS promised to testify and engage in activities that are forensic and revelatory. Unlike before, this is a new turn in the development of the narrative. Indeed, Craig Blomberg notices that the parallels between John 15–16 and the threat of persecution in Synoptic tradition indicate that the Fourth Gospel is in touch with a reliable historic tradition.[1] Scholars recognize that the hostility in 15:18–16:15 sets the context and tone of the promise for the Paraclete.[2] This hostility comes from two fronts—the world and the synagogue. But what does it mean to suggest that this hostility is described in terms of a hatred for not belonging (15:19), excommunication from the synagogue (16:1), and the presumption that being killed would be considered an acceptable service to God (16:2)? Furthermore, what is the relationship between the revelatory and forensic activities of the Paraclete with violence, rejection, and hostility from the world? Is this possibly a warning

---

1. Blomberg, *Historical Reliability*, 209–212; Burge, *Anointed Community*, 205–6. Persecution is found in the eschatological discourses of Mark 13; Matt 10:17–25; 24–25; Luke 21.

2. Burge holds that the forensic setting of the community, in its confrontation with a hostile world, led to a heighted revelatory role for the Spirit (Burge, *Anointed Community*, 208). See Brown, *John*, 2:699; Johnston, *Spirit-Paraclete*, 141–46; Mateos and Barreto, *Juan*, 677–78; Malina and Rohrbaugh, *John*, 236–40; Segovia, "John 15:18–16:4a," 216–17.

for all who dare to remain or enter the ethnic spaces of Jewish synagogues in the late first century? These are difficult questions because they force us to envision hostility and violence occurring in ethnic spaces—a situation that also happens in many religious communities today. This chapter will thus explore the Paraclete discourse within the context of violence in ethnic spaces. Plainly, we seek to know the significance of the Paraclete's activities within the context of hate, death, and rejection from the world.

Nevertheless, we must not forget that the role of the Spirit-Paraclete in these Johannine chapters is revelatory and forensic. However, the nature of this activity is debated. The first text of our analysis includes the Paraclete's testifying role in 15:26 which states:

> When the Paraclete comes, whom I will send to you from the Father, that is the Spirit of truth who proceeds from the Father, He will testify about me. And you all will testify because from the beginning you have been with me.
>
> Ὅταν ἔλθῃ ὁ παράκλητος ὃν ἐγὼ πέμψω ὑμῖν παρὰ τοῦ πατρός, τὸ πνεῦμα τῆς ἀληθείας ὃ παρὰ τοῦ πατρὸς ἐκπορεύεται, ἐκεῖνος μαρτυρήσει περὶ ἐμοῦ. καὶ ὑμεῖς δὲ μαρτυρεῖτε, ὅτι ἀπ᾽ ἀρχῆς μετ᾽ ἐμοῦ ἐστε.

Beasley-Murray and Millos explain that in these passages the Paraclete is on a mission to humankind, but not as an advocate in defense of the disciples.[3] In this perspective, the confrontation between the disciples and the world is reduced to tension in evangelism. In other words, the Paraclete does not forensically defend the disciples but, as Beasley-Murray states, will "bring to light the truth of the revelation of Jesus in his word, deed, death, and resurrection."[4] Tricia Brown also suggests that the Paraclete does not have a forensic role in 15:26. She argues that the Paraclete will support the disciples when they witness before the world, which is akin to a patron who provides benefits to clients in times of need.[5] Both Beasley-Murray and Tricia Brown do not take into account the hostile context of Jesus' words that begin in 15:18. We must however recognize that "hatred" from the world provides the rationale for sending the Spirit-Paraclete to the disciples.[6]

---

3. Beasley-Murray, *John*, 276–77; Millos, *Juan*, 1437–41; Hoeck, "Johannine Paraclete," 28–29.

4. Beasley-Murray, *John*, 276–77.

5. Brown, *Spirit in the Writings of John*, 218–20.

6. See Estrada, "Spirit as an Inner Witness," 77–94. Here I argue that the ones who need the witness of the Paraclete include the disciples and Johannine community who are undergoing a testing of their faith. The context of presses the readers to rethink the Paraclete's witness not in relation to evangelizing to the world, but in relation to the

Others argue that the Paraclete testifies to the world through the proclamation of the community.[7] Dodd and Raymond Brown hold on to the fact that this promise of the Paraclete is indeed a forensic witness against the world through the disciples and Johannine believers.[8] The Paraclete responds to the persecution through the disciples and believers in order to establish the guilt and sin of the world. The disciples and believers will not be passive victims but give voice to the Paraclete's witness.[9] Additionally, Lindars suggests that 15:26 is akin to a legal testimony in a court of law. He interprets this testifying activity as a special inspiration of the Spirit.[10]

Is the hostile experience solely limited to a theological rejection of the community's beliefs? This is Bultmann's claim, that hatred is to be understood as a rejection of revelation.[11] And second, who is the "world" that is supposed to be in hostile tension with the disciples? We will return to these questions later.

In the Paraclete's mission of John 16:7-15 the activities are twofold: There is a forensic activity directed against the world and a revelatory activity promised for the disciples. Jesus states the following:

> But I tell you the truth, it is to your advantage that I go away; for if I do not go away, the Paraclete will not come to you; but if I go, I will send Him to you. And He, when He comes, will convict the world concerning sin and righteousness and judgment; concerning sin, because they do not believe in Me; and concerning righteousness, because I go to the Father and you no longer see Me; and concerning judgment, because the ruler of this world has been judged.
>
> ἀλλ᾽ ἐγὼ τὴν ἀλήθειαν λέγω ὑμῖν, συμφέρει ὑμῖν ἵνα ἐγὼ ἀπέλθω. ἐὰν γὰρ μὴ ἀπέλθω, ὁ παράκλητος οὐκ ἐλεύσεται πρὸς ὑμᾶς. ἐὰν δὲ πορευθῶ, πέμψω αὐτὸν πρὸς ὑμᾶς. καὶ ἐλθὼν ἐκεῖνος ἐλέγξει τὸν κόσμον περὶ ἁμαρτίας καὶ περὶ δικαιοσύνης καὶ περὶ κρίσεως. περὶ ἁμαρτίας μέν, ὅτι οὐ πιστεύουσιν εἰς ἐμέ. περὶ δικαιοσύνης δέ, ὅτι πρὸς τὸν πατέρα ὑπάγω καὶ οὐκέτι θεωρεῖτέ με. περὶ δὲ κρίσεως, ὅτι ὁ ἄρχων τοῦ κόσμου τούτου κέκριται.

---

disciples and Johannine community's hostile context.

7. Bultmann, *John*, 553-54; Morris, *John*, 607; Harm, "Distinctive Titles," 125; Keener, *John*, 1021-22; Michaels, *John*, 825-26; Thompson, *John*, 334.

8. Dodd, *Interpretation*, 414; Brown, *John*, 2:690.

9. Brown, *John*, 2:698-701; Burge, *Anointed Community*, 206.

10. Lindars, *John*, 496-97.

11. Bultmann, *John*, 549; Segovia, "John 15:18-16:4a," 221-22.

Many hold different views on the significance of "ἐλέγξει" in v. 8, which is translated as "convict."[12] Some regard these passages in reference to the Paraclete's convicting role on the conscience of the world through the inspired utterances of a post-resurrection community.[13] Keener suggests that since Jesus sends the Spirit to the disciples in 16:7, the Spirit-Paraclete continues to prosecute the world through the apostolic preaching.[14] Millos follows a similar reading while noticing that this activity is necessary given the human condition.[15] Mateos and Barreto argue that the Spirit gives the disciples the possibility to love while at the same time proclaiming the world's judgement.[16] Bultmann however describes the Paraclete's activity as a cosmic lawsuit that aims to expose the world's guilt in the court of God, not the conscience of people.[17]

Others such as Raymond Brown and Tricia Brown suggest that the recipient of the Paraclete is not the world—it is the disciples. Raymond Brown states, "the idea that the world is to be convinced by the Paraclete contradicts the statement of 14:17 that the world cannot accept the Paraclete." Instead, the courtroom of the world is in the "mind of the disciples."[18] Likewise, Tricia Brown asserts that the "Paraclete will prove to the disciples the guilt of the world" just as Jesus "exposed the wrongness of the world."[19] These readings agree that the Paraclete's activity is a communicatory activity. However, they differ on the recipients, the location, and how this is made manifest.

---

12. For example, Lutkemeyer holds that is not to be understood forensically but rather in a social religious sense (Lutkemeyer, "Role of the Paraclete," 222). Harm reviews the three possible interpretations for the term but does not argue one or the other (Harm, "Distinctive Titles," 127). Carson outlines six different views that stem from four different translations of ἐλέγξει, which include: to prove, convict, convince, and expose. See Carson, "Function of the Paraclete," 547–66. Aloisi proposes a modified view from Carson. He points to similar verbal and propositional construction of John 16:8 with 8:46. See Aloisi, "Paraclete's Ministry of Conviction," 55–69, esp. 60.

13. Barrett, *St. John*, 405–7; Johnston, *Spirit-Paraclete*, 38; Lindars, *John*, 498; Morris, *John*, 619–20; Beasley-Murray, *John*, 280–81; Thompson, *John*, 338.

14. Keener, *John*, 1030.

15. Millos, *Juan*, 1458–60; Michaels, *John*, 834.

16. Mateos and Barreto, *Juan*, 682. Michaels notices a dynamic literary fusion between the "Jews" and the "world" within these chapters. He points out that Jesus' warning is mainly about the disciples' experience with the Jews with little attention to the fate awaiting them in the Graeco-Roman cities and Roman authorities. See Michaels, *John*, 836.

17. Bultmann, *John*, 561–62.

18. Brown, *John*, 2:711–12. See also Reese, "Role of the Paraclete," 40.

19. Brown, *Spirit in the Writings of John*, 223.

The last mention of the Paraclete takes a specific direction toward its role with the disciples. Jesus continues:

> I have many more things to say to you, but you cannot bear them now. But when he comes, the Spirit of truth, he will guide you into all the truth; for he will not speak on his own initiative, but whatever he hears, he will speak, and he will disclose to you what is to come. He will glorify me, for he will take of mine and will disclose to you. All things that the Father has are mine, therefore I said that he takes of mine and disclose to you.

> Ἔτι πολλὰ ἔχω ὑμῖν λέγειν, ἀλλ᾽ οὐ δύνασθε βαστάζειν ἄρτι. ὅταν δὲ ἔλθῃ ἐκεῖνος, τὸ πνεῦμα τῆς ἀληθείας, ὁδηγήσει ὑμᾶς ἐν τῇ ἀληθείᾳ πάσῃ. οὐ γὰρ λαλήσει ἀφ᾽ ἑαυτοῦ, ἀλλ᾽ ὅσα ἀκούσει λαλήσει, καὶ τὰ ἐρχόμενα ἀναγγελεῖ ὑμῖν. ἐκεῖνος ἐμὲ δοξάσει, ὅτι ἐκ τοῦ ἐμοῦ λήμψεται καὶ ἀναγγελεῖ ὑμῖν. πάντα ὅσα ἔχει ὁ πατὴρ ἐμά ἐστιν. διὰ τοῦτο εἶπον ὅτι ἐκ τοῦ ἐμοῦ λαμβάνει καὶ ἀναγγελεῖ ὑμῖν.

It must be noted that although the Spirit-Paraclete (also known as the Spirit of Truth) is promised to communicate to the disciples, debate centers on whether or not this includes future revelation (v. 13). Bultmann believes that the Spirit will neither contrast Jesus' words nor bring any new illumination, and certainly will not disclose new mysteries.[20] Beasley-Murray asserts that any notion of a prophetic ministry is "out of harmony with the general outlook of this gospel."[21] Millos explains that the Spirit will amplify the comprehension of Jesus' truth, not only to understand it, but to apply it to one's life and "nothing else."[22] Lindars however disagrees with these claims. He finds that these passages refer to the prophetic gift which was recognized in the early church.[23] Others who follow Lindars interpret the Paraclete's activity in reference to future prophetic revelation.[24] This includes Keener and Michaels, whom also notice the difficulties in determining whether the

---

20. Bultmann, *John*, 575; Barrett, *St. John*, 408.

21. Beasley-Murray, *John*, 283–84; Morris, *John*, 622; Lutkemeyer, "Role of the Paraclete," 228; Hoeck, "Johannine Paraclete," 34–36.

22. Millos states, "De modo que el Espíritu deje de revelar eventos futuros porque lo que tuvo que anunciar en ese sentido ya se hizo y ya no se puede añadirse nada más a la profecía ya cerrada" (Millos, *Juan*, 1469–70). See Brown, *John*, 2:714.

23. Lindars, *John*, 505.

24. Johnston, *Spirit-Paraclete*, 39; Brown, *Spirit in the Writings of John*, 232; Mateos and Barreto, *Juan*, 684; Stefan, "Paraclete and Prophecy," 273–96.

revelatory activity refers to eschatological events or detailed instruction on what the disciples will face.[25]

In review of the Spirit-Paraclete in John 15–16, we can observe some common agreements and differences. Most scholars recognize that hostility sets the scene for the Spirit-Paraclete sayings. There is also agreement that the Spirit-Paraclete is a testifier. Yet differences emerge on whether this testifying activity is missional, forensic, or in a supportive role for the disciples. There is also a recognition that the Spirit-Paraclete will engage in forensic activity by convicting the world on a variety of issues, but scholars again disagree on whether this activity is going to occur in the courtroom of God, in the human conscience, or in the conscience of the disciples. All agree that the revelation of the Spirit-Paraclete is Christocentric. The Spirit-Paraclete will lead the disciples into truth and will only communicate messages that coincide with Jesus' teaching. Scholars differ, though, on whether this includes revelation of the future. Although we can notice the range of views on the Spirit-Paraclete's revelatory activity, there is another crucial aspect that deserves our attention. That is, expanding upon the concrete images and experiences that set the stage for the Spirit-Paraclete's communicatory activity. This stage, as I argue, is an ethnically hostile world.

Why a focus on ethnic hostility as the context of these Paraclete sayings? Simply put, it is because Jesus describes the coming of the Paraclete within a context of hate, death, and rejection from all people—whom are categorized and described as the "world." I agree with Brown's conjecture that the catalyst for mentioning the Spirit in these passages is precisely the context of persecution from the world,[26] but my argument expands upon what we mean by the "world." This is not a vague concept or simply a part of a symbolic universe. It includes ethnic dynamics and realities. More specifically, it includes the subversive representation of the "other" as a violent group. We will thus examine the ethnic context of the Spirit-Paraclete passages in 15:18–16:15 with a focus on significance of "world" as ethnic classification language and "synagogues" as ethnic spaces of violence. After reviewing these dynamics, we will observe how the revelatory and forensic activities of the Spirit-Paraclete would be understood by the ethnically diverse but minoritized Johannine community that found itself being situated

---

25. Keener, *John*, 1041; Michaels, *John*, 837.

26. Brown, *John*, 2:699–700. He further notices that the role of bearing witness in times of persecution is akin to the promise of the Spirit in Matt 10:20; Mark 13:11; Luke 12:12. The difference, as he points out, is that the Synoptics describe the Spirit as defending the disciples before various authorities instead of the world. See also Burge, *Anointed Community*, 208; Johnston, *Spirit-Paraclete*, 141–46; Mateos and Barreto, *Juan*, 677–78; Malina and Rohrbaugh, *John*, 236–40.

in a context of hostility from various ethnic groups whom the gospel describes as the "world."

The "World" as Classification Ethnic Language in 15:18–25

It is difficult to avoid noticing that the Fourth Gospel views the first century Jewish people as Jesus' main opponents. The context of 15:18–16:15 however does not draw attention to the "Jews" as we had become accustomed in Jesus' public ministry. In fact, there is no mention of the "Jews" within John 14–17, only vague references in 15:25 and 16:2 which point to the Jewish law and the synagogue. The silence is noticeable. A different opponent emerges in the dialogue. Jesus urges his disciples to concern themselves with the "world" who will hate and persecute them. Why is there this focus on the world (κόσμος) with a mild inference to the Jewish law and hostility in the synagogue?

When we explore the Spirit-Paraclete sayings in 15:18–16:15, the world certainly takes a center stage as a new group of people who will pose a threat to the disciples. In fact, Jesus uses six conditional clauses prior to 15:26 that reveal the imminent danger from the world. The conditional statements are as follows:

15:18	If the world hates you, know that it has hated me before it hated you
15:19	If you were of the world, the world would love its own
15:20	If they persecuted me, they will also persecute you
15:20	If they kept my word, they will keep yours also
15:22	If I had not come and spoken to them, they would not have sin, but now they have no excuse for their sin.
15:24	If I had not done among them the works which no one else did, they would not have sin. But now they have both seen and hated me and my Father as well.
15:25	But they have done this to fulfill the word that is written in their law, "they hated me without a cause."

Jesus begins his discussion about a hatred he experienced from the world (v. 18). The world is described as having a hostile encounter with Jesus which will result in a similar experience for the disciples (vv. 18–21). The narrative, however, describes Jesus' detailed experiences, specifically that he has "spoken" and done "works" among them. But these activities do not seem to fit with a broader and more general understanding of κόσμος. So, what is the significance of the "world" here?

Certainly, when we explore κόσμος in Greek literature, it is used in reference for the universe in general[27] and for a sense of order—a distinct meaning that is not found in the New Testament.[28] Κόσμος is also found in reference to ornaments, whether worn by women, men, or metaphorically for an embellished speech.[29] But out of all the Jewish writers, Philo is one who frequently uses κόσμος. In particular, Philo's *De mundi opificio* utilizes κόσμος in reference to order,[30] adornment,[31] the intellect,[32] the created earth,[33] and to describe humanity as a "citizen of the world" (κοσμοπολίτης).[34] Philo's use of κοσμοπολίτης is striking because he equates Adam, whom he describes as the founder of the Jewish race, as the first human being and citizen of the world. Indeed, the entire world was his city.[35] But elsewhere, κοσμοπολίτης takes a pejorative sense in that in order to be a "citizen of the world," (or as he describes—a cosmopolitan), one needs not to be fixed upon divine affairs. Essentially, Philo claims that only the prophets and priests concern themselves with divine affairs because they are "born of God" (οἱ δὲ θεοῦ γεγόνασιν ἄνθρωποι).[36]

Is the Fourth Gospel imitating Philo's contrasting use of κοσμοπολίτης? Perhaps so. Nonetheless, we can observe the various and fluid uses of κόσμος within Philo. Scholars also notice that there seems to be a fusion

---

27. Xen. *Mem.* 1.1.11; Plato, *Tim.* 27a; 30b; *Epin.* 987b; Isocrates, *Paneg.* 4.179.

28. Homer, *Il.* 10.472; *Od.* 8.179; 13.77; Herodotus, *Hist.* 8.86; Plato, *Leg.* 8.846d. Plato's use of κόσμος appears in his description on the unification of all beings through order. He states, "Heaven and earth and gods and men are held together by communion and friendship, by orderliness (κοσμιότητα), temperance, and justice; and that is the reason, my friend, why they call the whole of this world by the name of order (κόσμον), not of disorder (ἀκοσμίαν) or dissoluteness" (*Gorg.* 507e–508a).

29. Homer, *Il.* 14.187; Hesiod, *Op.* 76; Herodotus, *Hist.* 3.123; 5.92; Isocrates, *Evag.* 9.9; Aristotle, *Poet.* 1457b; Plindar, *Ol.* 11. See also 1 Pet 3:3.

30. Philo, *De Opif.* 1.33.

31. Philo, *De Opif.* 1.53, 62, 139.

32. Philo, *De Opif.* 1.15, 17, 19–20, 24–26, 35–36, 55, 66. See Winden, "World of Ideas in Philo," 209–217.

33. Philo, *De Opif.* 1.3, 7, 9, 11–14, 16, 25–26, 52, 77–78, 89, 111, 131, 142–43, 146, 151, 171–72. He also uses the κοσμοποιία for "created world" in 1.3–4, 6, 129, 170.

34. Philo, *De Opif.* 1.3, 142–43;

35. Philo remarks, "If we call the original founder of our race not only the first man, but also the first citizen of the world (κοσμοπολίτην). For the world (κόσμος) was his house and his city" (*Opif.* 143).

36. Philo, *Gig.* 1.161.

of the "world" and the "Jews" in the Johannine dialogue, especially since this context uses the pronoun "them/their" (αὐτός) in vv. 22–25 and Jesus previously asserted that the Jews were "from this world."[37] Is Jesus warning the disciples about a future conflict with their own people? The use of γινώσκετε, which translated as an imperative in 15:18–20, conveys the idea that the disciples should not fail to understand that the world hates them. Jesus' maxim that a "slave is not greater than the master" in 15:20 informs the disciples that they should expect similar hostility and death.[38] He explains in v. 21, "all these things they will do to you on account of my name, and because they do not know the one who sent me." Furthermore, in vv. 22–25 Jesus also discloses to the disciples that the world is guilty of sin and has no excuse, even though the readers can recall that this echoes Jesus' activity with the Jews in his public ministry.[39]

The discussion suggests that association with Jesus will lead one to experience violence from the world. Yet it also includes an indirect reference to the Jews, who throughout Jesus' public ministry were hostile and challenging, although not in all occasions. Jesus even claims that the persecution and hatred of the "world" actually "fulfills what is written in their law that they hated me without a cause" (πληρωθῇ ὁ λόγος ὁ ἐν τῷ νόμῳ αὐτῶν γεγραμμένος ὅτι Ἐμίσησάν με δωρεάν [15:25]).[40] Barrett suggests that the mention of "their law" (νόμῳ αὐτῶν) in this passage points to a Jewish self-condemnation.[41] Beasley-Murray agrees, but adds that this mode of speech does not indicate that Jesus is disassociating himself from Jewish scripture.[42] Certainly, Jesus' appeal to the law is not new. It is a claim he had previously made during his public ministry.[43] However, Jesus does not mention the "Jews" in these statements. He simply describes the opponents as the "κόσμος." Does this confirm the suspicion that the Jews and the world are indeed identical in this discourse? The Jewish law is certainly being referenced, which seems to corroborate the fact that the "Jews" and the "world"

---

37. Lindars, *John*, 495; Brown, *John*, 2:696; Keener, *John*, 1018; Morris, *John*, 601–2; Michaels, *John*, 820–21; Burge, *Anointed Community*, 206; Bultmann, *John*, 548; Segovia, "John 15:18–16:4a," 225–26. See John 8:23.

38. Also found in Matt 10:24; Luke 6:40.

39. John 3:20; 7:7; 8:21, 26, 31–36; 9:41.

40. The reference of this passage is either Ps 35:19 [LXX 34:19] or Ps 69:4 [LXX 68:5]. Also found in *Pss. Sol.* 7.1. Lindars suggests that Ps 69:4 [LXX 68:5] is to be preferred given its wide use in the New Testament and previous citation in John 2:17; 19:28–30 (Lindars, *John*, 495).

41. Barrett, *St. John*, 402.

42. Beasley-Murray, *John*, 276.

43. John 5:37–39; 45–47; 7:19; 8:17; 10:34; 12:34–41.

are equivalent. Why not just use the designation "Jews" in this discourse instead? Why the allusion to the Jews and a distinct focus on κόσμος as fomenters of violence?

The gospel's use of κόσμος is not new. In fact, it occurs 78 times whereas the Synoptic Gospels utilize the term a combined total of 14 times.[44] When we explore κόσμος in the Fourth Gospel, Bultmann argues that it primarily means the world of humanity.[45] He also explains that, theologically, the world's essence is essentially non-existence, or "unreality," given its desire to cling to sin, darkness, bondage, death, and falsehood.[46] Millos notices that when Jesus speaks about the world hating the disciples, the use of κόσμος suggests that this will include a great multitude of people.[47] He also defines the world as those who live in a system of corruption and sin.[48] This reading is akin to Mateos and Barreto who recognize that the world is a "sistema opresor" and "sistema injusto."[49] John Ashton remarks that κόσμος is often used to contrast heaven with the earth in a vertical opposition.[50] But in other occasions, especially in John 15–17, κόσμος is set to contrast the community with the world.[51] Certainly, the Fourth Gospel contains various uses of the term.[52] But as Bultmann and Paul Rainbow assert, κόσμος conveys the concept of the human race.[53] Rainbow notices that the gospel thinks of the "world" collectively and in terms of God's creation that is in desperate need of salvation.[54] However, his reading later proposes that the "Jews"

---

44. Brown, *John*, 1:508.

45. Bultmann, *Theology of the New Testament*, 2:15; Barrett, *St. John*, 135; John 1:29; 3:16–17, 19; 4:42; 6:14, 33, 51; 7:4, 7; 8:12, 26; 9:5, 39; 10:36; 11:9; 12:19, 31, 46–47; 18:20.

46. Bultmann, *Theology of the New Testament*, 2:16–18.

47. Millos, *Juan*, 1425.

48. Millos, *Juan*, 1458–59.

49. Mateos and Barreto, *Juan*, 682–84.

50. Ashton, *Understanding*, 396; John 1:9–10; 3:31; 8:23; 11:27; 12:25; 13:1; 16:33; 17:5, 11, 16, 24; 18:36–37; 21:25.

51. Ashton, *Understanding*, 399. Lindars notes that the disciples are formed as a distinct category in society (Lindars, *John*, 493). John 14:17, 19, 22, 27, 30–31; 15:18–19; 16:8, 20, 28; 17:6, 9, 13–18, 21–23, 25.

52. For example, κόσμος does refer to the sphere of human existence (1:9; 3:19; 8:23; 9:5; 10:36; 11:9, 27; 12:25, 31, 46; 13:1; 14:30; 16:11, 21, 28, 33; 17:13, 16; 18:36–37), the created earth (1:10; 17:5, 11, 15, 18, 24; 21:25), humanity (1:29; 3:16–17; 4:42; 6:14; 7:4, 7; 8:26; 12:19, 47; 14:17, 19, 22, 27, 31; 15:18–19; 16:8, 20; 17:6, 9, 14, 21, 23, 25; 18:20), and in general for all creation (6:33, 51; 8:12; 9:39). See Köstenberger, *Theology of John's Gospel*, 281–82.

53. Rainbow, *Johannine Theology*, 121.

54. Rainbow, *Johannine Theology*, 122.

are presented in the gospel as representatives of the world.⁵⁵ Is Rainbow's reading the most probable, that the Jews are certainly representatives of the world? Or are the Jews part of the world? Why the fusion of these identities in the discourse?

In order to understand the rhetoric of Jesus' warning about a coming persecution, we must recognize that the world is not defining itself. It is being defined by Jesus in terms of its violent actions and rejection. When did the "world" hate, fail to know, or persecute Jesus? It was only the Jews that Jesus primarily had contact. When did Jesus ever perform miracles and speak to the entire world? Never, his activity was limited to the region of Galilee, Samaria, and Judea. When did the world ever persecute Jesus? Within the narrative the only hostility and threat of violence has come from the Jewish people and Jewish religious leaders. At this point in the narrative, Jesus had not been arrested nor crucified. Jesus certainly cannot be equating the "Jews" with the "world" as if there is no distinction. Despite this, Jesus simply does, and even defines the world as "haters." Strikingly, Jesus borrows the similar ethnic stereotype used against the Jews to describe the world.⁵⁶ Why is this so? Why such generalities and characterization? This is not hyperbolic. When we are thinking about characterization and representation of people, we must recognize that the use of the "world" in this dialogue is also an ethnic stereotype. But in what way is κόσμος operating in the dialogue? Is this perhaps a pejorative description? It most certainly is.

Edward Said reminds us that in interpreting and understanding the other, we must be mindful that descriptions are just representations that include dynamics of power and ethno-superiority. In Said's publication of *Orientalism*, he argues that the literary representations of Orientals in Western studies, the academy, and intellectual thought since the nineteenth century included a tendency of misrepresentation and misinterpretation. Primarily, it is found in the statements, authorizing views, descriptions, and teaching about the Orient in the academy and political discourse by Westerners. Said notices that in representing the Orient, the West had authority over the Orient and how the Orient was to be understood and defined. But even more, in the Westerner's description and representation of the Orient, the Orient also helped define the West as a "contrasting image, idea, personality, [and] experience."⁵⁷ As Said states, "European culture gained in strength and identity by setting itself off against the Orient as a sort of surrogate and

---

55. Rainbow, *Johannine Theology*, 136.

56. The Jews were called "haters of humanity" by Diodorus of Sicily (34.1.1–5; 40.3.4); Tacitus (*Hist.* 5.2–8). See Schäfer, *Judeophobia*, 6–11.

57. Said, *Orientalism*, 2.

even underground self."⁵⁸ As a consequence, the Oriental was also made Oriental through Western creation and representation.

This was more than just a Western creation on how the Orient was to be understood and perceived. The issue was about dynamics of power and the creation of identity through the negative portrayal of the other. Said notices that the representation of the Oriental for Western minds also left the Westerner in a superior position.⁵⁹ Their representations were not a natural depiction of the Orient but a deformation of the Orient. Said thus argues that there was no correct representation nor fidelity to Oriental culture, thought, or identity. The Oriental was never given an opportunity to speak for itself but was placed in a position where the Westerner spoke on its behalf.⁶⁰ This is a fundamental argument that Said makes throughout his monograph. That is, the tendency to construct the image of the Oriental in all its representations—which is really an attempt to present the Oriental negatively and in antithesis of Western identity.⁶¹ And in many ways, the West is that which the Orient is not.

But why the arbitrary construction of identity in terms of antithetical images and portraits between the East and West? Said indeed notices that the boundaries are arbitrary, but they are also more than that. They expose power in the creation of the "other." He states, "'they' become 'they' accordingly, and both their territory and their mentality are designate as different from 'ours.'"⁶² In other words, it is in the representation that one comes to define both the "other" in terms of what they are and also in terms of what they are not. In addition to this, these descriptions, representations, and even drawing of boundaries between "them" and "us," is also in itself an act of power. It is the power to define the other without giving the other an opportunity to speak for itself. Also embedded in this representation of the other is the act of placing oneself in a superior position and authority over them. Said recognizes in the literary history of representing the Orient that "they" are defined as something completely opposite to "us." He views this as a way in which the "Orient became known in the West as its great complementary opposite since antiquity."⁶³

What then are the implications for our study of the κόσμος in the Farewell Discourse? I argue that the κόσμος is "otherness" language that

58. Said, *Orientalism*, 3.
59. Said, *Orientalism*, 12.
60. Said, *Orientalism*, 21.
61. Said, *Orientalism*, 23–39.
62. Said, *Orientalism*, 54.
63. Said, *Orientalism*, 58.

embraces and envelops all ethnic groups who are in positions of power to harm or threaten the Johannine community with hate, death, and rejection. Unlike the Western characterizations and misrepresentations of the Oriental, Jesus describes the world from the perspective of the oppressed. Jesus is not in a privileged position, nor are the disciples and Johannine community the dominate group in Ephesus. Jesus has called the disciples "out of the world" (John 15:19) which means that they and the Johannine community are a minoritized community. Furthermore, as a minoritized community, they are also the ones who experience and encounter hostility and violence from the people in power. In this sense, there is a subversive representation of the dominate ethnic group who, in positions of power, are simply oppressors. This is why it is not appropriate to utilize the term "Jews" in this discourse but rather the broader ethnic term κόσμος which includes all ethnic groups who hold onto notions of ethnic superiority and violence over the oppressed. Those who are in power or who view themselves as religiously and ethnically superior are unmasked and exposed for what they really are to the disciples and Johannine community—they are the world.

With this in mind, what does this mean specifically and contextually? One becomes the "world" with the embrace of violence and power toward minority communities. No longer can the disciples or Johannine community presume that the world is restrictively a reference to the Jews—their own kin. It will include other ethnic groups such as Samaritans, Greeks, Romans, and many others. The world includes those who aim to violently oppress the minoritized community. The world is the oppressor and the disciples and Johannine people of God are the oppressed.

This reading of κόσμος however is not new. It elaborates upon Raymond Brown and Wayne Meeks's views of the Johannine community. In fact, Brown suggests that in the gospel κόσμος is a common term used for those who are not part of the Johannine community. He asserts that the term is not akin to "Jews" as if there was no distinction. Instead, it is a wider concept that refers to opposition from both Jews and Gentiles.[64] Brown proposes that the use of this language in the discourse reflects the community's alienation and isolation.[65] Meeks claims that the community had to distinguish themselves from others while also experiencing conflict, schisms, and defections.[66] He finds that the gospel utilizes a dualistic picture of a small group of believers isolated against the world. The world, in his estimation, includes those who are from "below" and are contrasted with Jesus who is

64. Brown, *Community*, 63–65.
65. Brown, *Community*, 64.
66. Meeks, "Man from Heaven," 59; See also Malina and Rohrbaugh, *John*, 236–40.

from "above" and not of this world.⁶⁷ Meeks also notices that "to come to faith in Jesus is for the Johannine groups a change in social location" and this also includes a "decisive break with the world."⁶⁸

I agree with Meeks's view that the community experienced alienation from Judaism and the "world." I also agree with Brown that the "world" is used as a term to contrast the community from all others. Yet the real issue in John 15:18–25 is not solely about sectarian or theological separation from the world. Both Brown and Meeks do not elaborate upon the ethnic implications and construction of identity with the Paraclete sayings. My point is that κόσμος is not solely a theological concept nor equivalent to "Ἰουδαῖος." Undeniably, within the New Testament, κόσμος is used within the context of nations or humanity in general.⁶⁹ But κόσμος within this dialogue stirs our ethnic imagination and does not narrow its restrictions or categorization to one particular ethnic group. Instead, it is ethnic classification language that subverts the ethnic identities of those who are in power and presume to be in a privileged and superior ethnic position.

Yet κόσμος as an ethnic classification term also does something else. In its aim to communicate otherness, difference, categorize, and classify any ethnic group that is not a part of "us," it also projects a fear of the other. The world could be anybody who is not "us." The world is defined and projected upon all people who are not members of the disciples or Johannine community.⁷⁰ This also means that the disciples and by extension—Johannine community—are being made aware that the hostility they will experience will come from all people—and no one distinct ethnic group will be the sole proprietor of conflict. The threat will come from various people, and the disciples and Johannine community must be aware about these coming dangers. As such, κόσμος within this context creates fear, mistrust, and suspicion of the "other," not because they are ethnically different, but because they possess the power to enact violence upon the minoritized community. As a result, it is for this reason that the Spirit-Paraclete must come to the disciples and Johannine community as a forensic defender, testifier, communicator of Jesus' teachings, and revealer of all things.

In this way, we can observe that the Spirit-Paraclete does more than just testify to the disciples or engage in a missional activity. The very presence of the Spirit-Paraclete, as a defender of the oppressed and orphaned,

---

67. Meeks, "Man from Heaven," 75–76.
68. Meeks, "Man from Heaven," 77.
69. Matt 4:8; 5:14; 13:38; 18:7; 26:13; Mark 14:9; 16:15; Luke 12:30; Rom 1:8; 3:6, 19; 11:12, 15; 1 Cor 1:20–21; 4:9, 13; Jas 1:27; 4:4; 2 Pet 2:20.
70. John 14:17, 19, 27; 15:18–19; 16:8–11.

comes to aid those who have fallen under the violent attack and brutal oppression of the world. The Spirit-Paraclete testifies to the disciples, and by extension the Johannine community, that the world in all its gruesome hatred and violence toward the minority community is nothing new. The disciples and Johannine community are not alone in their experiences. The Spirit-Paraclete testifies and reminds the disciples that Jesus was oppressed by the world as well. As a response, the Spirit-Paraclete comes from the Father as their advocate, standing alongside them, with them and in them as their defender. The Spirit-Paraclete reveals to the disciples that the people whom they see are not really who they may appear to be, they are the "world." The testimony of the Spirit includes the revelation of the disciples' true reality: that those who claim to be "religious," regardless of their attempts to worship God, are really unmasked for being the very hypocritical people who use legalities to justify their hatred, rejection, and oppression of the orphaned children of God.[71]

The Synagogue and the "Jews" in 16:1–6

When we continue to 16:1–6 the hatred and persecution from the world becomes more specific. Jesus tells the disciples that "they will put you out of the synagogues (ἀποσυνάγωγος)" and "kill you" (vv. 1–2). This is not the first time that this excommunication (ἀποσυνάγωγος) language emerges in the gospel. It is a rare word that only appears three times in the gospel and nowhere else in the New Testament or Septuagint. It is often translated as "put out of the synagogue,"[72] "banned from the synagogue,"[73] or in Spanish and a few English translations, "expelled from the synagogue."[74]

The first time that ἀποσυνάγωγος occurs is in 9:22, where we find a story of a blind man who Jesus healed. The religious authorities interrogate the parents of the formerly blind man because they want to know who healed their son. The parents knew that it was Jesus, but they avoid confessing to this fact. Instead, they tell the religious authorities to ask their son because he is old enough to speak for himself. The narrator explains the underlying motivation of the parent's response. The text states, "His parents said this

---

71. We see this most explicitly today, in 2019, when Evangelical "Christians" do not mind seeing Latinx immigrant children die in cages at the border in Texas. They think that by honoring US immigration law, they are honoring God.

72. NASB, NET, NIV, RSV, NKJV, ESV.

73. NJB, CSB.

74. NLT, NAB. Strikingly, the Spanish NIV (NVI), KJV (RV), and *Biblia de las Americas* (LBA) all translate the term with the phrase "expulsarán de la sinagoga" which is another way of saying "expelled from the synagogue."

because they were afraid of the Jews, for the Jews had already agreed that if anyone confessed him to be Christ, he was to be put out of the synagogue (ἀποσυνάγωγος)."

The second time that ἀποσυνάγωγος emerges is in 12:42. In this occasion there are certain Jewish rulers who were afraid to openly claim allegiance to Jesus. Like the parents of the man born blind, they too were afraid of being excommunicated (ἀποσυνάγωγος) from the synagogue. More specifically, the narrator mentions that the Jewish rulers were afraid of the Pharisees. This subtle comment in the gospel makes it seem as if the Pharisees were responsible for the synagogue expulsions, which certainly grants them more power and authority than they truly had during Jesus' ministry.[75]

Now in 16:2 the term ἀποσυνάγωγος appears for the third time. We notice that no Pharisees or Jews are mentioned in this discourse, but it is assumed. Jesus explains the reason for this warning was to prevent the disciples from "stumbling."[76] In fact, he explicitly restates his purpose in 16:4 with the similar language of 16:1. He states, "These things I have spoken to you so that when the hour comes you may remember that I have spoken of them." The disciples are exhorted to remember and know the reason why they are undergoing synagogue expulsion. This warning in 15:18–25 and 16:1–4 are Jesus' attempt to prevent the disciples from succumbing to the pressures of persecution in the synagogue.

It is, however, J. Louis Martyn with his monumental *History and Theology in the Fourth Gospel* who caused scholars to think about synagogue excommunication and its relationship to the Johannine community. As previously mentioned, Martyn believes that the gospel develops a new and unique interpretation by blending the experiences of the community's circumstances with the events that occurred during Jesus' life.[77] Martyn calls this doubling a "two-level drama."[78] According to Martyn, when we read the gospel we are reading the experience of the church engaged in a traumatic expulsion from the synagogue in the late first century.

---

75. See Sanders, *Judaism*, 393–98; Dunn, *Jesus, Paul, and the Law*, 66; Ashton, *Gospel of John and Christian Origins*, 45–46.

76. The term used for stumbling is σκανδαλίζω which carries notions of being offended or shocked. This term appears here and in 6:61 when Jesus spoke about "eating his flesh and drinking his blood." Jesus' teaching did not only shock the hearers, it led many followers to desert him. See Stahlin, "σκανδαλίζω," *TDNT* 7:344–52.

77. Martyn, *History and Theology*, 30.

78. Martyn, *History and Theology*, 40.

Evidence of this two-level drama is specifically found in the synagogue expulsions of 9:22, 12:42, and 16:2.[79] Specifically, Martyn argues that the term ἀποσυνάγωγος suggests that the person had been "made a synagogue excommunicate."[80] In other words, this is a characteristic of those who have been expelled. He considers 16:2 as evidence that "certain members of the Johannine church had already been detected as heretics and excommunicated from the synagogue."[81] Like Brown, he suggests that the threat of death in 16:2 was not just a warning of a future threat, but the reality of the Johannine community. As Martyn states, "an experience which so impressed John that he allowed it to be clearly reflected in dramatic form elsewhere in the gospel."[82]

Although Martyn's thesis has been recently challenged, it is difficult to avoid noticing how the horizons between Jesus' ministry in the gospel intersect with the possible Johannine experience with late first-century Judaism. If we are hearing the words of Jesus address the Johannine community in 16:2 as Martyn claims, then the community understands what it means to experience hate, death, and rejection by their fellow synagogue members. Yet the question we must ask is the following: why would we assume that only Jews would be persecuted and killed in the synagogue? Martyn's thesis rests upon the assumption that only Jewish Christians are being excommunicated from the synagogue. He does not take into consideration the possibility that the Johannine community was ethnically diverse and that those who were expelled would have also included God-fearing Gentiles. In fact, archeological and literary evidence suggests that the synagogues were not only ethnic Jewish spaces, but built by Gentiles, dedicated to Gentiles, and inhabited by Gentiles in the diaspora.

First, we must note that the term "synagogue" (συναγωγὴ) referred to a building that is set apart for religious purposes, a congregation, or a generic term for a gathering of people. Simply defined, it is a "gathering" or "assembly" that was later associated with a Jewish community space.[83] Although the origin of the synagogue is difficult to historically identify and define, Lee Levine suggests that by the first century it was primarily a communal institution where a wide range of Jewish activities found expression.[84] The synagogue was Jesus' frequent destination whenever he entered

---

79. Martyn, *History and Theology*, 47–48.
80. Martyn, *History and Theology*, 48.
81. Martyn, *History and Theology*, 66.
82. Martyn, *History and Theology*, 71.
83. See 1 Macc 2:42; 7:12; 14:28; Schrage, "συναγωγὴ," *TDNT* 8:798–805.
84. Levine, *Ancient Synagogue*, 23. Charlesworth notices that pre-70 CE synagogues

Capernaum, Nazareth, and Galilee. It was within a synagogue that Jesus taught, healed, and expelled demons.[85] It is not clear if all the portrayals of the synagogues in the gospel tradition reflect the late post-70 or a pre-70 CE period. However, we have much reason to suspect that there was continuity. Furthermore, it was Raimund Weill's discovery of a limestone inscription in Mount Ophel of Jerusalem, also known as the "Theodotus Inscription," that confirms this notion. The inscription provides evidence on the role and function of synagogues in Judea that are reflective of the gospel tradition. The inscription states:

> Theodotus, son of Vettanos, a priest and a leader of the synagogue son of a leader of the synagogue grandson of a leader of the synagogue, built the synagogue for the reading of the Torah and for teaching the commandments; furthermore, the guestroom, and the chambers, and the water installation for lodging needy strangers. Its foundation stone was laid by his ancestors, the elders, and Simonides. (CIJ 1404)

This pre-70 CE inscription confirms much of the synagogue activities we find in the gospels, particularly that of teaching and the role of a synagogue leader.[86] It describes a priest and synagogue leader by the name of Theodotus who established the synagogue as a place for reading the law, teaching the commandments, and refuge for visitors. And we can notice that the synagogue was a multi-purpose building that housed a variety of Jewish religious and social activities.

Synagogues were also distinctly ethnic spaces for Jews. When hostility emerged throughout the empire, Philo noticed that to attack a synagogue was to attack the Jewish people.[87] Even Jesus' description of the synagogue within the Fourth Gospel distinguishes the synagogue as an ethnic space. He states, "I always taught in the synagogues and temple, where all the Jews (ὅπου πάντες οἱ Ἰουδαῖοι συνέρχονται) come together" (John 18:20). Specifically, Rachel Hachlili also notices that after the Roman destruction of the Jerusalem Temple, the major feature of the synagogue was the Torah shrine. This receptacle would have distinguished the building as a Jewish place of

---

that have been found by archeologists in Gamla, Masada, Herodium, and Jericho (the oldest, dating back to 31 BCE). See Charlesworth, "Jesus Research and Archaeology," 27–30; Keener, *Acts*, 2:1298–1302.

85. Matt 4:23; 9:35; 12:9; 13:54; Mark 1:21–23, 39; 3:1; 6:2; Luke 4:15–20, 33, 44; 6:6; 13:10; John 6:59.

86. Kloppenborg, "Theodotos Synagogue Inscription," 278–79. Synagogue leaders include Jairus (Mark 5:22–38; Luke 8:49), unknown figures (Luke 13:14; Acts 13:14–15), Crispus (Acts 18:8), and Sosthenus (Acts 18:17).

87. Philo, *Legat.* 132–38, 371.

study, even though the structure looked like an indoor squared theater with the base floor as the focal point. Hachlili finds that synagogue buildings include benches along the walls for sitting, listening, and participating.[88] The Synoptics even mention that there were certain seating arrangements which the scribes and Pharisees seemed to enjoy.[89] Hachlili however points out that many homes were altered and renovated so that they too could serve as synagogues, a point that Josephus also states.[90] Although the architecture and artistic design of diaspora synagogues proves that there were no universal standard plans, the Torah shrine was the common element that would have marked the space as distinctly Jewish.[91]

This however does not suggest that the synagogues were sacred spaces or solely restricted to Jews. Levine cautions us about viewing the synagogues as sacred spaces, although synagogues principally served for religious activity.[92] He points out that other matters were deliberated within the synagogues, including the manumission of slaves.[93] Indeed, we find Philo and Josephus testifying of these Jewish religious and social activities throughout the diaspora.[94] Since the gospel tradition also narrates the presence of cripple and sick people within the synagogue, this alerts us to the notion that these spaces were not exclusive but open for all people. Synagogues had an open-door policy, given that Jesus himself was not restricted to one synagogue but freely ventured into them throughout Galilee and Judea. Having said this, would this mean that the open-door policy also provide Gentiles the opportunity to enter these ethnic spaces? Although we do not find mention of the Gentiles in synagogues within the gospel tradition, other evidence points us in the affirmative.

In Acts, for example, we find evidence that in the diaspora, Gentiles were also in synagogues. When Paul and Barnabas were in Antioch of Pisidia, it was the Jews and "God-fearers" who encouraged him to return and continue preaching in the synagogue the next Sabbath (Acts 13:43). Both Jews and Greeks were in the synagogue when Paul was preaching in Iconium as well. The Jews even tried to dissuade the Greeks from believing in the message of Paul (Acts 14:1–2). Later when Paul was in Thessalonica,

---

88. Hachlili, "Synagogues," 30–33.

89. Matt 23:6; Mark 12:39; Luke 11:43; 20:46. Matthew adds that the hypocrites would "sound trumpets in the synagogues" when they would give alms and "stand up to pray" so that they may be heard (Matt 6:2, 5).

90. Josephus, *Life*, 277, 280; *J.W.* 2.285, 289.

91. Hachlili, "Synagogues," 38.

92. Levine, *Ancient Synagogue*, 46.

93. *CIJ* 690; *Inscriptiones Graecae ad Res Romanas Pertinentes*, 1:881.

94. Philo, *Somn.* 2.127; *Mos.* 2.216; Josephus, *Ag. Ap.* 2.175.

he entered into the "synagogue of the Jews" and was able to persuade many "God-fearing Greeks" and noble women with the gospel (Acts 17:1–4). Shortly after, Paul enters another "synagogue of the Jews" in Brea and like before, several leading Greek women and men believed (Acts 17:10–12). We also notice that in the synagogue of Athens, Paul was able to reason with the Jews and the God-fearing Greeks (Acts 17:17). Finally, when Paul was in the synagogue at Corinth he was described as trying to persuade both Jews and Greeks (Acts 18:4).

What does this propose? Particularly, it posits that whenever Paul went into the synagogue throughout the diaspora, he not only found Jews, but also Greeks, Gentile women, and other God-fearers. This confirms not only the argument that Gentiles would have been found in the synagogue, but that the synagogue excommunication language in the Fourth Gospel would have resonated with more than just the Jews of the Johannine community. To quell any further doubts, archeological evidence also reveals that synagogues were also built by Gentiles and dedicated to Gentiles.

In Rome, a synagogue plaque dated in the late first century mentions that a Gentile woman not only built the synagogue, but also was a Jewish sympathizer. The inscription reads:

> This building, constructed by Julia Severa, was restored by Gaius Tyrronius Clades, head of the synagogue for life; and Lucius son of Lucius, head of the synagogue, and Popilius Rufus, archon, from their own funds and from money contributed the walls and the roof, and they made safe the little doors and all the remaining decorations. These men the synagogue honored with a golden shield on account of their virtuous life and their goodwill and zeal for the synagogue. (*CIJ* 766)

The inscription mentions that Julia Severa was the original builder of the synagogue although many others were also involved in its restoration and dedication. Julia is known to be the wife of Lucius Servenius Capito and priestess of a pagan cult.[95] Why would a Gentile woman who was also a pagan priestess build the synagogue? We are not sure. But this was not a rare, singular event. Other women philanthropists who provided funds to construct synagogues for the Jewish people include Tation. This inscription reads:

> In honor of Tation, daughter of Straton son of Empedon, who constructed, at her own expense, the assembly room, and the enclosure of the open-air courtyard and bestowed it on the Jews.

---

95. Feldman and Reinhold, *Jewish Life and Thought*, 70n4.

> The synagogue of the Jews honored Tation, daughter of Straton son of Empedon, with a gold crown and the privilege of a front seat. (*CIJ* 738)

The date of the inscription is unknown, however it confirms that Gentiles, and women in particular, were involved in the building and support of synagogues. Providing money to construct the synagogue also meant, according to this inscription, that one would have a permanent place as a Gentile woman within the synagogue.

We also find synagogues in Egypt and Rome dedicated to the political leaders and emperor. These particular synagogues demonstrate that there was a concern for the well-being of the empire. The inscriptions state:

> In honor of King Ptolemy and Queen Berenice, his sister and wife, and their children, the Jews built this house of prayer. (*CIJ* 1440)

> For the safety of our lords the Emperor and the Caesars, Lucius Septimius Severus Pius Parthicus Augustus, and Marcus Aurelius Antoninus and Lucius Septimius Geta, his sons, in accordance with the vow of the Jews. (*CIJ* 972)

What do these archeological and literary evidences suggest? Primarily, the evidence provides attestation of the gospel's description of synagogues as places where Jews gathered to read and learn scripture. Synagogues functioned like a Jewish multi-purpose buildings and were also open spaces that did not restrict access to Gentiles. In fact, this openness and acceptance of Gentile funding for synagogues confirms the only story we have within the gospel tradition that describes a Roman centurion who built a synagogue in Capernaum. Luke mentions that when the Jewish elders requested for Jesus' healing intervention, they did so because the centurion "loves our nation and it was he who built our synagogue" (7:5). Although some may doubt the reliability of this narrative, it is clear that Gentiles sponsored, supported, built, and received permanent places within the Jewish synagogue.[96] The centurion's support of a Jewish synagogue would not have been a unique phenomenon.

In addition to these aspects, Levine also points out that synagogues functioned as courtrooms.[97] We do notice that synagogues served as a quasi-judicial court in the gospel tradition. The synagogue was a hostile place for Jesus, followers of Jesus, Paul and his companions, and the churches in

---

96. Kloppenborg, "Theodotos Synagogue Inscription," 240–42.
97. Levine, *Ancient Synagogue*, 29.

Revelation.[98] In fact, Jesus warns the disciples that the synagogues would be hostile places that would practice flogging, arrest, and persecution.[99] But what about the Gentile? Would they be victims of the hostility in the synagogue? Or was this something limited to just the "Jewish Christians" as Martyn proposes? Did they too, by remaining or entering the synagogue, put themselves at risk and under threat of violence?

We cannot assume that only Jews would be persecuted in the synagogue. The synagogue did not lose function or relevance in early Christianity. As Rodney Stark argues, synagogues were the vital network of Jewish communities that the early Christian missionaries utilized for the growth of Christianity.[100] As the Acts narrative suggests, synagogues would have been the central place to reach Gentile God-fearers who would be sympathetic to the gospel. Synagogues were the ethnic spaces that Jews and God-fearing Gentiles would enter every Sabbath in order to hear the scriptures, celebrate with their community, or rest from an extensive journey. But for some reason, for the Johannine community it was also a space of violence. Synagogues were not used only as ethnic centers, they became places for the expression of ethnic violence. The synagogue was no longer a welcoming space. It was a hostile place for Jewish Christians, Greeks, Samaritans and other ethnic members of the Johannine community. In other words, what we hear in this "two-level drama" of John 16:2 is also the tension and persecution of ethnic groups who dared to join and remain in these ethnic spaces. This means that the very place where they thought they were welcomed, felt safe, or even a member of the Jewish community had now become a potential site of violence and death. From the disciple's perspective, the coming violence has filled their hearts with sorrow (John 16:6). It is from this perspective that we must hear and reimagine the promise of the Paraclete for an ethnically diverse Johannine community who would have been excommunicated from the synagogue.

What role does then Spirit-Paraclete therefore have within the context of hate, death and rejection in ethnic spaces? We must notice that Jesus does not want violence to catch the disciples and Johannine community off-guard. In fact, Jesus asserts that when violence does occur, he hopes that they would remember his words. In this scenario, it is racial violence that prompts memory. Racial violence in ethnic spaces draws the disciples and community to Jesus' teachings through the Spirit-Paraclete (v. 14).

---

98. Jesus (Matt 13:53–58; Mark 6:1–6; Luke 4:16–30); followers of Jesus (Acts 9:2; 22:19; 26:11); Paul and companions (Acts 13:44–46; 14:1–2; 19:8–9); and churches (Rev 2:9; 3:9).

99. Matt 10:17; Mark 13:9; Luke 12:11; 21:12; John 9:22; 12:42; 16:2.

100. Stark, *Rise of Christianity*, 49–72.

However, the Spirit-Paraclete does more than just help victims remember. The Spirit-Paraclete takes an active action against the world and in defense of the oppressed people of God. This defense continues in the manifestation of convicting the world of its sinful violence, oppressive injustice, and reality that its ruler stands judged (16:7–11). Although the disciples and Johannine community may feel alone as oppressed orphaned children, the Spirit-Paraclete is indeed with them. The Spirit-Paraclete's presence with the disciples and the community means that there is hope for justice and truth in a violent world.

This reading differs from Martyn's analysis of the Paraclete. He suggests that the Paraclete as "another" figure looks very much like Jesus and has no independent personality nor function.[101] The Spirit-Paraclete is an agent of justice, truth, and acts as a defender of the oppressed orphans of God. This is not just a replication of what was done in the past. It is an ongoing and continual revelation of truth and justice for the community in whatever new situation they face. Most certainly, we can agree with Martyn that the reason why the identity between Jesus and the Paraclete are similar is for the sake of the two-level drama. That is, since the disciples remain on the earth, this means that the Paraclete must be Jesus' "double" to continue the work of Jesus on earth while also being in heaven.[102] But what situation will prompt the manifestation of the Spirit-Paraclete? I argue that the Spirit-Paraclete most certainly emerges in situations of ethnic hatred, violence in ethnic spaces, and rejection by the "other." This is when the Spirit-Paraclete reveals herself most distinctly.

The Paraclete of the Oppressed

As argued in this chapter, Jesus' statement in 15:26–27 and 16:7–15 proposes that the Spirit-Paraclete will engage in the communicatory and forensic activities on behalf of and with those who experience violence in ethnic spaces and from all ethnic groups. The Paraclete is primarily a defender of the oppressed and rejected—the orphaned amongst us. Yet the hostility experienced has gone beyond the confines of one particular ethnic group. It is being experienced on all fronts and in various ways that create fear, mistrust, and suspicion of the "other." Yes, there was and perhaps still is tension in the synagogue but the violence can and will extend beyond these ethnic spaces. The perpetuators of violence are not identified nor should we

---

101. Martyn, *History and Theology*, 138.
102. Martyn, *History and Theology*, 138–41.

assume that only the "Jews" were instigating violence upon the Johannine community.

While scholars mainly focus on the Spirit-Paraclete's revelatory activities, my approach seeks to bring to the surface the ethnic scripts that are embedded within the text. In fact, we cannot understand the communicatory activities of the Paraclete apart from this hostile ethnic context. The disciples and Johannine community found themselves as a minoritized community that has been called out of the world (John 15:19). They were also an ethnically diverse community situated in a Greco-Roman world that had ethnic ideological views. In a sense, they were the minorities of the minorities. For this reason, Jesus warns them of the coming hostility from the world. This hostility would include violence in the confines of their ethnic spaces. They will experience violence in their synagogues, in their homes, by their fellow kin, and at the hands of the Empire. The world that Jesus warns them about is not a vague theological concept. The term "world" is ethnic classification language. This language not only creates suspicion and fear but subverts their identity by setting boundaries between "us," the disciples and Johannine community, and "them" which is the world. Indeed, these outsiders may be powerful and privileged, but they are nothing but the world—people who lose their identity when they utilize violence to achieve specific means. It also must be pointed out that the violence is not only an intra-ethnic conflict situated within the community spaces of the synagogue. Violence is also presumed to emerge with all people—a conflict that sets the disciples and Johannine community in continual ethnoreligious hostility with the world.

What then does the Paraclete have to do with hate, death, and rejection in ethnic spaces and from the world? Certain experiences will be so oppressive that it necessitates a response by the Spirit-Paraclete. The Spirit-Paraclete will indeed do something and not leave the disciples as victims. The Spirit-Paraclete will not be absent or passive, for Jesus promises that there will be a judicial response. The world will be judged. The world is being judged. Even more so, the world is being exposed for all its injustice and hypocrisy. Who will reveal this reality to the oppressed people of God if not the Spirit-Paraclete? Who will remind the disciples that the experience and trauma that they are undergoing is truly the work of the world if not the Spirit-Paraclete? And who will tell the diverse ethnic people of God that they are not rejected, hated, or abandoned by Jesus if not the Spirit-Paraclete? This activity of the Spirit-Paraclete occurs not just in the conscience of the disciples or before the courtroom of God. It also occurs in the proclamation of the community. It is made manifest during the courtroom trials of the community. The Spirit-Paraclete is active throughout the world as a prosecuting attorney in all spaces, promising to bring a legal case against the oppressive rulers which includes the Roman Empire. Where resistance to oppression is made through the proclamation of truth, the Spirit-Paraclete is promised to be present.[103]

---

103. For a contemporary example of what this looks like in the Christian community, see Estrada, "What Does the Paraclete Have to Do with Dreamers?," 67–81.

13

Delivering the Community from the Fear of the Other

JOHN 20:19–23

AT THE CONCLUSION OF THE FOURTH GOSPEL, WE HAVE VARIOUS resurrection appearances that demonstrate a preservation of unique Johannine material. In the context surrounding the giving of the Spirit in John 20:19–23, Jesus manifests himself to only ten disciples who are locked in a room because they were afraid of the Jews (v. 19). The text states:

> Thus when it was evening on that first day of the week, and when the doors were shut where the disciples were fearful of the Jews, Jesus came and stood in their midst and said, "Peace be with you." And when he said this, he showed them his hands and side. Then the disciples rejoiced when they saw the Lord. Jesus said to them again, "Peace be with you: just as the Father has sent me, I also send you." And when he said this, he breathed upon them and said, "Receive the Holy Spirit: If you forgive the sins of any, they have been forgiven; whoever you retain, they have been retained.
>
> Οὔσης οὖν ὀψίας τῇ ἡμέρᾳ ἐκείνῃ τῇ μιᾷ σαββάτων, καὶ τῶν θυρῶν κεκλεισμένων ὅπου ἦσαν οἱ μαθηταὶ διὰ τὸν φόβον τῶν Ἰουδαίων, ἦλθεν ὁ Ἰησοῦς καὶ ἔστη εἰς τὸ μέσον καὶ λέγει αὐτοῖς, Εἰρήνη ὑμῖν. καὶ τοῦτο εἰπὼν ἔδειξεν τὰς χεῖρας καὶ τὴν πλευρὰν αὐτοῖς. ἐχάρησαν οὖν οἱ μαθηταὶ ἰδόντες τὸν κύριον. εἶπεν οὖν αὐτοῖς [ὁ Ἰησοῦς] πάλιν, Εἰρήνη ὑμῖν· καθὼς ἀπέσταλκέν με ὁ πατήρ, κἀγὼ πέμπω

> ὑμᾶς. καὶ τοῦτο εἰπὼν ἐνεφύσησεν καὶ λέγει αὐτοῖς, Λάβετε πνεῦμα ἅγιον: ἄν τινων ἀφῆτε τὰς ἁμαρτίας ἀφέωνται αὐτοῖς, ἄν τινων κρατῆτε κεκράτηνται.

Jesus' presence provides the opportunity to demonstrate his resurrected body (v. 20). This appearance leads the disciples to rejoice because they have seen the "Lord." Right after this physical manifestation, Jesus commissions the disciples with a similar charge that he received from the Father (v. 21). It is at this moment that he breathes upon them the Holy Spirit and explains their role in the forgiveness of sins.

The giving of the Spirit in this resurrection scene presents a perspective that differs from Acts and the commission scenes of the Synoptic Gospels. In the Fourth Gospel, the disciples are not instructed to wait for the Spirit as we find in Acts 1:8. Instead, Jesus breathes upon them with the exhortation to receive "λάβετε" the Holy Spirit.[1] Furthermore, in the Fourth Gospel the disciples are together in a locked room because they were afraid of the "Jews" (φόβον τῶν Ἰουδαίων). The setting of John 20:19–23 is a context of fear, whereas the Synoptics describe fear occurring only at the tomb.[2] Considering this, how are we to understand the giving of the Holy Spirit in light of this "fear of the Jews"? Is the Fourth Gospel attempting to reinterpret Jesus' commission in light of those whom the disciples and Johannine community are afraid of? Furthermore, is this a commission to reach those who participated or condoned the synagogue excommunication, hatred, and death of their fellow members?

In this last analysis, I argue that the exhortation to receive the Spirit in John 20:22 is not just a desire to empower the disciples for mission or grant them the authorization to forgive sins. Although it includes these aspects, what is missing from the conversation is the opportunity to receive the Holy Spirit and become born into a new community that would have the fearless ability to reach the ethnically other. This aspect is of upmost importance, as it is required in order to continue Jesus' mission to the world. Even more so, this also means that the disciples and Johannine community cannot authentically imitate the Father's sending of the Son if they still hold onto a fear of the other, or in this case, a fear of the "Jews."

First, we will review how the Johannine commission scene is no more authentic or inauthentic from the Synoptic tradition. I will point out that

---

1. We must notice that Jesus' "breathing" (ἐνεφύσησεν) on the disciples echoes the moment when God breathed on the dirt of the earth to give life to Adam (Gen 2:7). This same term is also used to describe the "breathing" of the prophet Ezekiel in the valley of dry bones (Ezek 37:9) and God's "breathing" of the spirit into human beings (Wis 15:11).

2. Mark 16:8; Matt 28:8, 10.

the Johannine resurrection appearances puts forth a new perspective for a particular ethnic context. Second, we will closely review the significance of the Spirit in the commission scene by reviewing the scholarly views on the topic. This will include an argument on why the "fear of the Jews" must shape our understanding of Jesus' giving of the Holy Spirit. Lastly, we will explore how the giving of the Holy Spirit relates to Jesus' mission in the gospel as one who was sent by the Father. This chapter will conclude with some final observations on overcoming the "fear of the other" through the Spirit.

John 20:19–23: A New (Re)interpretation of the Great Commission?

From Jesus' resurrection appearance to the impartation of the Spirit, the Fourth Gospel is strikingly different from the Synoptic Gospels. The Johannine resurrection story begins with Mary Magdalene who for some reason unexplained, comes to the tomb early in the morning (20:1). Slightly after Mary Magdalene notices the empty tomb, she reports to the disciples that Jesus' body was taken (v. 2). It must be noted that Jesus' death would have been a profound loss to his followers and the violation of his tomb would have been another egregious act of disrespect. An empty tomb would have primarily suggested that Jesus' body was desecrated by bandits.[3] Thus when Peter and the Beloved Disciple see for themselves that the tomb was indeed empty, we can understand why they left and said nothing. Although the gospel explains that only the Beloved Disciple "believed," there is no evidence that he understood the resurrection implications of the empty tomb (vv. 8–10).[4] In actuality, they also leave Mary Magdalene weeping alone outside the tomb (v. 11). It is while she is alone that two angels appear and ask why she weeps (v. 13). Then she encounters another person, whom she misidentifies as the gardener, and hears the same question (v. 15). After

---

3. A Roman tomb dated to the first century states, "Caius Tullius Hesper made for himself this altar where his bones shall be interred. If anyone violate it or take anything out from it, I wish for him to live a long time with bodily pains, and for the gods of the underworld not to receive him when he has died" (*CIL* 6.36467). Julius Paulus states, "Whoever vandalizes a sepulcher or takes something from a sepulcher is, according to his social rank, either sent to the mines or exiled on the island" (*Opinions*, 1.21.2–5, 8–14). Malina and Rohrbaugh also point out that tampering with buried bodies would entail capital punishment (Malina and Rohrbaugh, *John*, 282).

4. Bultmann finds that the race to the tomb between Peter and the Beloved disciple is representative of the ethnic believing communities. Peter represents Jewish Christianity and the Beloved disciples represents Gentile Christianity. Since the Beloved Disciple had faith and Peter did not, this suggest that "readiness for faith is even greater with the Gentiles than it is with the Jews" (Bultmann, *John*, 685).

hearing the gardener call her by name, she recognizes that it is Jesus. While she attempts to cling to him, Jesus commands her to tell the disciples that he was going to ascend to the Father (v. 17). Mary Magdalene immediately leaves to inform the disciples that she "had seen the Lord" and spoken to him (v. 18).

Knowledge of Jesus' resurrection did not seem to have an impact upon the disciples. Instead, they are described as gathered behind locked doors "in fear of the Jews" (v. 19). This state of fear seems bizarre given that they had previously received a report from Mary Magdalene that Jesus had appeared. Is it possible that they were, as the Gospel of Peter suggests, afraid of the Jews because of false rumors that were being spread about them?[5] We are not sure if the Gospel of Peter is actually influenced or dependent on the Fourth Gospel for this description of the disciples. Nonetheless, according to the Fourth Gospel, it is in this state of fear that Jesus appears, saying on two occasions, "peace be with you" (vv. 19, 21). Jesus demonstrates his hands and side, which leads the disciples to be overwhelmed with joy (v. 20). Jesus states, "as the Father has sent me, I also send you." While saying this, he breathes upon them and continues, "receive the Holy Spirit" (Λάβετε πνεῦμα ἅγιον). This call to receive the Holy Spirit is an exhortation. It comes with the pronouncement that the disciples would have authority to forgive and retain sins. Did they respond and receive? We are not sure, and there is no reaction of the disciples as we are accustomed to seeing with other people or situations where the Spirit is received.[6] Instead, one is made aware that this appearance was only to ten disciples. Thomas was absent from the group and it takes an entire week before he gets the chance to see Jesus for himself (vv. 24–29). Yet the fear still lingers, and the disciples still gather together behind locked doors even though they had seen the Lord and knew that he was alive (v. 26). Why such fear?

In this brief review, we can observe that the Johannine resurrection episode departs from the Synoptics in a variety of ways. The story of Mary Magdalene conversing alone with Jesus is only found in the Fourth Gospel, although Barrett believes that it is influenced by Mark's resurrection story.[7]

5. It was believed according to the Jewish authorities that the disciples were going to set the temple on fire in response to Jesus' crucifixion. This is why the disciples were in fear and hiding in their homes, they preferred to weep in private than at the tomb (*Gos. Pet.* 7–15).

6. Similar exhortations to "receive the Spirit" include physical manifestations, reactions, or responses to the characters in Acts 1:8; 2:38; 8:15, 17, 19; 10:47; 19:2. Paul's use of the phrase is also found in his letters, but they do not aim to describe narrative encounters with the Spirit as we find in John or Acts (Rom 8:15; 1 Cor 2:12; 2 Cor 11:4; Gal 3:2, 14).

7. Barrett, *St. John*, 466.

In the Synoptics there are a variety of women who come to the tomb. Yet, none have a comparable dialogue as we find in the Fourth Gospel.[8] The differences are striking when we try to identify the divine figures that also appear at the tomb. None of the gospels agree on who or how many divine figures appeared.[9] It is difficult not only to find parallels between all the gospels, but also identify their literary relationship. The closest parallel account between the Fourth Gospel's description of Jesus' resurrection and the Synoptics is found in Luke when Jesus appears to all the disciples (Luke 24:36–43).[10] However, many Johannine stories are unique. The Fourth Gospel includes stories of Jesus appearing to the disciples a variety of times. As we have just reviewed, Jesus first appears to Mary Magdalene and then to the ten disciples who were gathered together behind locked doors (20:1–23). A week later Jesus appears with all the eleven disciples, including Thomas who confesses that Jesus is both "Lord and God" (vv. 24–29). Finally, Jesus appears a third time by the Sea of Tiberius where Jesus encourages the disciples to cast their nets for a miraculous catch and asks Peter if he loves him (21:1–25).[11]

The differences should not be understood as to presume that the Fourth Gospel is the only gospel that departs from some core tradition. Many resurrection stories in the biblical tradition are unique to each writer such as stories of the guards at the tomb (Matt 28:11–15), Jesus appearing on the road to Emmaus (Luke 24:13–45; Mark 16:12–13), the ascension accounts

---

8. In Mark 16:1–3, three women come to the tomb, including Mary Magdalene, Mary the mother of James, and Salome. They bring spices to anoint Jesus' body and know that they would need help to remove the stone that was covering the tomb. In Matthew 28:1–2, Mary Magdalene came with the other Mary to the tomb. An earthquake occurs, and the angels tell the women not to be afraid. Only two women come to the tomb in Matthew. Matthew also records a short conversation between Jesus and the women (Matt 28:9–10). According Luke 24:1–2, the women are not identified. Luke describes many women who come to the tomb with spices, find the stone removed from the tomb, enter, and leave the scene amazed.

9. Likewise, the gospel tradition does not agree on the number of divine figures who appear at the tomb. Mark describes a young man (νεανίσκον) in the tomb (Mark 16:5); Matthew describes an angel of the Lord (ἄγγελος γὰρ κυρίου) descending from heaven (Matt 28:2); Luke records two men (ἄνδρες δύο) in the tomb (Luke 24:4–5); and the Fourth Gospel describes two angels (δύο ἀγγέλους) in the tomb (John 20:12).

10. Lindars, *John*, 597; Morris, *John*, 744; Blomberg, *Historical Reliability*, 265.

11. There is a possible parallel between the miracle in John 21 with Luke 5:1–11, but there are also notable differences. What is similar between the stories is the basic plot: the disciples have difficulties catching fish, Jesus commands them to throw their nets again, and the miraculous catch of fish. The differences are numerous. However, Dale Allison suggests that the appearance of Jesus in John 21 and Luke 5 are variants of the same story. See Allison, *Resurrecting Jesus*, 255–59. For a review of the literary unity of John 19–21, see Segovia, "Final Farewell of Jesus," 166–90.

(Mark 16:15–19; Luke 24:44–53), Jesus appearing to over five hundred people (1 Cor 15:3–8), and various appearances that spanned for forty days (Acts 1:3). What do all these discrepancies and distinct traditions suggest? Does this propose that the resurrection stories are unreliable? Some scholars doubt that the Fourth Gospel preserves any historical tradition. Ashton bluntly states that in the Fourth Gospel "neither the resurrection itself nor the stories told to illustrate its significance are historical in any meaningful sense of the word."[12] Blomberg suggests that the resurrection accounts of the gospels pose problems for "would-be harmonizers."[13] Sanders is a bit agnostic. Faced with these diverging stories of where and to whom Jesus appeared, he suggests that we cannot construct what really happened.[14] And Dale Allison admits that our historical-critical tools are "too blunt" to determine what extent the particulars in the accounts preserve old or authentic memory.[15] Regardless of the difficulties that the various resurrection stories present, this may also suggest that the Fourth Gospel represents a perspective that is no more authentic or inauthentic than others. Although the differences between the gospels present challenges in trying to identify the historical realities of the reported events, it also reveals that the Johannine tradition has a unique and distinct interpretation for its own context and circumstance.

What then is the context and circumstance of the gospel's exhortation to receive the Spirit in John 20:22? Quite simply, it is the fear of the "other." We can see this more acutely when we focus on the Johannine commissioning scene and compare it to the commission episodes in the Synoptics and Acts. In particular, the earliest versions of Mark do not include Jesus' final words which suggests that there was no commission.[16] It is only in

---

12. Ashton, *Understanding*, 486.

13. Blomberg, *Historical Reliability*, 259. Dunn also points out that there are too many idiosyncratic and puzzling curious features about the data. There is however a "core spine" of events that point to a basic tradition. See Dunn, *Jesus Remembered*, 857–62.

14. Sanders, *Historical Figure of Jesus*, 278–80. Moloney points out that it is impossible to describe what happened in any concrete sense. He notices that the resurrection narratives show the unusual sign of the creative presence of later writings, reading, and listening communities. See Moloney, *Resurrection*, 139–147.

15. Allison, *Resurrecting Jesus*, 269. Keener outlines three possible outcomes on the differences between the gospels. First, the differences in accounts demonstrate that the writers were aware of the independent traditions; second, the divergent details suggest independent traditions; and third, explaining the similarities and differences in terms of multiple witnesses' surrounding a core historical event appears plausible and probable. See Keener, *John*, 1168; Brown, *John*, 2:978; Morris, *John*, 731; Brown, *Spirit in the Writings of John*, 104.

16. Metzger points out that there are about four different versions of the ending of

the longer ending of Mark 16:14–20 where Jesus appears to the disciples while they are sitting at a table. He commissions them to go into the world (κόσμον) and preach the gospel to all creation (κτίσει). This Markan mission to all creation is promised to be accompanied with signs which include the ability to cast out demons, speak in tongues, become unaffected by serpents and poisonous drinks, and heal the sick (vv. 17–18). There is a presumption that their mission will include manifestations of divine power, but the Spirit is not mentioned. Luke however presents the commission occurring in Jerusalem when the disciples were gathered together (Luke 24:44–53). There is an exegetical focus in this appearance. Jesus appears to the disciples in order to "open their minds to understand scripture" (v. 45). He explains the significance of his death and resurrection from the Law and the Prophets, and that the message of repentance and forgiveness of sins should be preached in all nations (εἰς πάντα τὰ ἔθνη). Jesus urges them to also wait for the Spirit that will "clothe them with power from on high" (v. 49). Then he walks out to Bethany, blesses the disciples, and ascends to heaven (vv. 50–51). Luke presents a different perspective in that Jesus is involved in explaining the significance of scripture with the promise for the later giving of the Spirit. According to Matthew, the disciples are already on a mountain in Galilee (Matt 28:16–20). It is there that they meet Jesus. Some disciples respond to Jesus' appearance by worshipping him, while others still doubted (v. 17). Jesus then states that he has all authority in heaven and earth and that they should make disciples of all nations (πάντα τὰ ἔθνη), baptizing them, and teaching them all that he commanded (vv. 18–19). In Matthew's account, the Spirit is mentioned only in the formula for early Christian baptism. There is no impartation or expectation that the Spirit will empower them in their commission.

Given this, what are the implications to our understanding of the Spirit and its relationship to Jesus' commission in the Fourth Gospel? Does this also suggest that the giving of the Spirit as found in John 20:19–23 is also a unique tradition? Certainly, the diversity of encounters reveals that no gospel writer has a more authentic preservation of Jesus' post-resurrection experiences and understanding of the Spirit in the commission. In Mark, the original ending has no resurrection appearance to the disciples. It is only in the longer ending of Mark that Jesus appears when the disciples are at a table. The power of the Spirit is promised to accompany the disciples, but the Spirit is not mentioned. In Luke, Jesus ascends to heaven from Bethany. Here he urges them to wait for the Spirit that is to come later. And

---

Mark. The last twelve verses of Mark are absent from the two oldest Greek manuscripts, the Old Latin codex Bobiensis, the Sinaitic Syriac manuscript, Armenian manuscripts, and the two oldest Gregorian manuscripts. See Metzger, *Textual Commentary*, 102–6.

in Matthew, there is no ascension. Jesus appears on a mountain in Galilee and commissions them to baptize disciples in the name of the "Father, Son, and Holy Spirit." All gospel writers preserve their own distinct tradition, albeit the possibility of influences, preservation, or revisions of a common core memory or experience.[17]

Gary Burge however presses the issue further and argues that the Fourth Gospel records the full giving of the Spirit-Paraclete which corresponds with Luke's account in Acts 2.[18] Burge highlights seven reasons why this is so.[19] However, at the end of Burges's analysis, that is, after building the case that John 20 is akin to Acts 2, he seems to cast doubt on his findings and notes that the evidence is not conclusive enough given that similar parallels could be made between John 20 and Luke 24. Nonetheless, he concludes that themes from both Luke 24 and Acts 2 appear to converge in John 20, especially since the Fourth Gospel has no sequel.[20] Burge asserts

---

17. For an outline to "core resurrection" elements found in the gospels, see Dunn, *Jesus Remembered*, 858–62; Moloney, *Resurrection*, 140; Allison, *Resurrecting Jesus*, 245, 269.

18. Burge, *Anointed Community*, 123. Bultmann suggests that in John 20:22, Easter and Pentecost are combined as one event (Bultmann, *John*, 692). See Dunn, *Baptism in the Holy Spirit*, 176. Although Brown considers it a "bad methodology to harmonize John with Acts," he does believe that they are describing the same event (Brown, *John*, 2:1038–39). Lindars views this giving of the Spirit as the disciples "Spirit-Baptism" (Lindars, *John*, 612). Beasley-Murray also makes a similar case, but he argues that the Lukan perspective is more authentic. He suggests that the Fourth Gospel was probably summarizing what happened during the Easter period and not what happened "five minutes on the first Easter Sunday evening" (Beasley-Murray, *John*, 382). Millos takes a different approach. He claims that John 20:22 does not suggests that the Spirit was immediately given; rather, it will be made available on the day of Pentecost. See Millos, *Juan*, 1777.

19. Burge points out that Jesus had already been glorified in John 20:22, which needed to occur before the Spirit was given, according to John 7:39. Second, Jesus is also portrayed as a re-creator when he "breathes" upon the disciples. Third, the promise Jesus would baptize in the Holy Spirit in John 1:33 is fulfilled in 20:22. Fourth, he finds that use of the term "receive/take" (Λάβετε) in 20:22 is frequently found to describe the reception of the Spirit elsewhere in the New Testament. Fifth, when Jesus pronounces "peace" upon the disciples, this fulfills the promise of the Paraclete who was also going to bring peace (John 14:27). Sixth, Burge states that early Christians only recalled one giving of the Spirit to inaugurate the church. And seventh, there are parallels between John 20 and Acts 2, which include the location, seclusion of the disciples, a commission, the ministry to forgive sins, and the utilization of the wind/breath metaphor. See Burge, *Anointed Community*, 125–30.

20. Burge, *Anointed Community*, 148. Michaels makes a similar point but also suggests that the Fourth Gospel seems to know nothing of Luke's Pentecost (Michaels, *John*, 1012).

that the Fourth Gospel "has developed a traditional resurrection scene into a singular event uniting the return, the ascension, and the Spirit."[21]

Although Burge attempts to make a case for viewing the giving of the Spirit in John 20:22 as a revision of Acts 2, others are not so generous. For instance, Barrett does not believe it is possible to harmonize John 20 with Acts 2. He states that the first Christians probably experienced the resurrection of Jesus, his exaltation, and the Spirit as one experience, which was only later described in separate elements and incidents as Acts narrates.[22] Felix Porsch also views the issue differently. He suggests that the giving of the Spirit is not the total fulfillment of the Paraclete promise, but only the beginning stage of its fulfillment.[23] Max Turner also casts doubt that John 20 is a Johannine version of Acts 2. He notices that the giving of the Spirit in John 20 occurs before all the conditions of the Paraclete described in John 14–16 are fulfilled. This means that this giving of the Spirit is not a true fulfillment of Jesus' promise about the Paraclete.[24] Blomberg takes a moderate approach. He believes that the gospel is describing a different event but finds it more likely that it is just as real and authentic to Acts 2.[25]

What we have observed from the scholars above is that it is difficult to detect the literary sources and relationship of all the gospel resurrection stories. Furthermore, it is very much debatable whether the Fourth Gospel envisions John 20 as a "Johannine Pentecost" akin to Acts 2. Perhaps we are looking at the issue incorrectly. Instead of attempting to find a literary relationship or influence between the gospels, perhaps the true issue at hand was more important than the need for the Johannine writer to borrow, draw upon, or become influenced by the resurrection stories of the Synoptic Gospels. The Fourth Gospel has its own resurrection tradition and does not find it necessary to draw from other sources because of the ethnic challenges it was facing in the late first century. And what is the probable reason that would motivate this preservation and understanding of the Spirit in this

21. Burge, *Anointed Community*, 131.

22. Barrett, *St. John*, 475.

23. Porsch, *Pneuma und Wort*, 363–78, esp. 377–78.

24. Turner, *Holy Spirit*, 92–99. Morris also notices that the circumstances between John 20 and Acts 2 are completely different. He proposes that the "Spirit continually manifests himself in new ways" and thus suggests that "John tells of one gift of the Spirit and Luke tells another" (Morris, *John*, 247–48).

25. Blomberg notices that there are three major reasons that should bar us from assuming that John 20 is a revision of Acts 2. First, the giving of the Spirt is primarily a climax of all previous promises of the Spirit-Paraclete; second, since Thomas is not present during the experience, this should not suggest that there is only one giving of the Spirit; and third, John 21 demonstrates that the disciples were still not ready for the mission. See Blomberg, *Historical Reliability*, 266–67.

Johannine commission scene? As this chapter proposes and will continue to argue, it was the fear of the "other." In other words, the giving of the Spirit was not solely an empowerment for mission. The added details about the "fear of the Jews" and setting of "locked doors" reveals to us the primary context of Jesus' giving of the Spirit.

The Spirit and "Fear of the Jews" in John 20:22

It must be noted, however, that not all scholars hold the view which I am proposing, and in general, the relationship between the "fear of the Jews" in 20:19, "locked doors" in vv. 19, 26, and the giving of the Spirit in v. 22 does not seem to garner any attention. Scholars rightly notice the link between the "breathing" of the Spirit upon the disciples and God's "breathing" upon Adam at creation in Genesis 2, but not all agree.[26] Michaels proposes that the giving of the Spirit is evidence of the resurrection—that Jesus is alive—and signifies an empowerment to do what Jesus has just sent them to do. He finds it doubtful that Genesis 2 is explicitly being held in view.[27] Johnston adds that John 20:22 is meant to be viewed both prospectively as well as retrospectively. That is, it denotes the age of the church with some people as chosen witnesses, with authority, and spiritual power.[28] Many agree that the giving of the Spirit was a fulfillment of the Fourth Gospel's promise in John 1:33, as John the Baptist pronounced.[29] Therefore, in light of the Baptist's claim, 20:22 is a Spirit-Baptism that brings to completion the promise

26. For example, Barrett believes that the Holy Spirit in this context is a parallel to the first creation of humanity, and as such, the giving of the Spirit suggests a new creative act (Barrett, *St. John*, 474). Lindars states that this creative act also entails the constitution of the Church as a kind of new creation (Lindars, *John*, 612). Keener suggests in this act "Jesus is creating a new humanity." He views this as the Spirit's regenerating and purifying activity that will empower the disciples to proclaim the risen Christ (Keener, *John*, 1204–5). Brown and Thompson also suggests that when Jesus breaths upon the disciples the Holy Spirit, this not only reflects the creation account in Genesis 2:7 but also describes the type of mission they will have in the world. They suggest that the disciples are recreated as the children of God who have the Spirit and confer the Spirit upon others (Brown, *John*, 2:1035–37; Thompson, *John*, 421). Tricia Brown suggest that we find a "pneumatizing of the disciples as a sort of new creation" (Brown, *Spirit in the Writings of John*, 111–13). Mateos and Barretto claim that Jesus is infusing the disciples with the Spirit that gives him life (Mateos and Barretto, *Juan*, 867).

27. Michaels, *John*, 1010–11. Likewise, Morris views the Spirit as the "equipment they would need for the discharge of their commission" (Morris, *John*, 747).

28. Johnston, *Spirit-Paraclete*, 38. Beasley-Murray also suggests that the giving of the Holy Spirit primarily represents the impartation of life that marks the new age. See Beasley-Murray, *John*, 381.

29. Johnston, *Spirit-Paraclete*, 11, 16; Thompson, *John*, 418.

of the Spirit. Others emphasize the relationship between the giving of the Spirit and authority.[30] Here Tricia Brown suggests that the true meaning of vv. 19–23 is tied to the power of the disciples as subordinate brokers. With the "spirit" they are able to give the "spirit" to others. As such, the disciples continue the mission of Jesus who functions as the primary broker of God's patronage.[31] And we find Bultmann focusing on the theme of judgement. He suggests that since the bestowal of the Spirit is accompanied by the giving of authority, this refers to the reality of judgement that continues from the judgement that Jesus inaugurated in his ministry.[32]

We can thus notice that the giving of the Spirit in John 20:22 is viewed differently by scholars. It is difficult to avoid noticing the allusion to Genesis 2:7 when Jesus breathes upon the disciples and exhorts them to receive the Holy Spirit. This "breathing" is a fulfillment and culmination of the Baptist's promise 1:33—and thus a Johannine Spirit-baptism that invites a response on part of the disciples. Early in the gospel Jesus is distinguished as one who has the Spirit. The presence of the Spirit upon Jesus marks the inauguration of salvation for all ethnic groups as promised by the prophet Isaiah. Yet the Spirit is also uncontrollable and unrestrained—it moves as it pleases. This means that the Spirit ventures where it desires and gives birth to all people, thus creating a new genealogical lineage (3:1–10). Is this happening here in John 20:22? Possibly, especially since the narrator explains that Jesus also gives the Spirit without measure (3:34).[33] But we can also notice that the Spirit engages in life-giving activity that supersedes the ethnic privileges of being connected to one's ancestors. The life-giving presence of the Spirit is made manifest as a result of Jesus' words (6:63). Even more, Jesus promises the coming Paraclete, also known as the Spirit of Truth, who will be with the disciples and in the disciples (14:16–17, 26; 15:26–27; 16:7–15). The presence of the Paraclete would include peace so that the hearts of the disciples would not be troubled (14:1, 27). Now, in John 20:22, the Spirit is made manifest as a result of Jesus' glorification. While Jesus breaths upon the disciples, he invites them to receive the Spirit while they are in a state of fear.

---

30. Moloney, *Resurrection*, 112.

31. Brown, *Spirit in the Writings of John*, 108.

32. Bultmann, *John*, 693.

33. Brown notices that one of the central issues in 3:34 is identifying the main speaker. Is this John the Baptist, Jesus, or the narrator? If we were to assume that the entire chapter is one continuous discussion, then this points to the Baptist. But if verses 31–36 continue from verses 3–21, then the perspective is that of Jesus or the evangelist. She does not attempt to solve this riddle but notices that it echoes the main theme of the Nicodemus narrative. See Brown, *Spirit in the Writings of John*, 126.

Yet the context of fear is often missed as a significant detail to the setting.[34] Bultmann suggests that the "fear of the Jews" is mentioned to emphasize the miraculous appearance of Jesus' arrival.[35] Millos speculates possible reasons why the disciples were gathered in fear. But he suggests that this "fear of the Jews" is really a fear of the religious leaders.[36] Of course, the question arises again, who are the Jews? As previously mentioned, the Jews are primarily an ethnic group. But the question we should really focus is the following: who are the Jews to the Johannine community? From the context of an ethnically diverse Johannine community in the late first century, this may refer to the Jewish religious authority.[37] But at its base, it primarily is ethnic language that refers to the other.[38] We must remember, that the mention of the "Jews" throughout the gospel reflects the reality of an ethnic struggle between anti-Jewish and pro-Jewish attitudes within the Johannine community. The Johannine community itself is also constructing its identity in contrast to the "Jews" and the "world" as children of God. At this point in the narrative, the Johannine community has now come to see itself as created and formed into a new ethnic lineage through the Spirit. However, one could argue that the context was joy given that the disciples had just seen and touched Jesus' body (v. 20). Indeed, there was joy amongst the disciples because of Jesus' resurrection, but the fear still lingered. They still met an entire week and continued to lock the doors in their gathering (v. 26). We therefore must hear within this "fear of the Jews" the reflection of the Johannine community's experience with the ethnically other, including one's own kin who had abandoned and excommunicated them from the synagogue.

One may wonder why the narrator decided to include this emotional detail of "fear." No other gospel records the disciples' "fear of the Jews" or any other ethnic group, especially since the Romans had just executed Jesus.[39]

---

34. See, for example, Barrett, *St. John*, 472; Morris, *John*, 745; Brown, *John*, 2:1020. Lindars suggests that the "motive is natural and introduced to emphasize the miraculous character of Jesus' arrival" (Lindars, *John*, 609–610). Beasley-Murray suggests that this detail was may have been added by the writer (Beasley-Murray, *John*, 378).

35. Bultmann, *John*, 690–91; Lindars, *John*, 609–610.

36. Millos, *Juan*, 1772.

37. Keener, *John*, 1200–1201.

38. See Culpepper, "Anti-Judaism in the Fourth Gospel," 68–69; Dunn, "Embarrassment of History," 51; Anderson, "Anti-Semitism," 309; Thatcher, "John and the Jews," 3–38; Wahlde, "Jews in the Gospel of John," 52; Reinhartz, *Befriending the Beloved Disciple*, 75–76; Leibig, "John and the Jews," 223.

39. Luke does record the disciples' fear. However, it is the result of seeing Jesus appear to them, not because they were afraid of the Jews or other ethnic group (Luke 24:36). Mark records the disciples having unbelief when Jesus appears (Mark 16:14). Matthew notices that some disciples worshiped Jesus while others had doubt (Matt

Tricia Brown suggest that this fear reveals a sense of hiddenness and shame. She points out that people in the Mediterranean societies are expected to have open doors. Since the doors in this scene are locked, this means that the disciples understood their behavior to be dishonorable, and thus the secrecy.[40] Keener suggests that by mentioning the locked doors (vv. 21, 26), it underlies the fear of the disciples which is in contrast to the boldness implied for their mission to the world.[41] One can understand why the disciples were in fear. Their messiah had just been betrayed, arrested in front of them, and executed by the Romans. They may have wondered if this same outcome of death was going to happen to them. But during Jesus' arrest there was no desire to arrest his followers. Peter was not even arrested for cutting off the ear of Malchus, the high priest's servant, with a sword in the garden.[42] In fact, Jesus made it clear to the soldiers that if they arrest him, then they should let his followers go (John 18:8).

Why then is there a "fear of the Jews" (φόβον τῶν Ἰουδαίων) as if the Jews were still pursuing the disciples or attempting to arrest them? We know that they were not. And we must keep in mind that the disciples are Jews, so it is redundant to mention this "fear of the Jews" as if the disciples were ethnically different. This statement however only makes sense when we think about the overall theme of "fear of the Jews" within the gospel itself. It is early in John 7:1 during a Jewish festival that some people from the crowds sought to apprehend and kill Jesus. They were looking for Jesus and a debate emerged over his true identity. Some publicly defended Jesus' identity by saying that he was a good man. But when resistance to this positive proclamation of his identity emerged, it led some to become silent. No one wanted to defend Jesus anymore against the charge that Jesus was leading the people astray. No one desired to openly speak about him for "fear of the Jews" (7:13). Who were these Jews? Of course, they would be people who are no different from those who were debating Jesus' identity and celebrating the Jewish festival. But from the vantage point of the reader, they know that these are the people who are ethnically different and hold the potential for resisting the claims of Jesus' true identity. Fear of the Jews in this context is a fear to publicly defend Jesus' identity amongst his own people. It is a fear that keeps one's mouth shut.

Then in 9:22 this "fear of the Jews" (ἐφοβοῦντο τοὺς Ἰουδαίους) also emerges. But in this context, it is a fear of the Jewish religious leaders who

---

28:17).

40. Brown, *Spirit in the Writings of John*, 106–7.

41. Keener, *John*, 1201.

42. Matt 26:51–52; Mark 14:47; Luke 22:49–51; John 18:9–10.

condoned and participated in eradicating members from the synagogue.[43] We must recall that in John 9, Jesus had recently healed a man who had been born blind. It is when the Jewish religious leaders interrogate and attempt to find out who had performed this healing that problems arise. The blind man knew that it was Jesus and he even called him a prophet (9:17). The Jewish religious authorities did not believe in the man's confession and sought his parents. When the religious authorities find the parents, they equivocate and do not admit that it was Jesus who had healed their son. Instead, they tell the religious leaders to go consult their son who was healed. In other words, when they had the opportunity to testify of Jesus' miraculous power before the Jewish religious authorities and cast away the claim that Jesus was a sinner, they balked. They did not speak the truth because they were "afraid of the Jews" given that these same religious leaders were involved in the synagogue expulsions. Fear kept them from proclaiming Jesus' miraculous power and agreeing with their son that Jesus was indeed a prophet sent from God.

And lastly, in 19:38 we find a secret disciple named Joseph of Arimathea who approached Pilate to ask for Jesus' body. He was a disciple of Jesus, but he was one who followed from the distance. Nowhere in the Fourth Gospel is Joseph mentioned, although he appears in the Synoptics as one who was a member of the Jewish council and sympathized with Jesus' message.[44] But perhaps he came to know about Jesus just like the way Nicodemus did, but would not approach or interact with Jesus in public because the impact it would have to his reputation. He nonetheless came to Pilate in order to bury Jesus' body. This move may appear respectful and an attempt to give proper honor to Jesus' body. But one must also keep in mind that it is the failure to defend the oppressed that leads to dead bodies. Joseph would not openly associate himself with Jesus or defend his identity before those who maligned his identity because he "feared the Jews" (φόβον τῶν Ἰουδαίων). What does

---

43. As Brown previously mentioned, the hostile experience of Jesus with the Jewish authorities and the hostile experiences of the Johannine Christians with the synagogue authorities are being fused here (Brown, *Community*, 41). The term ἀποσυνάγωγος, also mentioned in 9:22, suggests that the person had been "made a synagogue excommunicate" (Martyn, *History and Theology*, 47–48). Dunn also admits that the local historical context of John 9:22 is evidence of a serious rupture between the churches and synagogues (Dunn, *Neither Jew Nor Greek*, 649).

44. Mark describes Joseph of Arimathea as a prominent member of the Jewish council who was also waiting for the kingdom of God (15:43); Matthew describes him as a rich man who had become a disciple (27:57); and Luke agrees with details found in Mark and Matthew. Luke states that Joseph was a member of the Jewish council, a good and upright man, was waiting for the kingdom of God, and did not consent to the decision to hand Jesus over to the Romans for crucifixion (23:50–51).

fear do in this context? Fear keeps one from publicly associating oneself with Jesus. Fear keeps one away from defending Jesus' identity before those who falsely accuse him. And most certainly, fear also enables one to watch violence befall the innocent.

Why were the characters in the gospel so afraid? What did they fear so much that it led them to be silent in the midst of resistance, fake news about Jesus' identity, and violence against the innocent? Why did this fear paralyze them from speaking the truth and defending the oppressed? The invitation to receive the Spirit, in sum, is an invitation to be commissioned with the divine power of God's breath. It is only with the Spirit that the disciples would be able to overcome their paralyzing fear of what can happen at the hands of the ethnically other. Jesus summons the disciples to "receive the Holy Spirit." Yet did they receive it? There is no immediate response or reaction to the exhortation to receive the Spirit. There were no "speaking in tongues" or narrative affirmation that the disciples had indeed received the Spirit. We only know that a week later they were still afraid and continued to meet behind locked doors. Nonetheless, according to Jesus' commission, we know that the disciples and Johannine community needed to be infused with the Holy Spirit to propel them into the world and continue Jesus' mission on earth. Or said differently, the Fourth Gospel understands the mission of the disciples as one invigorated by the Spirit and focused toward those ethnic groups who cause much fear and have the power to do harm. As such, the breathing of the Holy Spirit upon the disciples is to be understood as a form of empowerment of divine life to reach those whom threaten human life. The disciples must receive the Spirit in order to continue the mission. And it is for this reason why Jesus prefaces the giving of the Spirit by telling the disciples, "just as the Father has sent (ἀπέσταλκέν) me, I send (πέμπω) you all" (20:21).

The Spirit and the Father's Sending of the Son

What does it mean to suggest that Jesus was sent by the Father? And how does this relate to the exhortation to receive the Holy Spirit? The language utilized to describe the "sending" in the Fourth Gospel is ἀποστέλλω and πέμπω, both terms appear in John 20:21. The term ἀποστέλλω is utilized to describe the Father's sending of Jesus, a term which can also be translated as "apostle" but primarily means "one who is commissioned."[45] It appears twenty eight times and used in reference to various people and aspects.[46]

45. Rengstorf, "ἀποστέλλω, (πέμπω)," *TDNT* 1:398.
46. John the Baptist (1:6; 3:28); Jewish religious leaders (1:19, 24; 5:33; 7:32; 18:24);

But ἀποστέλλω is found more frequently in relation to Jesus. That is, ἀποστέλλω primarily describes Jesus' relationship with the Father, as one who had been sent into the world with a specific mission and message.[47] Furthermore, the term used to describe Jesus' sending of the disciples is πέμπω which also means "to send."[48] It appears more frequently with thirty two mentions within the gospel. Like ἀποστέλλω, it too is utilized in reference to various people, but more commonly to explain the relationship between Jesus and the Father.[49] As previously mentioned, both of these terms appear in John 20:21. The gospel utilizes ἀποστέλλω to describe Jesus' relationship with the Father as one who is sent, and it uses πέμπω to describe Jesus' commission of the disciples. Is there a difference? Perhaps not. These terms are used interchangeably and primarily describe a network of relationships between people. As John 13:20 suggests, to be sent means that one comes on behalf of the sender. And to receive the sender also means to receive the one who sent the sender. Engaging, encountering, or receiving "the sent one" is to receive the "sender."

However, Jesus' identity as one who is "sent" by the Father is central to the Christology of the Fourth Gospel. It was Bultmann who proposed that the Fourth Gospel describes Jesus as a demythologized redeemer-revealer who is sent by God.[50] William Loader claims that Bultmann was fundamentally right in this aspect, but wrong in his demythologizing views.[51] Loader proposes that Jesus is to be understood as one who is sent to make the Father known, bring light and life and truth, and complete the Father's work.[52] Everything else, as he claims, revolves around this aspect. Indeed, Loader summarizes Johannine Christology as the following:

> The Father sends and authorizes the Son, who knows the Father, comes from the Father, makes the Father known, brings light and life and truth, completes his Father's work, returns to the Father—exalted, glorified, ascended—sends the disciples, and

---

disciples (4:38); pool of Siloam (9:7); and Lazarus's sisters, who send Jesus a message (11:3).

47. John 3:17, 34; 5:36, 38; 6:29, 57; 7:29; 8:42; 10:36; 11:42; 17:3, 8, 18, 21, 23, 25; 20:21.

48. Rengstorf, "ἀποστέλλω, (πέμπω)," TDNT 1:404–5.

49. Jewish religious leaders (1:22); John the Baptist (1:33); undefined person (13:16, 20); Jesus (4:34; 5:23, 24, 30, 37; 6:38, 39, 44; 7:16, 18, 28, 33; 8:16, 18, 26, 29; 9:4; 12:44, 45, 49; 13:20; 14:24; 15:21; 16:5); Holy Spirit (14:26; 15:26; 16:7).

50. Bultmann, "Die Bedeutung der neuerschlossenen," 404.

51. Loader, *Jesus in John's Gospel*, 37.

52. Loader, *Jesus in John's Gospel*, 143. See also "Central Structure of Johannine Christology," 188–216; Loader, *Christology of the Fourth Gospel*.

sends the Spirit to enable greater understanding, to equip for mission, and to build up the community of faith.[53]

What then does it mean for Jesus to be sent by the Father? According to Loader, this is Jesus' central identity that unites all the diverse images and activities of Jesus within the gospel. Jesus is primarily the envoy of the Father. But if this is Jesus' primary identity in the Fourth Gospel, what are the implications of this activity and what were the outcomes? Even more, how do these outcomes provide clues and insights as to what the disciples and Johannine community should expect as people sent by Jesus and potentially infused with the Holy Spirit?

The sending of the Son by the Father is briefly adumbrated in the opening prologue. It is here that Jesus' mission to the world is presumed to include rejection and potential success. That is, the Logos, who was with God and was God, comes to the world in order to enlighten humanity, but the world did not receive this enlightenment (1:1–9). This, however, does not mean that all within the world rejected him, some believed and thus gained the right to be children of God (vv. 11–13). The mission of the Logos also included a dwelling amongst his people—his own ethnic kin (v. 14). We further find in the gospel that the Father sends Jesus to the world with the mission to bring redemption, not condemnation (3:17). Jesus is sent on the Father's authority (7:28–29; 8:42), communicates the Father's words (3:34; 7:16; 8:26; 11:42; 14:24; 17:8), does the Father's work and will (4:34; 5:36–38; 6:38–39, 44; 8:29; 9:4), brings faith and honor to the Father (5:23–24, 30; 6:29; 12:44; 17:21, 23), brings life (6:57), and reveals the Father (12:45). Jesus' mission as one who is sent by the Father revolves around the Father's will, identity, words, and actions. Everything Jesus does and everywhere Jesus goes is done so with the assumption that he is the envoy of the Father. There is no person Jesus meets, nothing that he does or says to the Jewish, Samaritan, or Roman people that does not include this belief that he is the Father's envoy. In addition, there is also no city or region in which he enters that does not include this identity. Where Jesus goes—Galilee, Cana, Jerusalem, and Samaria—each region experiences the visitation of the Father through Jesus. Therefore, when Jews, Samaritans, and Roman authorities meet Jesus, they meet the Father and gain the opportunity to hear and see the Father's words and works.

The experiences of Jesus as one who was sent by the Father is not only central to his identity, it provides the disciples and Johannine community certain expectations. Therefore, is being sent by Jesus also a commission not to fear the other, but enter the spaces of the other even though there would

---

53. Loader, *Jesus in John's Gospel*, 144.

be rejection? Certainly! They must continue this mission and extend the words, works, and reveal the identity of the Son to all whom they encounter—regardless of location. Just like Jesus who became flesh and was sent into the world by the Father, this also means that he is commissioning the disciples and Johannine community to inhabit the spaces of the ethnically other. They must go outside of their own ethnocultural group and enter the world of the "other." Just as the Logos was sent into the world, they too must incarnate themselves in the world which is also the realm of the ethnically other. This was the mission of Jesus. Now, it is also the mission that Jesus expects for the disciples and Johannine community. They too must imitate the incarnation and dwell amongst the diverse ethnic people of Asia Minor. This also means that they too will enter and inhabit the spaces of resistance and rejection. But regardless of this hostility, this mission will not fail, because some will receive them and become children of God.

Conclusion

How does one overcome the fear of the other in an ethnically hostile and xenophobic world? How does one faithfully execute Jesus' commission if one still holds onto a fear of the "Jews" or any other ethnic group? From the Fourth Gospel's perspective, the fear of the other is overcome by the Holy Spirit. The Fourth Gospel presents its own Pentecost tradition by including the role of the Spirit in helping the disciples overcome their fear of the "Jews," which in the community's context also includes the ethnically other. The Spirit infuses the disciples with the divine life-giving power to proclaim the message of Jesus' identity, reach those who participate or condone the synagogue excommunication, or who enact violence against the innocent. The life-giving Spirit is provided for the disciples and Johannine community so that they may no longer have a fear of what may happen if they interact or engage with the other. They were afraid of the other amongst them when in reality, these "Jews" were the very people that Jesus came to grant eternal life. They must breathe in the divine Spirit in order to be created anew. Inversely, this also means that those who continue to be afraid or have trepidation of the other are those who have not received the Spirit. Did the disciples receive this Spirit? Did they inhale the divine breath of life? The gospel does not provide an affirmative answer to this question. We only know this answer from the Lukan Pentecost of Acts 2. But the ambiguity of this narrative also provides an opportunity for the Johannine community to expel their fear of the other and receive the divine Spirit for their work and mission in the world.

14

Yielding to the Holy Spirit

THE SPIRIT IN THE FOURTH GOSPEL CHALLENGES THE ETHNIC realities, relationships, and ideologies of the ancient world. We may assume that the main characterization of the Spirit in the Fourth Gospel solely emerges from the images of the Paraclete in John 14–16, but this is not true.[1] This study has argued that the portrayal of the Spirit has developed since the early public ministry of Jesus and continues to manifest as the divine breath that challenges the ethnic realities of the ancient world. This study also differs in its conclusions because the role of ethnicity is brought to the forefront of our analysis of the biblical text. The gospel has an ethnic agenda that is intrinsically linked to its articulation and description of the Spirit. We however would not be able to recognize this agenda without an ethnocritical approach which draws our attention to how elements of ethnic difference, rationalization, and prejudice of the Greco-Roman world ought to shape and influence our reading of the Spirit discourses in the Fourth Gospel.

But why such a concern with ethnicity in our study of the Spirit? Simply put, because in speaking about people who lived long ago, we conjure images of people with ethnic identities. These are the social imaginations that emerge in our reconstruction of the ancient world. Failing to take into account the ethnic dynamics of the ancient world not only assumes that an unexamined ethnic identity does not matter, but inadvertently supposes that the ethnic identity of the readers and narrative characters is irrelevant to the study of people in the ancient world. Our ethnic identity cannot be

---

1. See, for example, Köstenberger and Swain, who argue that the fullest characterization of the Spirit is in the Farewell Discourse in Köstenberger and Swain, *Father, Son, and Spirit*, 90–136; Köstenberger, *Theology of John's Gospel*, 393–400.

eradicated by theological identities. As we have noticed in our exploration of various scholars, not all recognize the significance of the ethnic context and its implications for our understanding of the Spirit. In fact, all meaning generated from the biblical text is also influenced and interpreted through a subjectivity that is racial and cultural, as well as ideological and theological.[2] Pentecostal scholars have alerted us to the role of the community in our understanding and interpretation of the biblical text.[3] I continue this motif but with a different focus. My focus is on how the ancients would have viewed ethnic groups and how these communities would have interpreted the ethnic implications of the Spirit in the Fourth Gospel. That is, any discussion on how the Johannine community would have heard the gospel cannot fail to discuss the contextual ethnic identity of its members, people who live in a flesh and blood context.

Scholars rightly notice how the Spirit in the Fourth Gospel intersects with many motifs that are historical, social, and theological. This includes polemical debates, sacramental issues, the death of the founding leader, the loss of faith, and tensions with the Jewish synagogue.[4] These perspectives, however, point to a striking realization that Johannine pneumatology emerges in relation to and reflection of a Johannine context. My contention is that this Johannine context is not ethno-neutral. The Greco-Roman world

---

2. For an analysis of the ethnic identity in theological hermeneutics, see Estrada, "Contextualized Hermeneutic," 341–55.

3. See Thomas, "What the Spirit Is Saying to the Church," 116–22; "Women, Pentecostals, and the Bible," 41–56, esp. 50; Cartledge, "Text-Community-Spirit," 130–45, esp. 133–35; Waddell, *Spirit in the Book of Revelation*, 101; Archer, *Pentecostal Hermeneutic*, 213; Moore, *Spirit of the Old Testament*, 15; Grey, *Three's a Crowd*, 114–33.

4. Barrett notices that the Spirit focuses on an eschatology and the experiences of the readers from a post-resurrection context (Barrett, *St. John*, 74–77; "Holy Spirit in the Fourth Gospel," 1–15). Brown interprets the Spirit in light of the community's dealing with the Parousia delay and the death of their founder (Brown, *John*, 2:1136–41; "Paraclete in the Fourth Gospel," 113). Johnston emphasizes the polemical context of the readers. He interprets the Spirit as the power of God in the experience of preaching, prophesying, and teaching (Johnston, *Spirit-Paraclete*, 3–4). Burge highlights the Christocentric emphasis of the Spirit. He notices that the anointed Christ was a pattern for the anointing Johannine community (Burge, *Anointed Community*, 45). Keener argues for a Judaic background of the Johannine Spirit, especially in terms of prophesy and purity (Keener, *Spirit in the Gospels*, 1–15). Tricia Brown finds the early Roman social context of patron-client relations as a model for interpreting the Spirit (Brown, *Spirit in the Writings of John*, 1–61). Smalley suggest that a unique pneumatology was needed to deal with community disintegration and debate revolving Jesus' identity (Smalley, "Paraclete," 89–92). Thompson points out that the Spirit is a distinct way of envisioning God's activity and presence in the world (Thompson, *God of the Gospel of John*, 145–83). Koester finds the Spirit relating to the role of faith, the presence of Christ and Father in the community, and empowering the community to know and bear witness (Koester, *Word of Life*, 134–60).

knew about ethnic difference. Furthermore, the Spirit cannot be understood apart from some portrait of the community, as many agree.[5] And it is true that how we perceive the Johannine community's context shapes how we interpret the role and function of the Spirit within Jesus' ministry. As this study demonstrates, I hold that the Johannine context includes an diverse community that is dealing with ethnic issues of identity, relations, and racial perceptions which were both positive and negative.

Having an ethnic conscience in our reading of scripture challenges us to reimagine how the Spirit was heard and understood by Jews, Greeks, and Samaritans. It urges us to rethink the situation of the Johannine community from an ethnic vantage point. As such, in our analysis of the gospel's background we affirm that the gospel stems from the memory of the Jewish apostle named John, also known as the Beloved Disciple.[6] This Johannine tradition was preserved, rewritten, and finalized by the end of the first century by the Beloved's followers in the urban Hellenistic environment of Ephesus. When we turn more specifically to the readers of the gospel, who are also described in scholarly literature as the Johannine community, some point out that they were primarily Jewish excommunicates. They propose that tensions with the Jewish synagogue reflected in the gospel mirrors the struggle between the church and the synagogue that became normative in the late first and second century.[7] Others suggest that the gospel is written with a broad audience in mind. They claim that the memory of the Johannine Jesus is presented in such a way that people from a Hellenistic background would easily comprehend the gospel.[8] The lack of consensus on the readers of the gospel also presents a new way of looking at the community. That is, the ability to read and understand the gospel regardless of one's ethnic background demonstrates a fundamental aspect of the implied audience. Not that it had no specific audience in mind but, as I argue, was composed for a community that included diverse ethnic members.[9] The gospel has a particular awareness of the multiethnic identity of the Johannine community

---

5. Meeks, "Man from Heaven," 76; Dodd, *Interpretation*, 3.

6. Irenaeus, *Haer*, 3.11.1; Eusebius, *Hist. eccl.* 2.22; 3.18, 20, 23, 24; 5.20; 6.14; 7.25.

7. Lindars, *Behind the Fourth Gospel*, 76–79; Martyn, *History and Theology*, 66; Ashton, *Understanding*, 100–133.

8. Brown, *Community*, 17–41; Bowman, *Samaritan Problem*, 57–89; Freed, "Did John Write his Gospel," 241–56; Purvis, "Fourth Gospel and the Samaritans," 161–98; Cullmann, *Johannine Circle*, 51; Bauckham, *Gospel*, 2.

9. Dodd, *Interpretation*, 55; Brown, *Community*, 40; Martyn, *History and Theology*, 66; Culpepper, *Anatomy*, 224–27; Lamb, *Text, Context, and the Johannine Community*, 203–4; Keener, *John*, 152–53.

and deliberately retells Jesus' ministry by including a distinct perspective of the Spirit that would resonate with these ethnic readers.

This ethnic dynamic within the gospel and reality of the Johannine community obliges us to explore how ethnic insights, expressions, and relations were viewed and perceived within the Greco-Roman world. It, however, must be noted that our concern is not anachronistic. These Johannine readers heard the gospel from within their experiences as people of their own ethnic environment. We have found that the concern for an ethnic identity and navigating race relations was a part of the social fabric of Greco-Roman world.[10] Ancient environmental theories promote the idea that southerners were physically too weak to rebel and northerners incapable of devising schemes to be victorious in battle.[11] It was assumed that the moderate climate and geographical location of Rome and Greece was the aptest environment for producing the world's most superior people.[12] Other prevailing views on ethnicity assumed that esteemed ancestors and lineage purity were deemed more superior to those who had questionable backgrounds. Immigration and the mingling of different ethnic groups were expected to inevitably develop inferior kin. The pedigree of one's origin was of prime importance and having a mixed lineage was not well esteemed in the ancient world. Genealogical purity and the preservation of lineage thus defined, proclaimed, and regulated how ethnic members would relate to others.[13]

The first-century Johannine readers knew of racial differences. The question is, what did they do about these ethnic ideologies as members of the Johannine community? Did they allow it to influence their views of the Jewish people, Samaritans, or Greeks within their midst? Did they hold onto racial hostilities toward their fellow members within the community? To assume that they would fail to observe the ethnic characters and racial

---

10. Radin, *Jews Among*, 49; Sherwin-White, *Racial Prejudice in Imperial Rome*, 1; Boatwright, *Peoples of the Roman World*, 6–7; McCoskey, *Race Antiquity and Its Legacy*, 9; Isaac, *Invention of Racism*, 1–37; Eliav-Feldon et al., *Origins of Racism*, 9; Kennedy, *Race and Ethnicity in the Classical World*, xiii–xv; Contrary to Hannaford, *Race*, 4–8; Snowden, *Blacks in Antiquity*, 2; *Before Color Prejudice*, 63.

11. Balsdon, *Romans and Aliens*, 59–60; McCoskey, *Race Antiquity and Its Legacy*, 45–48; Isaac, "Racism," 38–41.

12. Hippocrates, *Aer.* 5.10–28; 16.40–43; 23.20–30; Plato, *Tim.* 24c; *Leg.* 747d–e; Aristotle, *Pol.* 7.1327b; *Physiogn.* 806b15; Polybius, *Hist.* 4.21; Vitruvius, *On Architecture*, 6.1.11; Pliny, *Nat.* 2.80; Cicero, *Div.* 2.97; Seneca, *Ira.* 2.15; Ptolemy, *Tetra.* 2.2; Vegetius, *De Re Militari*, 1.2.

13. Euripides, *Ion.* 585–605; Plato, *Tim.* 18d–19a; *Resp.* 5.459d–e; 5.415a–c; *Menex.* 237b–238b; 245c–d; Aristotle, *Pol.* 1.1252b; 1.1254a–1255a; 5.1335b; Diodorus, 1.9.3; Livy, *His. Rom.* 38.17.9–12.

language within the Fourth Gospel truncates our exegetical analysis of the text. Incorporating the ethnic environment of the Greco-Roman world, including its positive and negative views of race relations, provides us with the exegetical rationale and opportunity to hear with ethnic ears the role of the Spirit for a Johannine community. It enables us to understand that the gospel is not only remembering Jesus' words anew; it is also attempting to forge out a new understanding of the Spirit in the midst of an ethnically diverse context and emerging race relations.

Ethnicity and the Spirit in John

How then is the Spirit heard in an ethnic context? When we explore the Spirit within Jesus' public ministry, we immediately find John the Baptist presenting Jesus as a bearer of the Spirit for a mission that had wider ethnic implications. The imagery of the Spirit's descent in John 1 echoes the prophetic hope of Isaiah which describes the anointed Servant who would bring imperial peace to the Jewish exiles and Gentiles. The Jewish religious leaders, who were present at John the Baptist's proclamation, no longer needed to concern themselves with interrogating the Baptist. They wondered what the Baptist was doing in the desert, but that should not alarm them. John the Baptist testifies to the religious leaders and crowds that the anointed Spirit-bearing redeemer had emerged onto the scene. The introduction of Jesus' public ministry commences with his identity confirmed as a bearer of the Spirit who aims to restore Israel and draw all Gentiles to a saving knowledge of God. The prophetic promise of the anointed Servant was being fulfilled and inaugurated with the Spirit's descent upon Jesus. The readers also see in John the Baptist a model for how they are to respond to the Jewish authorities, synagogue rulers, and fellow Jewish members who may challenge their particular ethnic embracing gospel. The readers are made aware that Jesus was anointed with the Spirit for a mission to redeem both Jews and Gentiles. The Spirit's descent was a confirmatory sign of an ethnic undertaking that was promised by the prophet. No longer must one doubt one's place and purpose within the inaugurate mission of Jesus. The Spirit not only serves as a sign that identifies Jesus for the Baptist; it gives the readers a signal that the mission Jesus undertakes includes all people. Since Jesus also promises to baptize believers in the Holy Spirit, this also means that the readers must be ready to continue the mission that Jesus started by reaching the entire Greco-Roman world. Jesus is the giver of the Spirit, and he exhorts the disciples at the end of the gospel to receive the Spirit. The hope for continuing

Jesus' mission anticipated in John 1 becomes a possible baptismal reality and commission when Jesus breathes upon the disciples in John 20.

When Jesus dialogues with the Pharisee named Nicodemus in John 3, the conversation focuses on the entrance requirements for the kingdom of God. Jesus ventures into this unprovoked topic with a Jewish leader to challenge the privileges that come with being born into a Jewish ancestry. Jesus needs to inform Nicodemus and his Pharisaic community that a Jewish genealogical pedigree no longer provides greater access or privileged rights as children of God. Those who debate, including those who have difficulties in negotiating the boundaries and liberties of converts or proselytes, are thus put on notice. The Spirit is the one who verifies and maternally incorporates people into the family of God. All ethnic genealogical relations are destabilized, questionable ancestry is made insignificant, and ethnic relations are now bound in unity because of the common birthing experience of the Spirit. It is now the Spirit that gives birth to all ethnic children of God. And although Jesus' inaugurated mission had commenced to redeem the world, this still does not mean that the issues between ethnic groups have been resolved. Believers within the Johannine community must also recognize the significance and insignificance of their respected ethnic ancestries. They no longer need to discriminate against one another, view each other as second-class converts, or suspect that non-Jewish ethnic members are not children of the same God. The Spirit's birthing activity of each member repudiates all attitudes of ethnic superiority and rebukes those who frown upon others for having interracial marriages. There are no longer any inferior ethnic members within the emerging Johannine community. All ethnic members within the community are bonded to one another as believers through the birthing experience of the Spirit. Anyone who doubts or prohibits the incorporation of the ethnically other calls into question their own born-again experience in the Spirit. In fact, they reveal that they still hold onto the presumption that ethnic identity alone is the defining marker that incorporates one into the family of God. And by doing so, they attest that they are not born of the Spirit nor know of anything related to the Spirit's maternal activity in granting rights to new members.

Yet this new birthing experience that bonds ethnic groups and eschews genealogical pedigrees does not mean that the deep historical ethnic tensions have been dissolved. In Jesus' venture into ethnic terrain in John 4, the memory of racial tension between the Jews and Samaritans follows. A Samaritan woman confronts Jesus with the issue of worship that needed to be resolved. Jesus' response points to the worship that God seeks, one that goes beyond what is done in temple complexes, ancestral mountains, and performed by people with pure ethnic lineages. Jesus points to a new future when all ethnic groups would inhabit the same space of worship through the Spirit. No longer was lineage purity, or the lack thereof, going to be the arbiter in determining the suitable people who could or could not participate in worship. To use ethnic purity, a focal point of segregation between Jews and Samaritans, as a means to justify the oppression and rejection of the worshipper is contrary to the presence of the Spirit. Within the memory of Samaritan and Jewish members of the community, the questions of proper worship are still a prime concern. They must recognize that lineage purity and violence against sacred spaces can never be condoned by the worshippers of the Father. Although ancestral temples are no longer useful, the Spirit still occupies the space of the community. One cannot hold racial prejudices against others or assume a certain racial superiority over others based on one's pure lineage. To do so would lead one to falsely assume that the Spirit is only inhabiting our ethnic spaces of worship. In fact, to worship in the Spirit is to participate in a Spirit-inhabited space that eschews violence and attitudes of ethnic superiority. The Spirit indiscriminately inhabits the space of the worshiping community and expects nothing less for the people of God. This worship that the Father seeks must recognize that the mestizo and refugee of besieged lands is not an inferior member. Although temples are gone, the symbols of ethnic segregation should not be found or preserved by the Johannine community. Even more, the memory of violence against one's community can never be used to initiate violence against the oppressor. The Father seeks worshippers who can remain together, ethnically united and without hostility, in their worship with and in the Spirit.

When we turn to John 6, we find that those who are impacted by Jesus' miraculous ministry are not immune to curiosity about his real ethnic identity. As Jesus provides bread and teaches the Jewish crowds his divine relationship with God, some are doubtful. They question his divine claims, urge him to provide bread from heaven as their ancestors experienced, and publicly remind him that they know his real father. Jesus, however, perceives that the crowds value the honor communicated to them through the fleshly relationship with their ancestors. Even more, the doubt of Jesus' claim that asserts divine relation with the Father had also reached his closest followers. They, too, need to move beyond the limitations and benefits of ethnic kinship. Jesus' identity cannot solely be circumscribed by this reality. Indeed, this is not to deny that ethnic kinship has its various benefits that provide honor, inheritance, the nurturing of children, economic security, and social union within the State. There are various privileges that are passed down to descendants. But the reality of death intrinsic to all flesh relations thwarts the tangible benefits it seems to provide. One cannot leverage ethnic privilege to force Jesus to act. And the members who doubt and struggle with the certainty of Jesus' relation with the Father no longer need to fret. They must not allow the lens of ethnic kinship to blind them from seeing Jesus' true identity and relation with the divine Father. If they hold to the privilege and prestige of their kinship they will fail to recognize that kinship privileges only bring death. What benefits therefore are in one's ancestral relations? When compared to the Spirit and giver of life, nothing. Solely relying upon the benefits of ethnic kinship will only result in death. Life does not come from the power of earthly fathers, nor is one's future dependent upon the acceptance or rejection of one's ancestral kin. Ethnic privilege and pedigree fail before the life-giving activity of the Spirit. It is the Spirit who breathes life to all ethnic bodies. And when the life is threated by one's ethnic kin because of association with Jesus, one is promised a new life and vitality that is infused by the Spirit. The source, sustenance, and breath that gives life to our bodies comes not from our ancestors, earthly father, or family. It comes from the divine Spirit of life.

Then in John 7 we find something different. Although Jesus encounters rejection from his own family, he dares to venture to the Jerusalem temple during the most festive occasions when the people reenacted the wilderness experience. In John 7 we encounter the invitation to partake of the Spirit. Yet this public exposure in the temple also meant that Jesus was putting his life at risk. The Jews were seeking to kill him. Officers wanted to arrest him. The crowds desired to apprehend him. Yet Jesus teaches in the temple and meets resistance from his own people. When Jesus informs the Jerusalem Jews that he was leaving, they accuse him of going to the Greeks. But this accusation of fleeing to the Greeks is not an embarrassment. Jesus does not seek to clarify the record. Instead, under the suspicion of ethnic outreach, he makes it evident that he indeed is receptive to all people. No amount of pressure would prevent him from proclaiming of those who thirst for new water. How many people respond to Jesus' invitation is not revealed, but the writer explains that this water was to be understood in terms of the Spirit. In a prelude to receive the Spirit in John 20, we see Jesus standing in the temple inviting all people to drink from him and partake of the Spirit. Jesus, the one rejected by his own ethnic people, dares to invite all those who hear his voice. It is ethnic suspicion that sets the scene for Jesus' final statement on the Spirit within his public ministry. As he cries out to those who participate in the Feast of Tabernacles, the readers hear that the Spirit has now been made available to all who thirst and are willing to believe in him. It is the Greek audience within the Johannine community that becomes acutely aware of Jesus' invitation, because they too have conflicts and perhaps experienced ethnic suspicion from the Jews. From the perspective of the Johannine community that was struggling with Greek-Jewish conflict and acculturation, they now can be assured that the Spirit has been offered to both ethnic communities. No amount of intra-ethnic conflict, suspicion, or racial hostility can prevent or suspend the invitation to partake of the Spirit. The Johannine community hears within Jesus' words the refreshing invitation to partake of the Spirit in light of their scorched ethnic conflict that has littered the diaspora lands.

When we turn to the Farewell Discourse in John 13–17, the presence and activity of the Spirit-Paraclete is clothed in kinship language. Jesus' departure and absence may appear to leave the disciples orphaned, placing their ethnic relations and identity in jeopardy, but the presence of the Paraclete sustains them as a newly begotten community who are also known as the children of God. The presence of the Paraclete binds together all disparate ethnic members into one household who all share the title "child of God." The disparate ethnic members in the Johannine community are not orphaned from their ethnic communities. They are not fatherless nor going to be vulnerable without a defender. They are divinely birthed children who have the Paraclete within them. They are given a new racial understanding of themselves and one another. To outsiders, they may appear as orphans, without an ethnic identity and kinship community. But to one another, they are children who have been born of God and born of the Spirit. Understanding the racial implications of the "orphan" and "children" language of the Farewell Discourse not only explains how the members within the community would define themselves, but also explains how the presence of the Paraclete sustains and unites all ethnic members in the family of God.

Then we find in John 15–16 the Johannine community understanding its identity in relation to the "other," also known as the "world." The world, however, is not a vague theological concept. This is ethnic classification language that reshapes the ethnic imagination of the Johannine readers. Because the disciples and Johannine community are set apart from the world who does not have the Paraclete, this also means that they are to understand themselves primarily as children of God. But as a newly created community of the Spirit, this does not mean that they will be free from violence and oppression. They should not only expect it; the Johannine community is already undergoing these traumatic experiences. Jesus' statement in 15:26–27 and 16:7–15 thus affirms that the Spirit-Paraclete will engage in communicatory and forensic activities. The Paraclete is to be understood as a defender of the oppressed and rejected—the orphaned people of God. The hostility that the disciples and Johannine community are expected to experience includes violence in the synagogues, that is, in the confines of ethnic spaces. This violence will emerge in their safe spaces, by their fellow kin, and at the hands of the Empire. As such, the Paraclete comes to their aid and does not leave them as victims. Resistance toward injustice and oppression is what Jesus promises that the Paraclete will do for the children of God.

And finally, the invitation to receive the Spirit in John 20 leaves open the possibility and expectation to continue the mission of Jesus in the world. But to do so, the disciples and community must eradicate all fear of the other. How can this be done? Overcoming the fear of the other can only be achieved by receiving the Spirit. In John 20 we find Jesus appearing to the disciples who were afraid of the "Jews," which is ironic given that they too are Jews. However, this fear of the Jews is really a reflection of the Johannine community's fear of the other. They too lived in an ethnically hostile and xenophobic world. They are made aware that in order to faithfully execute Jesus' commission they need to receive the Spirit. The gospel recognizes that the fear of the other can only be overcome by the Holy Spirit. This is the gospel's own particular "Johannine Pentecost" but without the physical manifestations as we find in Acts 2. This is not to suppose that, for the Fourth Gospel, the outward manifestations of the Spirit were irrelevant. To the contrary, the outward manifestation of the Spirit is found in the disciples' movement to the world. What truly demonstrates that the disciples receive the Spirit is if they could proclaim the gospel, reach those who engaged in violence against the community, and overcome their own fear of the other. Did the disciples and Johannine community do just this and confirm that they received the Spirit? We are not sure given that this part of the story is not found within the Fourth Gospel but only in Acts.

The Ethnic Spirit for Today

What new insights have we gained after exploring the Spirit in light of the ethnic and racial ideologies of the Greco-Roman world? We come to the realization that the Spirit as the divine presence of God addresses the challenges that result in having different ethnic bodies. The Spirit speaks to our ethnic challenges, rebukes our prejudices, and reveals the insufficiency that ethnic ideologies and stereotypes have in the formation of a new community of believers. This pneumatic perspective is not an anachronistic theme within the Fourth Gospel. It emerges when we recognize that to understand the Johannine context means that we must situate the Johannine community—a diverse one indeed—within the wider Greco-Roman context of racial ideologies. This racial context is not solely influenced by my ethnic context and identity. The Fourth Gospel with its language and distinction between Jews, Samaritans, and Greeks compels us to think about people groups. As such, we notice that this articulation of the Spirit was needed for a community that was undergoing ethnic challenges in their understanding of Jesus' mission and relationships with others, those within and outside the community. The Spirit is the divine wind of God that gives birth to all ethnic bodies for the purpose of gathering and forming a new community. Thus, to understand our role, identity, and relationship with others within the Spirit is to also confront the vicious and inhumane ideologies that have sought to divide and rank us.

I have sought to demonstrate the point that in order to fully understand why the Spirit is described and portrayed in such manner, we must understand the ideologies of ethnicity and race in the Greco-Roman world. Ethnicity matters in our exegesis. It matters because the gospel was written in such a way that it addresses the real issues and challenges of the ethnic readers who lived in a diverse world. From the inaugurated mission to all ethnic groups and the incorporation of each member, the Spirit is involved in the ethnic challenges they face as a Johannine community. Foreigners were easily oppressed and rejected in the ancient world because they were not pure-blooded people with native rights to the land. Violence against ethnic groups was justified on the basis of being from a far region. Ethnic groups with mixed ancestry and interracial relations were eschewed because it was assumed that they were reflective of humanity's deterioration. Many were so blinded by their ethnic privileges that they failed to recognize that life does not come from the pedigree of one's ancestors but from the Spirit. The Spirit, however, is offered to all ethnic communities and no amount of intra-ethnic conflict can stop Jesus from inviting those who live in a foreign land.

As the emerging Christian community expanded and traveled into various regions, they too needed to deal with these issues of ethnic inclusion and race relations. From the Fourth Gospel, we are made aware that the Johannine community received a pneumatic solution as they traversed through this challenge. From the description and portrayal of the Spirit, we too are reminded anew what it means for the Spirit to participate in the communal life of believers who come from diverse ethnic backgrounds. The Spirit's activity and description stir our imagination and compel us to act as we deal with race relations and oppressive ethnic ideologies that aim to dehumanize others based upon perceived differences. We can find in the ministry of Jesus how various racial ideologies of oppression and suspicion were being challenged by the Spirit. To participate in the mission of the Spirit, be born of the Spirit, worship in the Spirit, derive life from the Spirit, and drink from the wells of the Spirit means that one cannot harbor or participate in attitudes and practices that dehumanize, divide, and destroy ethnic bodies. As such, to be a member of the Johannine community, or any member within the early Christian community in the Greco-Roman world, means that one must denounce dehumanizing ideologies that would prevent one from being bound together as the people of God, with all the rights and privileges that come from being born of the divine Spirit.

How then do the readers of today respond? For one thing, any community that claims to bear the Spirit must be a vanguard for racial and ethnic equality and equity. To be born of the Spirit means that one adamantly rejects of all forms of ethnic superiority and dehumanizing practices that oppress the marginalized. Engaging in this resistance is to participate with the Spirit-Paraclete who is a defender of all orphans—the landless and refugees amongst us. Worshipping in the Spirit means that the sacred spaces of our communities cannot foster violence and segregationist attitudes toward the ethnically other. Ethnically hostile activities are to be eschewed by the community because they are antithetical to the life-giving identity of the Spirit. Failing to participate in the pneumatic activity as described in the Fourth Gospel is to maintain the old Greco-Roman structures of ethnic privilege, superiority, and systems of oppression. The multiethnic people of God who have the Spirit are empowered to foster ethnic equality and equity. Like the Spirit-Paraclete, they are to struggle for peace in the midst of contemporary ethnic ideologies that imitate and resurrect those old Greco-Roman racial ideologies.

This also means that racism and prejudice today are not simply wrong based solely on moral grounds. Racism and prejudice today are activities that run counter to the life-giving presence and activity of the Spirit. Racism and ethnic prejudice are by definition anti-pneumatic. That is, the diabolical work that dehumanizes and divides and sets up systems of privilege and pedigree are simply activities that run contrary to the inclusive, all-embracing, far-reaching, and life-breathing movement of the Spirit. This also leads us to wonder, can one still be "born again" and claim to be a Christian while still holding onto ethnic prejudice and ideologies of racial superiority? Can one claim to be a Christian and continue to support, champion, and uphold demagogues or politicians who utilize ideologies of racial superiority or foment fear of the immigrant? As I hope that this monograph has demonstrated—those who harbor racial superiority, fear of the foreigner, support, and engage in oppressive actions toward the ethnically other demonstrate that they truly do not have the Spirit. They may call themselves a Christian, but they are a life-less Christian who fight against the Spirit-Paraclete.

Bibliography

Aland, Barbara, and Kurt Aland. *The Text of the New Testament*. Grand Rapids: Eerdmans, 1987.
Allison, Dale, Jr. *Constructing Jesus: Memory, Imagination, and History*. Grand Rapids: Baker, 2010.
———. *Resurrecting Jesus: The Earliest Christian Tradition and Its Interpreters*. New York: T. & T. Clark, 2005.
Aloisi, John. "The Paraclete's Ministry of Conviction: Another Look at John 16:8–11." *Journal of the Evangelical Theological Society* 47.1 (2004) 55–69.
Anderson, Paul. "Anti-Semitism and Religious Violence as Flawed Interpretations of the Gospel of John." In *John and Judaism: A Contested Relationship in Context*, edited by Ray Alan Culpepper and Paul Anderson, 265–311. Atlanta: SBL, 2017.
———. *The Riddles of the Fourth Gospel*. Minneapolis: Fortress, 2011.
———. "The Sitz im Leben of the Johannine Bread of Life Discourse and Its Evolving Context." In *Critical Readings of John 6*, edited by R. Alan Culpepper, 1–57. Leiden: Brill, 1997.
Anderson, Robert, and Terry Giles. *The Keepers: An Introduction to the History and Culture of Samaritans*. Peabody, MA: Hendrickson, 2002.
Archer, Kenneth. *A Pentecostal Hermeneutic: Spirit, Scripture, and Community*. Cleveland, TN: CPT, 2009.
Ashton, John. *The Gospel of John and Christian Origins*. Minneapolis: Fortress, 2014.
———. *Understanding the Fourth Gospel*. 2nd ed. New York: Oxford University Press, 2008.
Badcock, F. J. "The Feast of Tabernacles." *The Journal of Theological Studies* 24.94 (1923) 169–74.
Balsdon, John P. V. D. *Romans and Aliens*. London: Duckworth, 1979.
Baltzer, Klaus. *Deutero-Isaiah*. Hermeneia. Minneapolis: Fortress, 2001.
Barrett, Charles. *The Gospel According to St. John: An Introduction with Commentary and Notes on the Greek Text*. London: Camelot, 1970.
———. "Holy Spirit in the Fourth Gospel." *Journal of Theological Studies* 1.1 (1950) 1–15.
Barth, Fredrik. *Ethnic Groups and Boundaries*. Long Grove, IL: Waveland, 1969.

Barton, Stephen. "Historical Criticism and Social Scientific Perspective." In *Hearing the New Testament: Strategies for Interpretation*, edited by Joel Green, 69–74. Grand Rapids: Eerdmans, 1995.

Bauckham, Richard, ed. *The Gospel for All Christians*. Grand Rapids: Eerdmans, 1998.

Beasley-Murray, George. *John*. Word Biblical Commentary 36. Nashville: Thomas Nelson, 1999.

Belle, Gilbert van. *The Signs Source in the Fourth Gospel: Historical Survey and Critical Evaluation of the Semeia Hypothesis*. Leuven: Leuven University Press, 1994.

Belleville, Linda. "Born of Water and Spirit: John 3:5." *Trinity Journal* 1.2 (1980) 125–41.

Bennema, Cornelis. "The Giving of the Spirit in John's Gospel—A New Proposal?" *Evangelical Quarterly* 74.3 (2002) 195–213.

———. "The Identity and Composition of Οἱ Ἰουδαῖοι in the Gospel of John." *Tyndale Bulletin* 60.2 (2009) 239–63.

Bernier, Jonathan. "Jesus, Ἀποσυνάγωγος, and Modes of Religiosity." In *John and Judaism: A Contested Relationship in Context*, edited by Ray Alan Culpepper and Paul Anderson, 127–33. Atlanta: SBL, 2017.

Berthelot, Katell. "Hecataeus of Abdera and Jewish 'Misanthropy.'" *Bulletin du Centre de recherche français à Jérusalem* 19 (2008) n.p.

———. "Misanthropy." In vol. 1 of *Antisemitism: A Historical Encyclopedia of Prejudice and Persecution*, edited by Richard S. Levy, 467. 2 vols. Santa Barbara: ABC-CLIO, 2005.

———. "Philo's Perception of the Roman Empire." *Journal for the Study of Judaism* 42 (2011) 166–87.

Bettenson, Henry, and Chris Maunder, eds. *Documents of the Christian Church*. Oxford: Oxford University Press, 1999.

Betz, Otto. *Der Paraklet*. Leiden: Brill, 1963.

Beutler, Johannes. "The Structure of John 6." In *Critical Readings of John 6*, edited by R. Alan Culpepper, 115–27. Leiden: Brill, 1997.

Blenkinsopp, Joseph. "Second Isaiah—Prophet of Universalism." *Journal for the Study of the Old Testament* 13.41 (1988) 83–103.

Blomberg, Craig. *The Historical Reliability of John's Gospel: Issues and Commentary*. Downers Grove, IL: InterVarsity, 2001.

Boatwright, Mary. *Peoples of the Roman World*. New York: Cambridge University Press, 2012.

Bowman, John. *The Samaritan Problem: Studies in the Relationships of Samaritanism, Judaism, and Early Christianity*. Eugene, OR: Pickwick, 1975.

Boyarin, Daniel. *Border Lines: The Partition of Judaeo-Christianity*. Philadelphia: University of Pennsylvania Press, 2007.

Brandfon, Fredric. "The Arch of Titus in The Roman Forum." *Change Over Time* 5.1 (2015) 6–27.

Bremmer, Jan. "Spartans and Jews: Abrahamic Cousins?" In *Abraham, the Nations, and the Hagarites: Jewish, Christian, and Islamic Perspectives on Kinship with Abraham*, edited by Martin Goodman, et al., 47–60. Leiden: Brill, 2010.

Bruner, Fredrick. *The Gospel of John*. Grand Rapids: Eerdmans, 2012.

Breck, John. *Spirit of Truth: The Origins of Johannine Pneumatology*. Crestwood, NY: St. Vladimir's Seminary Press, 1991.

Brown, Colin, ed. *New International Dictionary of New Testament Theology*. 4 vols. Grand Rapids: Zondervan, 1975–85.

Brown, Tricia Gates. *Spirit in the Writings of John*. New York: T. & T. Clark, 2003.
Brown, Raymond. *Community of the Beloved Disciple: The Life, Loves, and Hates of an Individual Church in New Testament Times*. New York: Paulist, 1979.
———. *The Gospel According to John*. 2 vols. Anchor Bible 29–29A. Garden City, NY: Doubleday, 1966–70.
———. *Introduction to the Gospel of John*. Edited by Francis Moloney. New York: Doubleday, 2003.
———. "The Paraclete in the Fourth Gospel." *New Testament Studies* 13 (1967) 113–32.
Browning, Robert. "Greeks and Others: From Antiquity to the Renaissance." In *Greeks and Barbarians*, edited by Thomas Harrison, 257–77. New York: Routledge, 2002.
Bruce, F. F. "Holy Spirit in Qumran Texts." *Annual of Leeds University Oriental Society* 6 (1968) 49–55.
Buch-Hansen, Gitte. *It Is the Spirit that Gives Life: A Stoic Understanding of Pneuma in John's Gospel*. Berlin: de Gruyter, 2010.
Buell, Denise. "Challenges and Strategies for Speaking about Ethnicity in the New Testament and New Testament Studies." *Svensk Exegetisk Årsbok* 79 (2014) 33–51.
———. "Early Christian Universalism and Modern Racism." In *The Origins of Racism in the West*, edited by Miriam Eliav-Feldon, et al., 109–131. New York: Cambridge University Press, 2009.
———. "Rethinking the Relevance of Race for Early Christian Self-Definition." *Harvard Theological Review* 94.4 (2001) 449–76.
———. *Why This New Race: Ethnic Reasoning in Early Christianity*. New York: Columbia University Press, 2007.
Buell, Denise, and Caroline Hodge. "The Politics of Interpretation: The Rhetoric of Race and Ethnicity in Paul." *Journal of Biblical Literature* 123.2 (2004) 235–51.
Bultmann, Rudolf. *The Gospel of John*. Philadelphia: Westminster, 1971.
———. *Theology of the New Testament*. Translated by Kendrick Grobel. 2 vols. 1951–55. Reprint, Waco, TX: Baylor University Press, 2007.
Burge, Gary. *The Anointed Community: The Holy Spirit in the Johannine Tradition*. Grand Rapids: Eerdmans, 1987.
Busine, Aude. "From Stones to Myth: Temple Destruction and Civic Identity in the Late Roman East." *Journal of Late Antiquity* 6.2 (2013) 325–46.
Carson, D. A. "The Function of the Paraclete in John 16:7–11." *Journal of Biblical Literature* 98.4 (1979) 547–66.
Cartledge, Mark. "Text-Community-Spirit: The Challenges Posed by Pentecostal Theological Method to Evangelical Theology." In *Spirit and Scripture: Exploring a Pneumatic Hermeneutic*, edited by Kevin L. Spawn and Archie T. Wright, 130–45. New York: T. & T. Clark, 2013.
Chapman, David. "Burial of Jesus." In *Dictionary of Jesus and the Gospels*, edited by Joel Green, et al., 97–100. 2nd ed. Downers Grove, IL: InterVarsity, 2013.
Charlesworth, James. "Jesus Research and Archaeology: A New Perspective." In *Jesus and Archaeology*, edited by James Charlesworth, 11–63. Grand Rapids: Eerdmans, 2006.
Childs, Brevard. *Isaiah*. Louisville: Westminster John Knox, 2001.
Cohen, Shaye. *The Beginning of Jewishness: Boundaries, Varieties, Uncertainties*. Berkley: University of California Press, 1999.
———. *From the Maccabees to the Mishnah*. Louisville: Westminster John Knox, 2014.
Collingwood, R. G. *The Idea of History*. Oxford: Oxford University Press, 1946.

Collins, John. *Between Athens and Jerusalem: Jewish Identity in the Hellenistic Diaspora.* Grand Rapids: Eerdmans, 2000.

Cortes, Juan. "Yet Another Look at John 7:37–38." *Catholic Biblical Quarterly* 29.1 (1967) 79–86.

Cosgrove, Charles. "Did Paul Value Ethnicity?" *Catholic Biblical Quarterly* 26 (2006) 268–90.

Courtney, Edward. *A Commentary on the Satires of Juvenal.* Berkley: California Classical Studies, 2013.

Crump, David. "Who Gets What? God or Disciples, Human Spirit or Holy Spirit in John 19:30." *Novum Testamentum* 51 (2009) 78–89.

Cullmann, Oscar. *The Johannine Circle: Its Place in Judaism among the Disciples of Jesus and in Early Christianity.* London: SCM, 1976.

Culpepper, Ray Alan. *Anatomy of the Fourth Gospel.* Philadelphia: Fortress, 1987.

———. "Anti-Judaism in the Fourth Gospel as a Theological Problem for Christian Interpreters." In *Anti-Judaism and the Fourth Gospel*, edited by Reimund Bieringer, et al., 61–82. Louisville: Westminster John Knox, 2001.

———. "The Gospel of John and the Jews." *Review & Expositor* 84.2 (1987) 273–88.

Daise, Michael. "'If Anyone Thirsts, Let That One Come to Me and Drink': The Literary Textual of John 7:37b–38a." *Journal of Biblical Literature* 122.4 (2003) 687–99.

Danzig, Gabriel. "Apologizing for Socrates: Plato and Xenophon on Socrates's Behavior in Court." *Transactions of the American Philological Association* 133.2 (2003) 281–321.

Delgado, Richard, and Jean Stefancic. *Critical Race Theory.* New York: New York University Press, 2012.

Dodd, Charles H. *The Interpretation of the Fourth Gospel.* New York: Cambridge University Press, 1970.

Domeris, Bill. "The Paraclete as an Ideological Construct: A Study in the Farewell Discourses." *Journal of Theology for Southern Africa* 67 (1989) 17–23.

Draper, J. A. "The Sociological Function of the Spirit/Paraclete in the Farewell Discourse in the Fourth Gospel." *Neotestamentica* 26.1 (1992) 13–29.

Drozdek, Adam. *Greek Philosophers as Theologians: The Divine Arche.* Burlington, VT: Ashgate, 1988.

Dube, Musa. "Reading for Decolonization John 4:1–42." In *John and Postcolonialism: Travel, Space, and Power*, edited by Musa Dube and Jeffrey Staley, 51–75. Sheffield: Sheffield Academic, 2002.

Dunn, James. *Baptism in the Holy Spirit: A Re-Examination of the New Testament Teaching on the Gift of the Spirit in Relation to Pentecostalism Today.* Philadelphia: Westminster, 1970.

———. "The Embarrassment of History: Reflections on the Problem of 'Anti-Judaism' in the Fourth Gospel." In *Anti-Judaism and the Fourth Gospel*, edited by Reimund Bieringer, et al., 41–60. Louisville: Westminster John Knox, 2001.

———. *Jesus, Paul, and the Law: Studies in Mark and Galatians.* Louisville: Westminster John Knox, 1990.

———. *Jesus Remembered.* Grand Rapids: Eerdmans, 2003.

———. *Neither Jew nor Greek: A Contested Identity.* Grand Rapids: Eerdmans, 2015.

Eliav-Feldon, Miriam, et al, eds. *The Origins of Racism in the West.* New York: Cambridge University Press, 2009.

Elliott, John. "Social-Scientific Criticism of the New Testament: More on Methods and Models." In *Social-Scientific Criticism of the New Testament and its Social World*, edited by John Elliott, 1–26. Atlanta: Scholars, 1985.

———. *What Is Social-Scientific Criticism?* Minneapolis: Fortress, 1993.

Eslinger, Lyle. "The Wooing of the Woman at the Well: Jesus, The Reader, and Reader-Response Criticism." In *The Gospel of John as Literature: An Anthology of Twentieth-Century Perspectives*, edited by Mark W. G. Stibbe, 165–82. Leiden: Brill, 1993.

Estrada, Rodolfo Galvan, III. "Is a Contextualized Hermeneutic the Future of Pentecostal Readings? The Implications of a Pentecostal Hermeneutic for a Chicano/Latino Community." *Pneuma* 37.3 (2015) 341–55.

———. "Renewing Theological Education: Developing Networks of Latino/a Ethnocultural Inclusion." *PentecoStudies: An Interdisciplinary Journal for Research on the Pentecostal & Charismatic Movements* 17.2 (2018) 134–57.

———. "The Spirit as an Inner Witness in John 15.26." *Journal of Pentecostal Theology* 22.1 (2013) 77–94.

———. "What Does the Paraclete Have to Do with Dreamers? A Pneumatological Paradigm for Latino/a Social-Political Advocacy." *Perspectivas: The Journal of the Hispanic Theological Initiative* 19 (2019) 67–81.

Faure, Alexander. "Die alttestamentlichen Zitate im 4. Evangelium und die Quellenscheidungshypothese." *Zeitschrift für die Neutestamentliche Wissenschaft* 21.1 (1922) 99–121.

Feldman, Louis. *Judaism and Hellenism Reconsidered*. Leiden: Brill, 2006.

———. "Josephus's Attitude toward the Samaritans: A Study in Ambivalence." In *Jewish Sects, Religious Movements, and Political Parties*, edited by Menachem Mor, 23–45. Omaha, NE: Creighton University Press, 1992.

Feldman, Louis, and Meyer Reinhold. *Jewish Life and Thought Among Greeks and Romans*. Edinburgh: T. & T. Clark, 1996.

Ferda, Tucker. "John the Baptist, Isaiah 40, and the Ingathering of the Exiles." *Journal for the Study of the Historical Jesus* 10 (2012) 154–88.

Fitzgerald, J. T. "Orphans in Mediterranean Antiquity and Early Christianity." *Acta Theologica* 23 (2016) 29–48.

Fitzmyer, Joseph. *The Gospel According to Luke 1–9*. New York: Doubleday, 1981.

Fortna, Robert. *The Gospel of Signs*. New York: Cambridge University Press, 1970.

———. "Source and Redaction in the Fourth Gospel's Portrayal of Jesus' Signs." *Journal of Biblical Literature* 89.2 (1970) 151–66.

Fowler, Russell. "Born of Water and Spirit (John 3:5)." *Expository Times* 82 (1971) 159.

France, Robert. *The Gospel of Matthew*. Grand Rapids: Eerdmans, 2007.

Freed, Edwin. "Did John Write His Gospel Partly to Win Samaritan Converts?" *Novum Testamentum* 12.3 (1970) 241–56.

———. *Old Testament Quotations in the Gospel of John*. Leiden: Brill, 1965.

Frey, Jörg. "Toward Reconfiguring Our Views on the 'Parting of the Ways': Ephesus as a Test Case." In *John and Judaism: A Contested Relationship in Context*, edited by Ray Alan Culpepper and Paul Anderson, 221–39. Atlanta: SBL, 2017.

Friedland, R., and R. D. Hecht. "The Politics of Sacred Place: Jerusalem's Temple Mount." In *Sacred Places and Profane Spaces: Essays on the Geographics of Judaism, Christianity, and Islam*, edited by Jamie Scott and Paul Simpson-Housley, 21–62. Westport, CT: Greenwood, 1991.

Fuglseth, Kåre Sigvald. *Johannine Sectarianism in Perspective: A Sociological, Historical, and Comparative Analysis of Temple and Social Relationships in the Gospel of John, Philo, and Qumran.* Leiden: Brill, 2005.

Gelston, Anthony. "Universalism in Second Isaiah." *The Journal of Theological Studies* 43.2 (1992) 377–98.

Goldenberg, David. "Racism, Color Symbolism, and Color Prejudice." In *The Origins of Racism in the West*, edited by Miriam Eliav-Feldon, et al., 88–108. New York: Cambridge University Press, 2009.

Goldingay, John. *The Theology of the Book of Isaiah.* Downers Grove, IL: InterVarsity, 2014.

Goldingay, John, and David Payne. *Isaiah 40-55.* Vol. 1. International Critical Commentary. New York: T. & T. Clark, 2006.

Goodman, Martin. *Judaism in the Roman World: Collected Essays.* Leiden: Brill, 2007.

Gordley, Matthew. "The Johannine Prologue and Jewish Didactic Hymn Traditions: A New Case for Reading the Prologue as a Hymn." *Journal of Biblical Literature* 128.4 (2009) 781–802.

Goulder, Michael. "Nicodemus." *Scottish Journal of Theology* 44.2 (1991) 153–68.

Grayston, Kenneth. "The Meaning of Paraklētos." *Journal for the Study of the New Testament* 13 (1981) 67–82.

Greene, Joseph. "Integrating Interpretations of John 7:37–39 into the Temple Theme: The Spirit as Efflux." *Neotestamentica* 47.2 (2013) 333–53.

Grese, William. "'Unless One Is Born Again': The Use of a Heavenly Journey in John 3." *Journal of Biblical Literature* 107.4 (1988) 677–93.

Grey, Jacqueline. *Three's a Crowd: Pentecostalism, Hermeneutics, and the Old Testament.* Eugene, OR: Pickwick, 2011.

Grigsby, Bruce. "'If Any Man Thirsts . . .': Observations on the Rabbinic Background of John 7:37–39." *Biblica* 67.1 (1986) 101–8.

Gruen, Erich. *Diaspora: Jews Amidst Greeks and Romans.* Cambridge, MA: Harvard University Press, 2002.

———. *Rethinking the Other in Antiquity.* New Jersey: Princeton University Press, 2011.

Guiding, Aileen. *Fourth Gospel and Jewish Worship: A Study of the Relation of St John's Gospel to the Ancient Jewish Lectionary System.* Oxford: Clarendon, 1960.

Hachlili, Rachel. "Synagogues: Before and After the Roman Destruction of the Temple." *Biblical Archeological Review* 41.3 (2015) 30–38.

Haenchen, Ernst. *John 1.* Hermeneia. Philadelphia: Fortress, 1984.

Hager, Paul. "Chrysippus's Theory of Pneuma." *Prudentia* 14.2 (1982) 97–108.

Hakola, Ramio. *Identity Matters: John, the Jews, and Jewishness.* Leiden: Brill, 2005.

Haley, Shelley. "Be Not Afraid of the Dark: Critical Race Theory and Classical Studies." In *Prejudice and Christian Beginnings: Investigating Race, Gender, and Ethnicity in Early Christian Studies*, edited by Laura Nasrallah and Elisabeth Schüssler Fiorenza, 27–49. Minneapolis: Fortress, 2010.

Hall, Jonathan. *Ethnic Identity in Greek Antiquity.* New York: Cambridge University Press, 2000.

———. *Hellenicity: Between Ethnicity and Culture.* Chicago: University of Chicago Press, 2002.

Hannaford, Ivan. *Race: The History of an Idea in the West.* Baltimore: Johns Hopkins University Press, 1996.

Hanson, K. C. "All in the Family: Kinship in Agrarian Roman Palestine." In *The Social World of the New Testament*, edited by Jerome Neyrey and Eric Stewart, 26–46. Peabody, MA: Hendrickson, 2008.

———. "How Honorable! How Shameful! A Cultural Analysis of Matthew's Makarisms and Reproaches." *Semeia* 68 (1996) 81–111.

Harm, Frederick. "Distinctive Titles of the Holy Spirit in the Writings of John." *Concordia Journal* 13.2 (1987) 119–35.

Harnack, Adolf von. *What Is Christianity?* Philadelphia: Fortress, 1957.

Harvey, Van. *The Historian and the Believer: The Morality of Historical Knowledge and Christian Belief*. Champaign, IL: University of Illinois Press, 1996.

Hoeck, Andreas. "The Johannine Paraclete: Herald of the Eschaton." *Journal of Biblical and Pneumatological Research* 4 (2012) 23–37.

Hope, Valerie. "Trophies and Tombstones: Commemorating the Roman Soldier." *World Archaeology* 35.1 (2003) 79–97.

Horrell, David. "Race, Nation, People: Ethnic Identity-Construction in 1 Peter 2:9." *New Testament Studies* 58 (2012) 123–43.

Hübner, Sabine. "Fatherless Antiquity? Perspectives on 'Fatherlessness' in the Ancient Mediterranean." In *Growing Up Fatherless in Antiquity*, edited by Sabine Hübner and David Ratzan, 3–28. New York: Cambridge University Press, 2009.

Hübner, Sabine, and David Ratzan. "Callirhoe's Dilemma: Remarriage and Stepfathers in the Greco-Roman East." In *Growing Up Fatherless in Antiquity*, edited by Sabine Hübner and David Ratzan, 61–82. New York: Cambridge University Press, 2009.

Humphreys, Sally. "Kinship." In *The Oxford Companion to Classical Civilization*, edited by Simon Hornblower, et al., 430. New York: Oxford University Press, 2014.

Hylen, Susan. *Allusion and Meaning in John 6*. Berlin: de Gruyter, 2005.

Isaac, Benjamin. *The Invention of Racism in Classical Antiquity*. Princeton, NJ: Princeton University Press, 2004.

———. "Racism: A Rationalization of Prejudice in Greece and Rome." In *The Origins of Racism in the West*, edited by Miriam Eliav-Feldon, et al., 32–56. New York: Cambridge University Press, 2009.

Johnston, George. "The Spirit-Paraclete in the Gospel of John." *Perspective* 9.1 (1968) 29–37.

———. *The Spirit-Paraclete in the Gospel of John*. New York: Cambridge University Press, 1970.

Jones, Christopher. *Kinship Diplomacy in the Ancient World*. Cambridge, MA: Harvard University Press, 1999.

Kaiser, Otto. *Isaiah 1–12*. Philadelphia: Westminster, 1972.

Kaminsky, Joel, and Anne Steward. "God of All the World: Universalism and Developing Monotheism in Isaiah 40–66." *Harvard Theological Review* 99.2 (2006) 139–63.

Keener, Craig. *Acts: An Exegetical Commentary 3:1–14:28*. Vol. 2. Grand Rapids: Baker, 2013.

———. "The Function of Johannine Pneumatology in the Context of Late First-Century Judaism." PhD diss., Duke University, 1991.

———. *The Gospel of John: A Commentary*. Vols. 1–2. Peabody, MA: Hendrickson, 2003.

———. "One New Temple in Christ (Ephesians 2:11–22; Acts 21:27–29; Mark 11:17; John 4:20–24)." *Asian Journal of Pentecostal Studies* 12.1 (2009) 75–92.

———. *The Spirit in the Gospels and Acts: Divine Purity and Power*. Peabody, MA: Hendrickson, 1997.

Kennedy, Rebecca. *Race and Ethnicity in the Classical World*. Indianapolis, IN: Hackett, 2013.

Kerferd, G. B. "Pneuma." In vol. 5 of *The Encyclopedia of Philosophy*, edited by Paul Edwards, 360. 8 vols. New York: Macmillan, 1967.

Kiley, Mark. "The Geography of Famine: John 6:22–25." *Revue Biblique* 102.2 (1995) 226–30.

Kilpatrick, G. D. "The Punctuation of John 7:37–38." *The Journal of Theological Studies* 11.2 (1960) 340–42.

Kim, Dongsoo. "The Paraclete: The Spirit of the Church." *Asian Journal of Pentecostal Studies* 5.2 (2002) 255–70.

Kim, Jean. "A Korean Feminist Reading of John 4:1–42." *Semeia* 78 (1997) 109–119.

Kittel, G., and G. Friedrich, eds. *Theological Dictionary of the New Testament*. Translated by G. W. Bromiley. 10 vols. Grand Rapids: Eerdmans, 1964–76.

Klauch, H-J. "Accuser, Judge, and Paraclete—On Conscience in Philo of Alexandria." *Verbum et Ecclesia* 20.1 (1999) 107–118.

Kloppenborg, John. "The Theodotos Synagogue Inscription and the Problem of First-Century Synagogue Buildings." In *Jesus and Archaeology*, edited by James Charlesworth, 236–82. Grand Rapids: Eerdmans, 2006.

Knoppers, Gary. *Jews and the Samaritans: The Origins and History of their Early Relations*. New York: Oxford University Press, 2013.

Koester, Craig. *The Word of Life: A Theology of John's Gospel*. Grand Rapids: Eerdmans, 2008.

Köstenberger, Andreas J. *A Theology of John's Gospel and Letters*. Grand Rapids: Zondervan, 2009.

Köstenberger, Andreas J., and Scott Swain. *Father, Son, and Spirit: The Trinity and John's Gospel*. Downers Grove, IL: InterVarsity, 2008.

Kraabel, A. Thomas. "New Evidence of a Samaritan Diaspora has been Found at Delos." *The Biblical Archeologist* 47.1 (1984) 44–46.

Krentz, Edgar. *The Historical-Critical Method*. Philadelphia: Fortress, 1975.

Krupat, Arnold. *Ethnocriticism: Ethnography, History, Literature*. Berkeley: University of California Press, 1992.

Lamb, David. *Text, Context, and the Johannine Community: A Sociolinguistic Analysis of the Johannine Writings*. New York: T. & T. Clark, 2015.

Leaney, Alfred R. C. "The Historical Background and Theological Meaning of the Paraclete." *Duke Divinity School Review* 37 (1972) 146–59.

Lee, Dorothy. "In the Spirit of Truth: Worship and Prayer in the Gospel of John and Early Fathers." *Vigiliae Christianae* 58.3 (2004) 277–97.

Leibig, Janis. "John and The Jews: Theological Antisemitism in the Fourth Gospel." *Journal of Ecumenical Studies* 20.2 (1983) 209–234.

Levine, Lee. *The Ancient Synagogue: The First Thousand Years*. New Haven: Yale University Press, 2005.

Levinson, John. *The Spirit in First-Century Judaism*. Leiden: Brill, 2002.

Lim, Sung. "Speak My Name: Anti-Colonial Mimicry and the Samaritan Woman in John 4:1–42." *Union Seminary Quarterly Review* 62.3–4 (2010) 35–51.

Lincoln, Andrew. *Truth on Trial: The Lawsuit Motif in the Fourth Gospel*. Peabody, MA: Hendrickson, 2000.

Lindars, Barnabas. *Behind the Fourth Gospel*. London: SPCK, 1971.

———. *The Gospel of John*. London: Oliphants, 1972.

Lindsey, Duane. "Isaiah's Songs of the Servant." *Bibliotheca Sacra* 133.553 (1982) 12–31.

Lingad, Celestino. *The Problems of Jewish Christians in the Johannine Community*. Rome: Gregorian University Press, 2001.

Lissarrague, François. "The Athenian Image of the Foreigner." In *Greeks and Barbarians*, edited by Thomas Harrison, 101–126. New York: Routledge, 2002.

Loader, William. "The Central Structure of Johannine Christology." *New Testament Studies* 30.2 (1984) 188–216.

———. *The Christology of the Fourth Gospel: Structures and Issues*. Frankfurt: Peter Lang, 1989.

———. *Jesus in John's Gospel: Structure and Issues in Johannine Christology*. Grand Rapids: Eerdmans, 2017.

Lutkemeyer, Lawrence. "The Role of the Paraclete (John 16:7–15)." *Catholic Biblical Quarterly* 8.2 (1946) 220–29.

Maccini, Robert. "A Reassessment of the Woman at the Well in John 4 in Light of the Samaritan Context." *Journal for the Study of the New Testament* 53 (1994) 35–46.

MacRae, George. "The Meaning and Evolution of the Feast of Tabernacles." *Catholic Biblical Quarterly* 22.3 (1960) 251–76.

Magen, Yitzhak. "Bells, Pendants, Snakes & Stones: A Samaritan Temple to the Lord on Mt. Gerizim." *Biblical Archeological Review* 36.6 (2010) 26–35.

Magness, Jodi. *The Archaeology of the Holy Land: From the Destruction of Solomon's Temple to the Muslim Conquest*. New York: Cambridge University Press, 2012.

Malina, Bruce. *Christian Origins and Cultural Anthropology: Practical Models for Biblical Interpretation*. Eugene, OR: Wipf & Stock, 2010.

———. *The New Testament World: Insights from Cultural Anthropology*. Louisville: Westminster John Knox, 2001.

———. "Normative Dissonance and Christian Origins." In *Social-Scientific Criticism of the New Testament and its Social World*, edited by John Elliott, 35–55. Atlanta: Scholars, 1985.

———. *The Social World of Jesus and the Gospels*. New York: Routledge, 1996.

Malina, Bruce, and Richard Rohrbaugh. *Social-Science Commentary on the Gospel of John*. Minneapolis: Fortress, 1998.

Marcus, Joel. "Johannine Christians and Baptist Sectarians within Late First-Century Judaism." In *John and Judaism: A Contested Relationship in Context*, edited by Ray Alan Culpepper and Paul Anderson, 155–63. Atlanta: SBL, 2017.

———. "Rivers of Living Water from Jesus' Belly (John 7:38)." *Journal of Biblical Literature* 117.2 (1998) 328–30.

Marcus, Ralph. "The 'Plain Meaning' of Isaiah 42:1–4." *Harvard Theological Review* 30.4 (1937) 249–59.

Martin, Gunther. "On the Date of Euripides's Ion." *Classical Quarterly* 60.2 (2010) 647–51.

Martyn, J. Louis. *History and Theology in the Fourth Gospel*. Louisville: Westminster John Knox, 2003.

Mateos, Juan, and Juan Barreto. *El Evangelio de Juan: Análisis Lingüísticos Y Comentario Exegético*. Madrid: Ediciones Cristiandad, 1982.

McCoskey, Denise Eileen. *Race Antiquity and Its Legacy*. New York: Oxford University Press, 2012.

McKnight, Scot. *A Light Among the Gentiles: Jewish Missionary Activity in the Second Temple Period.* Minneapolis: Fortress, 1991.

McPhee, Brian. "Walk, Don't Run: Jesus's Water Walking Is Unparalleled in Greco-Roman Mythology." *Journal of Biblical Literature* 135.4 (2016) 763–77.

Meeks, Wayne. "A Hermeneutic of Social Embodiment." In *In Search of the Early Christians: Selected Essays,* edited by Allen R. Hilton and H. Gregory Snyder, 185–95. New Haven: Yale University Press, 2002.

———. "The Man from Heaven in Johannine Sectarianism." In *In Search of the Early Christians: Selected Essays,* edited by Allen R. Hilton and H. Gregory Snyder, 55–90. New Haven: Yale University Press, 2002.

Menken, Maarten. "'Born of God' or 'Begotten by God'? A Translation Problem in the Johannine Writings." *Novum Testamentum* 51.4 (2009) 352–68.

———. "John 6:51c–58: Eucharist or Christology?" In *Critical Readings of John 6,* edited by R. Alan Culpepper, 183–204. Leiden: Brill, 1997.

———. "The Origin of the Old Testament Quotation in John 7:38." *Novum Testamentum* 38.2 (1996) 160–75.

Metzger, Bruce. *The Texts of the New Testament.* New York: Oxford University Press, 1968.

———. *A Textual Commentary on the Greek New Testament.* New York: UBS, 2002.

Meyers, Eric, and Mark Chancey. *Alexander to Constantine: Archaeology of the Land of the Bible.* New Haven: Yale University Press, 2012.

Michaels, J. Ramsey. *The Gospel of John.* Grand Rapids: Eerdmans, 2010.

Miller, J. Maxwell. "Reading the Bible Historically: The Historian's Approach." In *To Each its Own Meaning: An Introduction to Biblical Criticism,* edited by Steven McKenzie and Stephen Hayness, 17–32. Louisville: Westminster John Knox, 1993.

Miller, M. "Greek Kinship Terminology." *The Journal of Hellenic Studies* 73 (1953) 46–52.

Millos, Samuel Pérez. *Juan: Commentario Exegético Al Texto Greiego del Nuevo Testamento.* Barcelona: Editorial Clie, 2016.

Mitchell, Margaret. "Patristic Counter-Evidence to the Claim that 'The Gospels Were Written for All Christians.'" *New Testament Studies* 51 (2005) 36–79.

Moloney, Francis. *The Resurrection of the Messiah: A Narrative Commentary on the Resurrection Accounts in the Four Gospels.* New York: Paulist, 2013.

Moore, Rickie. *The Spirit of the Old Testament.* Dorset, UK: Deo, 2011.

Morris, Leon. *The Gospel According to John.* New International Commentary on the New Testament. Grand Rapids: Eerdmans, 1995.

Morrison, Donald. "Socrates." In *A Companion to Ancient Philosophy,* edited by Mary Louise Gill and Pierre Pellegrin, 101–118. Malden, MA: Blackwell, 2006.

Motyer, Stephen. "The Fourth Gospel and the Salvation of Israel." In *Anti-Judaism and the Fourth Gospel,* edited by Reimund Bieringer, et al., 83–100. Louisville: Westminster John Knox, 2001.

Munro, Winsome. "The Pharisee and the Samaritan in John: Polar or Parallel?" *Catholic Biblical Quarterly* 57.4 (1995) 710–28.

Navarro, Luis Sánchez. "Estructura testimonial del Evangelio de Juan." *Biblica* 86.4 (2005) 511–28.

Need, Stephen. "Re-Reading the Prologue Incarnation and Creation in John 1:1–18." *Theology Today* 106 (2003) 397–404.

Nel, Marius. "The Notion of the Holy Spirit as Paraclete from a Pentecostal Perspective." *In die Skriflig* 50 (2016) 1–8.
Neyrey, Jerome. *Honor and Shame in the Gospel of Matthew*. Louisville: Westminster John Knox, 1998.
———. "Jacob Traditions and the Interpretation of John 4:10–26." *Catholic Biblical Quarterly* 41.3 (1979) 419–37.
———. "Loss of Wealth, Loss of Family, Loss of Honor: The Cultural Context of the Original Makarisms in Q." In *The Social World of the New Testament*, edited by Jerome Neyrey and Eric Stewart, 87–102. Peabody, MA: Hendrickson, 2008.
———. "What's Wrong with This Picture? John 4, Cultural Stereotypes of Women, and Public and Private Spaces." In *A Feminist Companion to John 1–2*, edited by Amy-Jill Levine and Marianne Blickenstaff, 98–125. Sheffield: Sheffield Academic, 2003.
Nippel, Wilfried. "The Construction of the Other." In *Greeks and Barbarians*, edited by Thomas Harrison, 278–310. New York: Routledge, 2002.
Nir, Rivka. "Josephus's Account of John the Baptist: A Christian Interpolation." *Journal for the Study of the Historical Jesus* 10 (2012) 32–62.
Novakovic, Lidija. "Jews and Samaritans." In *The World of the New Testament: Cultural, Social, and Historical Contexts*, edited by Joel Green and Lee Martin McDonald, 207–216. Grand Rapids: Baker Academic, 2013.
O'Day, Gail. *Revelation in the Fourth Gospel: Narrative Mode and Theological Claim*. Minneapolis: Fortress, 1986.
Oswalt, John. *The Book of Isaiah 1–39*. Grand Rapids: Eerdmans, 1986.
———. *The Book of Isaiah 40–66*. Grand Rapids: Eerdmans, 1998.
———. "The Mission of Israel to the Nations." In *Through No Fault of Their Own? The Fate of Those Who Have Never Heard*, edited by W. V. Crockett and J. G. Sigountos, 85–95. Grand Rapids: Baker, 1993.
Oware, Matthew, and David James. "Ethnicity and Race." In *Dictionary of Race, Ethnicity, and Culture*, edited by Guido Bolaffie, et al., 99–102. London: Sage, 2003.
Padilla, Alvin. *Juan*. Minneapolis: Augsburg, 2011.
Patterson, Lee. *Kinship Myth in Ancient Greece*. Austin: University of Texas Press, 2010.
Peters, F. E. *Greek Philosophical Terms: A Historical Lexicon*. New York: New York University Press, 1967.
Polanski, Tomasz. "The Destruction of Cultural Heritage in the Kingdoms of Pontus and Kommagene during the Roman Conquest." *Iran and the Caucasus* 17.3 (2013) 239–52.
Porsch, Felix. *Pneuma und Wort: Ein Exegetischer Beitrag zur Pneumatologie des Johannesevangeliums*. Frankfurt: Knecht, 1974.
Powell, Mark Allen. *What Is Narrative Criticism?* Minneapolis: Fortress, 1990.
Pryke, John. "Spirit and Flesh in the Qumran Documents and Some New Testament Texts." *Revue de Qumrân* 5.3 (1965) 345–60.
Purvis, James. "Fourth Gospel and the Samaritans." *Novum Testamentum* 17.3 (1975) 161–98.
Radding, Jonah. "Paeanic Crises: Euripides's Ion and the Failure to Perform Identity." *American Journal of Philology* 138.3 (2017) 393–434.
Radin, Max. *The Jews Among the Greeks and Romans*. Philadelphia: Jewish Publication Society of America, 1915.
Rainbow, Paul. *Johannine Theology: The Gospel, The Epistles, and the Apocalypse*. Downers Grove, IL: InterVarsity, 2014.

Rand, J. A. Du. "A Story and a Community: Reading the First Farewell Discourse (John 13:31–14:31) From Narratological and Sociological Perspectives." *Neotestamentica* 26.1 (1992) 31–45.

Reese, Kelly. "The Role of the Paraclete in John 16:7–11." *The Theological Educator* 51 (1995) 39–48.

Rehm, Rush. *Greek Tragic Theater*. New York: Routledge, 1992.

Reinhartz, Adele. "'And the Word Was Begotten': Divine Epigenesis in the Gospel of John." *Semeia* 85 (1999) 83–103.

———. *Befriending the Beloved Disciple: A Jewish Reading of the Gospel of John*. New York: Continuum, 2001.

———. "Judaism in the Gospel of John." *Interpretation* 63.4 (2009) 382–93.

———. "Story and History: John, Judaism, and the Historical Imagination." In *John and Judaism: A Contested Relationship in Context*, edited by Ray Alan Culpepper and Paul Anderson, 113–26. Atlanta: SBL, 2017.

Reyes, Patrick. "Religious Education, Race, Dreams, and the Guild." *Religious Education* 114.3 (2019) 1–10.

Robbins, Gregory Allen. "Muratorian Fragment." In vol. 4 of *The Anchor Bible Dictionary*, edited by David Noel Freedman, 928–29. 6 vols. New York: Doubleday, 1992.

Roberts, Jim. *First Isaiah*. Hermeneia. Minneapolis: Fortress, 2015.

Rutledge, Steven. "The Roman Destruction of Sacred Sites." *Historia: Zeitschrift für Alte Geschichte* 56.2 (2007) 179–95.

Said, Edward. *Orientalism*. New York: Vintage, 1978.

Sanders, E. P. *The Historical Figure of Jesus*. New York: Penguin, 1995.

———. *Jesus and Judaism*. Philadelphia: Fortress, 1985.

———. *Judaism: Practice and Belief 63 BCE–66 CE*. Valley Forge, PA: Trinity, 1992.

Schäfer, Peter. *Judeophobia: Attitudes toward the Jews in the Ancient World*. Cambridge, MA: Harvard University Press, 1998.

Scheidel, Walter. "The Demographic Background." In *Growing Up Fatherless in Antiquity*, edited by Sabine Hübner and David Ratzan, 31–40. New York: Cambridge University Press, 2009.

Schipper, Jeremy. "Interpreting the Lamb Imagery in Isaiah 53." *Journal of Biblical Literature* 132.2 (2013) 315–25.

Schnabel, Eckhard. "Israel, the People of God, and the Nations." *Journal of the Evangelical Theological Society* 45.1 (2002) 35–57.

Schneiders, Sandra. "Born Anew." *Theology Today* 44.2 (1987) 89–96.

———. *Revelatory Text: Interpreting the New Testament as Sacred Scripture*. Wilmington, DE: Glazier, 1991.

Segovia, Fernando. *Farewell to the Word: The Johannine Call to Abide*. Minneapolis: Fortress, 1991.

———. "The Final Farewell of Jesus: A Reading of John 20:30–21:25." *Semeia* 53 (1991) 166–90.

———. "The Gospel of John." In *Postcolonial Commentary on the New Testament Writings*, edited by Fernando Segovia and R. S. Sugirtharajah, 156–93. New York: T. & T. Clark, 2007.

———. "John 15:18–16:4a: A First Addition to the Original Farewell Discourse?" *Catholic Biblical Quarterly* 45 (1983) 210–30.

———. "The Journey(s) of the Word of God: A Reading of the Plot of the Fourth Gospel." *Semeia* 53 (1991) 23–54.

Shapiro, H. A. "The Invention of Persian in Classical Athens." In *The Origins of Racism in the West*, edited by Miriam Eliav-Feldon, et al., 57–87. New York: Cambridge University Press, 2009.

Shelfer, Lochlan. "The Legal Precision of the Term 'παράκλητος.'" *Journal for the Study of the New Testament* 32.2 (2009) 131–50.

Sheridan, Ruth. "Issues in Translating οἱ Ἰουδαῖοι in the Fourth Gospel." *Journal of Biblical Literature* 132.3 (2013) 671–95.

———. "The Paraclete and Jesus in the Johannine Farewell Discourse." *Pacifica* 20.2 (2007) 125–41.

———. "The Paraclete as Successor in the Johannine Farewell Discourse: A Comparative Literary Analysis." *Australian eJournal of Theology* 18.2 (2011) 129–40.

Sherwin-White, Adrian. *Racial Prejudice in Imperial Rome*. New York: Cambridge University Press, 1970.

Sigismund, Marcus. "'Without Father, without Mother, without Genealogy': Fatherlessness in the Old and New Testament." In *Growing Up Fatherless in Antiquity*, edited by Sabine Hübner and David Ratzan, 83–102. New York: Cambridge University Press, 2009.

Smalley, Stephen. "The Paraclete: Pneumatology in the Johannine Gospel and Apocalypse." In *Exploring the Gospel of John*, edited by R. Alan Culpepper and C. Clifton Black, 289–300. Louisville: Westminster John Knox, 1996.

Smith, Amy. "Eurymedon and the Evolution of Political Personifications in the Early Classical Period." *The Journal of Hellenic Studies* 119 (1999) 128–41.

Smith, Dwight Moody. *John*. Abingdon New Testament Commentary. Nashville: Abingdon, 1999.

———. *John Among the Gospels*. Columbia, SC: University of South Carolina Press, 2001.

———. "The Setting and Shape of Johannine Narrative Source." *Journal of Biblical Literature* 95.2 (1976) 231–41.

———. "The Sources of the Gospel of John: An Assessment of the Present State of the Problem." *New Testament Studies* 10.3 (1964) 336–51.

———. *The Theology of the Gospel of John*. New York: Cambridge University Press, 1995.

Snowden, Frank. *Before Color Prejudice: The Ancient View of Blacks*. Cambridge, MA: Harvard University Press, 1983.

———. *Blacks in Antiquity: Ethiopians in the Greco-Roman Experience*. Cambridge, MA: Harvard University Press, 1970.

Spriggs, D. G. "The Meaning of Water in John 3:5." *Expository Times* 85 (1973) 149–50.

Stark, Rodney. *The Rise of Christianity: How the Obscure, Marginal Jesus Movement Became the Dominant Religious Force in the Western World in a Few Centuries*. New York: HarperCollins, 1997.

Stefan, Crinisor. "The Paraclete and Prophecy in the Johannine Community." *Pneuma* 27.2 (2005) 273–96.

Stein, Dina. "Collapsing Structures: Discourse and the Destruction of the Temple in the Babylonian Talmud." *Jewish Quarterly Review* 98.1 (2008) 1–28.

Stibbe, Mark. *John as Story Teller: Narrative Criticism and the Fourth Gospel*. New York: Cambridge University Press, 1994.

Stube, John Carson. *A Graeco-Roman Rhetorical Reading of the Farewell Discourse*. New York: T. & T. Clark, 2006.

Temple, Syndey. "Two Signs in the Fourth Gospel." *Journal of Biblical Literature* 81.2 (1962) 169–74.

Thatcher, Tom. "John and the Jews: Recent Research and Future Questions." In *John and Judaism: A Contested Relationship in Context*, edited by Ray Alan Culpepper and Paul Anderson, 3–38. Atlanta: SBL, 2017.

Thiel, Nathan. "'Israel' and 'Jew' as markers of Jewish Identity in Antiquity: The Problems of Insider/Outsider Classification." *Journal for the Study of Judaism* 45 (2014) 80–99.

Thomas, John Christopher. *The Spirit of the New Testament*. Dorset, UK: Deo, 2005.

———. "What the Spirit Is Saying to the Church—The Testimony of a Pentecostal in New Testament Studies." In *Spirit and Scripture: Exploring a Pneumatic Hermeneutic*, edited by Kevin L. Spawn and Archie T. Wright, 115–29. New York: T. & T. Clark, 2013.

———. "Women, Pentecostals, and the Bible: An Experiment in Pentecostal Hermeneutics." *Journal of Pentecostal Theology* 5.2 (1994) 41–56.

Thomas, Rosalind. "Genealogy." In *The Oxford Companion to Classical Civilization*, edited by Simon Hornblower, et al., 329. New York: Oxford University Press, 2014.

Thompson, Lloyd. "Roman Perception of Blacks." *Scholia: Studies in Classical Antiquity* (1993) 17–30.

Thompson, Marianne Meye. *The God of the Gospel of John*. Grand Rapids: Eerdmans, 2001.

———. *John: A Commentary*. Louisville: Westminster John Knox, 2015.

———. "Signs and Faith in the Fourth Gospel." *Bulletin of Biblical Research* (1991) 89–108.

Tilborg, Sjef van. *Reading John in Ephesus*. Leiden: Brill, 1996.

Tomson, Peter. "'Jews' in the Gospel of John as Compared with the Palestinian Talmud, the Synoptics, and Some New Testament Apocrypha." In *Anti-Judaism and the Fourth Gospel*, edited by Reimund Bieringer, et al., 176–211. Louisville: Westminster John Knox, 2001.

Trümper, Monika. "The Oldest Original Synagogue Building in the Diaspora: The Delos Synagogue Reconsidered." *Hesperia: The Journal of the American School of Classical Studies at Athens* 73.4 (2004) 513–98.

Turner, Max. *The Holy Spirit and Spiritual Gifts*. Peabody, MA: Hendrickson, 2009.

Vrede, Keith Vande. "A Contrast Between Nicodemus and John the Baptist in the Gospel of John." *Journal of the Evangelical Theological Society* 57.4 (2014) 715–26.

Waddell, Robby. *The Spirit in the Book of Revelation*. Dorset, UK: Deo, 2006.

Wahlde, Urban von. "The Jews in the Gospel of John: Fifteen Years of Research 1983–1998." *Ephemerides Theologicae Lovanienses* 76.1 (2000) 30–55.

Watt, Jan van der. "'Is Jesus the King of Israel?': Reflections on the Jewish Nature of the Gospel of John." In *John and Judaism: A Contested Relationship in Context*, edited by Ray Alan Culpepper and Paul Anderson, 39–56. Atlanta: SBL, 2017.

Webb, Robert. *John the Baptizer and Prophet: A Socio-Historical Study*. Sheffield: Sheffield Academic, 1991.

Weiss, Naomi. "A Psychoanalytical Reading of Euripides's Ion: Repetition, Development, and Identity." *Bulletin of the Institute of Classical Studies* 51 (2008) 39–50.

Weissenrieder, Annette. "Spirit and Rebirth in the Gospel of John." *Religion and Theology* 21 (2014) 58–85.

Wells, Jack. "Impiety in the Middle Republic: The Roman Response to Temple Plundering in Southern Italy." *The Classic Journal* 105.3 (2010) 229–43.
West, Cornel. *Race Matters*. Boston: Beacon, 2017.
Williams, Catrin. "John, Judaism, and 'Searching the Scriptures.'" In *John and Judaism: A Contested Relationship in Context*, edited by Ray Alan Culpepper and Paul Anderson, 77–100. Atlanta: SBL, 2017.
Wilson, Andrew. *The Nations in Deutero-Isaiah: A Study on Composition and Structure*. New York: Mellen, 1986.
Wimmer, Andreas. *Ethnic Boundary Making*. New York: Oxford University Press, 2013.
Winden, J. C. M. van. "The World of Ideas in Philo of Alexandria: An Interpretation of De Opificio Mundi 24–25." *Vigiliae Christianae* 37.3 (1983) 209–217.
Wink, Walter. *John the Baptist in the Gospel Tradition*. Eugene, OR: Wipf & Stock, 1968.
Witherington, Ben. "The Waters of Birth: John 3:5 and 1 John 5:6–8." *New Testament Studies* 35.1 (1989) 155–60.
Wöhrle, Georg. "Sons (and Daughters) without Fathers: Fatherlessness in the Homeric Epics." In *Growing Up Fatherless in Antiquity*, edited by Sabine Hübner and David Ratzan, 162–74. New York: Cambridge University Press, 2009.
Woll, D. Bruce. "The Departure of 'The Way': The First Farewell Discourse in the Gospel of John." *Journal of Biblical Literature* 99.2 (1980) 225–39.
Wong, Hertha D. "In Search of a Dialogic Criticism: Ethnocriticism and Native American Literatures." Review of Arnold Krupat, *Ethnocriticism: Ethnography, History, Literature*. *American Quarterly* 47.1 (1995) 159–64.

Ancient Document Index

Old Testament/Hebrew Bible

Genesis

Reference	Page
1:1-2	5
1:2	102
1:11-12	18
1:21	18
1:24-25	18
2:7-23	181
2:7	271
5:3-32	147
6:3	102
6:17	101
6:20	18
7:14	18
7:15	101
8:1	101
8:8	124
8:19	18
9:4	176
9:9	231
10:8—11:27	147
11:6	18
12:7	231
13:15	231
13:16	231
13:18	231
17:14	18
19:38	18
22:8	121
24:10-61	152
25:17	18
25:19	147
26:10	18
29:1-20	152
34:16	18
35:29	18
40:17	18
41:38	102
45:27	102
46:20-21	147
47:29—49:33	226

Exodus

Reference	Page
1:9	18
2:15-21	152
4:22	139
5:14	18
7:9	173
12:5	121
14:21	175
15:8	101
15:10	101

15:24	174	23:33–43	194		
16:2	174	23:35	194		
16:4–36	175	23:36	194		
16:4	173	23:42	194		
16:15	173				
17:1–6	207				
17:3	174	## Numbers			
19:12	175				
19:14	175	5:14	103		
19:20	175	5:30	103		
19:23	175	6:12	121		
20:17	156	6:24–36	241		
20:24	156	11:1	174		
22:22–27	240	11:17	102, 125		
22:22	240	11:25–29	102, 125		
24:1–2	175	11:26–29	124		
24:9	175	11:27–29	174		
24:10	175	11:31	101		
24:12–13	175	12:8	175		
24:15	175	14:1–3	174		
24:18	175	14:24	102		
28:1	145	16:12	102		
28:3	103	17:6	174		
29:38–46	121	17:20	174		
31:3	103	18:19	231		
32:1	175	20:8	192		
32:15	175	23:7	102		
33:11–23	175	24:2	102, 125		
34:2–4	175	25:12–13	231		
34:29	175	27:16	102		
35:31	103	27:18	102		
		29:12–28	194		

Leviticus

Deuteronomy

3:17	176		
4:32	121	2:30	102
14:12	121	8:3	174, 175
14:21	121	8:15	192
14:24–25	121	10:18	240
16:13	145	11:14	195
16:21	121	11:17	195
16:32	145	12:5	156
17:11	121	12:23	176
20:17–18	18	13:1–6	197
21:13–14	18	14:28–29	240
21:17	18	18:18	155, 172

24:17–22	240	16:13–14	102, 125
26:12–13	240	16:14–16	103
27:1–7	155	19:19	103
27:3	156	19:20–23	102, 125
27:19	240	30:12	102
28:12	195		
31:10–13	194		
32:6	139	## 2 Samuel	
32:18	141		
34:9	103, 125	3:2–5	145
		5:13–16	145
		7:14	139
## Joshua		9:6	145
		22:16	101
2:11	102	23:2	102
4:14	18		
11:21	18		
		## 1 Kings	
		8:35–36	195
## Judges		13:2	145
		17:14–16	172
3:10	102, 125	17:17	101
6:34	102, 125	18:12	102
8:33	194	18:35	101
9:23	103	19:11	101
9:37	194	20:5	102
11:29	102, 125	22:21–23	103
13:25	102	22:24	102
14:6	102, 125		
14:19	102, 125		
15:14	102, 125	## 2 Kings	
15:19	102		
16:14	102	2:9–15	102, 125
		2:16	102
		3:17	101
## Ruth		4:1	240
		4:3–6	172
4:18–22	147	4:42–44	172
		17	161
		17:24–41	158
## 1 Samuel		19:7	103
9:1	145		
10:6	102, 125	## 1 Chronicles	
10:10	102		
11:6	102	1:11—9:44	147
12:17	195		

5:26	102
9:1	145
12:18	102
12:19	125

2 Chronicles

6:6	156
15:1	102, 125
16:14	18, 136
18:20–22	103
18:23	102
20:14	102, 125
24:20	102, 125
36:22	102

Ezra

1:1	102
1:5	102
2:59–63	145
4	162
4:24	162
10:8	46
10:18–44	145

Nehemiah

8:13–18	195
9:8	231
9:20	192

Esther

2:10	18
3:13	18
6:13	18

Job

1:19	101
4:9	101
7:7	101
8:2	101
8:8	18
10:12	102
12:10	101
15:2	101
16:3	101
17:1	102
24:9	240
27:3	101
29:12	240
31:17–22	240
32:8	101, 103
33:4	102
34:14	102
40:30	18
43:8	101

Psalms

2:7	139, 141
7:8	18
10:6	101
10:14	240
10:17–18	240
17:7	18
17:16	101
29:3	172
30:6	102
32:6	101, 102
33:19	102
35:19	253
42:1–2	192
45:8	136
47:8	101
50:12–14	102
50:19	102
51:7	142
68:5	240
69:4	253
76:4	102
76:7–8	102
77:19	172
77:39	101
78:15–16	207
78:15	207

78:24	173	4:6	101
78:68	156	4:16	101
89:3–4	231	6:9	101
89:29–30	231	8:8	101
89:35–37	231	11:5	101
94:6	240	12:7	101
102:16	101		
103:4	101		
103:29	101	## Song of Solomon	
103:30	102		
104:6–8	231	4:12–15	142
105:33	102		
105:41	207		
106:25	101	## Isaiah	
107:29	172		
134:17	101	1:2	141
138:7	102	1:17	240
141:4	102	1:23	240
142:4	102	2:2–5	126
142:7	102	2:2	126
142:10	102	4:4	142
145:4	101	7:2	101
147:7	101	9:2	111
147:8	195	11:1–10	126
148:8	101	11:2	102, 103, 124, 126, 127
		12:3	192, 209
## Proverbs		19:13	102
		19:14	103
5:15–18	142	22:4	18
8:25	141	29:8	192
9:5	174	29:10	103
15:4	102	30:1	102
15:15	192	30:28	101
23:10	240	32:15	102, 127, 144
		33:11	101
		37:7	103
## Ecclesiasticus		40:3	110, 115
		40:4–5	110
1:6	101	42:1–6	112
1:14	101	42:1–4	112
1:17	101	42:1	102, 124, 126, 127
2:11	101	42:5	101
2:17	101	42:6	18, 111
2:26	101	44:3	102, 127, 144, 192, 209
3:19–21	101		
4:4	101	48:16	102, 124

49:6	18, 112	11:1	102
49:10	192, 209	11:5	102
51:10	175	11:19–20	143
53:7	121	11:19	101
53:12	121	11:24	102
55:1	192, 209	21:12	102
57:16	101	22:7	240
58:11	192	36:25–27	143, 192
59:21	102, 127	36:25–26	142, 144
60:1–3	112	36:26	101
60:5–7	112	36:27	102
60:10	112	37:1	102
60:11	112	37:5–10	101
60:12–14	112	37:9	271
60:14	112	37:14	102
60:16	112	38:12	208
61:1–5	127	43:5	102
61:1	102, 124	47:1–12	192, 208
63:10–11	102	47:1	195
63:14	102		
65:14	102		
66:9	141		

Jeremiah

Daniel

		1:3	18
		1:6	18
		2:1	102
4:11–12	101	2:3	102
5:24	195	2:35	101
5:28	240	3:5	18
7:6	240	4:8–9	102
11:19	121	4:18	102
22:3	240	5:11	102
28:11	102	5:12	102
31:33–34	143	5:14	102
33:8	142	5:23	101
34:5	136	6:4	102
48:1	18	7:15	102
		9:25	198
		10:17	101, 102

Ezekiel

Hosea

1:4	101		
2:2	102		
3:12	102	4:12	101, 103
3:14	102	5:4	103
3:24	102	5:7	141
8:3	102	11:1	139

12:2	101	14:8	192, 208
14:3	240	14:16–19	195
		14:17–18	195

Joel

Malachi

2:28–29	144		
2:28	192	2:15–16	102
3:1–2	102	3:1	198
3:6	82	3:5	240
3:18	192, 208		

Apocrypha

Amos

Baruch

4:7	195		
4:13	101	3:1	102
8:11–13	174	21:4	102

Jonah

Prayer of Azariah

1:4	101	3:39	102
4:8	101	3:86	102

Micah

Susanna

2:7	102	1:44	101, 102
3:8	102		

1 Esdras

Haggai

		2:1	101
1:14	101	2:5	101
2:5	102		

2 Esdras

Zechariah

		13:52	198
4:6	102		
7:10	240		
10:1	195	## Judith	
12:1	101		
12:10	102, 192	5:10	18
13:1	192, 195	6:2	18
13:2	103	6:5	18

6:19	18	\multicolumn{2}{c}{Sirach}
7:19	102		
8:20	18	9:9	102, 152
8:32	18	15:3	174
9:14	18	24:21	174
10:13	101	24:30–31	192
11:10	18	34:13	102
12:3	18	38:23	102
13:20	18	39:6	103
14:6	102	39:28	103
15:9	18	42:12	152
16:14	102	43:17	101
16:17	18	44:11–13	231
16:24	18	44:21	231
		45:25	231
		48:12	102, 124
		48:24	124
\multicolumn{2}{c}{1 Maccabees}	50:25–26	161
		50:27	197
2:42	261		
4:41–50	172		
7:12	261	\multicolumn{2}{c}{Tobit}
13:7	102		
14:28	261	3:6	101
14:41	172	4:3	102
		6:8	103
\multicolumn{2}{c}{2 Maccabees}	\multicolumn{2}{c}{Wisdom of Solomon}
3:12	41		
3:18	41	1:5	103
3:24	102	1:7	102
3:30	41	2:3	102
7:22–23	101	5:3	102
14:46	102	5:11	101
		5:23	101
		7:1–2	181
\multicolumn{2}{c}{3 Maccabees}	7:7	103
		9:17	102
1:9	41	11:20	101
2:14	41	12:1	102
		13:2	101
\multicolumn{2}{c}{4 Maccabees}	15:11	101, 271
		16:14	101
4:22	197	16:20	173
18:5	197	17:17	101

Pseudepigrapha

2 Baruch

29:3	198
29:8	172
77–87	226
77:13–16	192
77:19	162
78:1	162

1 Enoch

48:6	198
49:3	124
62:2	124
62:7	198
90:9–12	121
91–108	226

4 Ezra

7:28	198
8:8	142
13:32	198
13:40–48	162
14:27–48	226

Jubilees

1:20–23	104
1:23–25	143
8:19	208
10:1–15	226
14	124
16:21–31	194
20:1—23:1	226
35:1—36:18	226

Psalms of Solomon

7.1	253

Testament of Asher

1:3–9	218
3:2	218
5:3	220

Testament of Benjamin

3:8	121
6:1–7	218
10:3	220

Testament of Dan

1:3	220
1:6–8	217
2:1	226
5:1	217
5:7–8	226
6:8–10	220

Testament of Gad

4:1–7	226

Testament of Issachar

7:1–5	220
7:7	217

Testament of Joseph

1:1	226
19:8–11	121
19:8	121

Testament of Judah

14:1–8	217
18:7–12	218
19:4	217

20:1–5	217	\multicolumn{2}{c}{**Early Jewish Writings**}
24:2	124		
26:3	217	\multicolumn{2}{c}{*Josephus*}

Testament of Levi

Life

		10	158
1:2	226	12	137
4:1	226	191	137
4:9	217	277	263
13:5–7	226	280	263
18	124	352	66

Testament of Moses

Against Apion

1:15	226	1.200–204	205
		1.161	204
		1.162–63	204

Testament of Naphtali

		1.165–66	204
		1.177–81	204
1:2–5	226	2.58	202
4:1–5	226	2.69	66
9:2	226	2.80	201
		2.91–96	203
		2.112–13	201

Testament of Reuben

		2.121	203
		2.123–24	203
1:2–4	226	2.123	148
3:1–8	217	2.175	263
3:8	220	2.210	148
5:3	217	2.257	160
6:9	220	2.258–61	86, 87, 202
		2.258–59	160

Testament of Simeon

Antiquity of the Jews

1:2	226		
2:7	217	3.244	194
3:1–2	217, 226	3.245	194
4:7	217	4.202	136
5:1–5	226	4.209	194
		4.307–8	156
		6.29–30	122

Testament of Zebulun

		8.100	194
		9.288–91	159
9:8	217	9.290	158

10.183–84	159	19.284–86	84
11.19	162	19.287–91	84
11.75	195	20.97	173
11.132–33	122	20.118	165
11.154–57	195	20.169–70	173
11.173	122		
11.341	159		
12.10	165		
12.258–61	161		

Jewish Wars

13.46	195	1.63–65	163
13.72–73	161	1.110	137
13.74–75	165	1.123	75
13.171–72	114	2.119	114
13.171	137	2.162–66	114
13.241–42	195	2.162	137
13.254–58	163	2.166	137
13.254–56	162	2.226	75
13.257–58	75, 149	2.234–38	165
13.275–80	163	2.285	263
13.288	137	2.289	263
13.293–98	114	2.457	85
13.297–98	137	2.462–63	85
13.304	195	2.559–61	85
13.372	195	3.636–38	75
14.9	76, 149, 160	7.100–111	85
14.213–16	83, 201		
14.244–46	84, 201		

Philo

Against Flaccus

14:259–64	201		
14.259–61	84	13	214
14.262–64	84	22	84, 214
14.403	75, 149	23	84, 214
15.11	75	29	66
15.50	195	41–79	85
15.382	75	151	214
15.385	75	181	214
16.172	84, 201		
17.12–16	145		
17.41	114		
17.199	136		

Agriculture

18.11–17	114		
18.11–15	137	1.50–53	33
18.15	137		
18.29–30	165		
18.30	165		
18.116–19	110		
18.130–41	145		
19.278	84, 201		
19.284–91	88, 201		

Allegorical Interpretations

3.162	174
3.219	141

Confusion of Tongues

1.63	141
1.97	33

Creation of the World

1.3–4	252
1.3	252
1.6	252
1.7	252
1.9	252
1.11–14	252
1.15	252
1.16	252
1.17	252
1.19–20	252
1.20	33
1.23	214
1.24–26	252
1.25–26	252
1.25	33
1.29	99, 252
1.33	252
1.35–36	252
1.52	252
1.53	252
1.55	252
1.62	252
1.65	215
1.66	252
1.77–78	252
1.89	252
1.111	252
1.129	252
1.131	252
1.139	252
1.142–43	252
1.143	252
1.146	252
1.151	252
1.170	252
1.171–72	252

Dreams

1.75	33
2.127	263

Flight and Finding

198	33

Joseph

1.239	214

On Giants

10	99
22	100
23	100
27–48	100
27	100
47	100
53	100
161	149, 252

On the Change of Names

1.29	141
1.259–60	174

On the Decalogue

1.15–17	174

On the Embassy to Gaius

132–38	262

155–58		89	
159–160		90	
211		148	
371		262	

On the Life of Moses

1.147	148
2.17–25	148
2.134–35	214
2.138	142
2.216	263

Rewards and Punishment

1.166	214

Special Laws

1.237	214
1.303	33
2.208	195
2.211	195
3.169–71	152
3.178	152

That God is Unchangeable

1.57	33

That the Worse is Wont

80	99

Virtues

102–8	148
102–4	148
140–41	90
179	149

New Testament

Matthew

1:2–16	147, 184
1:18–20	5
3:7	109
3:11–12	109
3:14–15	109
3:16	109
3:17	109
4:1	5
4:8	258
4:15	15
4:23	262
5:14	258
5:21–24	138
6:2	263
6:5	263
6:32	15
9:35	262
10:5	15, 161
10:17–25	245
10:17	266
10:18	15
10:20	250
10:24	253
11:21–24	66
12:9	262
12:18	15
12:21	15
12:28	5
12:31–32	5
12:43	5
13:38	258
13:47	18
13:53–58	266
13:54–57	184
13:54	262
13:55	174
14:13–33	172
14:15	171
14:19	171
14:25	172
14:26	172
14:28–32	172
14:34–36	172

18:7	258	6:1–6	266
20:19	15	6:2	262
20:25	15	6:3	66, 174, 184
23:6	263	6:32–52	172
23:15	147	6:35–36	171
23:34	42	6:41	171
23:37	66	6:47	172
24:7	15	6:48	172
24:9	15	6:49	172
24:14	15	6:53–56	172
24:15–16	41	7:25	5
25:32	15	7:26	18
26:13	258	9:17–25	5
26:51–52	282	9:29	18
26:59–62	153	10:26	196
27:51	140	10:33	15
27:57	283	10:42	15
27:66	173	11:17	15
28:1–2	274	12:39	263
28:2	274	13	245
28:8	271	13:8	15
28:9–10	274	13:9	42, 266
28:10	271	13:10	15
28:11–15	274	13:11	250
28:16–20	276	13:14–15	41
28:17	276, 282	14:7	282
28:18–19	276	14:9	258
28:19	15, 42	14:24	121
		14:58	153
		14:70	66
		15:29	153
		15:38	140

Mark

1:5	109, 197	15:43	135, 283
1:8	109	16:1–3	274
1:9	109	16:5	274
1:11	109	16:8	271
1:12	5	16:12–13	274
1:21–23	262	16:14–20	276
1:23–26	5	16:14	281
1:39	262	16:15–19	275
3:1–6	138	16:15	42, 258
3:1	262	16:17–18	276
3:29	5		
4:22	196		
5:2	5	## Luke	
5:22–38	262		
5:8	5	1:3	40, 140

1:17	5
1:35	5
1:41	5
1:67	5
2:32	15
3:6	189
3:7	109
3:15	110
3:16–17	109
3:21	109
3:22	109
3:23–38	147, 184
4:1	5
4:14	5
4:15–20	262
4:16–30	266
4:22	174, 184
4:33	5, 262
4:44	262
5:1–11	274
6:6	262
6:40	253
7:5	15, 42, 265
7:11–16	240
8:17	196
8:29	5
8:49	262
9:12	171
9:16	171
9:39–42	5
9:51–56	161
10:13–15	66
11:43	263
12:10	5
12:11	266
12:12	196, 250
12:24–25	15
12:30	15, 258
13:10	262
13:11	5
13:14	138, 262
13:34	66
18:32	15
20:46	263
21	245
21:10	15
21:12	42, 266
21:24	41
22:25	15
22:49–51	282
23:2	15, 42
23:50–51	283
24:1–2	274
24:4–5	274
24:7	15
24:13–45	274
24:36–43	274
24:36	281
24:44–53	275, 276
24:45	276
24:47	42
24:49	276
24:50–51	276

John

1:1–18	48
1:1–9	286
1:5	111
1:6–8	113
1:6–7	111
1:6	284
1:7	111, 122
1:8	44
1:9–10	254
1:9	33, 111, 254
1:10	254
1:11–13	286
1:11	125, 187, 188
1:12–13	141
1:12	232
1:13	141, 187, 230, 231
1:14	187, 188, 286
1:15	111
1:18	28
1:19—3:36	200
1:19–42	113
1:19–34	200
1:19–31	120
1:19–28	109, 114
1:19–25	108
1:19	108, 114, 115, 116, 118, 132, 136, 284
1:21	115

1:22	115, 285	3:2	130, 132, 133, 136
1:24	44, 108, 114, 133, 136, 284	3:3–21	280
		3:3–8	4, 141
1:25–31	110	3:3	140, 141, 173, 188
1:25	114, 115	3:4	130, 140, 141
1:26–27	115	3:5	140, 141, 142
1:26	120, 125	3:6	140, 141
1:27	121	3:7	141
1:29–34	48	3:8	106, 140, 141, 231, 232
1:29–33	125		
1:29–31	121	3:9	130, 139
1:29	113, 121, 122, 124, 254	3:10	122
		3:11–21	130
1:30	121	3:13–21	130
1:31	122, 124	3:13	186
1:32–34	109, 124, 127	3:16–17	254
1:32–33	97, 106, 107	3:17	285, 286
1:32	109, 124	3:19	111, 254
1:33	109, 124, 173, 222, 277, 279, 280, 285	3:20	253
		3:22–26	38, 130
1:34	109, 124	3:22	48, 118, 130
1:35—2:12	200	3:25	118
1:35–42	109	3:26–30	48
1:35	113	3:26	132
1:37–42	27	3:28	284
1:37–39	109	3:30	44
1:38	38, 132	3:31–36	130, 280
1:41–42	38	3:31	254
1:43	113	3:34	106, 280, 285, 286
1:45	198	4:1—5:47	200
1:46	66	4:1–3	200
1:47	122	4:1	136
1:49	122, 132	4:2–42	41
1:51	186	4:4–42	200
2:1–10	133	4:9	41, 118, 155
2:6	118	4:10	33
2:11	48	4:14	33, 191
2:13	118	4:15	174
2:17	253	4:19	172
2:18–20	118	4:20–24	157
2:18	118	4:20	155, 157
2:20	118	4:21–23	154
2:23–25	133	4:22	118, 119, 156, 157
2:23	130	4:23–24	97, 152, 154, 156
2:24–25	133	4:24	106
3:1–21	130	4:31	132
3:1–10	97, 130, 280	4:33	199
3:1	118, 130, 132	4:34	285, 286

4:35-38	42	6:29	285, 286
4:38	285	6:30-31	173
4:42	254	6:30	173
4:43-54	200	6:31-32	174
4:44	184	6:31	172, 173, 178
4:54	48	6:32	172, 173, 178, 189
5:1	118	6:33	174, 186, 190, 254
5:2-9	197	6:34	174, 200
5:2	38, 46	6:35-59	173
5:10-18	118	6:35-50	171, 174, 175
5:10-16	197	6:35-39	189
5:10	118	6:35	174
5:15-16	118	6:36	118
5:18	118, 196, 197	6:37	172, 178, 189
5:23-24	285, 286	6:38-39	286
5:30	285, 286	6:38	186, 190, 285
5:33	284	6:39	285
5:36-38	286	6:40	172, 179, 189
5:36	285	6:41-42	186, 190, 200
5:37-39	253	6:41	118, 174, 175, 182
5:37	285	6:42	172, 179, 182, 184
5:38	285	6:43	175, 182, 200
5:45-47	253	6:44-46	179, 189
6:1—10:42	200	6:44	174, 178, 285, 286
6:1—7:9	200	6:45	172, 174, 178
6:1-15	171, 175	6:46	174, 175, 178
6:2-34	189	6:48	174
6:2-24	173	6:49-50	187
6:4	118, 171, 175	6:49	174, 178, 179
6:5	174	6:50-51	174, 186, 190
6:6	171	6:51-59	171
6:11	171	6:51-58	175, 185, 188
6:14	171, 172, 254	6:51	175, 254
6:16-21	171, 175	6:52	118, 175, 179
6:19-21	172	6:53-57	175
6:19-20	172	6:53-56	179
6:19	172	6:57	175, 178, 179, 189, 285, 286
6:20	172		
6:22-34	171	6:58	175, 178, 179, 186, 187, 190
6:22-24	172		
6:22	113	6:59	262
6:23	171	6:60-71	171, 175, 185
6:25	132, 172	6:60-66	38, 119, 189
6:26	174	6:60-61	190
6:27-59	171	6:61	200, 260
6:27-51	175	6:62-65	200
6:27-29	173	6:62-63	97, 169, 170
6:27	172, 173, 178, 189	6:62	186, 187, 189

6:63	106, 176, 185, 188, 189, 280	7:33–36	206
		7:33–34	198
6:64–66	185	7:33	285
6:64	118	7:34	206
6:65	189	7:35–36	196, 198
7:1–9	196, 199	7:35	41, 43, 118, 199
7:1	118, 196, 199, 282	7:36	206
7:2–9	194, 196	7:37–39	98, 191, 196
7:2	118	7:37	206
7:3–5	38	7:39	106, 192, 193, 207, 229, 277
7:4	196, 199, 254	7:40–44	196, 206
7:5	196, 199	7:40–42	184
7:7	199, 253, 254	7:40–41	135
7:8	199	7:43	118
7:9	196	7:44	135
7:10–13	196, 199	7:45–53	196
7:10	196	7:45–46	199
7:11	118, 196	7:45	196
7:12–13	196	7:47	135
7:12	197	7:50	134, 135
7:13	118, 197, 282	7:52	136
7:14–31	197	8:12	111, 254
7:14–24	196, 199	8:14	186
7:15–19	196	8:15	188
7:15–17	199	8:16	285
7:15	118, 197, 199	8:17	184, 197, 253
7:16	285, 286	8:18	285
7:17–19	197	8:19	188
7:17	197	8:21	253
7:18	285	8:22	118
7:19	118, 199, 253	8:23	253, 254
7:20–24	196	8:26	253, 254, 285, 286
7:20	118, 197	8:29	285, 286
7:21–24	197	8:30–31	118
7:23	199	8:31–45	116
7:25–30	196	8:31–36	253
7:25–29	199	8:31	38, 118
7:25–27	196, 198	8:33–44	231, 232
7:27	198, 199	8:33–37	231
7:28–36	196	8:37	118
7:28–29	198, 286	8:39	231
7:28	285	8:41	141
7:29	285	8:42	285, 286
7:30	198, 199	8:44–45	38
7:31–32	198	8:44	42, 118
7:31	118, 196	8:46	248
7:32	118, 136, 196, 199, 284	8:47	118

8:48	43, 118, 161	11:42	285, 286
8:52	118	11:45	118
8:55	118	11:48	15, 41, 42
8:56	184	11:50–52	15, 42
8:57	118	11:50	232
8:59	118	11:52	232
9:2	132, 141	11:53–54	118
9:4	132, 285, 286	11:54	118
9:5	254	11:55	118
9:7	39, 285	12:9–11	118
9:15–18	118	12:12	113
9:16	136	12:13	122
9:17	136, 283	12:16	229
9:18	118, 136	12:19	254
9:19	141	12:20–26	41, 43
9:20	141	12:20	198
9:22–23	37	12:23	229
9:22	37, 40, 42, 44, 49, 114, 118, 197, 259, 261, 266, 282	12:25	254
		12:31	254
		12:34–41	253
9:29	186	12:35	111
9:32	141	12:36	48
9:33–38	37	12:42–43	37, 116
9:34	141	12:42	40, 42, 44, 114, 136, 260, 261, 266
9:39	254		
9:40	136	12:44–50	48
9:41	253	12:44	285, 286
10:12	38	12:45	285, 286
10:16	43	12:46–47	254
10:19	118, 136	12:46	111, 254
10:20	118	12:47	254
10:24	118	12:49	285
10:31	118	13:1–20	225
10:33	118	13:1	229, 254
10:34	197, 253	13:2–20	229
10:36	173, 254, 285	13:16	285
11:1—17:26	200	13:20	285, 285
11:1—12:12	200	13:21	106
11:3	285	13:23	27, 28
11:8	118, 132	13:30	132
11:9	254	13:31—14:31	222
11:10	132	13:31–32	229
11:19	118	13:33	118, 229, 230
11:27	254	13:34–38	229
11:31	118	13:36	225
11:33	106, 118	13:38	114
11:36	118	14:1	230, 280
11:37	118	14:2–6	230

14:7	230	16:6	266
14:9	230	16:7–15	98, 225, 245, 247, 267, 280, 296
14:11	230	16:7–11	267
14:15–27	98	16:7	4, 213, 216, 285
14:16–17	216, 222, 223, 225, 233, 280	16:8–11	258
14:16	4, 213, 223	16:8	248, 254
14:17	4, 106, 220, 223, 248, 254, 258	16:11	254
		16:13	4, 12, 106, 220, 249
14:18	224, 234	16:14	266
14:19	254, 258	16:17–18	200
14:22	254	16:19–28	200
14:24	285, 286	16:20	254
14:26	4, 106, 213, 216, 222, 223, 225, 243, 280, 285	16:21	141, 254
		16:28	200, 254
		16:33	254
14:27	106, 254, 258, 277, 280	17:2	188
		17:3	285
14:30–31	222, 254	17:5	254
14:30	254	17:6	254
14:31	48, 222, 225, 254	17:8	285, 286
15:18—16:15	245, 250, 251	17:9	254
15:18—16:4	222	17:11	254
15:18–25	251, 258, 260	17:13–18	254
15:18–21	251	17:13	254
15:18–20	253	17:14	254
15:18–19	254, 258	17:15	254
15:18	246, 251	17:16	254
15:19	245, 251, 257, 268	17:18	254, 285
15:20	251, 253	17:21–23	254
15:21	253, 285	17:21	254, 285, 286
15:22–25	253	17:23	254, 285, 286
15:22	251	17:24	254
15:24	251	17:25	254, 285
15:25	184, 251, 253	18:1	48, 222
15:26–27	98, 216, 225, 245, 267, 280, 296	18:5	198
		18:7	198
15:26	4, 106, 213, 220, 246, 247, 251, 285	18:8	282
		18:9–10	282
16:1–6	259	18:12	118
16:1–4	260	18:14	118
16:1–2	259	18:15–16	27
16:1	175, 245, 260	18:20	118, 254, 262
16:2	37, 40, 42, 44, 245, 251, 260, 261, 266	18:24	284
		18:25	114
16:4–3	222	18:27	114
16:4	260	18:28	121
16:5	225, 285	18:31–33	48

18:31	118	20:17	186, 273
18:33	118	20:18	273
18:35–36	41	20:19–23	98, 270, 271, 272, 276, 280
18:35	15, 41, 42, 118	20:19	118, 197, 270, 273, 279
18:36–40	118	20:20	271, 273, 281
18:36–37	254	20:21	271, 273, 282, 284, 285
18:36	118	20:22	106, 222, 271, 275, 277, 278, 279, 280
18:37–38	48		
18:37	141	20:24–29	273, 274
18:38	118	20:26	273, 279, 281, 282
18:39	118	20:30–31	48
19:3	118	21:1–25	274
19:7–14	118	21:7	27
19:7	118	21:10–25	27
19:9	186	21:20–25	29
19:11	140	21:23	30
19:12	118	21:24	30, 31, 110
19:13	39	21:25	48, 254
19:14	118		
19:17	39		
19:19	118, 198		
19:20	118		
19:21	118		
19:23	140		

Acts

19:25–27	29
19:26	27
19:28–30	253	1:1	40
19:30	106	1:3	275
19:31	118	1:8	271, 273
19:34	208	2	278, 287
19:35	29	2:5	15
19:36	121	2:17	189
19:38–42	135	2:38	273
19:38	118, 135, 197, 283	2:46	166
19:39–42	132	3:1	166
19:39	133, 135	4:25	15
19:40	118, 136	4:27	15
19:42	118	4:36	18
20:1–23	274	5:42	166
20:1	272	6:1	198
20:2–10	27	6:13	41
20:2	272	7:7	15, 41
20:8–10	272	7:13	18
20:11	272	7:19	18
20:12	274	7:26	175
20:13	272	7:45	15
20:15	272	8:9	15
20:16	39	8:15	273

8:17	273	18:19–21	45
8:19	273	18:24–28	44, 45
8:32	121	18:24	18
9:2	266	18:25	110
9:15	15	19:1–20	45
9:29	198	19:1–7	44
10:22	15	19:2	273
10:35	15	19:3	110
10:45	15	19:8–10	44
10:47	273	19:8–9	266
11:1	15	19:10	198
11:18	15	19:17	198
11:20	198	19:34	191
13:14–15	262	20:17–38	226
13:19	15	20:21	198
13:26	18	21:11	15
13:43	263	21:19	15
13:44–46	266	21:21	15
13:46–48	15	21:25	15
14:1–2	263, 266	21:26–30	166
14:1	198	21:28	198
14:2	15	22:19	266
14:5	15	22:21	15
14:16	15	23:6	136
14:27	15	24:2	15
15:3	15	24:10	15
15:5	136	24:17	15, 166
15:7	15	24:28	166
15:12	15	25:8	166
15:14	15	26:4	15
15:17	15	26:5	140
15:19	15	26:11	266
15:20	176	26:17	15
15:23	15	26:20	15
16:1	198	26:21	166
16:3	198	26:23	15
17:1–4	264	28:19	15
17:4	198	28:28	15
17:10–12	264		
17:17	264		
17:26	15		
17:28	18		
17:29	18	1:3	188
18:2	18	1:8	258
18:4	198, 264	1:13	15
18:6	15	1:15	15
18:8	262	1:16	198
18:17	262		

Romans

2:9	198	5:7	121
2:10	198	9:20	66
2:14	15	10:4	192, 207
2:24	15	10:10	174
3:2–29	66	10:18	188
3:6	258	10:20	15
3:9	198	10:32	66, 198
3:19	258	11:7–9	181
3:29	15	12:2	15
4:13–18	81, 149	12:10	18
4:17–18	15	12:13	198
8:4	185	12:28	18
8:15	273	14:10	18
8:23	144	15:3–8	275
9:3	188		
9:5	188		
9:8	81, 149		

2 Corinthians

1:22	173
5:17	143
11:4	273
11:26	15, 18

9:24	15, 66
9:30	15
10:12	198
10:19	15
11:1	184
11:11–13	15
11:12	258
11:14	66, 188
11:15	258
11:25	15
15:9–12	15
15:16	15
15:18	15
15:27	15
16:4	15
16:26	15

Galatians

1:14	18
1:16	15
2:2	15
2:8–9	15
2:12	15
2:13–15	66
2:14–15	15
3:2	273
3:8	15
3:14	15, 273
3:26–29	81, 149
3:28	198
4:1–5	234
4:5	144
4:9	140
4:19	141
5:16	185
6:8	185
6:15	143

1 Corinthians

1:20–21	258
1:22–24	66
1:22	198
1:23	15
1:24	198
2:12	273
4:9	258
4:13	258
4:15	141
5:1	15

Ephesians

1:1	45
1:13	173
2:11	15
3:1	15
3:6	15
3:8	15
4:17	15
4:30	173

Philippians

3:5	18, 184

Colossians

1:27	15
3:11	198

1 Thessalonians

2:16	15
2:17	234
4:5	15

1 Timothy

1:3	45
2:7	15
3:16	15
5:1–16	240

2 Timothy

2:24	175
4:17	15

Titus

1:12	66
3:5	144

Philemon

1:10	141

Hebrews

8:5	166
9:8–10	166

James

1:17	140
1:27	240, 258
3:15	140
3:17	140
4:2	175
4:4	258

1 Peter

1:18–19	121
1:23	142
2:9	15, 18
2:12	15
2:22–24	121
3:3	252
4:3	15

2 Peter

2:20	258

1 John

2:1	4, 213, 216, 223, 232
2:12	232
2:28	232
3:1–2	232
3:1	233

3:5	142	17:15	15
3:7	232	18:3	15
3:9	81, 142, 149	18:23	15
3:10	232, 233	19:15	15
3:18	232	20:3	15, 173
4:4	232	20:8	15
4:5	233	21:24	15
4:6	4	21:26	15
5:2	232	22:1	192
5:21	232	22:2	15
		22:16	18

2 John

1:1	232
1:4	232
1:13	232

3 John

1:4	232

Revelation

2:1–7	45
2:9	49, 266
2:26	15
3:9	49, 266
5:6–13	121
5:9	15
6:16	121
7:3	173
7:9	15
7:14–17	121
10:11	15
11:2	15
11:9	15
11:18	15
12:5	15
13:7	15
14:6	15
14:8	15
15:4	15
16:19	15
17:14	121

Dead Sea Scrolls

Thanksgiving Hymn (1QH)

4:15	104
4:23–24	104
4:24	104
4:25	103
5:1–4	104
5:14	104
5:15–20	104
5:18	103, 156
6:10	104
6:12	103, 156
6:25	103, 104, 156
7:10	104
7:20	104
8:1–5	103
8:10–14	104
8:10–15	103
9:1–14	104
9:15	104
9:20–24	104
9:32	219
12:11	219
12:31	104
14:25	219
15:6	103
16:6–11	219
16:10–14	103
17:32	103, 156
18:8	104
20:11–32	156
20:11	103

War Scroll (1QM)

7:5	104
14:17	104

Rule of the Community (1QS)

1:5–7	220
3:7–9	103
3:13—4:26	217, 218
3:17–21	219
3:24	104
4:1–25	104
4:2–14	219
4:10–24	104
4:16–18	219
4:19–21	144
4:19	220
4:20–25	104, 218
4:20–22	103
4:23–25	219
7:18	104
7:22	104
8:2	220
8:16	103, 156
9:3–5	103
11:1–2	104

Damascus Document (CD)

2:12	103, 156
3:2	104
3:8	104
5:10–14	104
7:3–4	104

Rabbinic Writings

B. Berakot.

28b	36
47a	140

B. Sanhedrin

37a	208
43a	197

B. Sotah

47a	197

B. Yebamot

22a	140
47a	139
62a	140
97b	140

M. Berakot.

7.1	165
8.8	165

M. Bikkurim

1:4–5	148

M. Niddah

4.1	165

M. Šebiʿit

8.10	165

M. Sukkot

4:9–10	195
5:1	195

T. Sukkah

3.3–12	195

Pesiqta Rabbati

52	195

Greco-Roman Writings

Aeschylus

Persians

507	99

Prometheus Bound

1086	99

Seven Against Thebes

464	98

Aelius Aristides

Orations

46	201

Aetius

1.3.4	98

Alexander of Aphrodisias

De Mixtione

216	100

Apollonius

Argonautica

1.182–84	172

Apuleius

Apology

24	73

Aristotle

Colors

6.1	55

Generation of Animals

716a1–15	142
731b25	142
735b—736a	142
735b10	142
766b15—769a22	142

Movement of Animals

10	99

Nicomachean Ethics

1095b	183
1123b	183

Physiognomonics

806b15	71, 291

Poetics

1457b	252

Politics

1.1252b	79, 180, 291
1.1253a	88, 229
1.1254a–55a	79, 291
5.1303a	78
5.1335b	79, 291
7.1327b	71, 291

Cassius Dio

Roman History

40.47.3–4	164

Cicero

De Divinatine

2.97	73, 291

De Domo Suo

127–128	164

De Finibus

2.49	62

Pro Flaccus

67–69	119
67	90
68–69	90

De Officiis

1.53–55	180, 228
1.53	62
1.55	62
2.21	182
2.31	182
2.36	182

De Republica

1.58	57

Diodorus of Sicily

1.9.3	80, 160, 291
3.2.2—3.3.1	65
3.2.4—3.1	65
34.1.1–5	254
34.1.2	86
34.1.3–5	86, 202
34.1.3	86, 202
34.1	86, 119, 202
34.2	86
40.3.1–2	86, 202
40.3.4	255
40.3	205

Diogenes Laertius

1.33	56
7.1	99

Dionysius of Halicarnassus

Antiquitates Romanae.

1.89–90	147
1.89	75, 159
1.90	160
2.26.4	181
11.37.1	213

Euripides

Hecuba

571	99

Iphigenia at Aulis

760	99

Ion

1–75	237
25–35	236
63	239
70–74	237
265–70	238
290	239
295	239
314–25	237
535	238
570–80	238
585–605	76, 291
585–90	238
605–45	238
670–75	76, 239
1575–90	237

Supplicants

219–25	77, 160

Gaius

Institutes

1.55	181

Herodotus

Histories

2.104	204
3.123	252
5.92	252
6.16a	99
7.159	147
8.86	252
8.144.2	56

Hesiod

Works and Days

76	252
327–34	236

Hierocles

On Duties

4.28.21	152

Hippocrates

Air Water Places

1.10	68
3.1–40	68
4.1–48	68
5.10–28	69, 291
12.10–20	69
13.1	70
13.10–20	69
16.1–10	69
16.40–43	69, 291
17.1	70
18.1	70
19.30	70
23.20–30	70, 291
24.1–67	70
24.40–50	70
24.50–59	70
24.60	70

Homer

Iliad

2.867	56
5.696	98, 99
10.144	149
10.472	252
10.482	99
14.187	252
20.110	99
22.484–505	236
24.340–42	172

Odyssey

8.179	252
13.77	252
19.138	99

Horace

Satires

1.4.143	91

Hyginus

Poetic Astronomy

2.34	172

Isocrates

Panegyricus

4.179	252
50	56

Evagoras

9.9	252

Julius Caesar

Gallic War

2.15	57

Julius Paulus

Opinions

1.21.2–5	272
1.21.8–14	272

Juvenal

Satires

14.96–104	92, 119
15.1	63
15.45	63
15.80–90	64
15.80	64
15.110	63
15.120–30	64
15.130	64

Livy

1.1–2	75
1.4	75
1.8	75
4.13.3	173
31.29.15	56
38.17.9–12	80, 92, 160, 291
39.16.8–10	60
39.18	164
42.48	61

Lucian

Juppiter Tragoedus

37	65

Prometheus

17	65

Lucius Florus

Epitome of Roman History

1.47.7–8	91

Marcus Junianus Justinus

Epitome

36.2	203

Philostratus

Vita Apollonii

5.33	203

Pindar

Pythian Odes

4.161	172

Olympian Odes

11	252

Plato

Crito

50b	145
51c	146

Epinomis

987b	252

Gorgias

507e–8a	252

Laws

747d–e	71, 291
8.846d	252
12.949e–50a	78, 159
12.953a–b	78

Menexenus

237b–38b	78, 146, 291
238a–b	146
245c–d	78, 159, 291

Phaedo

89d–e	87

Republic

5.415a–c	77, 160, 291
5.459d–e	77, 160, 291

Statesman

271a	146

Timaeus

18d–19a	77, 160, 291
24c	71, 291
27a	252
30b	252

66e	98	*Lycurgus*
91c	98	
		16.1–2 ... 79

Pliny the Elder

Natural History

De Primo Frigido

7 ... 98

2.80	73, 291
3.39	55
7.30	61
24.1	60
29.7.15	56
29.13–14	60

De Stoicorum Repugnantiis

43 ... 100

Quaestionum Convivialum libri

Pliny the Younger

4.4–5.3 ... 201

Epistulae

10.50 ... 164

Polybius

History

Panegyricus

4.21	72, 291
27.6	61
31.10.4	99

1–5 ... 173

Plutarch

Porphyry

Alexander

De Abstinentia.

2.1–3.2 ... 149

2.26 ... 205

An seni respublica

Vita Pythagorae

783f ... 183

1.11 ... 204

Antonius

Ptolemy

69.4 ... 87

Tetrabiblos

2.2 ... 73, 291

Quintilian

Institutio Oratoria

7.3.5	100
8.1.3	62

Seneca

Hercules Furens

317–24	172

De Ira

2.15	291

Strabo

Geography

3.4.16	57
4.4.3–5	57

Suetonius

Divus Augustus

94.4	

Claudius

25.4	61

Tiberius

36	61

Tacitus

Annales

1.51	164
2.85	61
14.15	173

Germania

30.2	58
43.6	58
46	58, 80, 160

History

5.2–8	119, 255
5.2–3	88
5.3	88
5.4.2	201
5.4	88
5.5.1	203
5.5	89
5.8	88, 203

Thucydides

1.3	74
2.44.4	183
2.49.2	98
6.2–6	75, 147

Vegetius

Concerning Military Matters

1.2	73, 291

Vitruvius

On Architecture

6.1.3–5	72
6.1.3–4	72
6.1.9–10	72
6.1.9	72
6.1.10	72
6.1.11	73, 291

Virgil

Aeneid

3.161–71	75
4.239–41	172

Xenophon

Hellenica

6.2.27	99
7.4.32	99

Hiero

7.3	182

Memorabilia

1.1.11	252

Oeconomicus

7.19–21	152

Early Christian Writings

2 Clement

3:9	216
7:6	173

Didache

5.5	215
9	171

Eusebius

Ecclesiastical History

2.15	40
2.16	40
2.22	290
2.23	115
2.25	115
3.18	44, 290
3.20	44, 115, 290
3.23	44, 290
3.24	27, 40, 47, 290
3.32	115
3.39	40, 44
4.14	40
5.1–2	115
5.1	215
5.19	115
5.20	26, 290
5.24	27, 44
6.14	27, 40, 290
6.25	40
7.25	27, 290

Ignatius of Antioch

Romans

7:3	176

Philadelphians

4:1	176

Smyrnaeans

7:1	176

Irenaeus

Against Heresies

2.22.5	26
3.1.1	26, 40
3.5.1	40
3.11.1	40, 44
3.16.5	26
3.22.2	26
5.1.8	26

Justin

First Apology

66	176

Dialogue with Trypho

8.4	122, 198
69	197
80	110
110.1	198
131	192

Origen

Commentary on Matthew

1.8	40

Rufinus

Clementis quae feruntur Recognitiones

1.54	110
1.60	110

Tertullian

Against Judaism

13	192

New Testament Pseudepigrapha

Gospel of Peter

7–15	273

Gospel of Thomas

5	196

Papyri and Inscriptions

Papyrus Bouriant

25	241

Corpus Inscriptionum Judaicarum

690	263
738	264
766	264
972	264
1404	262
1440	264

Corpus Inscriptionum Latinarum

6.36467	272

www.ingramcontent.com/pod-product-compliance
Lightning Source LLC
Chambersburg PA
CBHW071151300426
44113CB00009B/1161